A BACK-TO-BASICS GUIDE TO CALM,
COMMON-SENSE, CONNECTED PARENTING BIRTH-8

Maggie Dent

Pennington Publications
PO Box 312, Murwillumbah, NSW 2484
www.maggiedent.com

First Published July 2014
Second reprint July 2016

© Copyright 2014 Maggie Dent

All rights reserved. If a small part of this book is reproduced for the purpose of education and training, newsletters, or to help someone, written permission is not required — provided the text is acknowledged and you are acting with integrity and respect. Written permission of the publisher is required for larger-scale reproduction or communication. Every reasonable effort has been made to contact the holders of copyright material reproduced in this book. The author and publisher will gladly receive information that will enable them to rectify any inadvertent errors or omissions in subsequent editions.

Edited by Carmen Myler
Design, layout and typesetting: Katharine Middleton, Ink Box Graphics
Illustrator: Linda True-Arrow

National Library of Australia Cataloguing-in-Publication entry:

Author: Dent, Maggie, author.
Title: 9 things a back-to-basics guide to calm, common-sense, connected parenting birth-8 / by Maggie Dent
ISBN: 9780975125878 (paperback)

Subjects: Child rearing.
            Child care.
            Child development.
            Child psychology.

Dewey Number: 649.1

I dedicate this book to my many nieces and nephews who are a special part of my life and who have been since they were born. I also include my non-biological nieces and nephews, other people's children who have allowed me to be Aunty Mag to them all — you know who you are. I love you all and my door is always open, with a cuppa and some fresh muffins just a half an hour away.

ACKNOWLEDGEMENT

I begin this parenting guide with a respectful acknowledgement to ancient knowledge that has been held by Indigenous people the world over. I pay my deepest respect to the traditional custodians of the land where I was born and raised — The Noongar peoples of Western Australia. And I also pay my respects to Aboriginal peoples and Torres Strait Islanders, past and present, who have also walked and cared for this land for over 40,000 years. A special message of love and respect to Aunty Janet Hayden and to my Noongar sisters — Fiona and Ched — thank you for your friendship. I am committed to supporting Aboriginal families and communities, to narrow the gap of disadvantage that has become a reality for too many Aboriginal children. Every child matters, no matter what.

A Canadian First Nations education professor once told me these wise words:

"In our culture, our babies and children are treated as miracles and gifts from Mother Earth. Not everyone who wants one receives one. The whole tribe takes an active role in raising that child as that child is 'ours' and we believe that experience is our children's greatest teacher. We don't 'don't' on our children as Western parents do — you only ever pick up a hot coal once."

CONTENTS

Introduction	1
1st Thing — Connected mothering	13
2nd Thing — The bountiful brain in infancy	51
3rd Thing — Go-slow childhoods	105
4th Thing — Roosters and lambs	141
5th Thing — The magic of movement and play	170
6th Thing — Gorgeous girls and beautiful boys	205
7th Thing — Expectations, belief systems and mindsets — positive memory pathways	238
8th Thing — Kindness and fairness really matters	260
9th Thing — The safe circle of community	298
Conclusion	315
Appendix 1	317
Reference list	319
Index	331

INTRODUCTION

> What a child really needs is good, positive emotional relationships with parents and others. They don't need a thousand activities. Children can learn facts and gain external skills at any time. But they only gain relationship skills when young.
> – Ruth Schmidt Neven, Director of the Centre for Child and Family Development, Melbourne, *Parents' Magazine*, November (2004).

It is a strange irony that in our massive information age, some really important basic information has been lost. This information impacts on a parent's ability to raise children who thrive — who can be happy, healthy, strong and kind. This guide is about 'the basics' that really matter and why they matter, and it has been created to offer support for those who are doing the most important job on earth — parenting. I am by no means an expert — even though I have helped raise four spunky sons to adulthood — I made many mistakes. My tertiary education prepared me to be a high school teacher and so when I began my intensive breeding program, I had absolutely no idea about birth, babies, breastfeeding or the developmental markers of healthy growth for babies, toddlers or children. In 1994 I completed a diploma in counselling and over the last 18 years, I have heard the anguish and wounds of many troubled children, adolescents and adults. These stories have strengthened my resolve to support families, especially parents, in the journey of parenthood. So often the unintended damage that happens to children before they start school, shapes their opportunities to thrive or to struggle.

We must never forget that child development cannot be hurried, no matter how inconvenient that may be for the adults of our 'hurry-up' world. Each child has a built-in timetable that dictates just when he or she will crawl, sit up and start to walk; and given a safe environment, their development will flow naturally. Children learn by doing and they will be noisy, untidy, messy and unpredictable. This is normal and at times parenting will be tiring, exhausting and frustrating. This too is normal. There is no 'perfect' in parenting.

Parenting cannot be perfect — nor can children. Being human means we are prone to experiencing this strange thing called 'life' as it happens and no matter how much we plan, dream and hope, things can go wrong. The modern world has become faster, busier and full of massive change and enormous choice and that's a bit difficult for both children and their parents. It takes a whole childhood for children to learn, to grow and to work out how to be whoever they are. When we try to hurry up childhood, our children's chances of thriving diminish — they will survive, just maybe not as well. There is no 'one right way' to parent and often what works this week with your child may not work next week. The main aim of this guide is to give you — the parent — information to help in your decision-making and to offer solutions to common concerns. A supportive network of parents who are on the same journey helps enormously — because in a way it still "takes a whole village to raise a child" and the stronger and healthier our communities, the better our children thrive.

It does not matter who a child's parents are, where they live, how much money they have or what culture they come from. All children, from the moment they are conceived, benefit from consistent, nurturing care from people who love and value them. When this loving care is present, a child will feel safe enough to explore the environment in which they live with guidance and the first six years are now proven to be the critical key to every child's potential. Indeed, there are some who believe that the first three years matter more than the first six — no matter what, this window is where the foundations for a happy, healthy life are laid down.

The early years of school, until children are eight, are also an important time to help those children who have readiness delays and so every one of the **9 Things** I will be talking about in this book, continue to be a valuable focus for parents, teachers and those who care for children.

WHY ARE WE CONCERNED ABOUT TODAY'S KIDS?

Child health researcher and former Australian of the Year Professor, Fiona Stanley has been warning this nation since 2000, that our children are struggling and yet the reality is they continue to struggle, especially children from lower socio-economic areas, and including our Indigenous children.

> "Health and behaviour problems among children have reached frightening levels and a national campaign is needed to avert a looming social crisis."
> — *The West Australian*, November 9th 2002.

Besides increases in obesity, asthma, allergies, aggressive behaviour, mental illness, autism and type 1 and 2 diabetes in children, the degree of significant developmental challenges for children beginning school has risen from:

- 5–10% around 20 years ago;
- 10–15% 10 years ago; to
- 22% of children starting school in 2015 who were deemed to be developmentally at risk in one or more domains (according to the Australian Early Development Census).

Doctors are increasingly medicating children with anti-depressants (even kids under five) and the number of children whose behaviour is too inappropriate and 'at risk' to remain in mainstream schooling continues to rise. In NSW alone, journalist Andrew Stevenson (2011) reported that, "the number of children in public schools with mental health disorders including depression and some serious behavioural disorders has almost doubled to 8000 students".

The AEDC (Australian Early Development Census)

In 2009, the then Australian Early Development Index (AEDI) was completed nationwide for the first time and the Australian Government subsequently committed to repeating it every three years. In the third round (now the AEDC) in 2015, information was collected on more than 300,000 Australian children (over 96% of the estimated five-year-old population) in their first year of full-time school.

According to these national reports results are publicly available and provide communities around Australia with information about how local children have developed by the time they start school, across five areas of early childhood development:

1. physical health and wellbeing,
2. social competence,
3. emotional maturity,
4. language and cognitive skills (school-based), and
5. communication skills and general knowledge.

The results are also reported at the community level. This can help communities understand how their local children are developing compared to children nationally. Communities can use the survey results to develop and evaluate their efforts to improve outcomes for children.

What the index shows us is that, in general, a significant proportion of our families and communities are struggling with lowering standards of decency, wellbeing, respect and empathy and the flow-on effect is less healthy relationships — with our selves, others and our world.

The current deep concern with the violence of young males on our streets at night is a sure sign that something isn't right in the way some children, especially boys, are being raised.

The AEDC results reflect that, "In 2015, boys were twice as likely as girls to be developmentally vulnerable on one or more (285% and 15%) and two or more domains (153% and 68%)".

The social media world, the celebrity and entertainment world (especially those that sexualise our children) and the consumer-driven, power-hungry elements of modern life are stealing from many communities their former healthy sense of belonging, of strong social capital and unconditional acceptance of people regardless of culture, age and gender.

Sadly, Western cultures are struggling with high levels of:

- **Alcohol and drug abuse**
- **Aggression and violence from childhood to adulthood**
- **Bullying, especially cyber bullying**
- **Family disconnection**
- **Family violence and abuse**
- **Mental illness, especially depression**
- **Chronic health issues like diabetes, obesity, asthma and allergies**
- **Homelessness**
- **Welfare dependency**
- **Suicide.**

Many of these life concerns have their beginnings in the first six years of life. Hard to believe, but true. The most effective way to improve the outcomes on all levels for every individual is to first better support families and especially parents. Many school principals I work with have deep concerns that parents have "dropped the ball" around parenting in constructive and healthy ways and teachers are being left to pick up the pieces while still needing to teach the curriculum. This includes both the vulnerable families who have always been struggling and the more affluent ones who have seemingly lost the 'basics' of parenting that they used to have.

The pursuit of perfection

The pursuit to be the 'perfect' parent is well-intentioned, however potentially unhealthy. If you want to be your child's best friend, you may be missing the enormously important role of being your child's first teacher and their parent guide. We are all born with strengths and flaws, and it is our responsibility to help our children work on their competences mentally, socially, emotionally, cognitively and spiritually.

The imperfect among us will be happy to read that 20th century pediatrician and child psychiatrist, Donald Winnicott hypothesised that it was not necessary to be a perfect mother to raise happy children, but rather to be a "good-enough mother".

Winnicott writes the good-enough mother, "(not necessarily the infant's own mother) is one who makes active adaptation to the infant's needs, an active adaptation that gradually lessens, according to the infant's growing ability to account for failure of adaptation and to tolerate the results of frustration".

Of course not all parents strive to be "good enough". As psychotherapist, Lori Gottlieb writes in her *Atlantic* article: "How to land your kid in therapy" (2011):

> *Paul Bohn, a psychiatrist at UCLA believes many parents will do anything to avoid having their kids experience even mild discomfort, anxiety, or disappointment—"anything less than pleasant," as he puts it—with the result that when, as adults, they experience the normal frustrations of life, they think something must be terribly wrong.*
>
> *Consider a toddler who's running in the park and trips on a rock, Bohn says. Some parents swoop in immediately, pick up the toddler, and comfort her in that moment of shock, before she even starts crying. But, Bohn explains, this actually prevents her from feeling secure—not just on the playground, but in life. If you don't let her experience that momentary confusion, give her the space to figure out what just happened (Oh, I tripped), and then briefly let her grapple with the frustration of having fallen and perhaps even try to pick herself up, she has no idea what discomfort feels like, and will have no framework for how to recover when she feels discomfort later in life. These toddlers become the college kids who text their parents with an SOS if the slightest thing goes wrong, instead of attempting to figure out how to deal with it themselves. If, on the other hand, the child trips on the rock, and the parents let her try to reorient for a second before going over to comfort her, the child learns: "That was scary for a second, but I'm okay now. If something unpleasant happens, I can get through it". In many cases, Bohn says, the child recovers fine on her own—but parents never learn this, because they're too busy protecting their kid when she doesn't need protection.*

Parenting is a unique journey where we nurture and guide our children to become competent and capable at managing this strange beast called life. At times there is great joy and delight and at other times deep disappointment and sadness. In a way, happiness is sweeter because we have known the reverse. The more children actually experience, the more resilient they grow. Life experience is a wonderful teacher that every parent needs to embrace.

Gottlieb (2011) writes about Dan Kindlon, a child psychologist and lecturer at Harvard, who, "warns against what he calls our 'discomfort with discomfort' in his book, *Too Much of a Good Thing: Raising Children of Character* in an Indulgent Age". She refers to Kindlon's belief that if kids can't experience painful feelings, they won't develop "psychological immunity".

"It's like the way our body's immune system develops," he explained. "You have to be exposed to pathogens, or your body won't know how to respond to an attack. Kids also need exposure to discomfort, failure, and struggle." (Gottlieb, 2011)

Gottlieb describes meeting 'teacups', who are fragile young adults who have had perfect childhoods and who have been adored by their parents and yet struggle because they no longer feel special and very happy. Adversity is not all bad, and can be a great teacher – no matter what age we are. I explore the growth of resilience in children extensively in my book, *Real Kids in an Unreal World* (2008), if you are interested in learning how to build this in your children.

A final message here is about over-parenting — when we lose ourselves in our children's lives. Many family therapists share stories of family angst as the 'helicopter parent' struggles with letting go as adolescence appears — the transition to adulthood. Dr Kindlon believes many of us don't really want our kids to leave, because we rely on them in various ways to fill the emotional holes in our own lives (ouch!). Kindlon is concerned we devote inordinate amounts of time, energy, and resources to our children, but for whose benefit?

Despite the spate of articles in recent years exploring why so many people in their 20s seem reluctant to grow up, leave home and live independently, the problem may be less about kids refusing to separate and individuate than that their *parents* resist doing so. Parenting is about preparing our children to become independent, capable, resilient adults and yes, letting go is hard. However, for the health and wellbeing of our precious children, letting go is what is best. Common sense supports this ancient view of the unique dance called, parenting and each child is a one-of-a-kind miracle who is both a student and teacher to us. It is not just a one-way journey.

Feel ok that you are a 'good enough' parent and relax when things go wrong — it is a valuable teachable moment. Indeed, Daniel Siegel and Tina Payne Bryson in their wonderful parenting book, *The Whole Brain Child* (2011) argue that the tough moments are our greatest opportunity to teach.

> When your child is disrespectful and talks back to you, when you are asked to come in for a meeting with the principal, when you find crayon scribbles all over your wall: these are survive moments, no question about it. But at the same time, they are opportunities – even gifts – because a 'survive moment' is also a 'thrive moment', when the important meaningful well-work of parenting takes place.
> — Siegel & Bryson (2011)

When my boys were growing up, I made many mistakes and struggled with guilt at the times when I could have done more and been more. I wished I could have taken away my sons' pain at dark moments in their lives. However, they have grown to be independent, capable and resilient. That is what they value and they enjoy reminding me of my many moments when my mothering was flawed!

MY AIM IN PRODUCING THIS GUIDE

Let's begin with a fact: parenting is hard work no matter who you are, how much money you have, where you live or how old you are. There will be days when you will be challenged to the depth of your being and thankfully there will be days when you will feel ecstatic and overcome with joy in a way that words will fail to capture.

The original impulse for this book was the number of times after parenting seminars I had a mum or a dad say to me, "Gee, I wish I had known about that before I had kids!"

In fact, while I was researching this guide, I asked parents within my Facebook community what they wished they knew before they became parents. I've sprinkled some of their responses throughout the book.

The main aim of this guide is to provide information that gives all children the good start in life that they truly deserve. It aims to help prevent or at least reduce the factors that contribute to all of the concerns outlined above — so in nature, it is preventative and resilience building. The guide aims to give parents information that is based on evidence-rich research, supported by paediatricians, OTs, early years' educators and child psychologists, while being easy to understand. We have been raising children for a very long time and (according to the developmental research) families and communities were doing a better job 20 years ago **with less**. There is no "one-size-fits-all" solution for the many parenting dilemmas that appear, as each child is a unique, never-been-here-before human being. This is a quick reference guide full of practical suggestions and ideas that can make a difference in the early years of life.

Not only do we want our children to be happy, healthy, strong and kind, we also want them to be confident, caring and capable. I am passionate that children under six engage in meaningful and fair relationships with family and community because this will help them not only navigate the school journey competently, but also the bigger journey of life.

Woven into this guide is the intention to build early mental and psychological strength, strong human connectedness and permission for children under eight to be children — not little pseudo adults, not projects to be managed or problems to be solved — but *children*. The nature of children is that they are a work in progress — so at times the parenting journey will be noisy, chaotic, dirty, exhausting, unpredictable, confusing and challenging. There will be moments when you may feel like locking yourself in the toilet wishing you had never begun breeding and then there will be moments when you can scarcely breathe because of the overwhelming love you feel for your child.

Parents are the most important teachers children ever have — and their main job is to teach and guide children, not to control and police. In a way, children learn really fast with a degree of 'benign neglect'. This means that we allow our kids to learn from experiences that can sometimes be painful — so many of us can remember when we learned about respecting the wooden see-saw after it hit us in the chin! Indeed a great message to remind our kids after things 'go wrong' is — so what did you learn from that moment, that experience, that event?'

WILMA THE WALLABY — OUR WISE GUIDE TO HEALTHY MOTHERING

Throughout this guide, we have used the character of Wilma the Wallaby to illustrate key points in a friendly and visual way. Wilma is representative of the gentle wisdom of all good grandmothers, aunties and wise women who have walked this earth before us. She is full of kindness, calmness and insight, and her genuine intention is to support all parents, especially mums, to take kind, fair and respectful care of their wee ones so that they grow up to be happy, healthy, strong and kind.

Healthy mothering is essential for optimal development for any child. There is a deep and primal hunger in every child for a loving and safe connection to their birth mother. Much of Wilma's wisdom comes from that place of 'mothering' — in traditional communities, the mothering role was shared and many women contributed to this essential bond of belonging. Research shows that healthy mothering can absolutely occur without a biological connection and this is why choosing carers for your children, especially under five, is such an important decision for families, no matter where they live. It is the *art of mothering* that matters, dads can mother, grandparents and foster carers can also mother. It is the mothering that occurs before a child turns three that is particularly important in the whole parenting journey.

> **WILMA WALLABY**
>
> "Families who play together will feel belonging and kids need to know they belong and that they matter."

Many of us did not have a Wilma as our primary mother to learn from. Some had absent mothers or mothers who were ill, who struggled with addictions or family violence, or — as I did — with a cold, emotionally unavailable mother. This guide is especially useful in helping those parents adopt healthier patterns of 'mothering' than what was modelled for them, in the hope that their children can have a better start in life.

Wilma believes that by guiding and teaching children well before they go to school, you give them the best possible start in life and she believes that a circle of supportive women is one of the best protective factors a mother can have. Wilma is the voice of common sense that seems to be lost in much of today's parenting. Wilma believes that all children matter, no matter what, and that there is no race, no competition. Indeed, Wilma believes in seeing babies, toddlers and children as miracles — not everyone is blessed with a miracle.

In ancient Indigenous cultures, women took care of all the babies and children until the boys were ready to begin their journey to manhood. This required women to be more in the feminine side of their psyche, and for men to be more in the protective, warrior side of their psyche. As times have changed and women have careers that take them outside of the home, we have needed to use our masculine side a little more to strive and contribute in the workforce. This has created a gap in the family for more nurturance energy, and men have begun filling this essential role in the family.

With honest communication, parents can still offer children a balance of the traits of masculine and feminine; they are both needed for the healthy development of children. It is the first three to six years that make the most significant impact on children in terms of their need for healthy 'mothering'. In Scandinavia, they have a national focus on creating flexible workplaces for working mums and dads who have children under six, to encourage parents to spend as much time as possible with their own children. At-home dads are becoming more and more common and they can fill the same mothering needs as a woman — except breastfeeding obviously! What is important is the role of significant, consistent, nurturing mother figures like Wilma — even if sometimes he's a William! If both parents are working full-time, the choice of child care needs to meet the 'mothering' needs of young children, whether it be with extended family, nannies, family day care or child care. I had three amazing carers who shared my mothering journey and that allowed me to work outside of home at times while my boys were under six.

So allow Wilma to be a voice of common sense and sound wisdom — the voice of the healthy, even ancient 'mother' who encourages, affirms and inspires all parents as they make the journey along the road of parenting. If you don't have a Wilma in your life and you are living with babies, toddlers or children under eight, hopefully this book will allow you to tap into wise mother wisdom to reassure you when making the endless decisions needed day by day as a mother or father.

We all want the best for our children and in my experience it is what we do 80% of the time, rather than what we do 20% of the time, that defines our parenting. When things muck up, when your children haven't eaten any vegetables on a given day, when they don't have a bath, when they eat trans fatty acids in the biscuits you bought because they were starving and you had a bit of a shouty moment, give yourself a break. Inwardly tell yourself that it's a 20% moment or a 20% day and then move on. Your survival, especially as a mum, is critical to the long-term wellbeing of your children. So if you are sick, go to bed. Yes, you can stagger out at some point and heat up a frozen pizza or chicken nuggets, and yes — sit your children in front of the TV and have them watch back-to-back kids' DVDs and then go back to bed until you are well. This will not permanently scar them or set their developmental markers back, however, it may allow you to recover quicker so that you can get back to being a Wilma mum, an 80%er who gets it right most of the time.

I can reassure you as an 80% mum myself, your children can turn out really well and that being a good-enough mum may actually be better than one who strives to be perfect. So when a 20% moment happens, maybe pause sometimes and ask yourself — "what would Wilma do right now?"

I have used 'Did you know?' boxes throughout the guide to signpost key important facts about essential child development needs that can help parents in their decision-making without drowning you in theory, tertiary language and terminology that would see you constantly Googling to find out what the heck they are talking about!

If you need to search for information please go to: *www.raisingchildren.net.au/articles* — this is an excellent site to provide you with grounded, well-researched information at a click. They even have fabulous little videos and audios to help you connect and care for your precious children.

DID YOU KNOW?

Every single child is a unique, one-of-a-kind child. There is never another child the same — even identical twins. This means that parenting decisions have to be flexible and creative to meet the needs of each child, at any given time of their development, and given the environment and circumstances that are happening at that moment.

So remember:

TOP TIPS

* Every parent will have moments when parenting will be hard work.
* Every parent will make mistakes on occasion.
* Every parent is human and can only do the best they can with what they know.
* Every parent wants their children to grow up healthy, strong, kind and capable.
* Every parent needs to teach their child that life and people are not perfect.
* Every parent will need some extra help at times to be a better parent.
* Every parent benefits from a supportive network of caring people in his/her community.

What I wish I had known ... "That despite all the advice given, no-one knows it all because there is no right answer. That it is OK to be wrong and learn as you go " - Rebecca

The 9 things Wilma wants you to know so that you can become a calm, connected, common-sense parent:

1. Connected mothering
2. The bountiful brain in infancy
3. Go-slow childhoods
4. Roosters and lambs
5. The magic of movement and play
6. Gorgeous girls and beautiful boys
7. Expectations, belief systems and mindsets – positive memory pathways
8. Kindness and fairness really matters
9. The safe circle of community

1st Thing

CONNECTED MOTHERING

BIRTH UNTIL 3

OK, before the uproar begins, let's get this straight. Fathers can mother, extended family members can mother and so can others who are closely connected to a child. This whole chapter simply affirms the importance and significance of babies, toddlers and young children receiving connected mothering, whether biological or otherwise, especially in the first three years of life.

> In the tribal context, women's business was taken very seriously. Each woman was supported by other women, especially when they were expecting or had a new baby. They were given food, care and respect because they were bringing a miracle into the tribe, a new life. This was something that was deeply respected and honoured, and seen as a sacred privilege.
> — Maggie Dent, *Real Kids in an Unreal World* (2008).

I went to an early years' conference in Canada in 2012, which explored mental health and wellbeing of children under five. A common theme throughout was that mothering has changed. It is a bit ironic that parents-to-be often attend several classes about the birth of their baby and no classes about parenting after that. I can remember during my first pregnancy having the odd thought: 'this won't change my life much'; and 'how hard can it be with just one baby if I'm used to teaching 150 smelly, confused and often horny adolescents?'

On my first shopping trip after the birth of my son, I remember being absorbed with the nappy bag and ensuring I had all the right things in it. On arriving at my local supermarket after I took out my handbag and the new nappy bag, I turned to get my son and take him on his first shopping outing. Bugger! I had left him at home. This was the first of my 'aha' moments where I realised that this parenting journey was going to be a lot harder than I thought.

Unfortunately for me, my own mother had been emotionally unavailable and distant, and had difficulty with alcohol so I did not have an immediate primary Wilma to call on for help. Thankfully my older sister stepped in as my Wilma or things could have been a lot more difficult and challenging for me. I felt very much like this mum:

> No one tells you what it's going to be like to have a baby. Well, one person did when I was six months pregnant (my OB, of all people), but I didn't listen to her. I had too many visions of lovingly gazing down at my precious, sleeping little one, too much optimism about my optimism being able to trump any newborn behavior, and too much biology demanding to be reproduced to be able to fathom how challenging and exhausting on so many levels it can be (and certainly has been in our house). Why don't parents talk about how hard and even awful having a baby can be? And yes, it can be *awful!* The sleep deprivation, the often unending crying without knowing why, the never having a single moment to yourself even to pee, much less take a shower and wash your hair... it is relentless. Yet, by not talking about what parenting is really like – the good, the bad and the ugly – we're actually doing a disservice to new moms and dads who are wholly unprepared for what they're getting into.
>
> Thankfully though, enough time has passed that I'm growing accustomed to things, including accepting the enormity of all that I'll never understand or be able to control. That's one of the gifts of being a parent.
>
> And there are many. Layers of selfishness you never knew you had, disappear. A love unlike one you've ever known cracks even the most open of hearts wider still. New and deeper meanings of the words patience, resilience, sacrifice and perspective confound your earlier understandings, and the meaning of life smacks you upside the head and brings you humbly, reverently and eventually, gratefully to your knees.
>
> I'm certain that I wouldn't have learned these things had I not had a child. Yet it is also a tremendous, difficult and terrible challenge. One doesn't come without the other; let's do every future mom and dad a favor and be sure to talk about both.
>
> — Jennifer Hamady, *The Truth About Being a Parent* (2014).

Essentially, parenting begins at conception; their unique DNA template that lies within as well as the experiences and the environment that surrounds them shapes the start of our baby's journey. This journey is one that takes a baby who is completely dependent on others, to an adult who is independent and it flows from:

Belonging ⇨ Living ⇨ Growing ⇨ Leaving

> When an infant receives too little direct loving contact this can cause the area of his brain that regulates emotion, self image and beliefs about relationships to become atrophied with serious, long-lasting – often permanent – consequences for behaviour. Touch deprivation releases steroids that damage the hippocampus leading to cognitive and behavioural problems later in life.
> — Robin Grille, *Parenting for a Peaceful World* (Second edition, 2013).

What babies need in order to thrive in our modern world is to live in a society that values them and really cares for them. That might seem like an obvious thing in our Western world but many of the decisions made by governments are made for the economic best interests of the country, rather than what is best for society's most vulnerable — our children. Quite ironically, the better our babies and toddlers are loved and cared for, the better the economy prospers because these children will grow into capable, responsible and healthy adults.

Sally Goddard Blythe is the director of *The Institute for Neuro-Physiological Psychology* in the UK and her main area of work is with children experiencing specific learning disabilities (dyslexia, developmental coordination disorder, attention deficit disorder, under-achievement, etc.). She believes that our modern world is making it more and more difficult for babies and toddlers to spend significant time with their parents, where she believes the healthiest 'mothering' can occur. On reading Goddard Blythe's book, *What Babies and Children Really Need* (2008), it turns out that what they really need — time — is what many modern mothers cannot provide, simply because we live in a society that does not allow for that need.

The situation in Australia is a little easier than in the UK and USA, although for many Australian mums, returning to work is an economic necessity. The pressure for women to be part of the workforce is enormous in these countries and in the UK particularly there is pressure for women to re-join the workforce when their babies are very, very young. Women can have careers and they can have children. However having it all at the same time can be incredibly stressful and challenging, and it simply may not be what is best for babies, especially in the first 12 months of life. We need to have conversations about how we can better support mums and dads of young children to combine parenting and working. With the rapid advances in technology, more flexibility is now possible for working parents and as any employer will tell you, a happy mum or dad is a much more productive worker.

Many mums who do plan to stay home for the first three to five years of their child's life tell me that other mums often look at them as though they have lost their capacity for logical thought. This is captured beautifully by Mary Jessica Hammes who reviewed Goddard Blythe's book back in 2009:

I particularly liked the way she addressed how motherhood suffers generally from a sense of support and worth. She writes about how she dreaded social events when her children were young, knowing the inevitable response when she was asked about her career.

"I soon came to expect the glazed look of fading interest that would pass across the questioner's face when I replied, 'I have three small children'," she writes. "It was as if I had just issued them with a certificate which confirmed my intellectual level was the same age as that of my youngest child...there is something fundamentally wrong with a society which regards motherhood as a temporary mental aberration which will only be restored to normalcy when she returns to the world beyond children."

I was very lucky to be financially able to be an at-home mum for around seven years. When I returned to the workforce my passion for teaching, for supporting other parents with their children and my own maturity and growth allowed me to be a very late bloomer in terms of career development. There were times when I did some non-mothering activities, like play basketball, tutoring, learn to be a radio announcer with the ABC and become a volunteer at the Albany hospice. When I was away from my children, a very special lady called Kate who became a surrogate grandma to my boys would come to our house to care for them. Finding similar supports for today's mothers of young children is really important because we were never meant to go on a parenting journey without a network of support — and yes, it still takes a village to raise healthy children. Sometimes, we just have to create the village from non-biological people and in my work in rural communities around Australia, I salute the excellent work that is happening with our NGOs in supporting today's parents.

My team today consists of mums who blend work and family, and our priority is always family first and work second. I did not begin travelling for work until my boys were much older and I also had a very supportive husband for when I was away. He now comes with me often because family is still incredibly important to me. Creating pathways that work for both women and men, while raising their children requires good communication and flexibility. There is no one right way, there is no one-size-fits-all and we are all doing the best we can.

For those mums who choose to or have to work, this guide will give you an enormous support so that you can raise happy, healthy kids. It will help you make decisions that will not only be great for you; they will be great for your children too. I have had parents contact me who said they wished they had known how important healthy attachment was in the first three years of life, because they could have been an at-home mum or an at-home dad, or worked part-time. One paediatric specialist says he believes the number one important factor in parenting babies and toddlers is that you need to spend a lot of time with at least one person "who is completely nuts about you!"

Belonging is another way of explaining attachment, which is the relationship between a key adult and a child, and then their wider community. Babies, toddlers and children need to have 'big people' they can trust to nurture and care for them. These people help guide and teach them all that they will need to know in life so they can become independent, capable adults who will hopefully in many cases find mates, breed and ensure the survival of the species.

> A secure attachment happens when parents are able to be sensitive to their child's cues, responsive to his needs and treat him lovingly. This pays instant dividends in both child development and also in behaviour.
> — Jo Jackson King, *Raising the Best Possible Child* (2010).

Primary attachments are the big people of central importance to a child's life — typically parents. It is helpful for parents of babies and toddlers to have a circle of caring adults who can share the raising of children. This allows for support, guidance and respite, which helps every parent, especially tired mummies, cope with this intensive time of life. For children who are in long-day child care, the early years' educators who form a loving, caring connection to a young child are technically a source of primary attachment, often called secondary attachment figures.

Attachment is the 'super glue' that holds a child in close proximity to a parent/caregiver. A child is meant to pursue **proximity**, which means being close to their big person so that they feel safe and are safe. Attachment is as important to healthy child development as eating or sleeping. Indeed in much of the most recent research, strong attachment and bondedness can be shown to be the most significant influence on emotional wellbeing, mental health and physical health for life.

> You are teaching one of the few human beings who will be entirely entrusted to you, how to laugh, learn and love people. There is nothing more worthwhile that you will ever do.
> — Steve and Shaaron Biddulph, *Love, Laughter and Parenting* (2001).

There seems to be some confusion in the parenting world about what works best in building young children's socialisation skills — or their ability to get on with other children. Child psychologist Dr Louise Porter, believes that children are technically unable to master social skills until around three years of age and she recommends that young children play with tiny clusters of other children — the child's age plus one (Porter, 1994).

Dr Gordon Neufeld is very concerned that we can cause problems when we force socialisation on young children:

> Premature socialization was always considered by developmentalists to be the greatest sin in raising children ....[w]hen you put children together prematurely before they can hold on to themselves, then they become like [the others] and it crushes the individuality rather than hones it.
> — Dr Gordon Neufeld (in Mrozek, 2012).

We are highly sociable beings and we quite naturally identify that some of our relationships have a higher priority than others — that is why I am so passionate that babies, toddlers and young children have strong attachment to their key caregivers. When they default to their safe grown-ups, they learn by interacting with and modelling from the adults they spend most time with. Invisibly, this is how children develop their own unique sense of self. If children are spending the majority of their lives with other children, rather than their key attachment adults, they can quite easily substitute their socialisation growth and development away from adults, especially adults who are strongly invested in them to other children.

> The problem is that the more children are peer attached, the less attached they are to adults – and this can result in children becoming very hostile to being parented or taught.
> —Neufeld (in Mrozek, 2012).

Essentially, Neufeld's message for parents is that if you are placing your child into long-based child care so that they will be 'socialised', you may like to know that your child will benefit more from being around caring parents than peers. That way they are developing a strong sense of self, which means that when they immerse themselves into environments with other children, they can mix, mingle and play without needing to defer their needs and wants to others. Their inner sense of security will be strong and they will be more respectful of the adults and teachers who will be caring for them.

> The first issue is always to establish strong, deep emotional connections with those who are raising you. And that should be our emphasis in society. If we did this, we would send our children to school late, not early.
> —Neufeld (in Mrozek, 2012).

At the conference in Canada, which I mentioned in the introduction, Professor W. Thomas Boyce gave an address entitled, *What the Genes Remember: The New Epigenetics of the Early Years*. In groundbreaking studies, they have been able to show that childhood adversity, particularly poor attachment (by age 3.5) can change the genes, especially the serotonin transporter gene, and this will increase the chances of the following occurring:

- School failure
- Chronic illness like diabetes and cancer
- Heart disease and cardiac deaths.

I was pretty stunned at that moment. To think that our DNA can change due to environmental influences challenged my previous learning about the nurture vs nature debate. Essentially, this means that no matter what DNA a child is born with, the influences of nurture or environmental influences can change that coding. Obviously it works both ways — safe, loving environments can change the DNA positively and environments where babies and toddlers feel threatened or unsafe set them on a trajectory towards ill health on many levels.

Children who are securely attached to their parents are more likely to:

- be able to cope well with stress
- have satisfying relationships
- have healthy self-esteem
- have good mental health
- reach their full intellectual potential
- have fewer behavioural problems
- have fewer discipline problems
- have fewer problems separating from parents when it is developmentally appropriate.

— Robin Grille, *Heart to Heart Parenting* (2008).

WHAT HELPS BUILD STRONG ATTACHMENT OR HEALTHY MOTHERING?

.We have been breeding for a very, very long time, however nothing has changed in terms of how to build a strong, safe connection to babies and toddlers. Put simply, with skin-to-skin, face-to-face, endless soothing, caressing, gentle sounds and constant reassurance that you (their big person) are close, you will meet their needs. What is really occurring with emotionally responsive parenting is the building of trust — the most important thing in almost any human relationship.

> Many of the infant and child behaviours that are challenging parents in our culture are unheard of in cultures that practise high-touch nurturing. Babies are biologically programmed to expect the same high-touch nurturing that evolved millions of years ago.
> — Pam Leo, "Connection Parenting", in *Kindred Magazine* (June-August 2008).

Tips for connecting:

- Create a caring bond as soon as possible with: lots of skin-to-skin contact; soothing when obviously distressed — not when the bottom lip quivers; enormous amounts of comfort touch such as rocking to sleep when they are distressed; singing soothing lullabies; tender stroking; pushing the pram backwards and forwards; and simple, genuine loving attention.
- Create pathways of comfort with sheepskins, cuddly blankets, soft toys, their hands or thumbs and maybe a comforter dummy.
- Involve others to help in the first two years only if they can be loving, caring and comfortable with safe, nurturing touch. This might include tickling, blowing raspberries, singing and playing, "Round and Round the Garden".
- Gazing deeply into your baby's face while making loving conversation is incredibly powerful for baby.
- Avoid forcing young ones when they are experiencing separation distress — this hurts a young child much like a physical pain.

WHAT ELSE DOES THIS ENTAIL?

Routines make it easier.

Try following a similar routine each day. For example, give your baby her breakfast, change her nappy, take her for a walk, play with her, take a nap, and so on.

Talk, smile and sing!

Describe what you're doing as you're doing it. Read aloud, catching her eye as you do.

Play every day.

Try the mirror-game: if your baby smiles, smile back; if she coos, coo back. Older babies love peek-a-boo and pat-a-cake. You can let her lead the play when she's able.

Repetition

Anything you do over and over teaches your baby "what the world is like". Lots of angry faces or lots of smiles: what will she learn about the world from you?

'Match' your baby.

Watch your baby to see the state she's in and approach her in the same way. If she's alert and active, approach her in a playful way. If she's quiet or upset, approach her quietly. If she startles when you speak, try a gentler way of speaking.

Babies need touch.

Babies need touch, just like they need food. The more you touch, hold and respond to your baby, the healthier, happier and smarter he'll be.
Touch helps his brain develop. It releases soothing hormones in Him — and in you. Hold your baby close as often as possible. If using a baby carrier, follow the instructions carefully.

Eye contact

Look into your baby's eyes often. It helps build a loving connection between you.

What's your baby saying?

When your baby coos, he's asking you to chat. When he cries, he's asking you to feed him, keep him warm, change him or hold him — or he's telling you he's sick or in pain.
He is saying, "stop what you're doing" if he turns away from you, cries, squirms, opens and closes his hands, pushes you, or flails his arms. Over time, you'll learn your baby's language.

A special personality.

As your baby grows, you'll get to know her personality. What does she like to play with? How does she calm herself? Let those who watch your baby for you know what your baby likes and dislikes.

— Source: Licia Rando, *Caring and Connected Parenting* (2010).

One of the saddest realities of our modern world is that the busyness of life has stolen many of the sacred moments that allow babies and toddlers to feel the deep and abiding presence of a significant loved one. Without the ability to be present to a baby or a toddler, it is very difficult — indeed impossible — to 'attune' to a child's unique sense of self, thus being able to meet <u>their needs</u> based on this attunement, not on what you learnt from their sibling, or what somebody else has told you about their baby, or what the maternal nurse has told you should do. Healthy attachment through attunement is essential to ensure every baby is set on the pathway to thrive and become a child who is happy, healthy, strong, kind and capable.

The ability to linger when feeding a baby, whether by bottle or breast, to gaze lovingly into a baby's face, to smother a baby's brow with endless gentle kisses and to make soothing low sounds of reassurance while a baby is being changed, dressed or settled are disappearing due to the pressures and interruptions of our chaotic world. Many mums of young babies and toddlers tell me that they feel they are drowning under exhaustion and stress. The first 12 months of a baby's life is when parents have the most disturbed sleep and sleep deprivation is one of the biggest stressors of being a parent. This was why the tribal approach to raising children was pure magic. There was always another woman who could give you respite, time for a little nap, time to have a shower so you could wash your hair or time to drink that cup of tea while it was still hot.

Tired and exhausted mums and dads are often unable to meet the needs of their babies and toddlers with calmness and unconditional love. It is very difficult to be joyful and patient when you are completely sleep deprived and exhausted. Healthy attachment needs human connectedness that is saturated with warm, loving interaction, respectful and child-centred care and an unhurried, calm environment.

> The parts of the brain concerned with regulations of emotion and deeply held attitudes to human relations are particularly dependent on human contact in order to develop. A mother's joyful interactions with her baby actually provide an essential building block to these areas of the brain.
>
> — Grille (2013).

CRYING BABIES AND TODDLERS

It is all very well to talk about warm, loving interactions and the tender moments of delight that we have with our babies, however this would be a lousy guide for parents if it did not include some information about crying. If there is one thing I wish someone had told me before I started breeding, it is that healthy babies still cry a lot. Apparently, it is quite common for young babies to cry for two to three hours a day — some more and some less. I also wish someone had told me that crying can increase when babies are around six to eight weeks old, with no obvious reason at all. I am sure I decided I was the worst mother on Earth around six to eight weeks after my first son was born.

Many parents of babies tell me how confused they are with the information they get from midwives, maternal nurses, well-meaning family members, parenting books and of course Google. In a recent survey, around one third of the 700 parents who responded, stated that they were uncertain how to respond when their baby cried. Apparently, this uncertainty was based around the fear that they may spoil their child and create bad habits. If one of the key essential requirements of early parenting is to ensure that your baby feels secure and that they can rely on you to care for them and meet their needs, then spoiling your baby is impossible. Remember the key is to respond sensitively to their needs on a regular basis, knowing that sometimes you will achieve that much more easily than other times. Comforting does not just mean picking a crying baby up, it also means patting, singing, rocking, stroking and making soothing 'shh, shh' noises. Like many parents, I have memories of putting a crying baby boy into the car while I was still in my nightie, driving around and around in the middle of the night because all else had failed. Thankfully, I was never pulled over by the police because I am sure they would have noticed the nursing pads under my nightie.

> **WILMA WALLABY**
> "The first three years are the most important years of a child's life — please spend lots of time giving them the best start in life."

Margot Sunderland in her excellent book, *The Science of Parenting* (2007), warns against allowing babies to get to a highly distressed state for more than a short time as all the brain chemicals flood their little brains and their primitive brain response is likened to being abandoned from the tribe and that death is imminent. She warns that this type of distress, if it happens, often can wire a child to be hypersensitive to stress for the rest of their lives and increase the chances of depression, self-harm and addictive behaviours — so sensitive is the developing brain of our babies and toddlers! They are unable to soothe themselves when they are distressed and need big people, especially the big people who love them, to help manage these big ugly feelings that frighten them. Even the most loving and attentive parents can find crying babies day after day enormously taxing and exhausting especially when they are sleep-deprived themselves. For mothers without partners this is an especially challenging time. The more support parents of new babies can get from either family or community, the better.

Wilma suggests that the best soothing options we have as parents are:

- Burping
- Swaddling
- Riding in car
- Singing, talking
- Rocking, swaying
- Increase warmth in the room
- Playing soft familiar music
- Making soothing sounds
- Rubbing, patting, stroking
- Rhythmic noise and vibration
- Walking with baby in your arms
- Body sack or carriage
- Gentle baby massage
- Warm baths.

— Source: Licia Rando, *Caring and Connected Parenting* (2010).

For more information on crying babies, go to: *www.raisingchildren.net.au* and search 'crying'.

Also check out Pinky McKay's website: *www.pinkymckay.com*. As well as having a whole book on sleep called, *Sleeping Like a Baby*, Pinky also offers some excellent online resources, does one-on-one consultations and runs seminars, particularly around breastfeeding and sleeping.

> # DID YOU KNOW:
> Did you know that some babies sleep better when they are tightly swaddled, while others sleep better by not being tightly swaddled?

SLEEP AND WHAT HELPS

It seems that everyone has opinions and ideas on how to get babies to sleep. One thing is for sure, babies need to sleep lots in order to grow well. Such rapid growth occurs in the first few years of life physically, emotionally and cognitively. Babies must experience the REM (or rapid eye movement) stage of sleep in order for the necessary growth hormones to facilitate optimum development. Quite simply, without enough sleep our nervous systems cannot function as well and we are prone to distress.

Poor sleep also often leads to poor appetite and if prolonged, poor sleep definitely compromises our immune systems and makes us even more vulnerable to illness and disease. Babies and toddlers who sleep well, play and explore in their world much more contentedly and freely. Poor sleep for both baby and parent can have a negative impact on healthy attachment.

Another thing I wish I'd known when I had my first son was how a baby's biological body clock works. Circadian rhythms develop over time as the brain and other organic systems mature. This is a complex interplay that involves: hormones, external cues like light, touch and smell, temperature and food intake. It can take up to two to three months before babies have their circadian rhythms sorted out in such a way that they have good sleep patterns. The first 'big one' is helping your baby learn the difference between day and night. There is nothing more frustrating than having a cheeky eight-week-old wanting to play between 1 AM and 5 AM, and then proceeding to sleep nearly all day! This too is quite normal development.

Understanding sleep cycles

All humans have different sleep cycles when sleeping at night. Without going into too much depth, babies tend to have five stages of sleep. The first four stages are varying depths of non-REM sleep followed by one REM deep sleep stage. Stages one and two are when the baby is drowsy and sleeping lightly, and can be easily disturbed by noises or movement. Stages three and four are deep sleep phases and in that relaxed state, babies may be difficult to rouse. The final stage, stage five, is REM sleep. This is a light sleep stage where there is increased brain activity and dreaming, and sometimes a baby may make little movements that looked like they are waking up however it is really important not to disturb them. This stage of sleep is where the growth hormones are released. This sequence of sleep patterns tends to begin from around three months of age and continues throughout one's life.

The length of sleep cycles can vary up to around three months of age. During the day, your baby will generally complete the cycle every 20 to 40 minutes. After three months, the cycle length changes to around 30 to 60 minutes until the end of the first year. At night the sleep cycles tend to be longer, especially in the first half of the evening. It is a challenging irony that the longest patch of sleep our babies tend to have is before adults get to bed or very soon after.

The best kept secret about babies' sleep is that as they move between cycles and experience states of wakefulness — during which they may have their eyes open, be grizzling or even full-on crying — they are not ready to be fully awake as they have not had enough sleep. This is where our soothing techniques come into play as we gently help them move into the next cycle of sleep. If a baby gets distressed, then it will be very difficult for them to soothe themselves back to sleep without possibly needing more than just patting.

Helping babies to self settle can take enormous patience however it is better for everyone concerned. If a baby expects to be picked up every time they come to a light phase of wakefulness, then they will become distressed if that does not occur. No matter how well informed you are around sleep patterns for babies, there are times when illness, temperament or stressful environments may mean your baby will have horrendous nights with very little sleep. You are not failing as a mum or a dad if this occurs. You merely have to survive until the baby grows fatter and older, when they will be able to sleep more settled for longer.

Toddlers can also be notoriously poor sleepers and sometimes it is better for everyone if they sleep wherever they feel safest. Co-sleeping with babies is not recommended due to the risk of babies being suffocated accidentally. Nothing could be more tragic than such an event happening.

However, statistics indicate that almost half of all two-week-old infants end up in their parents' bed, so if you do make the choice to co-sleep, it's very important that you educate yourself about the risks and take precautions, such as those outlined below from the *Raising Children Network*.

It is never advisable to sleep with your baby if you or your partner smoke or take drugs (including alcohol).

Co-sleeping precautions:

- Put your baby on his back to sleep (never on his tummy or side).
- Make sure his head is uncovered during sleep.
- Keep the sleep environment smoke-free.
- Don't sleep with your baby on the couch. This is very dangerous, because your baby can get trapped between you and the cushions and can suffocate.
- Make sure your bed is firm. Don't use a waterbed, or anything soft underneath (for example, a lamb's wool underlay).
- Use lightweight blankets, not heavy quilts or doonas.
- Make sure that bedding can't cover your baby's head.
- Don't use any pillows.
- An infant sleeping bag can be used instead of bedding, so that your baby doesn't share adult bedding.
- Put your baby beside one parent, not between parents, so there's less chance she'll slip under the bedding.

- Put your baby where he can't fall out of bed, but not against pillows or a wall. Babies can suffocate under pillows and have died after becoming trapped between the bed and the wall. A safer alternative is to put the mattress on the floor.
- A 'side car crib' that attaches to your bed provides a separate sleeping surface but keeps your baby close for breastfeeding.

— Sourced from the Raising Children Network's comprehensive and quality-assured Australian parenting website http://raisingchildren.net.au

Bedtime rituals

Sleep patterns for toddlers and children can vary and change due to the stressors of modern life. Having a regular routine that leads up to bedtime is incredibly helpful to calm busy children and prepare them to fall asleep. Feeling safe and secure helps everyone sleep better. I am a firm believer in bedtime rituals that reassure children they are loved and safe.

My favourite bedtime ritual is:

I love you more than every star in the night skies. I love you more than every grain of sand on every beach in the whole wide world. And I love you more than all the hairs on all the bears.

It is important that children hear their favourite bedtime ritual often, however if you have had a lousy day, and you are feeling stressed and grumpy, it will not reassure your child at all. Actually it may give them nightmares!

I once had a lady who came to speak to me after one of my seminars. She said she had a four-year-old son and she paused and looked a little uncomfortable and then said, "It's not that I don't like him, we just are not close. Do you have any suggestions that may help me?"

I suggested that she tried the bedtime ritual and I am sure she left thinking that would not be very helpful. One week later, I was surprised to see the same mum at another seminar in another town and she came to speak to me.

She said she wanted to tell me what happened so that I could tell other parents what happened when she began the bedtime ritual. Apparently the first night when she did the ritual, her son looked at her suspiciously, probably wondering where the heck she pulled that new thing from. On the second night, her son looked again as if to say, "Oh, she is doing it again!" However, this mum said the following morning after just two nights with the new bedtime ritual, her son came to her while she was washing the dishes, and he wrapped his arms around her thigh and put his head against her leg and said, "Mummy I have got one more for us. You love me more than all the fluff on all the fabric in the whole world". As she told me this, her eyes teared up and she said, "It took just two nights for my son and I to fall in love. I can't thank you enough".

Over the years, I have heard so many examples of how much parents love their children — more than all the Hot Wheels in the world; more than all the hairs on daddy's back; more than all the scales on all the fish in all the seas; more than all the bears, the stars, the fish and smelly feet in all the world. The concept of love is not easy for children to understand, especially when we have had to sanction them or growl at them. Through the eyes of a child, that can sometimes seem like you don't love them.

> An article in *The West Australian* newspaper (October 22nd 2005, p62) showed that kids are likely to rate a hug from mum as of higher importance than the latest X-Box game. Special education and behaviour management lecturer Jonathon Sargeant from New England University found in his PhD study 'cuddles, affection and happy parents' were high on the list of what pleased children the most.
> — Maggie Dent, *Nurturing Kids' Hearts and Souls* (2005).

In a way, children see love as connection — where they sense that you not only see them, but that you feel them invisibly and strongly. Many people talk about having quality time with their children and while that is a good thing, I recommend 'micro-moments of loving connectedness' that happen often, rather than quality time that is created by an adult. Children live in the present moment and when we come and join them, even briefly, in that amazing place it makes their hearts sing. When we can come to them and share in their childlike view of the world, children know we love them. Many parents who have to work tell me how they struggle with feeling guilty that they are unable to spend a lot of time with their children. The same goes for those who work away from home like FIFOs (fly-in-fly-out workers) in our mining towns and those in the military services. There are many ways, some really tiny, that build a heart connection with our children. I was blessed to spend hours of my childhood in the ute driving around the farm with my dad as a captive audience for my endless chatter and questioning about everything. No wonder he struggled with his hearing as he got older.

A child can feel unloved by a parent who really loves them a lot! This is an interesting phenomenon that I have noticed again and again over my years as a counsellor. The parent thinks it is obvious how much they love their child because of all the things they do for them and because they know how they feel about their child. Children can feel gratitude for what is done for them but still feel unloved.

WHEN THE LOVING IS NOT HAPPENING — POST-NATAL DEPRESSION

Often in my counselling work and in my women's retreats, I come across mums whose journey in the first six months of their baby's life was a blur of exhaustion, sadness, overwhelm and at times, it was almost too much to bear. These mums had experienced postpartum depression, sometimes called PND. The list of symptoms associated with PND can sometimes look similar to a new mum who does not have PND.

Symptoms

- fatigue
- disinterest in her baby
- sleeplessness
- enormous sadness
- tearfulness
- anxiety
- hopelessness
- feelings of worthlessness and guilt
- irritability
- irrational moments of anger and rage
- appetite change
- poor concentration
- strong need to withdraw.

Marcy Axness in her book, *Parenting for Peace* (2012) states that PND can almost always be detected by a single, simple screening question — "Is the mother feeling joy?" Given that implicit memory pathways have such a powerful unconscious effect on us as adults, then possibly a mother whose own birth and postpartum relationship with her mum when she was born was joyous, uncomplicated and uninterrupted, could be less likely to suffer PND. Contrary to most common conventional wisdom, there is little evidence that hormonal fluctuations actually cause PND; rather they can reflect, amplify and extend it. This is explored in greater depth in the next chapter, THE BOUNTIFUL BRAIN IN INFANCY.

Daniel Siegel in his book, *Mindsight* (2010), explores how our perceptions and memories can be changed with therapy — and that our emotional memories, which many children retain from their birth experience, can be healed and transformed so that the painful implicit memory pathway can also be changed. I have worked with many children who struggled by being incredibly stubborn, driven and seemingly always at war with their parents — only to find that their birth included the experience of being stuck and/or at risk of dying. This emotional memory can sometimes create an irrational mindset to avoid feeling powerless ever again. I have found that well-trained kinesiologists are our best practitioners to help unravel some of these implicit patterns and memories that come from the birth experience.

What is real is that PND is a mental illness that requires professional help as soon as possible, along with enormous compassion and support from family and friends. So often, mums who experienced PND express the same sense of failure and guilt as those who are unable to breastfeed even though they want to. The mothering journey is one that challenges us often and every mum will have times when she feels helpless and powerless. I can remember vividly how powerless I felt during my first son's delivery when he got stuck — thankfully I had amazing, experienced midwives who I was able to surrender to, and who guided me on what to do to ensure his safe delivery. I can also remember those same feelings when I was carrying my second son as I kept going into labour from around 27 weeks, for no obvious reason. I am a strong type-A personality, however I recognised early on that I was unable to control this journey of mothering and that I needed to learn from the wise Wilmas who have walked this journey before me. I learnt patience, humility and profound gratitude for those that helped me mother my four miracles. If you are a mum who still struggles feeling guilty because you had PND, or because you needed a Caesarean instead of a vaginal delivery or you were unable to breastfeed as you had wanted, again I recommend that you visit a good kinesiologist or therapist who is recognised at helping women heal. I have had women tell me they have had significant healing by using *TRE — Trauma Release Exercises* as taught by trauma specialist, Dr David Berceli.

> External conflict comes to an end with the dawn of internal peace.
> — Dr David Berceli

Dr Berceli has discovered in his work that the shock of many traumatic experiences in our lives, including when we have fallen off a bike and knocked out our front teeth, stays in our nervous system until they have been discharged. He refers to how indigenous peoples have a deep respect for the energy of the body and they often avoid suppressing it. Sometimes, for example, grieving will involve loud wailing, stomping the ground or dancing vigorously. These are incredibly healthy ways to discharge big emotions from the body. In the Western world we tend to avoid expressing big emotions and we subdue them and suppress them until they reach a tipping point and often they explode in frightening moments of spontaneous rage. Dr Berceli noticed in his studies that women in traditional communities tended to have a spontaneous tremor experience after childbirth. He wondered if this powerful release of birth trauma from the body was one of the reasons why women in traditional communities very rarely experience PND.

As well as TRE exercises, I also recommend simple energy techniques — like *EFT (Emotional Freedom Techniques)* and *SET* (simple energy techniques) — that are easy to learn to use on yourself. I began using these techniques back in 1999 and found that they were the best way to release trauma experiences from the body as well as the mind. For more information on these techniques or how to participate in a weekend seminar about them, visit *www.eftdownunder.com*. I have enormous respect for psychologist Steve Wells and Dr David Lake and each year I try to spend a weekend tapping, laughing and learning how to move irrational, disturbing emotions from the body.

We need to keep a close eye on our new mums for any signs of PND because the sooner it is identified and help received the better for everybody. Remember it is not a sign of poor mothering and it is not a sign of weakness — it is a serious mental illness. Asking for help is a sign of strength and courage, however mums have told me that they thought all of the feelings they were feeling were just the normal feelings of being sleep deprived with a demanding baby. Please keep an eye on new mums exhibiting any of the obvious signs and symptoms, please step forward with an open heart to help them overcome this additional challenge they could not anticipate.

HOW DO YOU ENSURE YOUR CHILD FEELS LOVED?

Firstly, remember that every child is unique. What works for one child may not work for another. Secondly, the metaphor of a 'love cup' is really helpful to remember; if your child's love cup is full they feel loved. If their love cup is not full, they may feel disconnected, unloved and un-special —hug them! Unfortunately, I cannot remember being held tenderly by my mother when I was young. I am a highly kinaesthetic person so this was a serious deprivation in my life. If I had been more dependent on vision or sound as my first sense it may have been less of a problem for me. Physical touch and intimacy is really important for my wellbeing and I am now blessed to be surrounded by an abundance of it in my life.

An excellent book that explains how to fill your child's love cup is *The 5 Love Languages of Children* (2012) by Gary Chapman and Ross Campbell. There are five ways that we fill our children's love cups:

1. **Physical touch** — children and teenagers who really love physical touch will often touch you, sometimes in an annoying way! This is why some boys love to fight or wrestle with their dad; it is an intimate safe touch that fills their love cup. Teenagers who needed touch to feel loved as a child STILL need it. Ask them what works best for them.

2. **Words of affirmation** — hearing words of love, encouragement, guidance and appreciation works for some children. They are sensitive to tone and criticism, often very sensitive. They need to hear, "I love you" often!

3. **Quality time** — if this is the primary way your child feels loved they may sometimes drive you nuts with wanting your full attention. They value real eye contact, one-on-one time, real conversations, sharing feelings and bedtime rituals.
4. **Gifts** — these children are very attached to the gifts you have bought them over the years and rather than be concerned with cost, size or shape, they are more tuned into the thought you put into purchasing the gift. Be very careful about buying meaningful gifts and of bribery and manipulation as your child will know the difference!
5. **Acts of service** — these children respond to acts of service. They notice and mention when you cook their favourite meal, come to watch them play sport or make their school lunch in good time. The main motivation must be love, not manipulation or to get something. Also be mindful of making requests and not commands.

I recommend that you read *The 5 Love Languages of Children* and explore with your child their preferred love language; see how you can build on their feelings of being loved.

Families can also use the love cup metaphor. Ask your children what makes them feel happy, calm and really valued. What family rituals support this state of wellbeing? As a teacher I learned about the importance of happy family memories by asking my students to create a timeline of their lives so far. What staggered me was that most of the significant moments on their timelines were painful or unpleasant times. It was much harder for them to remember the good things, and this tendency was expressed over and over again. My suggestion to parents is to consciously build in special moments and family rituals that are more likely to be remembered because of their repetition. For more on family rituals and making memories that matter see the next chapter,

THE BOUNTIFUL BRAIN IN INFANCY.

Dr Vanessa Lapointe, a Canadian child psychologist I deeply respect, stresses the need for us to always work to preserve and nurture our connection with our children and to avoid anything that separates them from us. Her key guidelines for parents and those who care for children are:

<u>Guiding Principles</u>

- Children find their way to independence through dependence — if we force independence in the hope that it will yield independence, we foster emotional immaturity.
- Children need us to be the 'alpha' in the family — or the big person.
- Big people must always be the answer to little people's troubles — even if you have no idea what the answer is! The child must believe you have the answer!

- When a challenging moment happens, focus on the **why** rather than the **what**.
- It is always about the relationship: **CHOOSE TO DO NO HARM!**

— Dr Vanessa Lapointe, *Beyond Behaviour: Understanding Children from the Inside Out* (2012).

Babies, toddlers and children live in the present moment and one of the best ways to ensure that they feel loved and emotionally connected to you as their parents is to meet them in the present moment rather than during adult-prescribed quality time. This concept of meeting children with a specific intention to nurture connection through how we interact with them comes from Neufeld's work, especially his book, *Hold On to Your Kids* (2005). Neufeld believes so much of the parenting practices of today create experiences of separation for our young children, rather than experiences that connect and bond us with our children. When this occurs repeatedly, children's trust in us is broken and the relationship will be weakened. I have renamed the bridges from Neufeld's work as "love bridges" — which build stronger heart connections with our children to ensure that they feel safe and secure within their families. If you can keep in mind that, when you are dealing with challenging behaviour in your child, your priority is to work at the relationship first and the behaviour second; this will ensure that you will be on the right track to use discipline in a way that benefits everyone.

BUILDING LOVE BRIDGES WITH OUR CHILDREN

- Wink at children, make funny faces, give them high fives or thumbs up – non-verbal messages of connection.
- Parents can give small symbols to hold onto in their absence like kisses in the child's hands.
- Create a unique bedtime ritual… "I love you more than…".
- Send them rainbows when you are away.
- Create an imaginary giant protector/guardian angel to watch over your child.
- Have a picture of you with your child in a locket or plastic sleeve they can keep in their bag.
- Record readable stories or messages on smart phones if you're away.
- Take small bites out of their toast or a bite out of their sandwich.
- Leave notes or funny pictures in their lunch box or on the bathroom mirror.
- Hide special messages around the house when you go away.
- Spontaneously join them in drawing or colouring in.
- Join them on the couch randomly to watch their favourite show.

- Engage in spontaneous hugs, cuddles and tickles.
- Launch a 'surprise bedroom attack' (for older children!)

Surprise bedroom attack...

The 'surprise bedroom attack' involves waiting about five minutes after the lights go out, then creeping into your child's bedroom and throwing yourself onto your child in the dark, covering them with kisses, tickles and perhaps even blowing raspberries on their stomach — and then you race out the room. A small warning about the surprise bedroom attack — which is recommended for a child who has had a really lousy day — avoid the joint mum and dad attack without careful planning. I do know a couple who ended up with mild concussion when they executed their simultaneous surprise attack for their full-on 'rooster' son after he had had a very difficult day. Although, apparently when their heads collided their son thought it was hilarious and cheered up enormously! I would suggest you also be mindful of doing this to your sensitive 'lamb' children or you may actually create an anxiety disorder. The aim of the surprise bedroom attack is to demonstrate your deep and profound love for your child — no matter what.

Experience vs stuff

The consumer world has put enormous pressure on parents to buy toys and 'stuff' to make their child stimulated and smart. Also, in some places there is pressure to schedule lots of classes and activities — also designed to make your child smarter and cleverer. Much of this pressure is unwarranted as babies and toddlers find their own world fascinating — ice-cream containers, plastic cups, cellophane paper, boxes, balls — things with different shapes and textures are all teachable toys. So save your money to buy good food and quality toys like wooden blocks, jigsaw puzzles and Duplo, which allow children to gradually become more and more competent. These toys may look boring to adults however they can be used in different ways by a small child and you can use them for every baby or child you have or one that visits! Children also learn by modelling adult behaviour so think of dress-up clothes, plastic lawnmowers and chainsaws, dolls that look like babies, little prams and kitchen items. Children can learn from using real pots and pans, wooden spoons and plastic bowls. Many young toddlers can spend hours playing in the plastics cupboard, with a basket of pegs or a set of car keys. A great take on what 10-month-olds really want for Christmas can be found online at *www.theuglyvolvo.com/a-ten-month-olds-letter-to-santa/*

A couple of the things this baby wanted were:

- I would love a set of house keys. To eat, obviously. Only metal house keys will do. Please do not buy me plastic ones. I am not an idiot. I know that plastic house keys are not real keys.
- Glasses — I pull these off the face of every person I meet, only to have them pried from my fingers and reclaimed by their original owners. I would love a pair of my own. Again, these are going to be for eating.
- Dog hair — This stuff is the best. I keep trying to pull it off but she moves frequently, making collection difficult. My favorite thing to do with it is put it in my mouth and then immediately realize that I didn't want it in my mouth.
- The hole in the hallway floor board — Such a strange existential dilemma. I spend hours looking at this hole and poking at it with my fingers. I know that I cannot "have" a hole, as a hole is not a thing that can be had. A hole is an absence. And yet this is supposed to be a list of the things I want, and I want this hole in the hardwood floor the way Gandhi wanted peace. The way the dog wants to lick my face. The way my mother wants me to stop pulling off her eyeglasses.

Safe base

Babies and toddlers often like to play within reach of their significant caregiver. As they feel braver, they venture away to explore and then come back to their 'safe base'. As they build in courage, they will be able to play for longer without having Mum or a carer in sight. Children differ in their ability to play by themselves and 'lambs' or more sensitive children may take longer to be brave. However, with loving support and encouragement they will grow in this ability. When a child can trust their 'safe base' and the proximity to their significant loving adult, then they tend to be braver and more courageous. Lapointe (2012) again stresses the importance of the following:

1. Children are meant to **pursue** proximity.
2. Adults are meant to **provide** proximity.
3. The purpose of attachment is to keep the child safe and make the child feel safe.
4. Attachment is as important to healthy child development as eating or sleeping.
5. **Attachment is the 'super glue' that holds a child in close proximity to a parent/caregiver.**

It does seem almost ironic that a child learns independence by being completely dependent on their significant big person. However, that is how Mother Nature planned it to be. As children grow older they still have a primary need to feel that they are loved and valued. In a way, it is like building bridges that show we are connected even when we have to teach our children right ways and boundaries.

A great way for parents to build connection rather than separation is to acknowledge our children. This is much better than just endless praise, which has been shown to de-motivate our children and turn them into praise 'junkies'. It is amazing how powerful it is to a toddler or young child when a smiling adult comes really close to them and makes strong eye contact with them. Just watch their face light up. Being 'present' to young children is how they know they are loved. This is explored in much more depth in the chapter, ROOSTERS AND LAMBS, where I discuss compassionate communication.

RELATIONSHIPS WITH SELF AND OTHERS

> What began as a pattern of interaction in relationships becomes generalised into expectations of the world, coded unconsciously, part of the structure of the mind. It becomes a kind of internal map of the self, of the other, of self with other.
> — Anne Manne, *Motherhood* (2005).

Families live with constant change. Relationships with self, with partners and with children are constantly evolving and changing. Life is unpredictable. Children are also innately unpredictable. Every age in childhood brings with it a new gift and a new challenge. Do you remember wishing your toddler could walk and then a few months later, getting exhausted chasing them? And wishing your daughter could talk and then soon wishing she would be quiet? Such is the nature of parenthood — a constant cycle of change.

> As parents, we are valuable, indispensable, needed. The ongoing, always-at-the-ready, nature of being a parent makes it extremely challenging to always be emotionally available for our children. But that is precisely what they need – a parent who is emotionally available. This is the single most important thing we can do to create a happy peaceful home and a secure child.
> — Justin Coulson, *What Your Child Needs from You* (2012).

The safe circle of care provides opportunities to support the healthy development of babies and toddlers. The things that worked in the past, before our modern technological world emerged, still allow healthy development to occur. This includes child-centred learning experiences rather than adult-driven ones. Babies do not need massive, expensive machine-made toys or DVDs to be stimulated. The everyday and natural world is fascinating for growing babies and toddlers, especially with things like baskets of clothes pegs, coloured paper, sand, pebbles, water, the plastics cupboard, cuddly comfort teddies and stuffed animals.

> **WILMA WALLABY**
>
> "Our kids need real experiences with real people or with pets, dirt, puddles, mud, trees, leaves and fresh air to grow healthy brains, minds and bodies."

Resist the overzealousness of well-meaning thinking, assuming that you need to be always entertaining your children or stimulating them. It is the biggest con of the toy world — "stimulate your child to make them smart". The market for parents as consumers is massive and the way to make parents put their hands in their pocket to spend their money is to make you feel guilty or frightened. If you don't buy enough of their toys to stimulate your baby or toddler, then the supposition is you are a lousy parent and your child will end up on the rubbish tip of life. Nothing could be further from the truth. This will be explored in more depth in the next chapter about THE BOUNTIFUL BRAIN IN INFANCY.

THINGS FOR OVER-3S

Learning for life

The early years are when children begin to build a toolkit of life skills. Building up the toolkit starts from birth and sometimes it is the little things, like getting themselves a drink of water when they need to, that are the big things. It is interesting to notice that in traditional Aboriginal culture, children were encouraged to become self-reliant earlier than in non-Aboriginal families. Small milestones build a child's belief in their competence to accomplish tasks, which in turn helps build their self-esteem. Adults should avoid the one or two word commands and rather converse with their toddlers and young children about things such as:

- "To be safe we hold hands when we cross busy roads."
- "Why do we wash our hands after going to the toilet?"
- "Why are vegetables good for us?"

- "What does sour taste like?"
- "Sleep makes our brains and our bodies healthy and smart — so let's get to sleep!"
- "What are seat belts used for?"
- "How do you know when you are thirsty or hungry?"
- "You seem angry that Sam has taken your toy from you — how else can you show your anger without biting Sam?"
- "Shall we clean up all these toys before we have lunch, or shall we do it after we have lunch?"

The more tools in a child's toolkit, the more resilient the child will be. The first tools deal with practical things like being able to dress and feed themselves, going to the toilet unaided, and being able to play with others. Building tools in our child's toolkit takes enormous patience and time. Sometimes when our children are learning to dress themselves, it could seem like they have terrible parents who allow their shirt to be on inside out, maybe even their pants, or their boots to be on the wrong feet. Be careful never to judge how a child is dressed as a sign of poor parenting — if the child has done it himself, it's a sign of great parenting!

All learning is sequential for babies and toddlers, and it takes time for things to become solid memory. Repetition of meaningful experiences is the key to building the required neural pathways. Many early years' teachers are concerned that more children are coming to preschool and kindergarten without having mastered basic toilet training skills, with poor organisational skills and struggling to feed themselves. Early years' educators also express concern that parents are expecting them to take on the responsibility of toilet training their young children during the day. Sometimes, these same parents are happy to leave a nappy on once they collect their children at the end of the day. This can be very confusing for toddlers. Remember it still takes a village to raise a child and everyone can contribute to a child's capacity to manage themselves — everyone needs to help them build life skills to go in their lifelong toolkit.

> All children learn, grow and master life skills at differing rates. There is no competition in raising children – there never has been and never should be. However a parent who keeps doing things for a child when they can do it themselves – even if slower and messier – is hindering their child's development and confidence.

Children need to keep building up the tools in their toolkit for every year of their lives. I am still learning new life skills and I am almost 60. Sometimes you will meet a three-year-old who is able to do things an eight-year-old cannot do. The more time and energy we invest in the early years in building our children's capacity to be capable, the sooner they'll master new skills and their self-confidence will grow.

Self-mastery as explored in my '10 resilience building blocks model' is only achieved with young children through much time, energy and guidance from their significant big people. This skill building can happen at home with committed parents or carers, and it can also happen in early years' centres, or family day care in the company of quality trained and passionate early years' educators. Quality early years' educators are focused on the whole child and are fully aware of the incredibly important role they play in early childhood. Best practice in early years' education creates standout children when they transition to school. There is no need to change best practice — which includes play-based learning environments, child-centred and adult- directed activities, plenty of nature time, and immersing children in real-life experiences. However I will explore more of that later in some of the other chapters. Remember, some children develop abilities and capacity in different areas much earlier than others and it is important to avoid comparing your child with someone else's. As you will read in the chapter about gender, many three-year-old girls run rings around their five-year-old brothers in many areas of development. By around the age of eight, these differences seem to have disappeared.

Some of the life skills that are important to start developing as young as possible are the following:

- Communication skills, both listening and speaking
- Thinking skills
- Dressing themselves
- Basic organisational skills, e.g. putting their shoes in their bag
- Social skills like listening, waiting
- Sense of humour
- Pre-literacy preparation — singing, rhyming, repetition, conversation
- Personal hygiene
- Patterns around food — ability to feed themselves
- Family rituals
- Protective behaviours — knowing about boundaries around their private parts
- Life understanding around family, school and life challenges like loss, death and transitions
- Practical skills including gross and fine motor skills
- Emotional literacy
- How to be a good friend.

Another important life skill involves the art of finding solutions. This is about helping children to discover other choices that they could make in response to a challenge, whether a disagreement with a friend or a toy that has broken.

A commitment to search for solutions begins with the adult.

> Children will not enter school ready to learn unless families, schools and communities provide the environments and experiences that support the physical, social, emotional, language, literacy and cognitive development of infants, toddlers and preschool.
> — From the US National School Readiness Indicators Initiative cited in ARACY, School Readiness (2007).

Children do not yet have a frontal lobe in their brains where reasoning and problem solving takes place but they can develop thinking skills that empower them to manage some situations themselves. There is a great temptation for parents to rescue their children from struggles and challenges, however this denies them vital opportunities to learn life management skills for themselves.

Essential life skills involve using manners, etiquette, road rules, practising good hygiene — such as bathing and cleaning teeth — doing up buttons and tying shoelaces. These are the little things that other children may use to tease a child. Parents must be proactive to help their children gain essential life skills so the children are able to take care of their own age-appropriate needs — and not expect child care, kindergarten or preschool to be places where children learn these vital life skills. A child can be bullied and teased if they are unable to complete basic tasks when at preschool. This can be very painful and may leave scars that later impact on his or her ability to be resilient. Peer-based sanctions and observations can, however, serve as great motivators as well. Children who notice they are the only ones in the class who cannot tie up their shoelaces are suddenly very keen to learn this skill — one of my sons mastered it overnight when he was in Grade One. I had failed him by using elastic sided boots instead of lace-up shoes — too many busy lads to keep in lace-up shoes in my house!

We continue to face an uncertain future with depleting oil supplies and the effects of global warming. It is more important than ever that we prepare our children by helping them to develop life skills that build on environmental appreciation and ecological sustainability. The return of home vegetable gardens is a great place to start. Children love to be involved

WILMA WALLABY

"Before you fix a problem for a child, help them to explore ways to overcome it for themselves."

anywhere there is dirt; and watching seeds turn into shoots and seedlings is quite magical for small children. If space is limited then even pots with fresh herbs are a great experience for children; and to pick fresh herbs and take them into the kitchen can provide an important life awareness to take into adulthood. There are children who have no idea where milk comes from, or even what many fruit and vegetables are. Gardening is a great way to be alongside your children as they play, and it helps ground us and slow us down as well. This outside activity can also help children develop an understanding of the seasons and the amazing flow of natural life. These may seem small things to adults, however they are big for children. Outside activities can also plant a seed of possibility for a child, which may develop into a potential career path later in life. I know of zoologists who have grown from being frog-gatherers and lizard-catchers as children. Steve Irwin's passion for wildlife would have started early in his childhood as he followed his father's love of the natural world. I wonder what creatures were hiding in his bedroom at times!

Much of the essential learning that takes place in childhood, especially in the early years, is building emotional and social competence. We now know there are many ways of being intelligent and one of these is emotional intelligence (EQ). Research shows that 80% of a person's potential to be successful in life has to do with their EQ and not their IQ (Daniel Goleman). We can encourage emotional intelligence and competence from an early age because this builds resilience for later in life. This will be covered in more depth in the chapter on KINDNESS AND FAIRNESS REALLY MATTERS.

> **WILMA WALLABY**
>
> "Kids need a lot of practice to master life skills so be patient and encourage them to keep trying. Failure is normal in life and does not mean we are bad or useless."

In some areas of today's world, parenting has become some form of competition and many parents, particularly mums, are seeking to create the perfect child. This is a good example of an unrealistic, unhealthy expectation that can cause enormous angst for mum and baby. Many mums tell me how confused and overwhelmed they are with the pressure, mainly from other mums, to be a perfect mother. Some have shared with me that they feel in playgroups, for example, that very few mothers are brave enough to admit how exhausted they are, how some days they really struggle with their children, and that they sometimes yell and smack in complete frustration and overwhelm. This is why I recommend that every mum with a baby or toddler should find a Wilma, a wise gentle supportive woman who has experienced cracked nipples, sleepless nights, vomiting babies and despair at what's happened to her body since she surrendered it to the journey of being a mother. Wilma will often be an older mum but she also may just be someone in your life who's embarked on parenting earlier than you; above all she needs to be an ally.

I send strong messages out everywhere I go that we need to heal the sisterhood, to remove the judgement, the bitchiness, the "tut, tut, tut" in the school car park and the hurtful gossiping that goes on behind each other's backs. Women were never in competition with each other as mothers — traditionally they were a circle of rock-solid, unconditional support. In our information-overloaded world, parents are drowning in confusion and even well-meaning experts are shaking their heads at the confusion. I am no expert, however I am committed to supporting families and communities in the healthy raising of our children with as little stress and as much love is possible. Yes, I am a Wilma and common sense is still important in our homes. Google is not a Wilma!

I really like the way that child psychologist Dr Louise Porter in her book, *Children are People Too*, has expressed similar views around childhood. If we are able to have more realistic expectations around our children — accepting deeply that there is no perfect; and that there will be challenging moments; and that we will make mistakes — I am sure we can reduce some of the pressure on today's parents. Porter noticed the following four triggers in young children that occur simply because children are children:

1. Children are naturally exuberant and excitable and can crash into each other and hurt each other—often they feel a need to retaliate.
2. Children learn through exploration both physically and socially and some of their actions like throwing food on the floor are a result of this, rather than a deliberate act of defiance.
3. Children under three years of age may not know any better—yet. They are still learning.
4. Sometimes children lose control of themselves—just like some adults do. Yes, they know what they should do, but they lose control—like a person on a diet who cannot resist a bucket of hot chips.

WHEN CHILDREN ARE HARD WORK...

Children are just kids and sometimes they struggle to behave as we would like! This does not mean they are bad — they are simply struggling with managing their world. Kids need help to manage how they cope with the environment and the people who are in their environment. For a more detailed exploration of discipline see the chapter where I explore KINDNESS AND FAIRNESS.

Swiss/American developmental psychologist Aletha Solter (1989) believes there are three main reasons for inappropriate behaviour in children. And the first one is there will be an unmet need.

Firstly, consider — from the child's perspective — is there an unmet need?

A child may be:

- wet
- tired
- thirsty
- hungry
- bored
- needing love and attention

How can I help meet that need?

You might say to your child:

- "Will a hug help?"
- "Here is a drink of water. Does that help?"
- "Do you feel sick? Let me feel your head?"
- "Let's go outside for a while."
- "Can I help you with something?"
- "Tell me what you need right now."

Secondly, children often repeat the same inappropriate behaviour because they don't know any other way to behave in the same or similar situation. We as adults need to give them more information to help them make a better choice next time. For example, Johnny bites Sarah in the sandpit because she was sitting on his truck. She gets off quickly, so his need is met however biting others is not OK and Johnny needs to know that. Simply chastising him or growling at him **does not give him other options** to guide him in knowing what to do when someone interferes with his toys again. So we need to show him how to put his hands up and say, "No" or "Get off please" or maybe give a gentle shove. Until we show other ways of managing the conflict, we have not helped him avoid behaving inappropriately.

Thirdly, sometimes children behave poorly because their nervous system is stressed or threatened. Painful feelings can result from stress or unhealed trauma such as anger and frustration, feeling powerless or weak, feeling unsafe or threatened, or that no one cares. The nervous system will be producing stress hormones such as cortisol and adrenalin. Too much stress or distress in a child can cause long-term damage.

> Studies show that some children are dealing with far too much stress in their lives, because of biological, social, psychological and/or environmental reasons. Some children are constantly pushing too hard on the gas or the brake pedal, jumping erratically from one level (of arousal) to another or not hard enough.
> — Lillas & Turnbull (2009).

> These children have to work much harder to pay attention and risk falling further and further behind or having greater and greater social problems exacerbate the drain on their already over-stretched nervous system.
> — Dr Stuart Shanker, presentation to Early Childhood Australia (2011).

The good news is that there are clear indicators of what helps children manage their nervous systems. Maybe next time you see a child throwing a spectacular tantrum in a shop you might nod understandingly towards the parent while thinking, "that child is just discharging excess emotions from their nervous system!"

Non-verbal gestures of support are also powerful. I used to pull an exaggerated sad or angry face that often worked as a wonderful distraction in the moment. Otherwise I simply opened my arms for a hug. I think the most important thing is that we need to respond to meltdowns in a caring way, knowing that our child is simply not coping with their world in this moment, and it may have nothing at all to do with us. As the 'alpha' in the house, they will always look to us to solve their problems until they are empowered to do so for themselves. Remember every day is a new day and a strategy that works one day may not work the next day; however, that doesn't mean you are a lousy parent.

Flexibility and creativity are two great assets in a parent's toolkit. It goes without saying that a sense of humour is also a great asset in that same toolkit. It's just really hard to find when you have sleep deprivation, a cracked nipple, constipation or a really sick little toddler whose only comfort is lying on your chest every minute of a very long day and night.

David Swanson in his book, *Help — My Kid is Driving Me Crazy*, writes that children have five reasons to manipulate their parents:

1. To obtain love, attention and nurturance.
2. For self-preservation — to achieve something he/she likes or to stop losing something he/she likes.
3. To bring about a self-prosperous condition — (I WIN. I want it now!) desire, excitement, anxiety.

4. To gain a sense of empowerment — to cover feeling insecure, sad, anxious.
5. To even the score — when a child vents pent-up feelings on those around him/her.

— Swanson (2009).

DADS MATTER

It's easy to be a father — but it takes a special man to be a real dad. Every child wants a good dad.

Dads and men who can enact the role of dads are incredibly important in children's lives. Having a positive father figure in kid's lives is now being shown as significantly important at reducing psychological and behavioural problems later in life. These father figures "who show an interest in children, help them to feel special, express unconditional love and who can give safe authentic love and respect to kids, can actually inspire them for the rest of their lives". These words come from Dr Bruce Robinson, author of *Fathering in the Fast Lane* and *Daughters and their Dads*, who became a passionate advocate for the role of fathers in our society when he noticed how many men who were approaching the end of their lives due to life-threatening illness, expressed deep regret about their relationships with their daughters. Research shows that children who have significant father figures in their world do statistically better in life — they have a lower risk of drug addiction, crime, bad attitudes to school, and low self-esteem and depression.

I share Steve Biddulph's concerns too that many of our boys are lacking the significant presence of good men in their childhoods and adolescence. In a nutshell, boys need some things in particular from their fathers.

Boys need:

- to feel part of a team — belonging
- opportunities to explore and investigate how things work
- to kick balls, run races and pit themselves physically against a challenge
- structure and help getting organised
- goals and good coaching
- safe environments and a zero-tolerance attitude to ridicule and shaming

— Ian Grant, *Growing Great Boys* (2006).

> Every boy needs a dad to 'download the software' of how to be a man.
> — Steve Biddulph

Connected mothering

We have always known that men are important in the lives of boys because they enable them to journey to manhood. It is the more recent research around dads and the role they play in their daughter's lives that many men have no idea about.

> Many men do not realise the profound and long lasting impact their relationship has in shaping their daughter's life, particularly her relationships with men. From her father, a daughter learns self-respect and acceptance, how to relax around and be affectionate with men without being sexual, that men and women can negotiate fairly and what to expect from a male-female relationship.
> — Bruce Robinson, *Daughters and their Dads* (2008).

Studies show that girls who have healthy, warm relationships with their dads:

- begin menstruating later in puberty
- become sexually active later
- have a healthy self-esteem
- are more confident naturally
- work better in work environments
- negotiate better without needing to flash their breasts or flutter their eyelashes.

> For your daughter, you will be the first man she will fall in love with and many girls seek a man who is either a lot like her dad or the total opposite. The way a father treats a daughter determines how high she sets the bar in male relationships.
> — Robinson (2008).

For boys, you are modelling for your sons how to become a good man or how to become a lousy man. Remember you do not have to have a biological connection to be a father figure in girls' and boys' lives. You simply have to turn up with an open heart and connect.

> Your daughter needs the best of who you are; your strength, your courage, your intelligence, and your fearlessness. She needs your empathy, assertiveness, and self-confidence. She needs you. Our daughters need the support that only fathers can provide–and if you are willing to guide your daughter, to stand between her and toxic culture, to take her to a healthier place, your rewards will be unmatched.
> — Meg Meeker, *The Wisdom of a Paediatrician. The Heart of a Mother* blog, August 29th 2013. Accessed at: www.drmegmeeker.blogspot.com.au

Things good dads, uncles and grandads can do with kids

- Play with kids from babies to teens
- Get them to help you do stuff around the house
- Take them away to play outside or to the park
- Take them fishing
- Kick, throw and play lots with balls
- Teach kids how to help do 'man' things
- Help make kids know right from wrong
- Make kids laugh
- Play rough and tumble with boys
- Give great hugs
- Teach them how to watch clouds or star gaze
- Tell kids you love them
- Fix things like cars, bikes and taps
- Be soft and sad sometimes.

There is no question that children benefit the most from loving, consistent relationships and yes, it is helpful to have relationships with both men and women in your lives. What matters most, the absolute most, is that children are exposed to consistent, loving relationships and that they be protected from toxic and unsafe relationships regardless of gender. As you journey through your life as a parent, be mindful of who is present in your children's lives.

Every human is wired to be a social being first and with strong connected mothering in the first three years of life, children will have the best start possible to become happy, healthy, strong and kind. When we use the less-than-perfect parenting moments as wonderful opportunities for growing and learning, everyone benefits.

A reminder that needs to be made as we come to finish this chapter is your children are watching you! Even when you are not talking to them, they are gathering information and learning how to behave by watching you and listening to you, and they will model that behaviour. They make a note of it all: when you told that lie about being too busy to attend Grandma's party; when you had a rant about your boss; or when you swore your head off. The good news is they will also have seen your moments of tenderness, compassionate care, and gestures of unconditional love and kindness. Ideally the latter will be greater than the former, but when it isn't — when we stuff up, as we all inevitably do — it is important to take responsibility for our mistakes and to apologise. We're only human after all.

To conclude this chapter on connected mothering I am including a quote from Robin Grille to affirm that children need what they have always needed to grow up to be healthy and happy. They need humans who have a deep commitment to being significant, connected adults who embrace the choice they made to be parents. When we hold our role as parents as something we cherish, respect and honour, the choices we make will come from the right place and we will be good enough parents.

> It's time to take our children back.
>
> It's time to review our shallow sense of economics and bring relationships into the equation. Our assets and techno goods are wonderful, but they are not more important than our children, not more important than time to ourselves, not more important than our need for loving relationships and time to just hang out together.
> It is time to take our children back.
>
> — Grille (2008).

TOP TIPS

- Healthy attachment and consistent, loving care for babies and toddlers shapes children for life.
- Healthy mothering ensures healthy attachment.
- Healthy babies can cry a lot.
- Most babies take time to be sound sleepers.
- PND is a mental illness and not a sign of poor mothering.
- Real experiences are great teachers for babies and toddlers.
- Meeting the needs of babies and toddlers can be difficult.
- Positive father figures are really important.

WHAT I WISH I HAD KNOWN ... "I WOULD HAVE BOUGHT LOTS OF LOVELY NIGHTIES AND NOT GOT DRESSED FOR THE FIRST SIX WEEKS AND JUST ENJOYED MY BABY AND NOT WORRIED ABOUT HOW I LOOKED, MY STRETCHED BODY OR THE HOUSEWORK."
– Linda

2nd Thing

THE BOUNTIFUL BRAIN IN INFANCY

> Your child is not a blank slate or an empty vessel who needs to be filled up with copious amounts of excellent information. Your child comes to you with a nascent intellect that is consolidating energy and waiting to unfold in good time like a flower in the bud. You would never pry open a rosebud to somehow optimise or improve upon it. Instead you would make sure it has the best soil and nourishing fertiliser to support its optimal unfolding.
> — Reproduced from *Parenting for Peace* (2012), by Marcy Axness, with permission of Sentient Publications, LLC.

THE WONDERS OF THE DEVELOPING BRAIN AND WHAT REALLY MATTERS IN THE FIRST SIX YEARS

A healthy understanding of what happens inside our babies' brains from the moment of birth is incredibly helpful to shape the way we parent. Our babies are born with around 200 billion brain cells called neurons but with very few connectors, or synapses, in between. In a way, this means that the baby's brain is half-baked and the reason that the human brain is born this way, unlike any other species on earth, is so the baby's head can come down the birth canal to be born. If nature waited until the connectors had joined the many billions of neurons, the size of the baby's head would be impossible to give birth to. For a baby to create connectors between two neurons, the secret ingredient is experience and this experience needs to be repeated in order for that neural highway to become fixed and stable. Much of the massive growth surge takes place in the first five years of life.

In Norman Doidge's book, *The Brain that Changes Itself* (2007), he explores the plasticity of the brain — the process whereby the brain grows and prunes itself due to the role of experiences —and there is good news for parents. Doidge asserts that anything that a baby or toddler has missed out on learning or mastering by the age of five can possibly be learned after that because anything that is done repeatedly will make the brain change. This is why early intervention is so vitally important for children with developmental delays, especially those who are on the autism spectrum.

Doidge also explores the topographical organisation of the brain and the 'brain maps' that are made. *Mindsight* author Daniel Siegel, explains this concept of brain maps well for the layperson. For example, he illustrates how the map containing all the brain cells and connectors associated with the right thumb, sits right next to the brain map for the right pointer finger and so on. The complete map of the right hand is actually found on the left side of the brain, which is why cross-patterning is such a vital part of brain development; it cannot occur without movement, both unilateral and opposite. Through research, scientists discovered a cluster of brain maps that proved to be very interesting. This cluster involves the maps to do with repetition, rote learning, sequencing and patterning, which sit right beside the brain maps to do with eloquence of speech, eye contact and the understanding of symbols This realisation has transformed the way that stroke patients are rehabilitated. By having patients spend hours doing boring, repetitive tasks the brain is able to open up the eloquence of speech map much more quickly than previously possible (Doidge, 2007).

In a way, this new brain mapping knowledge validates why movement, especially repetitive movement and also repetitive rhyming, is so important in early childhood development. This amazing new understanding about brain maps shows how essential clapping, rocking, hopping, playing lullabies and singing songs that include touch are in the development of clever brains for children. **No screen can build these pathways**. This is why massive interaction with humans and possibly pets has such a profound influence on a child's chances of reaching their optimal potential. In the classrooms of old, activities like clapping games, folk dancing, playing musical instruments and singing together were very common. No wonder Australia looked better on the international scales back then. Out in the playground there was also an acceptance that vigourous play was a good thing and many students spent hours using elastics and skipping ropes. We are seeing less of this in today's schools with many countries choosing to place an early (and damaging!) emphasis on formalised learning, more crowded curriculums, and play-based learning diminishing in the process. In homes, technology has the potential to erode this critical brain development not just from the early years but from childhood as a whole. There is very little cross-patterning movement occurring when a small child is playing with a tablet or an iPad.

A leading researcher in children's neurobiology and development, Dr Jack Shonkoff, stresses that it is much better to build a healthy brain as early as possible in life than to try and make changes to it later in life, although with new neuroplasticity that is possible.

> ... Without understating the potential lifelong influences of early experience, it is essential that policymakers understand the concept of adult neuroplasticity. This is especially true for brain circuits that are specialized for selected aspects of learning, which can continue to make adaptations in response to new experiences after their sensitive developmental periods have passed (84–86). It is also important to note that changes in mature brain circuits require highly tailored inputs and focused efforts to secure maximal attention. Stated simply, building brain circuitry correctly from the beginning is easier and generally leads to better outcomes, but it is never too late to invest in remediation. The proposed emphasis on explicit capacity building in parents with limited education, described earlier in this paper, draws on these concepts, particularly as they apply to skills that are mediated by the prefrontal cortex.
> — J.P. Shonkoff, *Leveraging the biology of adversity to address the roots of disparities in health and development* (2012).

The early years are where the connectors are built, making brain maps or cognitive maps. Being hurried, overstimulated or stressed, impacts negatively on how a child's brain maps form as well as the emotional triggers that accompany experiences. Not only are babies and toddlers creating brain maps, they are creating perceptions, beliefs and concepts that shape how they will interpret the world. The biggest threats to the developing baby and toddler brain are abandonment, deprivation and abuse. The emotional memories a baby makes can come from pre-birth and they can be incorrect but more on that later.

Babies and toddlers have three underdeveloped brains:

1. **Reptilian brain** — This involves the instinctive behaviour related to survival.

- Hunger
- Digestion/elimination
- Breathing
- Circulation
- Temperature
- Movement/posture/balance
- Territorial instincts
- Fight or flight

2. **Mammalian or limbic brain** — This triggers strong emotions that need to be managed well by the rational or 'higher' brain when it is developed.

- It helps to control the flight or fight response
- Rage
- Fear
- Separation distress
- Caring and nurturing
- Social bonding
- Playfulness
- Explorative urge
- Lust in adults

3. **Rational or higher brain** (not complete until our late 20s).

Also known as the frontal lobes or neo cortex its functions and capabilities include:

- Creativity
- Imagination
- Problem-solving and planning
- Reasoning and reflection
- Self-awareness
- Kindness, empathy and concern

— Margot Sunderland, *The Science of Parenting* (2007).

...Findings from various areas of developmental psychology suggest that everything that happens to us – the music we hear, the people we love, the books we read, the kind of discipline we receive, the emotions we feel – profoundly affects the way the brain develops.
— Daniel J. Siegel and Tina Payne Bryson, *The Whole-Brain Child* (2011).

The way that you parent will have a major impact on how these three brains grow and develop, especially in the first five years of life. When we view the emotional immaturity of our children as a sign of the immaturity of the brain we can see that it's normal for children to have times when they feel incredibly overwhelmed and upset with things that seem very minor to us. This is because they are young children with a young child's brain not a young child with an adult brain. As the prefrontal cortex or the higher brain is not complete until the late 20s, it is important to see that children will often struggle making emotionally sound decisions.

Our challenge is to remember that we have a higher brain, or an 'upstairs' brain, and that it is important we use it when working with our children who don't have one. When we become reactive, exhausted and overwhelmed, we find it difficult to interpret their behaviour through the calm rational higher brain. That's when real problems can occur.

The brain's plasticity process of growing and pruning happens right throughout life, however the peak windows of massive pruning and growing occur under five years of age and in early adolescence. In a nutshell, the more actual real-life experiences that a baby or child has, the denser the brain grows.

> **WILMA WALLABY**
> "Babies, toddlers and children are wired to learn at their own pace in their own way if they are in a safe, interesting environment. They are never 'not learning'."

Harvard University's Center on the Developing Child has a great, short video on their website demonstrating this process. The site explains:

> *The basic architecture of the brain is constructed through a process that begins early in life and continues into adulthood. Simpler circuits come first and more complex brain circuits build on them later. Genes provide the basic blueprint, but experiences influence how or whether genes are expressed. Together, they shape the quality of brain architecture and establish either a sturdy or a fragile foundation for all of the learning,*

health, and behavior that follow. Plasticity, or the ability for the brain to reorganize and adapt, is greatest in the first years of life and decreases with age. Healthy development in the early years provides the building blocks for educational achievement, economic productivity, responsible citizenship, lifelong health, strong communities, and successful parenting of the next generation.

Source: http://developingchild.harvard.edu/index.php/resources/multimedia/videos/three_core_concepts/brain_architecture/

Even when a child may be sitting still — s/he is still learning because his/her brain is processing new information and how it fits with prior learning. Please take some time to watch a child's face when s/he meets something they have never met before. It is priceless!

> Babies create hypotheses, test them and then relentlessly appraise their findings with the vigour of a seasoned scientist. This means that infants are extraordinarily delightful, surprisingly aggressive learners. They pick up everything.
> — John Medina, *Brain Rules for Baby* (2014). http://brainrules.net/

This same need for repetition can be seen when children like to have the same story read over and over again. Boring for mums and dads, however so important for the plasticity of the child's brain. So remember, repetition is excellent for the developing brain and each child will learn differently, so avoid comparing your children.

John Medina writes that babies are really good at imitation. Often they can reproduce a behaviour after only witnessing it once — this is called, deferred imitation. This is an astonishing skill and it develops rapidly and research shows that a 13-month-old child can remember an event one week after a single exposure. However by the time she is almost a year-and-a-half old she can imitate an event for many months after a single exposure. This affirms why parental modelling is extremely important. However, it should also create a deep sense of concern around what these little ones are downloading if they are spending hours watching TV. In the chapter on KINDNESS AND FAIRNESS, I explore what research is telling us about the negative influences of some TV programs that are targeted to children under five.

It may be really useful to dispel some of the myths that exist in our world today about brain development and babies and toddlers.

The myths:

1. *Exposing your infant or toddler to language DVDs will boost their vocabulary* — in actual fact some DVDs have been shown to reduce toddlers vocabulary. The words our little people hear need to come from a real living human being.

2. *Playing Mozart to your womb will improve your baby's future maths scores* — your baby will simply remember Mozart after birth — along with many other things she hears, smells, and tastes in the womb. the greatest thing you can do to ensure your child does well in maths later is to teach impulse control in her early years.
3. *To boost their brainpower children need French lessons by the age of three and a room piled with 'brain- friendly' toys and a library of educational DVDs* — possibly the greatest paediatric brain–boosting technology in the world is a cardboard box, a fresh box of crayons and two hours. The worst is probably your flat screen TV.
4. *Continually telling your children they are smart will boost their confidence* — actually they become less willing to work on challenging problems. Praise their effort instead.
5. *Children somehow will find their own happiness* — the greatest predictor of happiness is having friends. How do you make and keep friends? By being good at deciphering nonverbal communication. Learning a musical instrument boosts this ability by 50 percent. Text messaging may destroy it.

— Source: Medina (2014). http://brainrules.net/

You may have noticed how a toddler will use the same toy, rattle or ever your car keys over and over again before getting bored. Essentially what is happening is that repeated experiences encourage that growth of connectors between the neurons discussed earlier.

Take for example a baby who can see a light on the ceiling each time he is put on the floor to play. Over time, his brain will wire together various neurons that let him 'know' what the light does — he or she can then predict what that thing does, even without knowing the name of it. In time, he will not pay that light much attention because he has 'learnt' what it does, and the inquisitive baby brain will be looking for something new to learn about. The repeated activity is important as the brain benefits from practice, as it strengthens to new connectors.

This is partly why babies and toddlers do not need to be surrounded by plastic toys and brightly coloured things. They are fascinated by anything they have not seen before or something that is in the wrong place. Indeed there is some concern that the increases in childhood anxiety and ADHD could be influenced by the unnecessary overstimulation, albeit well-meaning, of babies and toddlers with brightly coloured, noisy and many-textured toys and things that dangle above their head in their prams, in their cars and on their highchairs. A Wilma secret is to place a child in one of those places without any distractions and when they start to get bored we start adding things for them to play with, usually one by one, and you will find you can keep them happy for much longer.

> **DID YOU KNOW?**
> Under five years of age is the best window for learning several languages because of the massive plasticity that is occurring. Children's brains will be able to learn them easily; however they will lose their competence if the languages are not spoken, ie without practice!

It is really sad to see how parents are blatantly marketed to, so that they buy products to make their child smarter, to be stimulated and that are 'educational'. This pressure causes enormous angst at times. Essentially babies and toddlers are never 'not' learning from their environment and the interactions with the significant big people in their lives. By targeting parents' guilt and often their fears, the toy industry is making billions of dollars from people who are trying to do the best thing for their little people. It is really important to remember that no matter what is suggested or recommended by people who make money out of the products, that every single child is different and the way they interact and experience life is not something we can control or shape completely.

> The *Neurons to Neighborhoods* report was very emphatic in stating that children are born ready to learn. We don't have to make them ready to learn. We don't have to teach them how to learn. They are wired from the beginning to learn and they're wired to experience and to master the world around them.
> — Shonkoff (2012).

As written on The Developing Child website once again:

"One of the most essential experiences in shaping the architecture of the developing brain is 'serve and return' interaction between children and significant adults in their lives. Young children naturally reach out for interaction through babbling, facial expressions, and gestures, and adults respond with the same kind of vocalizing and gesturing back at them. This back-and-forth process is fundamental to the wiring of the brain, especially in the earliest years." -Source: *www.developingchild.harvard.edu* (do a site search on the term 'serve & return' to watch the accompanying video.)

This incredibly powerful interaction with loving, safe people is the fastest way to support our babies' and toddlers' brain development. Because babies are human beings, deeply embedded into their DNA is a wiring to survive first, and to be smart and happy after that. This means that if a baby is distressed or struggling with a stressful environment, the architecture of their brain will be very different to a child who was surrounded by a loving family in a safe home.

> Extensive evidence that personal experiences and environmental exposures are embedded biologically (for better or for worse) and the cumulative knowledge of more than four decades of intervention research provide a promising opportunity to mobilize evolving scientific insights to catalyze a new era of more effective early childhood policy and practice. Drawing on emerging hypotheses about causal mechanisms that link early adversity with lifelong impairments in learning, behavior and health, this paper proposes an enhanced theory of change to promote better outcomes for vulnerable, young children by strengthening caregiver and community capacities to reduce or mitigate the impacts of toxic stress, rather than simply providing developmental enrichment for the children and parenting education for their mothers.
> — Shonkoff (2012).

Babies' right hemisphere of the brain is developing rapidly in the first three years. The right hemisphere develops in response to face-to-face social experience, with extended shared eye gaze. Isn't it fascinating how powerful the extended shared eye gazing is in terms of early brain development of our babies? This is one of the reasons why many people recommend a 'go-slow' approach to parenting in the early years. It is equally fascinating that babies are wired to 'lock on' to human faces even through to toddlerhood. As I travel extensively, I spend a lot of time in airports where I find babies and toddlers everywhere. It is interesting to watch how quickly they turn to you if you lock into their eyes with a non-threatening gaze. I love smiling and winking at babies and toddlers, and they connect so quickly; it's quite funny to watch. It must be sad for some babies and toddlers in today's modern plugged-in, screen-focused world because so few adult faces are available for them to connect to. These moments of interaction with the safe stranger are still important in the way that their brains are being built. This is why indigenous communities have surrounded children with large numbers of family or kin, maybe without even knowing it, because it helps to build healthy brains. The right hemisphere governs self-regulatory systems. If babies are placed in front of screens, ignored or isolated, they are missing critical experiences.

> What moulds our brain? Experience. Even into old age our experiences actually change the physical structure of our brain. The brain has 100 billion neurons, each with an average of 10,000 connections to the other neurons. The ways in which particular

circuits in the brain activated determines the nature of our mental activity, ranging from perceiving sites or sounds to more abstract thought and reasoning. When neurons fire together, they grow new connections between them. Over time, the connections that result from firing, lead to rewiring in the brain. This is incredibly exciting news!

— Siegel and Payne Bryson (2011).

Now that you have a fundamental understanding of how building connectors between the neurons in your baby's brain is important on all sorts of levels, and that repeated experience builds stronger connections, maybe you will appreciate this little poem:

MY PLASTICS CUPBOARD

I am a lucky kid.
My mum has given me a plastics cupboard.
It's mine and no one else's and that's really special.
I know I am only two and some grown ups think I don't know much
But my plastics cupboard knows I am smart.

I know exactly what's in my plastics cupboard and that's 'cos
I can remember.
It took me a while to be able to remember everything
But I can now and that makes me feel smart.

Every time I go into my plastics cupboard, it is like a whole new adventure
even though I know everything that's in my cupboard.
There are many different shapes amongst the things in my plastics cupboard
and every time I go in there, I find different ways of putting things together.
How cool is that?

When I first was given my plastics cupboard I would reach in and pull things
out onto the floor.
It was such fun and I could make a really big mess.
Now I like climbing right into my cupboard and pretending I'm hiding from
my mum.
How cool is that?

I have noticed that the things in my plastics cupboard come in all different
colours as well as shapes.
Some days I put all the same coloured things together.
Other days I put all the things that are the same shape together.
How cool is that?

Because the plastics cupboard is mine I can move things around and I can also put some of my own toys in the plastics cupboard.
Sometimes I hide Ted and Dora in my cupboard so that they can play in there together while I'm not there.
How cool is that?

My plastics cupboard is in the kitchen of our home.
It is really close to where my mum does the cooking.
I like playing in my plastics cupboard with my mum close by. I think she does too.
One day when I got into my plastics cupboard I found something strange. I sat for a while trying to work out what it was.
My mum came over and explained that it was a whisk. I had a lot of fun with that whisk that day.

Another day I found some really strange things.
That took me a very long time to work out.
Again my mum came and helped me.
The things were biscuit cutters that came in all sorts of shapes. Later my mum and I used the shapes to bake some biscuits for Daddy.
How cool was that?

Some days I find that my mum has put a new plastic container into my plastics cupboard without telling me.
It is my cupboard and I need to know what is going on in my cupboard.
I even know when one of my containers is missing.

I love my plastics cupboard.
It is like a new adventure every day.
I am a very lucky kid to have my very own plastics cupboard and I just wish every kid could have a plastics cupboard just like me.
How cool would that be?

— Maggie Dent (2014)

There is a major growth spurt in the frontal lobes of a child's brain in the first two years of life. This time is a great window of opportunity for establishing nerve pathways that underpin learning and language development and also for establishing anti-anxiety chemical systems in the brain.
— Sunderland (2007).

Babies and toddlers are learning constantly from everything they see, hear, taste, touch and smell because our senses are VITALLY important in brain growth. Have you ever noticed a young child's face the first time they taste something new, touch a kitten for the first time or see something bright and unusual? That's a WOW moment to them. Build as many WOW moments as possible from real-life experiences like plastics cupboards, peg baskets, cardboard boxes, cellophane paper and human interaction.

As I have said in the previous chapter, parents do not have to buy things to stimulate their baby or young child! Their sensory world is constantly processing because almost everything is being reviewed and explored. Indeed, there are some child development experts who argue that we are overstimulating babies and toddlers with too many toys, too much TV and too much talking and this could be contributing to the high levels of children with ADHD and anxiety disorders. In our consumer-driven world this concept of not needing to buy things to stimulate our children must seem almost foreign and ridiculous. However, in a way it is good news — save your money and invest in fabulous high-quality food and fuel for your car so you can take your child out into the real world and allow them to find truly fascinating things that exist in nature.

> ...Findings from various areas in developmental psychology, suggest that everything that happens to us – the music we hear, the people we love, the books we read, the kind of discipline we receive, the emotions we feel – profoundly affects the way the brain develops.
> — Siegel and Payne Bryson (2011).

On a family visit to my sister's home a couple of years ago, I watched her granddaughter do some amazing brain building right in front of us. She was probably just two years of age. She was wandering around in my sister's garden and on the lawn she found an empty ice-cream container. When she picked it up you could almost hear her brain ticking over, "What is it? What can I do with it?" Then she put it on her head and walked off, and it fell off. She tried it twice more and obviously that was not very exciting or interesting. She paused, again looking at this container. And then she put it on the lawn upside down and stood on it. Then she jumped off with a, "Ta dah!" When she had achieved this new experience she looked to her nanny as if to say, "Wow, look what I can do." She proceeded to do that several times until she tired of it, and then just left it and went in search of something else that she might be able to explore.

The bountiful brain in infancy

> Children cannot push themselves on until they have done very thoroughly what it is they need to do. Until they have reached the state of boredom they are still motivated by unfinished business and can't move on. Boredom when they finally attain it provides the push to move on – but the push comes from within
> – not without.
> — Janet Gonzalez-Mena, et al., *Infants, Toddlers and Caregivers* (2007).

The bountiful brain of a baby or toddler is not just learning the names of things and how things work; it is also learning how to manage the emotional world that is taking shape inside their minds. In their excellent book, *The Whole-Brain Child*, Siegel and Bryson explore integration and what that means and why it is important that parents to understand.

BRAIN CHEMICALS

Our brain is amazing. Not only is it constantly learning, changing, copying and seeking, it also governs the moods we feel. The brain makes things called neurotransmitters or brain chemicals. Neurotransmitters and hormones play an interactive ever-interchanging game that impacts the nervous system. The diagram below offers a very simplistic approach to how this affects our children and us.

Certain activities in the classroom or home will influence chemical and hormone release.

Positive

- Serotonin
- Dopamine
- Endorphins

Negative

- Cortisol
- Adrenoline
- Noradrenaline

Neurotransmitters influence both explicit and implicit memory.

Cortisol is the stress hormone and it gets released with adrenaline. When our children are struggling with high levels of cortisol they don't feel too good and it also lowers language functioning. We all will struggle with cortisol in different ways but temperament is a fair indicator of how we will manage heightened levels of cortisol. Some children will become upset really easily, possibly get worried and be clingy. Others may become defensive and over-reactive, which in turn creates more cortisol. So if we can now see some of our children's meltdowns and disasters as merely a function of their brain maybe we can be a little bit kinder and more understanding. Many of the techniques explored in this book suggest promoting serotonin and calmness before confronting the conflict or aiming to find a solution.

Adrenaline is "at least partly responsible for the revved up, 'red cordial' high" that we sometimes see in our children, according to Andrew Fuller's, *Tricky Kids* (2007). Adrenaline is a really important brain chemical to have when you are about to be attacked by a grizzly because it activates the amygdala, which is the flight-or-fight area of the brain — and it provides enormous energy for the body to escape a life-threatening situation. Sometimes children can get an adrenaline rush. Unfortunately there's not much you can do until you have lessened the amount of adrenaline, possibly by creating some serotonin, dopamine or even some endorphins. Fuller lists the following characteristics of children with high levels of adrenaline — I know some adults who have this too!

High levels of adrenaline

- exhibits silly, 'hyper' behaviour
- has difficulty getting to sleep
- has lots of energy
- runs off if upset
- has squabbles and little conflicts
- shows lots of busyness but not much gets done
- is reluctant to try new things.

— Andrew Fuller, *Tricky Kids* (2007).

The above list reads a bit like what our children are like after a birthday party!

Noradrenaline, broadly, affects our heart rate, and has been linked to our capacity to stay awake, pay attention, our responses around motivation and reward, and also learning and memory.

Serotonin could almost be called the most powerful antidepressant available because it has a calming effect on the nervous system and on our children's moods and behaviours. When children feel safe and loved they will have good levels of serotonin. Safe touch, good food, fun times with the family, and being acknowledged and encouraged by your parents, all create serotonin. So too do some high-fat, high-sugar foods. I am sure you've had the urge to down a burger or far too many Tim Tams after you've had a very late night, possibly involving a beverage or two. High-sugar drinks, caffeine and alcoholic beverages, too, can lift serotonin levels. Serotonin is also made when we relax, when we breathe deeply and when we get a good massage.

Dopamine creates a switched-on, having fun, "I am really interested" kind of state in the body. The biggest killers for dopamine are stress, boredom, fear or threat. Fuller offers some suggestions for parents to help lift kids' dopamine levels:

- sports that involve repetitive movements like table tennis, swimming and handball
- solving challenges and problems
- social interaction, especially play
- giving rewards or prizes
- some dietary supplements including tyrosine, omega 3 and 6. (Fuller, 2007).

Endorphins are another feel-good brain chemical; created by laughter, positive human interaction, and safe touch and are sometimes triggered spontaneously via the senses of smell and hearing. If you smell a smell that is buried in your implicit memory from childhood — say the smell of your favourite dish Mum cooked, fresh bread or maybe Grandma's apple pie — just a tiny whiff is enough to flood the body with endorphins. The same goes for when we hear a song that is linked to implicit memories of great moments in our childhood.

As parents we can be 'manipulating with love' the mood levels of our children with this knowledge. This is one of the reasons why I encourage parents to lighten up — to don a cape, or a psychedelic wig or a tiara. The immediate rush of positive brain chemicals turns the level of cortisol right down and the mood within the home will change with it. When there is a lot of stress, tension and maybe shouting, cortisol levels go through the roof and our children can display enormous distress.

WHAT IS INTEGRATION AND WHY DOES THAT MATTER?

Integration is about taking the distinct parts of your brain and helping them work together as a whole. It is similar to what happens in the body, which has different organs to perform different jobs. Tantrums, meltdowns, aggression and most of the other challenging experiences of parenting — and life — are the result of loss of integration also known as disintegration. It's easy to see when our kids aren't integrated — they become overwhelmed by their emotions, confused and chaotic.

We want our children to become better integrated so that they use the whole brain in a coordinated way. For example, we want them to be horizontally integrated so that their left-brain logic can work well with their right-brain emotion. We also want them to be vertically integrated so that the physically higher parts of their brain, which let them thoughtfully consider their actions, work well with lower parts which are more concerned with instinct, gut reaction and survival.

> *An integrated brain results in improved decision-making, better control of body and emotions, for self-understanding, stronger relationships, and success in school.*
> — Siegel and Payne Bryson (2011).

It is really important to remember that the human brain is not complete until the mid to late 20s and that when a two-year-old has a meltdown it is most likely an overwhelming moment of poor integration of the developing brain. Remember that the rage, fear and separation distress system is set up at birth to support a baby's survival, not to cause their mum and dad great distress. These systems were designed to ensure that infants were not eaten by predators or harmed by any other potential danger in their world. These days, the distress systems can be triggered when a door slams loudly, when they are unable to dress themselves or when you walk out of the room unexpectedly. In the chapter on GO—SLOW PARENTING, I explore stress and distress in children's lives in much more depth.

> *Parents would never dream of leaving their baby in a room full of toxic fumes that could damage their child's brain. Yet many parents leave their baby in a state of prolonged, uncomforted distress, not knowing that he is at risk from toxic levels of stress chemicals washing over his brain.*
> — Sunderland (2007).

We all function better when we experience harmony rather than states of chaos or rigidity, when our sense of being able to cope is threatened. The same goes for our children. When they experience too much chaos or when their world is full of rigidity and they are unable to get their needs met, this creates emotional distress that the body will respond to loudly and vigorously. Again, this is when a loss of integration occurs.

Siegel writes about the importance of understanding horizontal and vertical integration in the brain. And while that might sound incredibly complicated it is really empowering when a parent understands these concepts.

Horizontal integration

Most people have heard that we have a left and right brain. Put simply, the left brain loves and yearns for order. It tends to be logical, literal, linguistic and linear. This is the part of our brain that loves lists and the need to explain things logically and with reason. The right brain tends to be holistic and non-verbal, preparing to send and receive messages that allow us to communicate through facial expressions, eye contact, tone of voice, posture and gestures. A right brain prefers to be concerned with the big picture — the meaning and feel of an experience — rather than the details in the right order. Some suggest that the right brain is more intuitive and emotional, however it is probably more accurate to talk about this side of the brain being more directly influenced by the body and the lower brain areas, which allows it to receive and interpret emotional information. Obviously two halves make a whole and so when we have good integration into two hemispheres it will be easier for us to manage our world. When a child has a significant meltdown or is extremely upset there is little point in us trying to appeal to their left brain or their logical brain. For example, if you have a sobbing four-year-old who is sure there is a monster going to kill them in their bedroom at night, there would be no point rationalising that there is no monster. The first thing to do is to soothe their nervous system which connects to their right brain and when that feels calmer you may then appeal to their left brain to explain the unlikelihood of a monster coming to kill them. Acknowledging irrational feelings and allowing children to feel loved is incredibly important — denying or minimising big ugly feelings denies an opportunity to teach children how to manage such feelings.

An excellent technique that Siegel teaches to help in situations like the one above is called, "name it to tame it". This works by having a child retell their frightening or scary experience in their own words, with you helping them clarify their experience. Remember the experience is valid and real for the child, no matter how ridiculous we can see it through the eyes of the rational brain. Some children might prefer to draw it or to use play to express what happened.

The tricky thing for parents is to remain calm when their children are distressed. Sometimes it is helpful to arrange some time out, calling it "calm down time", before exploring the conflict. This will allow a much better integration of the left and right brain. This is a great habit to introduce into family life as early as possible. I created a quiet space out in my garden for times when I felt myself losing contact with my upstairs brain. I would often take a cup of tea outside to my quiet place BEFORE things became too volatile or tense. Funnily enough there were times when I headed out to my special spot to find that one of my sons was already there! Modelling is such a powerful tool in our parenting journey.

Vertical integration

I have already touched a little on vertical integration in this chapter when I was talking about the upstairs brain, "three brains" or the triune brain. This is about the need to integrate the 'upstairs' and 'downstairs' brain. The downstairs brain includes the brain stem of the limbic region, which is the lower part of the brain. Scientists tend to talk about the lower areas as being more primitive because they are responsible for the basic functions like breathing, blinking, and other innate reactions and impulses like the fight-flight response (our basic survival instinct) and strong feelings like anger and fear. Our upstairs brain is completely different because it is more evolved and sophisticated, and allows our children to have the following qualities when they mature:

1. sound decision-making and planning
2. control over emotions in the body
3. self-understanding and awareness
4. empathy and compassion
5. impulse control
6. morality.

The upstairs brain is where the prefrontal cortex is shaped by the experiences we have within our human relationships. It is also deeply influenced by the loving guidance of parents or other significant carers, who have such an enormous influence on the mature person we become one day. We need to have appropriate expectations of a child whose prefrontal cortex is still developing, and we need to have understanding and compassion for when their behaviour is annoying, tiring and frustrating. Sometimes a child's tantrum can come from the sheer frustration of not being unable to understand, manage or cope with whatever is happening at that point in time. This does not mean they are a bad child or even a naughty child; it is simply a child who is not coping well partly because of an underdeveloped upstairs brain.

> It is very important for kids to learn about and understand their feelings. It is true that feelings need to be recognised for what they are – temporarily, changing conditions. They are states not rates. We need to help children understand that the clouds of their emotions can and will roll on by.
> — Siegel and Payne Bryson (2011).

Tantrums are a downstairs brain performance for most children. However, some tantrums are an 'upstairs tantrum' — when a child consciously decides to throw a tantrum to get what s/he wants. Despite dramatic and seemingly desperate pleas s/he could instantly stop the tantrum if s/he wanted to. This is an example of a child who has not lost control of their emotional world, which is what happens with a downstairs tantrum. The best advice for dealing with such a tantrum is, "never negotiate with a terrorist!" This tantrum requires firm boundaries and a clear discussion about appropriate and inappropriate behaviour. This is impossible with a downstairs tantrum. The best approach to a downstairs tantrums is as I discussed earlier: to connect with the child and help soothe them so that you can calm the overwhelmed lower brain before you try to use your left logical brain to help the child makes sense of the meltdown or to find a solution that feels right for the child.

Sunderland wrote that while we need to give children clear boundaries, rules and consequences for unacceptable behaviour we also need be careful not to damage their will. Rather than seeing a toddler who is saying "won't" and "no" a lot around the age of two or three as bad, it can be seen as a precursor for the capacity to stand up for yourself, the passion to know what you want in life and the drive to follow it through.

> Children who move into total compliance at the toddler stage often suffer later in life from not having developed a separate self. They may be very skilled at adapting to the needs and feelings of others but with little or no notion about what they want and feel for themselves. This can happen with overly strict parenting, where an infant is too frightened to protest or with parenting which employs all manner of subtle forms of withdrawal of love and approval to get obedience.
> — Sunderland (2007).

Using empathy with a crying baby or an upset toddler is obviously the best way to help manage those situations, although in reality — let's be honest — it isn't always possible. Remember it is what we do 80% of the time rather than the other 20% that shapes our children's lives. If we yell or walk away in anger, we can come back later when we have calmed down and apologise to our children explaining that our downstairs brain won over our upstairs brain, but that our upstairs brain is back in control.

Indeed, scientists are becoming more open to the belief that empathy has its roots in a complex system of optical mirror neurons and that children learn it by observing people who are caring and compassionate. It can help young children develop a sense of morality and empathy by giving them some hypothetical situations to consider. Would it be okay to run a red light if there was an emergency? Would it be okay to push a child over who was running close to a busy road? Our capacity to think logically and rationally is improved by more opportunities to do so. If we always tell our children what the answer or the solution is to their problems, we are denying them the opportunity for their brain to figure things out for themselves.

Children's ability to develop empathy can be negatively influenced by watching TV programs that include relational aggression like name calling, exclusion and putdowns. Some of the programs that were shown to negatively influence children's playground behaviour after being watched were *Clifford the Big*

Red Dog, *Arthur* and *Sponge Bob Square Pants* — all very popular children's programs. I write in more detail about this research in the chapter on KINDNESS AND FAIRNESS. Children see TV programs as real life not as entertainment as adults do. This is brain plasticity in action.

Babies and toddlers need repeated experiences in which they can self-direct and build the neural connections in the brain that create memory. When children are bored they are wired to move on to something else, to continue to engage their inquisitive brains. Learning how to manage boredom is a vital stage of development that over-stimulated babies and children need to master. Early over-stimulation, especially from huge plasma televisions, excessive noise levels in the house, and high levels of chaos and confusion in the family environment can all cause the baby's brain to flood with stress hormones. This can cause them to be distressed and it can hard wire them to be overly sensitive to stress for the rest of their lives. Stress and distress is explored more deeply in the chapter, GO-SLOW CHILDHOODS.

Siegel (2011) explores a couple of other myths about the brain. The first myth is that memory is like a mental filing cabinet in the brain and as he says it would be convenient if it was like this but it simply is not how it works.

> ... Memory is all about associations. As an association machine, the brain processes something in the present moment - an idea, a feeling the smell or an image - and links that experience with similar experiences from the past. These past experiences strongly influence how we understand what we see and what we feel... Memory shapes our current perceptions by causing us to anticipate what will happen next. Our past absolutely shapes our present and future.
> — Siegel and Payne Bryson (2011).

The second myth that Siegel likes to dispel is that memories are a bit like a photocopy machine. This is the assumption that when we recall a memory it will be an exact and accurate reproduction of what took place in the past. Unfortunately that is not quite how it happens. Technically:

> ... Whenever you retrieve a memory, you alter it. What you recall may be close to exactly what happened, but the very act of recalling an experience changes it, sometimes in significant ways. To put it scientifically, memory retrieval activates a neural cluster similar to, but not identical with, the one created at the time of the encoding. Thus memories are distorted - sometimes slightly and sometimes greatly - even though you believe you are being accurate.
> — Siegel and Payne Bryson (2011).

EXPLICIT AND IMPLICIT MEMORIES

There is another fascinating side to memories that can help you understand how your child becomes a unique human being, rather than a close clone of their parents or siblings. There are two types of memories — implicit and explicit — and these interweave and work together all the time.

Think of driving your car, something that we do almost without thinking after we have had a lot of experience. This 'knowing' becomes largely automatic and is known as implicit memory. The ability to recall learning to drive, all those years ago is explicit memory. Most of the time when we are recalling past experiences we tend to be using our explicit memory, which is a conscious recognition of what happened in the past.

In many ways it's the implicit memory that can cause our children to have emotional meltdowns and irrationally big, ugly feelings. Take for example when one of my lads was about three and we were visiting a toyshop. His oldest brother found a really ugly monster mask, which he put on and suddenly appeared in front of the three-year-old making a horrible grunting noise. Now, that three-year-old took off so fast — his flight or fight response was activated — and no matter what I called out to him as he ran, he was hell bent on escaping that threat! I managed to catch him just before he ran across the very busy car park outside.

When he was 10 years of age, he attended a fancy dress birthday party. Once again, as a bit of a joke one of the boys put on a gorilla suit and unexpectedly appeared in the window beside my son. His implicit memory kicked in and he took off like a rocket, terrified and consumed with irrational fear. This can happen to children who have been frightened by a dog, a scary movie, a large spider or a snake because essentially these hypersensitive memory pathways can trigger distress sometimes for the rest of our lives. So keep in mind if your child is behaving in an incredibly irrational or unusually unreasonable way, consider whether there could be an implicit memory somewhere in their brain that could explain why they are behaving in such a way. It is really helpful if you explain to them how the brain works.

I have had enormous success diffusing these irrational implicit memories by using simple energy techniques whereby the child or an adult taps on acupressure points while we explore the original scary experience. There is an excellent resource called, "Rose and the Night Monster" that parents and those who care for children can use to help release emotionally overwhelming memory pathways. To find out more, visit *www.eftdownunder.com*. Keep in mind that it is helpful for children to explore their big ugly feelings rather than suppress them or deny them. This is why I like the simple energy techniques so much, because as the child explores their feelings while they tap those acupressure points, they noticeably calm down. Indeed some of the best parenting that you can do will be at times when your children are greatly distressed rather than when they are incredibly happy.

A mum shared a story with me once. Her eight-year-old son was playing outside in the street with the neighbourhood children, some of them older than him. He came rushing into the house obviously upset and said to his mum, "Some of those kids say they hate me!" The mum immediately tried to use her left brain to explain that it didn't matter because she loved him, and his dad loved him and his family loved him. The son got up and ran into his bedroom and slammed the door. The mum was really confused and sought the help of a friend who works as a family support person. She explained to the mum that what the boy really needed was to be heard and to actually experience the ugly feelings. By reassuring him with logic (think left brain) she was probably leaving her son feeling misunderstood and frustrated. So the mum went into his bedroom and this time she simply listened mindfully without saying anything and said she was sorry she didn't listen before. Shortly afterwards the boy ran out and said he was going back out to play. This is a good example of what happens when we deny children the opportunity to experience big ugly feelings because they will come up later in life often when we are not around.

The reverse occurs with implicit memory in that positive memories can work in our favour. This is why loving family rituals are incredibly powerful at building that loving connectedness that children yearn for. It is also why I encourage parents to create family rituals like building the love bridges that I explored in the previous chapter. This is why I encourage families to have dogs as pets because a good dog may well be the most unconditionally loving creature your child may ever meet. The dog will love you no matter what — even after you've wet the bed, not eaten vegetables and punched your sister out of frustration. That dog just keeps on wagging its tail, and seeing you through the eyes of unconditional love and acceptance. So many family stories are anchored through a loving pet rather than through the people in the house.

The joy of pets

Our family dog Jess was a hyperactive fox terrier. In days gone by, when the boys would come home from university she would do amazing laps around the garden or inside the house. Her complete excitement at their return was a sheer delight to see. I was a little bit jealous because my hugs did not seem to give my boys the same exquisite joy as Jessie's laps around the house!

When the boys would take care of her during the times I was travelling she was always happy to see them return at night. Coming home to an empty house is never pleasant and a welcoming pet can make a lousy day seem OK. On one of our trips away, when the boys needed to take care of her, she had been allowed to sleep on a blanket in the oldest boy's bedroom; this was my tough, career-focused son who usually complained about her! Jess lived to be 14 years of age and in many ways was like a four-legged sister to the boys. Secretly, we all still miss her and I am profoundly thankful for all that she taught them and me.

Pets open our hearts to tenderness and kindness. Among our family photos many include family pets and animal friends. These pets not only become part of the family, they are key teachers in the areas of care, kindness and unconditional love. No wonder animals are brought into aged care facilities and hospitals, to help people smile and feel happy. Never underestimate the emotional intelligence that can be created and developed through sharing the world of animals.

> Joy is the result of human connection. With high levels of bodily arousal, optimal levels of epinephrine rushing through the body, and optimal levels of dopamine and opioids cascading over the brain, we feel intensely alive, wide awake and with tons of energy to do what we want to do.
> — Sunderland (2007).

Eric Jensen in his book, *Enriching the Brain* (2006), writes that memories are anchored much more deeply when there are strong emotions present. This would make sense in terms of what I've just written about powerful scary memories and how they anchor so deeply in the brain. Many children who struggle to remember their childhood when they have grown up sometimes mistakenly think that maybe something awful happened, which the mind has suppressed to protect them. More likely they have had a bland and quite normal childhood without an abundance of peak moments of suffering or joy. Technically, in the brain there is a foundation or genetic system for joy but how it unfolds depends on the interaction of those genes with social experiences. To give children this solid foundation early in life will help them be resilient and buoyant when life gives them challenge. I agree with Sunderland when she writes:

> Joy is a bodily state and the repeated activation of this state in children especially enables them to access many other wonderful human gifts – to be spontaneous, to have the drive and hope to follow a dream, to feel awe and wonder and sheer delight in response to the beautiful and amazing things in the world.

My challenge to you is to consciously build memories that are drowned in moments of profound joy and delight so that your child can remember them when s/he is an adult.

MAKING MEMORIES THAT MATTER

> As the brain matures, however we start to evaluate the world in terms of what has gone before: now there is a two-way street between the outside and our personal memories... a clear, connected, conceptual framework for how we see ourselves, the rest of the world and our life story as a 'connected chain': a narrative. But an increasingly prevalent tragedy is that this sequence of events can be thrown into reverse gear [like with dementia].
> — Prof Susan Greenfield, *ID: The Quest for Meaning in the 21st Century* (2008).

From the beginning of time, traditional kinship communities have used celebration around food as rites of passage and markers of significant events in the lives of their community members. One of the most significant markers in every child's life is their birthday every year (except for those poor kids who are born on 29th February in a leap year). What makes a birthday special for children is not how much money you spend on them, but the heightened moments of joy that this is a day that celebrates them. I am concerned about what is happening in some parts of the world at young children's birthday parties. A couple of the changes that have occurred in recent times are that adults stay the whole time. If we want to build child-friendly memories I am going to suggest that it needs to be about the children rather than the adults, and the extra pressure of having to cater for adults is probably the last thing busy parents need on their child's birthday. There can be many other gatherings where mums and dads and children are present however a child's birthday needs to have the child at the centre for one day in the year, surrounded by other children.

Creating family rituals around what happens on birthdays needs to happen when children are quite young. What happens when they first wake up? Do you have a special birthday hat that they can wear at breakfast? Where do they find their presents? Do you have a treasure hunt with clues so they can find their presents? When do they unwrap their presents? Maybe they choose what they have for dinner on the day of their birthday? Remember young children do not need to have a giant birthday party every year inviting all the children in their class. If you explain to your children they can have a big party once every three years and the other two years they have close family for dinner to celebrate their birthday — it makes them really appreciate when they do have a big birthday party because it doesn't happen all the time. So often children's birthday parties become overwhelming especially for young children under five and often they end up in tears and tantrums because our precious little children are not always very good at social and emotional intelligence due to the delay in the growth of the prefrontal cortex.

I am a huge fan of birthday parties in the park — not only because being outside has a natural calming effect on everyone. It saves you from having to micromanage highly excited young children with lots of games because they tend to play much more freely in a park. The noise level is also a lot lower and the absolute best part of having birthday parties in the park is that when you get home your house has not been trashed!

There are so many mini rituals or fun habits that can help create the happy memories you want your child to have from their childhood. Rituals for when we leave, rituals for when we arrive, rituals for family film nights, rituals for play time outside in the garden, and even bath time and bedtime rituals. We were lucky to live next door to a family who had two beautiful little girls. Every night these two little girls would go down to the bottom of the garden where they would leave breadcrumbs for the fairies they believe lived at the bottom of the garden. We could often hear them as they headed off down the back path. What was really beautiful was the dog went down every time after they had delivered the breadcrumbs and ate them so they would never find any breadcrumbs left behind by the fairies at the bottom of the garden.

Other important opportunities to build family rituals that are engaging and fun are around Easter and Christmas holidays, and of course any religious or cultural holidays that your family might engage in. My family has lots of memories of spending Easters with my sister and her family, which meant there were eight cousins all together — with fun being the number one aim. On Easter Sunday we used to hide the Easter eggs all around the garden or if we were camping around the campsite and great mirth was had as the Easter egg hunt took place. Several years ago when we had Easter together with the cousins aged 16 to 30 my sister and I hid Easter eggs in the garden. When we came in and told everyone what we'd done, one of the older cousins asked, "Aren't we a bit old for that now?" However, before he got the final word out there was a massive stampede as all of these big cousins raced outside to search for the eggs — with the same tussles and rugby tackles that used to occur when they were smaller. Such is the power of repeated rituals and how they can trigger joyful moments when our children grow into much bigger bodies.

Creating rituals doesn't have to be a big deal. I accidentally created an end-of-term treat for my sons one year after a particularly challenging and busy term of school. I took the boys to a local cafe and bought them hot chocolate sundaes to say, "well done". After all, their reports were good, no one had been suspended and there'd been no broken bones or stitches during the term. They enjoyed it so much they asked if we could have it at the end of each school term from then on. What was really interesting was that rather than get really tired and crabby in those last weeks at the end of the school term, the boys were counting down the days till the end of term treat with great excitement. When my older son moved to Perth for university, he rang a few weeks before the end of the first school term and asked that we didn't have end-of-school treat until he came home.

Building memories that last occurs when you repeat significantly positive experiences. There are many families that return to the same campsite or the same family farm for repeated holidays throughout childhood — not just because they can't think of anywhere else to go, but because memories are made from doing the same fun thing year after year. Think bike riding around the campsite with a heap kids that you only ever meet at that time each year, swinging off the flying fox into the river, climbing trees, building cubbies, hunting for prawns in the estuary in the dark, playing spotlight or fox holes on the beach with lots of kids (and often quite a few dads), or playing on the swings from dawn till dusk — this is the stuff that builds positive memories that your child can draw on later in life as evidence that they had a fabulous childhood.

Families who like to visit different places on their holidays can still lock in the same strong memories by taking their holiday rituals wherever they go. My dad had a habit on holidays of waking us up really early so that we could, "get a good day's loafing in!" This is also what children will draw on when they become a parent. The same goes for family games like SCRABBLE® or Monopoly, kicking a football outside, playing cricket in summer, going fishing, bush barbecues in the back paddock or yard, collecting mushrooms or heating up marshmallows over the campfire on a chilly winter's night. I am deeply saddened that many of these wonderful memory-making moments are at risk of disappearing as our children spend hours on iPads and tablets rather than playing with the children and adults who love them the most. The first five to seven years of brain development are critical and the optimal conditions this development requires mean our precious children need: lots of movement; complete sensory immersion; saturation of language and music; autonomy and freedom in their play; and of course a strong, healthy attachment to their parents or their secondary attachment people. An environment with low stress in a community that values children supports parents and this this will give them the best start in life. We want this for every single child ever born.

90% of the growth of the human brain occurs in the first 5 years of life...

With emotionally responsive parenting, vital connections will form in his brain enabling him to cope well with stress in later life, form fulfilling relationships, manage anger well, be kind and compassionate, have the will and motivation to follow his ambitions and his dreams, experience the deepest calm, love intimately and be in peace.

— Sunderland (2007).

Scientist, Baroness Susan Greenfield, shares my concern around the distraction of technology and also the pressure to live life 'instantly', right away and immediately. Baroness Greenfield writes of her sense that the world is 'fun' focused with not so much time to think deeply.

> This is not to say that thinking deeply isn't enjoyable – but the pleasure is of a different type from that of surrendering to sensations... the appreciation and savouring of 'meaning': some cerebral light flashes on as you start to see one thing in terms of something else, and place an event or behaviour in a new, wider context. Really 'understanding' something, be it in science or literature, usually devolves from that 'a ha' moment, from making a connection: by contrast, having fun is usually based on the opposite on *dissolving* connections, splitting the here-and-now moment from the past and the future... and above all splitting the sense of self, of a particular identity, in favour of abandonment to the raw sensory experience.
> — Greenfield (2008).

Baroness Greenfield is concerned about how these new technologies can impact on how our brains create our sense of unique individuality. For example, if every child plays the same game with their technology over and over again is it possible their brains will be wired very similarly? In a way we could be interfering with the sacred and creative pathways that allow every single unique human being to be unique. So rather than having a world full of 'somebodys' — people who've been created with very different experiences in different environments — if children's use of technology went untethered and they were fed the same stream of mainstream media, one view is we may end up with a world full of 'anybodys' and 'nobodys' who are all wired the same, with the same interests and the same implicit memories.

This seemingly far-fetched concept needs to be imagined because our world needs people to be different so that we can meet the challenging new times ahead. We need creative thinkers and innovative minds who will be able to think outside the box. We need to be able to function separately from the technology.

How the Net is changing our brains

In his book, *The Shallows* (2010), Nicholas Carr writes about how the Internet is changing the way we think, read and remember. He talks of the Net's capacity as a "high-speed system for delivering responses and rewards" when we get an SMS, a 'like' on a Facebook post, or a response to a comment we posted on a news site, for example.

"The Net's interactivity gives us powerful new tools for finding information, expressing ourselves and conversing with others. It also turns us into lab rats constantly pressing levers to get tiny pellets of social or intellectual nourishment," Carr writes.

He also discusses a 2008 study into the effects of the Internet on 6,000 young people, which reported that the generation of children who have grown up with the Web read differently from prior generations. Rather than reading left to right, they skim and skip around scan for "pertinent information of interest." (Tapscott in Carr, 2010).

In that same year, a professor of psychiatry at UCLA, Gary Small, led a research project that compared brain scans of regular Web surfers to those of novice users, while they searched the Web. They also compared the brain activity of the subjects as they read books. Regular Web users had much broader brain activity than the new users while they were surfing the Web, but showed no significant difference between groups while reading a book.

This is the really interesting part of the study: the novice Web users then spent one hour a day for five days searching the Internet. After less than one week of practice, the brain scans revealed, "the exact same neural circuitry in the front part of the brain became active in the Internet-naïve subjects," according to Small. "Five hours on the Internet, and the naïve subjects had already rewired their brains." (Carr, 2010).

Academic and journalist, Dr Aleks Krotoski in her book, *Untangling the Web* (2013), sees the concerns raised by the likes of Baroness Greenfield and Carr as quite 'dystopian'. She cites among the benefits of technology: bringing families closer together; developing new ways of intimacy and community online; and freeing up brain space for greater cognitive use (even if we do unfortunately, she points out, fill this space with watching funny videos about cats).

I am not against technology. I agree that it can help families connect and I love that it enables me to connect with people all over the world to share my message. However, we must ask if its use is rewiring adult brains in as little as five hours, then what effect might this have on our children's developing minds?

I also wonder what will happen to us if we ever have to do without technology, when we have been wired to seek entertainment by ourselves on a screen? It's like trying to find our way in life without the GPS!

It is essential to keep the use of technology as low as possible in the first three to five years so that the full integration of the brain with the body and the heart can take place as completely as possible.

As Carr again writes, "How sad it would be, particularly when it comes to the nurturing of our children's minds, if we were to accept without question the idea that 'human elements' are outmoded and dispensable".

I know of a five-year-old boy who has been raised on an iPad and a TV in his bedroom who did not know what "that white thing in the sky" was. This poor child's reality meant that he did not even know what a cloud was! Scary, but true. I wonder if he knew what the iCloud was?

PARENT MEMORIES AND HOW THEY INFLUENCE OUR PARENTING

Every parent has had parents and a childhood, and no matter how fabulous your mum and dad may have been as parents, we all come with scars from our childhood. Now that you understand how memories are formed and how memories influence our behaviour, especially implicit memories, you may appreciate why parenting is so challenging. In any given moment a mum or a dad may be triggered by an experience that makes them react from an unconscious place deep within their mind and they can make a choice that they deeply regret later. Essentially we all have unfinished business from our childhood and it is not until you live in close proximity to children that you have helped to create that these buttons tend to be pressed as often as they do. Many of us make decisions as parents to either copy or reject whatever our own mum or dad did as a parent.

> Parents who express anger or disappointment about any mistreatment they received as children are less likely to pass on this mistreatment to their own children. If we can be honest with ourselves about our emotional wounds and if we allow ourselves in our grief, we free ourselves from the tendency to repeat history.
> — Grille (2013).

My own mum was emotionally unavailable, aloof and struggled so much with her own happiness that she self-medicated with alcohol. By the time I arrived as the fifth child of six she was pretty weary and absent on many levels. I have many memories of beltings from Mum and thought that she was abusive. However, when I grew older I found that most children raised in the 50s and 60s were frequently given the same firm physical discipline. My mum was a very poor communicator and so being frozen out and being ignored were two very significant wounds that I experienced as a child. When I reached adolescence, I was a pretty angry and aloof young lady with a very low self-esteem even though I displayed confidence academically, in the arts and in my sports.

When I became a mum, I remember choosing to be present and to be as loving and as available as I could be. Then one afternoon when my oldest son was throwing a particularly spectacular tantrum when he was around two-and-a-half, I swung round to hit him in the head — I stopped with my arm midflight, with a hideous thought, "Oh no. I have turned into my mum!" That single experience was enough for me to realise that I needed some help to release the pent-up anger, rage, sadness and remorse from my challenging relationship with my mum. I spent many weekends doing personal development programs; I went to counselling and I explored 'my story' of my childhood deeply with my sister. We discovered that we had slightly different stories and very different wounds. While I had been the challenging child, who questioned my mum's behaviour, argued with her and demanded attention wherever I could, my sister had been the good girl, secretly jealous of my courage and bravery. While our relationship with Mum was challenging on some levels, she was an excellent cook, a competent gardener, an avid reader, a passionate bird lover and a highly intuitive woman, and all these wonderful and positive attributes are very much a part of the women we have become, and for that we are deeply grateful.

In time I came to a profoundly peaceful place with my relationship with my mum when I realised that she had done the best she could, with what she knew and with what she had experienced being the fifth child of 12 children raised in poverty. Forgiveness came easily once this realisation anchored in my brain. To be the best parents possible for your child, I encourage you to explore honestly the story you have in your head by reading good books, attending seminars and workshops, and finding a professional who can help you with some of the most challenging moments that you experience as a parent. This will enable you to parent from a grounded and loving place, rather than a reactive and defensive place. With more knowledge, understanding and a bucket load of compassion, we can really re-wire the memory pathways in our mind so that we can navigate a better and more loving journey in our own homes. We all want to be the best parents we can be because we all want what is best our children.

> Our ability to have sensitive, reciprocal communication nurtures a child's sense of security, and these trusting secure relationships help children do well in many areas of their lives. Our ability to communicate effectively in creating security in our children is most strongly predicted by our having made sense of the events of our early life. Making sense of our life enables us to understand and integrate our own childhood experiences, positive or negative, and to accept them as part of our ongoing life story. We can't change what happened to us as children but we can change the way we think about those events.
> — Daniel J. Siegel and Mary Hartzell, *Parenting from the Inside Out* (2003).

HONOURING CHILDREN'S IMAGINATIONS AS VALUABLE

You may not have considered that an imagination is a product of our brain, however, it most certainly is. Those delightful moments of joy that children experience within their imaginations are important parts of being young.

Do you remember that horrifying moment when you learned that Father Christmas was not real? Or maybe you remember a time when a grown-up tried to tell you that wishes never come true or when you were shown how a magic trick really worked? If you can remember any of these experiences you will also recall disappointment, sadness and the poignant moment of grief that accompanied that moment. Sadly, imagination is being killed off in our Western world by busy parents, overuse of technological creations like television, computers, smart phones, tablets and DVDs, and the pressures of consumerism.

Children's imaginations, especially when a child is under seven, help them experience a form of mindful joy. They are totally unaware of the concerns of later life. More than that, a child's imagination can nurture, protect and insulate them from many of the harsh realities of the adult modern world that surrounds them. It can feed their growing spirits, and build on emotional and social competencies that will help them in adolescence and adulthood. Imagination and the holistic growth of healthy, happy, resilient children have suffered greatly in the last couple of generations. Modernism, the rise of a popular culture that honours 'fast and quick' living, the 'must have' mentality, and family and community disintegration have all taken their toll on children.

I firmly believe that a rich imaginative childhood is essential for the evolving brain. It helps to create the neuronal templates that ensure emotional stability, social awareness and the spiritual strength to cope with life in this chaotic, constantly changing world.

Put simply, the imagination helps children explore and interpret life experiences as they strive for a sense of meaning. This search for meaning is not a logical process. We need to remember that children do not see the world as we do, and thank God for that! Children have a unique way of seeing the world that enables them to stay curious, and full of wonderment and spontaneity.

We lose something when we only see the world through the eyes of an educated, sensible and logical adult. To demonstrate how children search for meaning from within their imaginary world, let's run through the following scenario.

A little girl lines up her dolls and teddy bears. She then assumes the voice of an adult and proceeds to teach her 'students' about the importance of being tidy. Watching carefully we notice that she is modelling a significant adult in her life. She copies the voice, body language, words and intonations that she experiences so strongly in her life. And she copies so well! Sometimes she uses a growly voice to scold an inattentive doll, "Are you listening to me?" She may then immediately become tender and console the wounded doll, reassuring it with kind words and a hug. I have noticed this pattern of events many times. Interestingly, it is the child who makes up the part about consoling, probably in response to what they wish had happened to them when they were scolded. In this play they are able to explore their emotional worlds and attempt to make sense of how adults behave and how their world could be improved.

Children's imaginations can create new ways of seeing the world and of coping with things that challenge them. Indeed, Marjorie Taylor in her book, *Imaginary Companions and the Children Who Create Them* (1999) explains that people who had imaginary friends as younger children appear to be mentally and emotionally more stable as adults. Rather than store, suppress or distort their experiences, they explored them with their imaginary friends. This allowed the child to diffuse any unexpressed emotion and to find a sense of meaning out of their experiences. Professor Susan Harter and Christine Chao from the University of Denver argue that children may fashion their imaginary companion in one of two ways: one possible way is to create an imaginary friend who is helpless and incompetent and who makes the child feel strong or better by comparison; or they may create a friend who is extremely competent so that the child has a powerful ally, which bolsters their self esteem.

> "Think of the imaginary companion as providing a window on your child's thoughts and feelings."
> — Marjorie Taylor (1999).

Marjorie Taylor believed that the main reason children created imaginary friends was simply to experience fun and companionship. Essentially they can be great boredom beaters and, for a lonely child, fill the need to have someone to play with. These views support the role of imaginary friends in the healthy development of a child's personality. Furthermore, most imaginary friends disappear before six years of age.

I was once doing a radio interview about how important the imagination is in children's lives when a mum rang to give us the story of her daughter's imaginary friend. Apparently around the age of four her daughter created an imaginary friend called Claire. She was so real to her daughter that she needed a place set at the table every night for dinner; she also went to school with her and needed to have a seatbelt put on when they were in the car. The mother said she did 'use' the imaginary friend at times to motivate her daughter to eat vegetables or to get her bag ready to school because, "Claire has already done it!" Then one afternoon on their way home from school the daughter became very distressed and was screaming and crying. The mum stopped the car and ran around to see what the problem was and amongst the sobs, her daughter said, "Mummy, you have shut Claire's leg in the car door!" So, quickly the mum pretended to take Claire out of the car seat and console her outside the car, silently hoping that she didn't need to take Claire to the emergency department.

When her daughter was preparing for her 21st birthday and they were writing out invitations her mum wrote one to Claire and passed it to her daughter saying, "Wouldn't it be great if she could come?" The daughter looked up with tears in her eyes and said, "Thank you Mum for letting Claire be such a special part of my life". They hugged deeply and the mum said it would be a peak moment forever in her life.

Another caller phoned the same day to say that when the neighbour's children used to come over and play in the garden they used to tell her they were having afternoon tea with Mrs Brown. Many years later that family left and another family arrived and their young children also went and played in her garden. Without her ever telling them about Mrs Brown and the tea parties, they came rushing in one afternoon with great excitement to say that they had been having afternoon tea with Mrs Brown! Such is the beauty and the wonder of children's imaginations.

From the age of two, we use the imagination to process life experiences, achieve mastery of our emotions, enrich our social understandings, develop communication skills and create wonderful possibilities for our future lives. Even though young children's imaginations are more fertile than those of adults, teenagers and adults can still use the imagination for support. It can support our emotional and mental wellbeing right through life.

It is important that we bear witness to a child's way of experiencing the world and that we allow a childlike way to flow through us, to imbue us and to change us. A child's delight at their first touch of a cat's fur, hearing thunder or experiencing a colourful sunrise can soften the hardest adult heart — if we simply stay fully present in the moment. Being in touch with awe, wonder and micro moments of ecstasy, once again, help shape the brain so that it will anticipate such profoundly beautiful moments right throughout life.

Research suggests that the brain can be wired one of two ways by the most significant experiences that children can remember. One is the pain-thinking way and this happens when the child struggles with many painful events, mainly from deprivation, abandonment and significant abuse. In a way, this is how they will unconsciously expect their life to be forever. Those who have experienced the significant moments of joy and delight that I have been sharing, have what we call a joy-seeking pathway in their neuronal maps. They will anticipate much happier events and experiences as a consequence of experiencing them when they were children.

> When imagination and play collide, spontaneously, magic happens for real children.
> — Maggie Dent, *Nurturing Kids' Hearts and Souls* (2005).

Children under seven years of age have an exquisite imagination — and indeed this is often called the "magical child window" in childhood. As we keep on speeding up childhood and being in a hurry to make them grow up, especially in our test-driven education systems, I am deeply concerned about messing up some of the brain development that shapes our wellbeing, especially our mental wellbeing later in life. This sacred window is highly fertile and woven closely into their real world so that the two constantly merge, ebb and flow together. Young children who are asked to breathe out their worries as part of therapy sound like steam trains. When you ask teenagers to do the same you can barely hear any breath at all! Imagination is an enormous source of comfort and protection for children.

> In their book, ***Magical Parent, Magical Child*** (2003), Michael Mendizza and Joseph Chilton Pearce point out that the kinds of qualities essential to an innovative peacemaker – curiosity, playfulness, willingness to experiment, flexibility, humour, receptiveness to new ideas, eagerness to learn – all rely upon imagination. Just as chips and candy are junk food for the child's developing body, so are television and computer images junk food for her developing imagination.
> — Reproduced from *Parenting for Peace* (2012), by Marcy Axness, with permission of Sentient Publications, LLC

An absence of a rich imaginary world has been shown to add to the possibility of mental illness and poor motivation when faced with challenge. Some modern parents have stopped sharing traditional fairy tales and nursery rhymes because they sometimes have awful things in them. Georgie Porgie made the girls cry; in "Rock-a-bye Baby", the baby fell out of the tree; and Hansel was almost eaten by a witch. Some researchers believe that traditional tales and nursery rhymes were preparing children better for how to be resilient later in life. They showed children that evil existed, that persistence was often needed to overcome adversity, and that life hurts at times. Maybe our need to overprotect our children and be politically correct is making them softer and less prepared for life as an adult.

We cannot measure the health of a child's imagination, however, children who struggle, especially in times of challenge, may very well be the product of a modern world that is hell bent on stealing childhood from our children. We see how happy some children appear to be who live in poverty in developing countries — they have the magical window of childhood as a profoundly important part of their journey on our earth. While we cannot analyse a child's imaginary world from the perspective of the educated logical mind of the adult, we need to be quietly reassured that, "imaginative thought is an integral part of every day cognition and human experience" (Taylor, 1999). It is woven into the threads of our lives, without conscious thought or intention, and enriches our lives. It is more than a form of escape or a source of entertainment; imagination plays a very important part in the creation of a preferable future. Its role in modern thinking and consciousness is undisputed.

The poem below has been published widely on the Internet. Its original author and source is not known but it was allegedly written by a young man who committed suicide two weeks after writing it. Despite its murky origins, I use it here because it illustrates my point about imagination beautifully:

> *He always wanted to say things. But no one understood.*
> *He always wanted to explain things. But no one cared.*
> *So he drew.*
> *Sometimes he would just draw and it wasn't anything.*
> *He wanted to carve it in stone or write it in the sky.*
> *He would lie out on the grass and look up in the sky*
> *and it would be only him and the sky and things that needed saying.*
> *And it was after that he drew the picture. It was a beautiful picture*
> *He kept it under the pillow and would let no one see it.*
> *And he would look at it every night and think about it, and when*
> *it was dark, and his eyes were closed, he could still see it.*
> *And it was all of him, and he loved it.*
> *When he started school he brought it with him. Not to show anyone,*
> *but just to have it with him like a friend.*
> *It was funny about school.*
> *He sat in a square, brown desk like all the other square, brown desks*
> *and he thought it should be red.*
> *And his room was a square, brown room. Like all the other rooms.*
> *And it was tight and close. And stiff.*
> *He hated to hold the pencil and the chalk, with his arm stiff*
> *and his feet flat on the floor, stiff, with the teacher watching, watching.*
> *And then he had to write numbers. And they weren't anything.*
> *They were worse than the letters that could be something if you*
> *put them together.*
> *And the numbers were tight and square and he hated the whole thing.*

The teacher came and spoke to him. She told him to wear a tie like all the other boys.
He said he didn't like them and she said it didn't matter.
After that they drew. And he drew all yellow and it was the way he felt about morning. And it was beautiful.
The teacher came and smiled at him "What's this?" she said "Why don't you draw something like Ken's drawing, Isn't that beautiful?"
It was all questions.
After that his mother bought him a tie and he always drew airplanes and rocket ships like everyone else.
And he threw the old picture away.
And when he lay out alone looking at the sky, it was big and blue and all of everything, but he wasn't anymore.
He was square inside and brown, and his hands were stiff, and he was like everyone else.
And the thing inside him that needed saying didn't need saying anymore.
It had stopped pushing. It was crushed. Stiff.
Like everything else.

HUMOUR HELPS BUILD MEMORIES

The more warm, unconditional, constant and physically affectionate your relationship is with your child, the stronger the release of opioids, oxytocin and prolactin in the brain. As a result your child is likely to feel increasingly at ease and comfortable with himself.
— Sunderland (2007).

Another way to build such a warm, affectionate relationship with your children is by maintaining a lightness in your home; humour and laughter are the best teachers. In global resilience studies, having a sense of humour is recognised as being a very valuable life skill. It is a huge protective factor in homes and schoolyards where it can protect children from drowning in big ugly feelings, feeling overwhelmed and also helping with unwanted harassment or bullying. There are so many benefits that can be gained on many levels from laughter.

Laughter:
- transforms emotional states
- stimulates endorphins and creates wellbeing

- increases levels of serotonin and dopamine I
- is a key coping skill, especially for boys
- is an anti-bullying strategy
- encourages lightening up for serious moments
- is a bonding experience when shared in groups
- builds inclusivity and connectedness
- releases tension and stress
- is a key element in effective communication, especially in close relationships
- is an antidote to violence.

Laughter can transform negative emotional states faster than almost any other strategy or technique a parent can use. It is unfortunate that a sense of humour does not arrive in a box underneath the Christmas tree; it would be so much easier than cultivating it as a child has to do, along with so many life skills. There are times when young children use inappropriate humour in certain circumstances. Risqué or 'shed' humour has a very important place in the Australian psychology and larrikin humour helps to negate our depreciatory humour and language patterns. Culturally, we tend to 'put things down' or deflate compliments, "Wow, you have scrubbed up pretty good tonight, darling!" can be an Australian compliment that is genuinely meant to be kind. An overt compliment like, "Wow, you look beautiful tonight!" could get you a quick kick in the knee! This cultural nuance needs humour and without it people can easily take offence. Apprentice tradespeople are sometimes the brunt of antics and pranks by older staff. Some young lads are asked to find the left-handed screwdriver or the striped paint. When people realise it's a joke, those with a sense of humour are able to laugh about it rather than feel shame and deep embarrassment, which is what can happen without a sense of humour.

> The fun aspects of play also serve an important role in developing a child's psychology. The more pleasurable experiences that a child has, the more chance they have of developing a pleasure-seeking response to unknown experiences. The opposite can also occur, where the more painful experiences the child has, the more likely it is that they will seek pain rather than pleasure out of new experiences. This becomes an unconscious process that happens quite spontaneously. It is influenced by the core concepts that a child has come to believe.
> — John Joseph, *Learning in the Emotional Rooms* (2005).

Sharing simple riddles and jokes with young children is an excellent way to nurture a sense of humour. There will be times when the children share a joke that is a little inappropriate and it's important to avoid shaming or overtly sanctioning their attempts.

One way to encourage laughter and lightness in the home is to have funny books and riddle books beside the toilet. Make sure they do not have sexist, racist or gender jokes as children can see this as an appropriate way to have fun by laughing at others.

> "No man has ever been shot while doing the dishes."
> "Five out of four people have trouble with fractions."
> "If one synchronised swimmer drowns does that mean all the others have to?"
> "What happens if you get scared half to death twice?"
> "Marriage is the chief cause of divorce."
> "Be careful not to be too open-minded — your brains might fall out."

By reading these books and sharing the funny bits with family, children can learn the nuances of joke telling and of being humorous. This is a very important part of communication among friends and family. Only practice can improve anyone's ability to be humorous. Stressed and tired parents tend to lose their sense of humour so that's why it helps having aunts, uncles and grandparents who can make our kids laugh!

The capacity to laugh deeply and in an uninhibited way is another life skill that takes developing. Children who feel safe and valued can even fall over when they get an attack of giggles or laughter. A positive gauge of the wellbeing of a child can be how often they smile and laugh. It is something that is very difficult to fake as children — if they are unhappy or frightened, their faces show it. As adults we need to treasure these exquisite moments of joy.

Laughter and lightness in homes and classrooms demonstrates security and builds connectedness. We now have laughter therapy groups that help people to laugh again; such is the healing potential of triggering those positive brain chemicals.

> In Fact, "playful parenting" is one of the best ways to prepare your children for relationships and encourage them to connect with others. That's because it gives them positive experiences being with the people they spend the most time with: their parents... With every fun, enjoyable experience you give your children while they are with the family, you provide them with positive reinforcement about what it means to be a loving relationship with others. One reason has to do with the chemical in your brain called dopamine.
> — Siegel and Payne Bryson (2011).

I recommend that parents use props and puppets to increase the levels of lightness in the house. Wearing a witch hat can warn children that Mum is feeling grumpy and her tiara will help children know she's feeling happy. Puppets can cheer up any place, as they become a metaphor that can communicate so powerfully. I know teachers who have the clean-up puppet, the quiet time mouse, the Tigger puppet for exercise time, and the serious owl for proper chats about values. Be adventuresome and lighten up, your children will come with you. In the process you too could make your spirit and heart happier, and help your stress levels dissolve away.

A few helpful props can lighten up your home so perhaps get yourself a few capes, a tiara or two, a psychedelic wig, a crazy hat, some weird fake glasses or plastic moustache or beard! Sometimes it is fun to just put them on and pretend you haven't noticed — children think is really funny. If your children are displaying signs of exhaustion towards the end of the school term that's a great time to bring out costumes and lighten things up. This may also be a time to remind your children about the power of a great cubby, treasure hunt, a picnic on the back lawn or a water fight on a hot day. Technically, adults are the alpha people in the house and as such, we can use our prefrontal cortex to change the environment in such a way as to cheer everyone up. You are the happiness police and the choices you make around your home can and do contribute enormously to the wellbeing of your children.

> We want the happy moments. They are essential for family life so that we can flourish as families. But we need the difficult times as well. They help us recognise and appreciate the good times for what they are, and they help us develop and grow. It is something of a paradox, but our eventual levels of happiness are raised because we are willing to have them lowered through years of dirty nappies, tantrums and attitude.
> — Justin Coulson, *What Your Child Needs From You* (2012).

LANGUAGE ACQUISITION AND LEARNING TO READ

> The foundations for learning to read are set down from the moment a child first hears the sounds of people talking, the tunes of songs, and the rhythms and repetitions of rhymes and stories.
> — Mem Fox.

The ability to communicate is a profoundly important skill for human beings because we are wired to be social beings who live together in families within larger units called communities. For us to be able to cooperate and exist with some degree of harmony, we must be able to communicate. For the brain, the ability to communicate is incredibly complex and we seem to have some serious concerns in our modern world at the delays many of our beautiful children are having with their ability to communicate verbally. This challenge will also make it difficult to learn to read. Our precious children, especially our babies and toddlers, are downloading not just our verbal language but also our non-verbal language. Indeed without the non-verbal connection with loving, caring parents, children can sometimes struggle with verbal language. Yet again, we come back to the fundamental need of healthy attachment as being the number one thing that shapes our babies and toddlers early growth and development and that has life-long influences.

Even before I began my parenting journey, when I was in the company of babies or toddlers I was fascinated that I could utter really strange noises and speak in a language I did not know that I knew. This language is called 'parenteze' and it is great to see that neuroscience can now show how important parenteze, or baby talk, is to developing the 'tracts', or processing neuro-highways, that later help children to speak and to read. When parents make "goo goo, ga ga" noises, it helps babies work out HOW to speak and how sounds are formed. When combined with the repetition and sequencing the brain needs, it is like creating the fertile soil required to grow the future seeds of language and words. Dr Martha Burns, a neuroscientist who specialises in reading, strongly affirms how essential nursery rhymes are in the development of phonological awareness — the building blocks for reading. It helps build a sense of syllables in a natural fun way.

Indeed, Swiss dyslexia expert, Dr Nora Raschle believes that a key indicator of a child's ability to read later is: "Can they rhyme at four years of age?" Tongue twisters are also excellent for building phonological awareness, as well as building children's working memories. They used to be practised regularly in classrooms, indeed they still can be. The good news is teachers don't need an iPad, computer or interactive whiteboard to do them!

> **WILMA WALLABY**
>
> "Enjoy your kids as often as you can — play with them, laugh with them and celebrate them. Before you know it, they have grown up and flown from the nest."

Tongue twisters

SHE SELLS SEA SHELLS ON THE SEA SHORE,
BUT THE SEA SHELLS THAT SHE SELLS,
ON THE SEA SHORE ARE NOT THE REAL ONES

and

A big bug bit the little beetle but the little beetle bit the big bug back.

or

Peter Piper picked a peck of pickled peppers.
Did Peter Piper pick a peck of pickled peppers?
If Peter Piper picked a peck of pickled peppers,
Where's the peck of pickled peppers Peter Piper picked?

and

How much wood would a woodchuck chuck
If a woodchuck could chuck wood?
He would chuck, he would, as much as he could,
And chuck as much as a woodchuck would
If a woodchuck could chuck wood.

At a 2013 conference, neuroscientist, Dr Martha Burns presented on, "Reading and the Brain" and she emphasised the unbelievable importance of *language saturation*, repetitive rhyming, and quiet environments for babies, toddlers and young children. Research shows that under-threes are unable to take language from the TV and that auditory processing, which is vital for so much other development, is seriously impacted in a negative way from noisy screen environments. Children surrounded by such noisy environments can develop 'muddy maps' in their brain, which can increase reading problems including dyslexia if a child has a predisposition to dyslexia. Too much visual and auditory stimulation can lead to delays in other areas of the brain's development. We must remember that early brain development in all areas of growth for our babies, toddlers and young children is essential for children to be able to transition into preschool, then school and finally into life.

Many health professionals have been in touch with me sharing my concerns about the 'hurry up' occurring in early childhood. This is about a shift that has occurred in allowing our children to have 'go-slow' toddler-hoods; to experience rich and engaging play in child-friendly environments; and to have early years' educators focus on the whole child, rather than just the "brain that sits on a seat". Many parents are also anxious to get their children reading and learning formally as soon as possible, without really understanding how language is formed within the brain and how effective brain integration is essential before we learn to read. Professor Patricia Kuhl, co-director of the Institute for Learning and Brain Sciences at the University of Washington, discovered an interesting phenomenon, which Medina wrote about in his excellent book, *Brain Rules for Baby* (2014):

> At birth your baby can distinguish between the sounds of every language that has ever been invented. In other words we are not born with a capacity to speak a specific

language. We are born with the capacity to speak any language... Unfortunately things don't stay that way. And by their first birthdays, Professor Kuhl found babies could no longer distinguish between the sounds of every language on the planet. They can only distinguish between those to which they have been exposed to in the first six months... In general, this means the brain appears to have a limited window of opportunity in an astonishingly early timeframe.

It was these same studies that determined a baby's brain can only take language through social interaction with a live human being. It seems a baby cannot be fooled by DVDs or CDs. "The brain needs the information-rich, give-and-take stimulation that only another human being can provide," Medina writes.

Tucked into this data is a bombshell of an idea, one with empirical support across the developmental sciences. *Human learning in its most native state is primarily a relational exercise.* Intelligence is not developed in the electronic crucibles of cold, lifeless machines but in the arms of warm, loving people. You can literally rewire a child's brain through exposure to relationships.
— Medina (2014). http://brainrules.net/

In her aforementioned presentation, Dr Burns showed some technical slides about the brain to show that the left brain is where we process the ability to do maths, reading, understanding of symbol systems and sequencing. The first three years of life is when children build the essential neuronal highways that process the 'traffic' of stimuli and experiences. Real experiences that involve all the senses are profoundly important — listening, movement, sequencing like nursery rhymes and lullabies, rocking, swinging and face-to-face interaction.

The saturation in language in a calm environment was mentioned by Dr Burns, "as being the most important preparation for future capacity to read well". The neuronal tracts, or highways, take time to mature due to exposure to amount and quality of real-life experiences, and when the tract is mature, it is then 'ready' to learn to read. This maturity is known as readiness, and children who have English as a second language, boys, or those exposed to chronic distress often have delayed readiness.

To recall the words of some nursery rhymes you might remember, see Appendix 1.

Australian speech pathologist Amanda Styles wrote to me about her concerns for the children she has worked with over 20 years who have "developmental difficulties, ranging from speech and language difficulties, learning disorders, ADHD, Autism Spectrum Disorders, and emotional and behavioural problems".

Amanda has noticed that more children than ever are exhibiting developmental difficulties and believes that this is because of changes in the parenting and educational landscape, where the seeds of their brain development around language, concentration and learning have not been sown in an optimal way.

> Instead of having the much-needed time to further develop their oral language development, self-regulatory skills and social-emotional maturity through the much-needed play experiences that preschooling has previously provided, their attention is pushed towards formal literacy and numeracy training. They do not have the verbal and social prerequisites to cope with this level of teaching. It is like asking a child with a physical disability to run a race they are not yet physically able to run. They cannot run that race. Similarly, these children with developmental difficulties are cognitively not ready to cope with the demands of formal learning.
> — Amanda Styles

So from the moment your baby begins life outside of their mum's womb, we are shaping their brains with every choice we make.

Language saturation with plenty of movement, in the company of human beings who offer a loving, warm relationship must be the number-one priority of every parent.

Every decision you make in the first three years needs to take these things into consideration. It is as simple and complex as that. This intricate dance is what allows our children to grow healthy on all levels, especially the brain.

> In homes where there is heavy TV use, children are less likely to read every day; and when they do read they tend to read for much shorter times. These children are the most likely group to not read at all.
> — Rideout, Vandewater & Wartella, *Zero to Six: Electronic Media in the lives of Infants and Toddlers and Preschoolers* (2003).

There is a well-known study that shows the greater the amount of language a child hears the better they will read. The study also revealed that lower socio-economic families speak less than those who have more favourable economic circumstances. It was estimated that there was a difference of 30 million words over the first five years. This demonstrates how powerful saturation with language really is in the critical early years of life (Hart and Rissley, 1995).

Having endless conversations — which means two-sided conversations with our babies and toddlers — is the first way we saturate them with sound. Indeed in traditional communities, before written language, songs and stories held deep and profound meaning about everything the child would need to know in their entire life —history, culture, the right ways to behave, their connection to earth and how to read their environment. In the Yolngu culture in the Northern Territory they still sing songs about creatures that have been extinct for 20,000 years — now that is serious communication and information sharing.

It is helpful if you can develop an interest in storytelling in the early years. Having special storybooks that become favourites, help children develop a passion for special stories. There are so many beautiful picture books now written by Aboriginal authors that teach cultural stories as well as building much-needed respect for the Aboriginal culture, the Australian landscape, flora and fauna. One of my sons loved, *Franklin the Turtle*. He had nearly all the books and his special favourites were, *Franklin Gets Lost* and *Franklin Afraid of the Dark*. When it came to packing up the family home and moving, my then 14-year-old son was not quite ready to have his Franklin books packed away into storage. They were kept in a drawer in his new abode. He highly valued his special books from his childhood; they were keepers of memories.

> For as long as he could remember
> Wombat had wanted to be in the Nativity.
> Now, at last, he was old enough to take part.
> So, with his heart full of hope
> And his head full of dreams,
> He hurried along to the auditions.
> — Mem Fox, *Wombat Divine* (1995).

Reading stories to children has always been important, however the need to read in a highly animated way with texts that use rhyme, especially in the first three years, is seen as even more important than just reading any old story. Thank goodness for Mem Fox because not only are her fabulous children's picture books full of rhyme and things that young children love — they are short! If you have a child who wants to listen to the same book over and over again, for weeks and weeks, please be assured that this is fabulous for their beautiful brains. Every single time you read that book something else is happening with the wiring of the brain. Just because we get bored, we must not change the way our child is interacting with that book.

> ...Books that make a child's eyes sparkle, a child's hand to want to grab. If reading is to benefit a child, it must become part of that child's life, not as a task to be mastered, not as a mark or a grade on a school report, but as a living activity, as normal as eating or sleeping.
> — Dorothy Butler, *Babies Need Books* (1980).

There are two key elements to nurturing a love of reading in our children. One is the love of reading, which can only come from someone who models a deep passion and love of reading. The second is the art of reading and that can be a little more complicated. Good readers are **phonemically aware**, understand the **alphabetic principle**, apply these skills in a rapid and fluent manner, **possess strong vocabularies** and syntactical and grammatical skills, and relate reading to their own experiences.

As a secondary English teacher I felt for those students who arrived in high school unable to read. Basic literacy is very important in developing resilience because the ability to read and write increases our chances of life success. We need a basic level of literacy to read road maps, signs, bills, emails and text messages, and to fill in application forms and other documents or contracts. Literacy begins very early with reading to and having conversations with, young children. This takes take time and effort, and cannot happen in a week — it requires consistent effort. Children not only pick up nuances of language patterns, they learn to sit still and listen. To master these skills before preschool is really helpful for children; it happens largely through plenty of interaction with adults and other children.

> Reading a "good book" that absorbs you can help you build a wider conceptual framework with which to see the self and our world.
> — Greenfield (2008).

Reading to children is not just about building their phonological awareness, saturating them with language and giving them a love of reading. Research shows that it does so much more than that. When we read a good book, the act of reading can place the reader in the body of the characters, particularly the main protagonist and, at significant points of challenge in the book, our brain can alter our somatosensory and motor cortex connectivity. Essentially, this means that we experience bodily sensations when we are immersed in a good book and it can make us rethink who we are or what we might have done if we had been a character. Indeed being deeply immersed in a book that explores significant themes of life can change who we are by deepening us and expanding our awareness. And it doesn't matter if our children of primary and secondary school ages are reading their books on a screen or a Kindle; they will still experience the same immersion in it if it is a high-quality text. In a way, what I have just written sounds like an advertisement for English teachers, however as a teacher, I was deeply passionate about the effects that good-quality texts had on adolescents at such a bumpy time in their lives.

Baroness Susan Greenfield writes of the journeys that we take when we read good books:

> True, such journeys are indeed passive; but they do allow us to make an eventual comparison, to see one journey in terms of another, and hence to reach an ever wider 'understanding', a multi-faceted context within which everything that one encounters and experiences is then evaluated, has 'significance'. And as we've seen, we can view 'understanding' as seeing one thing in terms of another; 'significance' would occur when something could be linked to something else. The more connections, the deeper the significance and the greater the understanding.
> — Greenfield (2008).

It can be challenging if you you have a reluctant reader in your house. Educational researcher Dr Lorraine Hammond explained in a seminar I attended that for a child to be able to read they need to have lobe 39 turned on in the brain. This particular lobe enables sight and sound to be processed at the same time, and it quite naturally turns itself on somewhere between ages four and 14. This made a lot of sense as to why some children struggle and others find it easy, even when they are in the same family with the same gene pool and the same environment. Hammond's latest research demonstrates that children need movement in order to develop the fundamental skills needed for reading and I write about the more in the chapter on **MOVEMENT AND PLAY**.

Once a child has struggled with reading and they have noticed that other children are doing it really well, they can create a negative mindset around reading. Once again, the brain does not like being stressed or doing things that it finds difficult. Unfortunately, the only way to improve your ability to read, once your readiness has kicked in, is to actually spend time reading. I am sure that some children who struggled to read at five years of age may be able to read by age seven, but because they have developed a negative mindset and resist reading, then the ability to improve will be seriously hindered. So below are a few tips if you have such a child in your house. If these tips do not work, remember there are many other reasons why your child may be struggling with learning to read and getting professional help is incredibly important. I have worked with young lads who could not read at 13 only to find they had a serious issue with visual processing and that with a pair of glasses everything changed.

One of the secrets to getting reluctant readers reading is obviously to find material that they enjoy.

Reluctant readers want to:

- choose their own books from a narrowed choice
- have teacher read aloud the entire book — with no questions!

- compare movie to book
- read illustrated books & comics
- do art activities based on books
- read atypical nonfiction material.

Top tips for helping reluctant readers

1. Find funny books that have short fun quotes or fun facts.
2. Find books about things they love.
3. Read every day — alternating parent and child if they are struggling.
4. Let them read comics, magazines.
5. Validate their feelings.
6. Choose technology that encourages reading.
7. Help them change their attitude (i.e. try my, "I Can Read Easily" audio track, available for download from *www.maggiedent.com* or on my "School Mastery" CD).

If we didn't know chocolate was delicious we'd never crave for it – so it is with books. Books all need to feel smooth, smell nice, look enticing and present their readers with real rewards for the effort of reading them.

— Mem Fox.

THE SEEKING MECHANISM

When you contemplate your child's growing intelligence, other than memory or fluid intelligence, consider these 5 ingredients in the human intelligence 'stew'.

1. The desire to explore (and the freedom to do so)
2. Self control
3. Creativity
4. Verbal communication
5. Decoding nonverbal communication.

— Medina (2014). http://brainrules.net/

The willingness to explore the world is a baby or toddler's greatest source of stimulation and when parents fill their homes with bought toys or gadgets they weaken this powerful urge to explore. You'll recall earlier that I wrote about how babies' brains are born with 200 billion neurons (brain cells) and very few connectors (axons and dendrites).

This willingness is called the 'seeking mechanism' and it can be strengthened or crushed in early childhood. If parents tend to buy toys that work one way; or limit their child's creative or unstructured play opportunities; or miss the opportunities to share a young child's delights at things like a dead leaf, a broken stick or a feather on the ground — then the seeking mechanism will simply weaken. When the seeking mechanism has been nurtured, together with a strong imagination, adult humans can tackle almost any adversity because they have the inner capacity to work out a different way of conquering that adversity. People who have had this crushed early in their lives seem to be powerless to re-build their lives when bad things happen like divorce, natural disaster or serious illness. The human brain can be wired in either direction and a strong seeking mechanism is something to celebrate.

> In humans the seeking system can activate an appetite for life, an energy to explore the new, and an eagerness to seek out the fruits of the world. It also stimulates curiosity or intense interest in something and this is sustained motivation and directed sense of purpose that help us to achieve our goals.
> — Sunderland (2007).

Sometimes a child's seeking mechanism will seem to make choices that cause their parents great angst. Think of the toilet blocked up with toilet paper, the lipstick drawing on your wall, or Dad's tools all painted different colours — these are great examples of a healthy seeking mechanism in young children. Know your child did not think, "How can I annoy my parents?" They simply had fascinating thoughts about a possible experience and they set off to test their amazing hypotheses. We can crush the seeking mechanism quite easily.

A friend told me once that her three-year-old son had begun drawing flowers. He loved to draw flowers and his parents encouraged him to follow his passion. When he first attended preschool at age five his preschool teacher, quite innocently, asked him when he was drawing flowers, "Is that all you ever draw?" He never drew flowers again.

My suggestion to cope with the more challenging moments is to always remember — **"Wow, my child has a creative mind and a strong seeking mechanism!"**

In *Brain Rules for Baby*, Medina celebrates the desire to explore that babies are innately born with. Indeed, in thousands of experiments it has been shown that, "babies learn about their environment through a series of increasingly self-corrected ideas. Just like scientists they make sensory observations, make predictions about what they observe, design and deploy experiments capable of testing their predictions, evaluate their tests and add that knowledge to self generated growing database. The style is naturally aggressive, wonderfully flexible and annoyingly persistent."

> # DID YOU KNOW?
> Babies are biologically wired to learn - they don't need to be taught how to learn, they simply know. In a way babies and toddlers are scientists. They are constantly creating hypotheses, testing these hypotheses without any fear of failure.

I am deeply concerned about some of today's technologically wired children who have missed these vital developments because they have been using screens excessively from an early age. Humans are social beings and without lots of early interaction with other humans, they may struggle to create healthy, committed relationships later in life. So many of the basic building blocks around emotional awareness, belief systems, cultural and family patterns, and the influence of emotional memories happen before five! Fortunately, the human brain remains plastic for life and with concentrated effort from significant people, some of these gaps can be strengthened. Many unacceptable learned behaviours can be un-learned, however it makes life more of a challenge to do this rather than learning more appropriate behaviours when one is a child.

SELF-REGULATION AND WHY IT MATTERS

Essentially self-regulation means regulation of the self by the self. For quite some time now it has been apparent that behavioural management techniques that rely heavily on punishment and reward are relatively ineffective in reducing children's problematic behaviours both in our homes and our classrooms. In many cases, they can actually exacerbate the problem. Over the past decade it has also become increasingly clear that the cause of many of these behaviours lies in poor self-regulation.

In 2005, Angela Duckworth and Martin Seligman reported that self-discipline is a stronger predictor of school performance than IQ; not just in terms of grades, but even such things as school attendance, hours spent doing homework, or the amount of time spent watching TV. So if self-regulation is so important for our children to do well at school and in life, we need to understand how we help build it in the early years of their life.

> Self-regulation is basically self-control. That is, inhibiting impulses: physical (e.g. drives, appetites and emotions), behavioural (actions), and mental (thoughts, beliefs and desires)
> — Dr Stuart Shanker.

Dr Stuart Shanker has visited Australia a couple of times in the last few years and some of you will have heard his Australian lectures. I feel very excited and relieved by his views. His key message is that children's capacity to self-regulate largely determines how well they will perform at school, much more than whether they can count, or be good at picture recognition or colour-in within the lines.

You can hear him for yourself by searching on YouTube for an interview and talk published on 'tvoparents' channel: "Self- Regulation [sic] and Kindergarten" and "People for Education Keynote Address: Stuart Shanker".

Dr Shanker believes that kids vary how much 'gas' or energy they have and can use in coping with life, e.g. in the famous marshmallow test — this is the one where they gave four-year-olds a marshmallow, and told them if they didn't eat it for 15 minutes, they could have a second one. All the children were tracked later in life and the ones who could wait had performed much better at school, in work and very importantly, in relationships. Dr Shanker believes that kids who burn less energy, have more energy to manage delayed gratification.

Dr Shanker believes that high-energy foods, especially the habitual use of them, cause problems with kids' mechanisms to self-regulate especially high sugar foods and drinks. This means that the child will be "too aroused" to manage their impulses and regulate their emotions — they will have energy to burn. This shows up in children's tantrums, the meltdowns, the clinginess, the fighting and in the inability to play well. We must help children to develop their own capacity to self-regulate as this greatly increases children's ability to do well at school and in later life.

The less gas the child has, the more energy he'll need to use to cope, and this will affect his capacity to learn.

Essentially, there are five domains that are contributing to a child's ability to self-regulate and there can be overlaps and interactions that happen spontaneously, in different ways throughout the day. The five domains are:

1. Biological
2. Emotional
3. Cognitive
4. Social
5. Pro-social.

There are six stages of energy and kids need to be at level four — relaxed alertness — to be able to do well in school.
Inhibition
1. **Asleep**
2. **Drowsy**
3. **Hypoalert**
4. **Calm, focused and alert**
5. **Hyperalert**
6. **Flooded.**

Activation

Why do some kids burn more energy?

There are many factors, all covered in great depth in my 2003 book, *Saving our Children from Our Chaotic World: Teaching Children the Magic of Silence and Stillness*. Kath Walker also covers them in her excellent book, *What's The Hurry?* (2005).

> *The child with poor impulse control becomes an attractive mark for bullies because he is easy to upset and slow to soothe, which is a big boost for the ego of the bully.*
> — Jo Jackson King, *Raising the Best Possible Child* (2010).

There are many things that will sap a child's energy: poor attachment to their mother, over-scheduled lives, overstimulation, poor sleep patterns, too much TV/screen time, low-quality food, lack of predictable routines and boundaries, abuse, shouting, shaming, and unrealistic expectations. You will notice that many of these contributors have been explored in this book or they will be by the time you have finished.

If a child is sensitive to auditory stimuli — this will wear them out — they may be at operating at level three, but their biology may make it hard to get to level four.

"The better kids self-regulate, the better their self-control and the better they will manage themselves, their social environment and the better they will learn at school," according to Dr Shanker.

INSTANT ENERGY takes kids to level 3 or 5

As I've stated, high-energy foods are problematic, especially high-sugar cereals, foods and drinks. When our children have a high-sugar breakfast with a high-sugar juice drink, technically we have set them up to have poor self-regulation when they get to school. Protein is a much better choice at breakfast.

How do kids manage their energy states? Dr Shanker argues there are TOO MANY STRESSORS for today's children. Now you can see why I love Dr Shanker — he and I sing from the same song sheet! TV is like a high-calorie food for kids — it drains their energy for other things.

> Sitting in front of a television runs counter to all of those brain-nurturing pursuits and is in fact a highly unnatural activity for a young child: sitting motionless for 30, 60, 90 minutes at a time watching the flicker of electronic signals play across a backlit screen was never part of Nature's plan for the unfolding of social and cognitive intelligence.
> — Reproduced from *Parenting for Peace* (2012), by Marcy Axness, with permission of Sentient Publications, LLC.

WHAT HELPS build self-regulation in our children?

- MUSIC
- DRAMA
- ART
- NATURE
- SPORT
- SAFE TOUCH
- DEEP, LOVING RELATIONSHIPS
- REAL PLAY

WHAT DOESN'T?

- TV
- VIDEO GAMES AND IPADS, TABLETS AND SMART PHONES
- TOO MUCH PRESSURE/STRESS
- NOT ENOUGH HUMAN CONNECTION
- POOR QUALITY FOOD
- LACK OF GOOD SLEEP

Poor self-regulation appears to be contributing to the epidemic in childhood anxiety that is sweeping the Western world. Shanker has deep concerns about the effect of the screen world on these disturbing trends. Essentially, he explains, the brain uses 15% of the body's available energy and the vision sense uses 65% of that. This means that when we use too much visual stimulus we drain the brain from energy to think, reflect, problem solve, calm and self-regulate. So the brain fatigue causes the nervous system to go into stress. Shanker defines anxiety as "a chronic state of low level fear," and feeling stressed and having serious energy depletion are huge contributors to childhood anxiety challenges (Shanker, 2014).

There are three main ways to help our children improve their self-regulation according to Shanker:

1. Identify and reduce stressors
2. Develop self awareness about shifts in energy
3. Teach and encourage self-regulation techniques especially deep breathing, using meditation and improving sleep patterns.

> *Parents cannot change every gene, nor modify every neural tic – and yet what children experience day after day sculpts their neural circuitry.*
> — © Daniel Goleman, 1996, 'Emotional Intelligence', used by permission of Bloomsbury Publishing Plc.

We need to reduce the pressure and the stress on our children when they are young so that they can develop a healthy relationship with themselves, with others and with our world that allows them healthy self-regulation, so that they can get on with people while they learn and grow. Our modern, often chaotic world is drowning our families in stress and tension that impacts on how our precious babies meet the world in the first years of life.

So if you want your child to reach their full capacity in life, they need these basics wired into the brain before three years of age if possible, and if not by then, seven is the last window where teachers can catch up on any missing links while your child is within the school system.

From birth, create a quiet home environment where baby can hear clearly and then saturate them with sounds, gestures and safe touch. This is what builds the brain connectors in the best way possible.

The most important thing to remember from this chapter is that babies' and young children's brains are fragile and they are easily influenced, either positively or negatively, by the relationships they experience within the environments in which they live and play. Stress must be avoided as much as possible as it can shape our children to be wired to be hypersensitive for the rest of their life. Their beautiful, bountiful brains are ALWAYS learning and they need more quietness and spaces for individual curiosity and exploration to grow to be as healthy and capable as possible. The brain's plasticity is always in play, continually shaping and pruning, and so we can always grow new abilities and capacities by merely changing what children do. The developing human brain is bountiful and fragile at the same time.

TOP TIPS

* Babies' brains are born 'half-baked' and in the first five years 90% of the brain's growth will occur.
* The baby technically has three parts to its brain with the prefrontal cortex not completed until s/he is in their 20s.
* Babies are wired to learn – they are like scientists and adventurers.
* Neuroplasticity means that brains can be changed through experience at any time in your life.
* The best teacher for our babies' brains is experience, often repeated experience, in the early years.
* There are two levels of brain integration – vertical and horizontal.
* Memories matter, and how we create them and access them throughout life is important.
* Stress can damage a developing baby's brain.
* Babies' brains develop best with massive social interaction with human beings who use the language(s) dominant in that family.
* Mindsets are formed in the early years, which can enhance or hinder a child's growth and development.
* Self-regulation can be nurtured in children and can help them right through life.

WHAT I WISH I HAD KNOWN... "TALK TO YOUR KIDS... AND NEVER STOP TALKING TO THEM. TELL THEM WHY YOU ARE DOING SOMETHING, BE IT PUNISHMENT OR REWARD, TELL THEM HOW YOU FEEL, ABOUT THEM SUCCEEDING AT SPORT OR WALKING TO THE SHOP ALONE OR DRIVING A CAR FOR THE FIRST TIME. ADMIT TO THEM THAT YOU ARE LEARNING ALONG THE WAY AS WELL AND THAT IF YOU CONSIDER EACH OTHER, ALL DECISIONS MADE WILL BE EASIER ON EVERYONE. THEY CAN'T UNDERSTAND AND ACCEPT IF THEY DON'T KNOW WHY THINGS ARE HAPPENING." – Alison

3rd Thing
GO—SLOW CHILDHOODS

> Increasingly, scientists are linking stress in infancy and childhood to the soaring numbers of people suffering from anxiety and depressive disorders from adolescence onward.
> — Margot Sunderland, *The Science of Parenting* (2007).

All parents want the best for their children — we want them to grow up healthy, happy and kind, and to live meaningful lives as adults. We want them to be able to manage living in our chaotic world and avoid becoming overwhelmed by the speediness and busyness of modern life. One of the best ways to do this is by calming our children's lives. Stress is a new challenge to children's health and social wellbeing in our modern world. The 'hurried child' and the over-scheduled child are modern developments. Somewhere over the last 10 years, parenting has become a type of competition — thanks largely to parenting being more highly scrutinised and idealised in media. The hidden stress this places on growing children causes many other issues that delay healthy development and growth on all levels: emotionally, socially, mentally and cognitively. We have sped up the pace of life and living. We live in an **instant** world where we expect everything NOW. Communication, food, pain relief, results, well-behaved children — you name it, we expect things instantly. This expectation works silently and unconsciously creates stress when things do not happen straight away.

> I firmly believe that much of the stress and anxiety present in children's lives comes from hidden pressures and overzealous expectations of well-meaning parents, and sometimes teachers. Adults want to hurry up the innate and unique development of children in a busy, instant world.
> — Maggie Dent, *Real Kids in an Unreal World* (2008).

Children take **all** of childhood to grow — to learn how to think, learn, process information, behave appropriately, manage their lives, dress themselves, find their way home and learn who they are! We cannot rush this vital development. The key message from this chapter is do everything you possibly can to slow life down while your children are under five years of age. There will be days when it feels like you are having a 'groundhog day' because of the endless repetition that needs to occur so that you can meet the needs of your baby or toddler. This is completely normal and very helpful for your precious child to allow them to develop in the healthiest way possible. If you have days when you are striving to get ahead as a mother, just remember that it's almost impossible to get ahead because your baby or toddler is already wearing the next load of washing and there is probably a 'skiddy' in your son's underpants as I write. So take some deep breaths from time to time and tell yourself "go slow — there is no race, there is no competition and this too will pass!"

> **DID YOU KNOW?**
> Safe, loving environments & relationships reduce stress for our precious kids.

As well as building deep connectedness or love for a baby or toddler, it is important to create a calm environment for the child so they can thrive.

BABIES AND TODDLERS

> The single most universal fear for a child to experience – separation from their key caregivers, real or perceived.
> — Dr Vanessa Lapointe, "The Wishing Star" Lapointe Developmental Clinic

Babies and toddlers build their sense of security in the world through the people who care for them. This is the main reason why healthy attachment and safe attunement to our precious little people is so important. Daniel Siegel in his book, *Mindsight* (2010), explains that babies first develop a 'me map' of the world and, because of the immaturity of a baby's brain, they believe that 'me' includes the mother and baby as one. This is why babies get so distressed when they experience a sense of separation from their birth mother or the person who has taken the role of the mother. Around eight to ten months, the baby's mind starts to perceive a new map. This is the 'you and me' map, which means the baby now knows that the primary carer is separate from them. As the baby grows into toddlerhood they start forming their third map which is the 'we map'. When there are disruptions to the formations of these maps within a baby's brain, the way they see the world will be a little distorted and possibly unstable. The more secure a baby feels as these mind maps are created, the less stress they will experience, the calmer they will be and the happier they will be.

Robin Grille in his book, *Heart to Heart Parenting* (2008), outlines some of the things that are going on in a baby's consciousness that I think are very helpful for is to keep in mind:

- Babies feel everything far more intensely than do adults.
- Babies cannot lie, put on an act or pretend like older children. What you see is what you get — complete emotional honesty.
- Babies cannot plan or think ahead — all they do is to react.
- Babies are incapable of influencing or manipulating anyone.
- Babies do not understand time.
- Babies have very little ability to soothe themselves.
- Babies have no strong defences against pain or sorrow as they do not yet have the fight or flight response.
- If babies learn that reaching out is rewarding they will become strong communicators, able to connect with people more effectively.

OLDER CHILDREN

Modern life is really putting pressure, usually invisible, on our children — especially sensitive children. Children's brains are immature and unable to cope with the stressors of modern adult living and they often misinterpret adult challenges as being about them or their fault. Consistent stress becomes distress and the brain is seriously affected. Irrational behaviour, unstable emotions, sleeplessness and defiance are potential signs that a child is stressed, and struggling.

Daniel Goleman in his now famous book, *Emotional Intelligence*, writes that, "Happy, calm children learn best". Homes that consciously create calm and quiet times are building enormous support structures that will help children feel safe, allow them to enjoy their own quiet company and lower the stress levels within their growing bodies. Overexposure to TV and screens is overstimulating many little minds and bodies. Interestingly, research that has been conducted on overexposure to TV was conducted at a time when the size of TVs was very different to what it is today. The enormous screens and the digital processing mean that TVs and other screens are even more stimulating to the developing brains of babies, toddlers and young children. Remember always, the baby's brain is very underdeveloped and everything that s/he internalises through their senses will shape how that unique little miracle will interact with the world. This early overstimulation is thought to be a significant contributor to the inattentiveness, poor attention and restlessness of many of today's children when they turn up in our classrooms.

I was disturbed when I read Bruce Lipton's book, The Biology of Belief (2005). Lipton writes that babies' and toddlers' brains download everything they hear and see from TV — even when they are asleep in the room or they may appear to not be paying attention. That means all the violent images and sound bites of stories on the news and other adult programs are downloaded into their memory banks — and because they are so vulnerable, it causes them to skew the way they see the world.

Guidelines endorsed by the Australian Government recommend NO television (or screens from other devices) for children under two; no more than one hour a day for children between two and five; and no more than two hours a day for children over five.

Please avoid TV as much as possible in the early years and then be very vigilant on what programs your child's sensitive minds watch or are exposed to. Also keep your noise levels down in the home — voices, radios and volume on TV and other devices.

We have to remember how very noisy our modern world has become and just be mindful of how noise may impact on our young children's developing minds — and on our efforts to be conscious, present parents. Philosopher Damon Young wrote in Distraction, a publication from the Art of Living series (2010).

> …A Cornell University study concluded that children from schools under aeroplane flight paths have more difficulty learning language. As they adapt to the noise of the jet engines, they 'filter out' the human voice and its expressive nuances. The din doesn't simply silence us — it can deprive us of our capacity to speak and be heard. And these industrial distractions are accompanied by those of advertising and leisure — Music blares in lifts, malls and train stations, and cafés and bars have wall-sized televisions. In these circumstances, intimate conversation is hampered, along with quiet reflection. If this cacophony doesn't directly fracture our consciousness, it hampers our efforts to determine what will — to clearly and decisively seek what's valuable. (Young, 2010).

Overstimulation from too much activity, too many toys and too much talking can also cause children to become anxious. They need time to exist, explore and process the world on their own terms — and so do we.

STRESS IN CHILDREN

Learning how to cope with adversity is an important part of healthy development. While moderate, short-lived stress responses in the body can promote growth, toxic stress is the strong, unrelieved activation of the body's stress management system in the absence of protective adult support. Without caring adults to buffer children, the unrelenting stress caused by extreme poverty, neglect, abuse, or severe maternal depression can weaken the architecture of the developing brain, with long-term consequences for learning, behavior, and both physical and mental health.

— Source: "Toxic Stress Derails Healthy Development," Three core concepts in early development series. Center on the Developing Child, Harvard University. Accessed at: http://developingchild.harvard.edu/resources/multimedia/videos/three_core_concepts/toxic_stress/

Soothing and reassuring a distressed baby releases oxytocin and opioids that give the child a sense of wellbeing. Biting, hitting and running away are examples of reactions to big negative feelings flooding a child's brain. They need help to manage these painful feelings especially when they don't deserve it!

Comforting a crying baby activates the vagus nerve, which is found in the brain stem. As soothing takes place, the vagus nerve will rapidly restore order to key body systems that have been disrupted by distress, rebalancing the digestive system, heart rate, breathing and functioning of the immune system.

The main pathways that allow us to understand and manage our emotions are created in early childhood. Anne Manne in her book, *Motherhood*, writes that we now understand that children can suffer from post-traumatic stress disorder or have long-term damage from a single episode of terrible trauma. This can happen without any outward signs and the child may appear unharmed.

Babies and children who are "frozen out", or who experience rejection, whether it is physical, emotional or verbal, are at great risk of struggling socially and emotionally for the rest of their lives.

— Anne Manne, *Motherhood* (2005).

Their inability to be empathetic or to form caring, loving relationships is seriously and often permanently impaired. This lack of emotional skills in their kit bag can increase the chances of them making very poor decisions in life. The result can be enormous suffering, especially around violent behaviour, criminality, addictive patterns and abuse.

> Abused and neglected children have extremely high rates of disorganised and disorientated attachments, which is highly correlated with the development of personality disorders.
> — Manne (2005).

There is much research available now that shows how amazing the neurotransmitters in our brains are. These brain chemicals whizz around our body influencing how we feel at any given moment. Children are particularly susceptible to external stressors because they are rushed and hurried like no other generation. The ability to measure the stress hormone cortisol via a saliva test has shown how stressed many of our children are in their everyday lives. It is not a simple case of looking at environments and guessing how our children are managing things — we have a biological indicator. Some children find large-group child care stressful, and yet children from dysfunctional homes have shown to have reduced levels of cortisol, meaning less stress, in the same environment.

WILMA WALLABY

"Every child is different in how they like to be soothed — remember there is great power in teddy bears."

> So many grown-ups can't manage stress well. Because no-one helped them enough with stress and distress in childhood, they never set up effective stress regulating systems in their brains.
> — Sunderland (2007).

Sunderland explores in her excellent book how there are particular ways of responding to children that help them to establish pathways in their brains that enable them to manage emotions well, think rationally under pressure and to calm themselves down without recourse to angry outbursts, attacks of anxiety or, in later life, alcohol, smoking and drug problems.

Obviously emotionally responsive and caring parenting especially in the first three to five years of life will build these protective pathways for toddlers. We must remember that in the first years, a baby's brain is very immature and often the primitive or reptilian brain will simply take over when a baby is feeling threatened or overwhelmed. Imagine a massive storm suddenly descending upon you — that is how their little brains feel when this occurs! They need help to come out of a massive cortisol download, not chastising and lectures about being bad or naughty.

The impact of early distress, especially from abandonment, threats or violence, may lead to permanent brain impairment in the early years.

A recent research paper also suggests that chronic levels of distress from abusive or troubled childhoods may be present in the genes of the next generation. This may explain partially the generational patterns of abuse and deprivation that do occur.

WILMA WALLABY

"Everyone loves 'quiet time'. It feels good and it helps our minds and our bodies to take a rest from the game of life. A calm mind is often a kind mind — and that helps our kids cope better."

> Society reaps what it sows in the way it nurtures its children. Stress sculpts the brain to exhibit several anti-social, though adaptive, behaviours ... stress can set off a ripple of hormonal changes that permanently wire a child's brain to cope with a malevolent world. Through this chain of events, violence and abuse pass from generation to generation as well as from one society to the next.
> — Martin H. Teicher, "Scars that Won't Heal", *Scientific American* (March 2002).

An overactive stress response system originating in childhood underlies many mental disorders later in life:

- Depression
- Persistent states of anxiety
- Phobias and obsessions
- Physical symptoms and illness
- Being cut off emotionally
- Lethargy and lack of get up and go
- Lack of desire and excitement
- Lack of spontaneity.

> Early distress can cause cell death in a very important structure of the brain. The hippocampus, situated within the lower mammalian brain, plays a role in long-term memory and brain scans of a very stressed child resemble that of an aged person.
> — Sunderland (2007).

Negative neurotransmitters make it very difficult for children to learn. Low dopamine and noradrenalin levels make it more difficult for a child to focus and concentrate, which can lead to learning difficulties in comparison with other children. There is significant research that suggests there is a link between ADHD and low levels of dopamine. It seems that children with ADHD need more dopamine to sustain their concentration, and they have a tendency to lose their dopamine faster than other children. It is interesting to see that the activities that build dopamine in our early years' centres and primary schools are being reduced — outside play; frequent movement in the classroom; and music, drama and the arts. This may be one of the reasons why there has been such a significant increase in the number of children (mostly boys) aged four to six who are being suspended and expelled for aggressive and inappropriate behaviour in centres and schools across Australia. Boys tend to be kinaesthetic learners as do Indigenous children and, without opportunities to move, we may be creating brain-antagonistic environments for them thereby setting them up to fail. Maybe they are not failing school so much as school is failing them. In the chapter on MOVEMENT AND PLAY I explore this in much more depth.

> Low serotonin levels are a key component in many forms of aggression and violent behaviour. Opioids are vital to diminish feelings of fear and stress, so deactivation of opioids in parts of the brain leads to increases in negative feelings and stress, and decreases in positive feelings.
> — Sunderland (2007).

Distress (chronic stress)

1. Halves neuron development
2. Reduces effectiveness of the dendrites
3. Reduces brain to 'survival' mode rather than upper cognitive processing
4. Reduces blood supply to the brain
5. Stimulates emotional meltdowns
6. Impedes immune system.

> Stress is the body's response to a perception of a lack of control over an aversive situation. Distress is when there are chronic levels of elevated stress.
> — Eric Jensen, *Enriching The Brain* (2006).

What happens to the body when it enters 'Flight or Fight' state? (Distress)

- Breathing becomes shallow
- The heart rate increases
- Blood pressure rises
- Adrenaline and cortisol hormones are released into the blood
- The senses are heightened
- The liver releases stored sugar into the blood
- Muscles tense and tighten
- Blood flow increases to the brain and major muscles and is constricted to the extremities.

— Patrice Thomas, *Stress in Early Childhood* (2006).

The above impacts on children and adolescents' developing brains can be profound. A distressed child, who every morning turns up to school with only has half as many spaces for new learning as a child who is not distressed, has their capacity for learning impeded and is at a disadvantage. There is a massive cumulative effect over time of missed learning. Not only is the space for new learning reduced but the integration of the learning is negatively affected and that too has a significant cumulative influence. A toxic teacher or a threatening school environment can have a serious long-term, debilitating effect on student learning on all levels — cognitive, social and emotional. We must strive for safer schools with a more calming and nurturing focus, rather than better-looking buildings!

Bruce Lipton in his brilliant book, *The Biology of Belief* (2005), showed that cells in our body can only do one thing — focus on either growth or protection, in order to ensure survival:

> ...children who are experiencing frequent stress will have increased illness because the adrenal hormones will directly suppress the immune system to conserve energy supplies in order to survive their stressful experience.

This is why a child who experiences the distress of a death of a parent will feel dumber for ages — sometimes up to 18 months. The body will preserve its cognitive energy in order to manage the deep challenges of processing a death of a loved one.

I was recently in a rural community running a seminar about death and loss and children, and a teacher came and shared something interesting. He said that his primary school had been vandalised and destroyed in a fire and although the students were re-located to a nearby school they had gone backwards so rapidly academically it was frightening!

Professor Margaret Sims from the University of New England conducted several studies into the stress levels of children while she was at Edith Cowan University in Western Australia. Professor Sims measured the cortisol levels (a brain chemical present when a person is stressed) by using saliva tests on children in child care settings. She points out in her writing on the subject that a range of research studies have linked chronically high or low cortisol levels to long-term health, social-emotional and behavioural problems (2007). Her work fits in with my common-sense approach to parenting and education — the better the care, the healthier the child.

Professor Sims characterises a high quality child-care environment as being warm, responsive and respectful staff/child relationships, and good communication between parents and staff (Horin, 2008).

Research shows that social dislocation and change can be highly stressful for individuals, especially children. Moving preschools, schools, homes or countries may be contributing to a retardation or delay in some children's intellectual, social and emotional growth. Distress can cause long-term damage to the brain's adaptive systems and these are crucial for resilient behaviour like decision-making, reflection and flexible thinking. Studies clearly link distress with lowered cognitive capacity. Children need routines and consistent patterns of family routine to feel safe, and it also helps them to play often with other children and to make friends. This allows their nervous systems to relax and not continually flooding with the stress chemicals cortisol or adrenaline or both.

> When we feel too stressed we are less likely to show exploratory, curious, novelty seeking behaviours.
> — Sunderland (2007).

Sunderland lists six triggers for poor behaviour in children:

1. Tiredness and hunger
2. An immature brain
3. Unmet psychological needs
4. Intense emotions
5. Parental stress
6. A parenting style that activates the alarm systems in a child's lower brain.

The opposite of stress and feeling threatened is feeling calm or safe and happy. Brain chemicals are also responsible for this feeling! The good neurochemicals are called endorphins.

The question of comforters

Now to explore comforters in the early years of children's lives — a question I am asked so often. Babies and toddlers often need to have comforters to help soothe them when their significant loving carer is absent or busy. It's quite amusing to see little ones sitting in front of the washing machine and then the drier waiting for their favourite blanket to be washed and dried but that shows how important a comforter can be. Please be careful not to shame children that they should be "big enough" or "old enough" to stop needing a comforter — especially our boys. In particular, dads who have shamed their sons this way can do some serious damage that can impact him later in life. Shame from a significant male in a boy's life can figure in self-harm and even suicide.

We never know when something unexpected will happen that will mean a young child's parents are unable to care for them — sudden illness or accidents for example. Children who have comforters are easier to soothe and feel safer and have less chance of being scarred by such an event.

You are never too old to have a teddy to have as a special friend and confidante. A lovely mother told me of how her daughter has a teddy that has been well-loved and well-travelled. When she married her new husband he was happy for her teddy to sit on the marital bed — knowing how important the bear was in her world. The fact that she's 26 and the bear has only one ear and one eye — makes no difference at all.

Modelling calm

> *Pausing and taking three long, slow deep breaths or sighing three times in a row calms the vagus nerve in the brain and will settle our cortisol levels. Model it from birth and your child will automatically do that as a way to calm himself.*
> — Maggie Dent, *Saving Our Children from Our Chaotic World* (2003).

We need to be very mindful of the things that cause stress in children's lives and we need to protect them in the vulnerable early years. Gradually they will grow braver and stronger, but in their own time. If we were able to model quietness, stillness and calmness then our children will normalise this behaviour. We all need to slow down, and smell the roses. We only have one chance at rearing our children from birth to five — plenty of time to be busy when they are older and better able to cope with stress and chaos.

Main sources of stress and anxiety in children:

- Hurried, over-scheduled world
- Temperaments and personality

- Absence of healthy love and attachment
- Too much pressure on children to perform
- Stressed parents who rush
- Not enough calm, still, quiet solo time
- Poor sleep patterns
- Too much stimulation from TV, toys and adult commands
- Not enough consistency and routines
- Too much social change or social dislocation
- Shaming language
- Threats of abuse and violence
- Death and loss experiences.

> Children who are over scheduled into weekly activities may inadvertently be learning that life is about having every moment of their lives filled with entertainment and prescribed activities. Consequently, opportunities to show initiative, play alone and/or create experiences for themselves appear to have become lost.
> — Kathy Walker, *What's The Hurry?* (2005).

There has been a significant increase in the number of children suffering from anxiety and stress-related illnesses and hypersensitive behaviours. The modern world has created environments that have helped overload children's stress-regulating systems — and being aware of how to reduce some of the stressful events in children's lives will help reduce stress and anxiety. Busy parents who have poor stress-regulating systems often contribute to the increased levels of stress in their children. Prolonged sleep deprivation compromises our immune systems and parents of sleepless babies often display heightened levels of stress, and run the risk of becoming ill. Heart disease, high blood pressure, anxiety disorders, autoimmune disease, chronic fatigue and many mental illnesses are all believed to be affected by stress. We all know that the flight or fight response is naturally programmed into our bodies to help us act quickly in emergency situations. As the body and the mind have become overloaded with the fast pace of our modern life, they often stay in this heightened state of tension, for long periods of time. This means that the normal body function of cell replacement, rest and renewal for revitalisation, do not occur. The heightened level of cortisol in the body influences how we think, sleep and even how we digest our food, unfortunately all negatively. We are asking for illness by living this way.

> Research shows that if a child's need for comfort is not met with emotional responsiveness and soothing, this system can over time become wired for bodily hyperarousal. This can make life a stressful and exhaustive affair.
> — Sunderland (2007).

I believe there is a lot of violence in the world because there are a lot of people walking around this planet with poor frontal lobe functioning, poor stress-regulating systems and unexpressed emotional distress from their childhoods. We know that much of this damage comes from the first five years of life when children did not have their needs met in a loving, consistent way in a supportive environment.

Many children with broken hearts behave in angry, aggressive ways because of their changed brain chemistry. Grief can result in the withdrawal of opioids in key parts of the brain, along with reduced levels of other bonding chemicals. This causes a marked increase in negative feelings, as well as a reduction in positive feelings (Sunderland, 2007).

Experiences of shaming can debilitate us, especially during adolescence when brain changes create more confusion and vulnerability for our fledgling adults. They will simply shame themselves and almost all adolescents struggle with crippling self-doubt and self-criticism that will be fuelled by shaming from early childhood.

Aletha Solter (*Helping Young Children Flourish*, 1989) believes there are three main reasons for inappropriate behaviour in children:

1. Unmet needs — hungry, thirsty, need for attention, need for stimulation
2. Insufficient information — not sure how else to behave or child is too young to understand or remember rules
3. Painful feelings resulting from stress or unhealed trauma

The stressed or threatened nervous system will produce stress hormones like cortisol and adrenalin.

The brain adapts to chronic stressors with either of two extremes:

1. Numbness — listless, apathetic, unresponsive — disappearing
2. Hypervigilance — edgy, suspicious or overactive — acting out

> A child will be more likely to suffer from depression, stress and anxiety disorders, and a lower IQ, if exposed to prolong distress.
> — Jensen (2006).

- Rage, fear and separation are primitive responses that are set up in the primitive brain to support a baby's survival…
- The brain floods with cortisol and can lead to a state of hyperarousal and of feeling very unsafe in the world…
- When a child is not given enough help with his intense lower brain feelings his brain will not develop the pathways to enable him to manage stressful situations effectively.

Setting boundaries and having consistent carers with similar expectations of how to behave helps reduce stress for toddlers and children. It is very confusing for children when they receive different instructions and discipline from different people. Stress is a response to the perception of lack of control. Children are susceptible to stress because they seldom have much control over their environment.

Remember that children are children — not little adults. They can get confused, frightened and hurt quite easily. They need safe, consistent adults in their lives to help them manage difficult challenges — often little things that an adult may not notice can upset a child, especially a sensitive child.

> Adequate nurturing and the absence of intense early stress permit our brains to develop in a manner that is less aggressive and more emotionally stable, social and empathetic.
> — Teicher (2002).

SOOTHING, CALMING AND RELAXATION

The opposite of stress and distress is calmness and feeling relaxed. If a child clings to you s/he is trying to bring down a high body arousal level and high levels of stress chemicals. S/he is trying to activate the positive brain chemicals that activate feelings of wellbeing. Research shows that children who have been soothed quickly and frequently, tend to become self-soothers and manage stress better (Sunderland, 2007). Due to the neuroplasticity of the human brain, calmness can be learned at any stage of life.

Top tips for soothing: Key ways to trigger oxytocin – the love neurotransmitter

1. Calm adults
2. Touch and massage — especially 'tickle point' (high on back — stroke gently)
3. Rocking

4. Sucking
5. Physical comforters — soft toys, dummies, blankets
6. Warmth, approx 21 degrees C — (or cooling if child has a temperature)
7. Low soothing sounds, familiar songs
8. Bathing in warm bath
9. Novelty — laughter
10. Avoid overstimulation, especially loud voices, noises, too much chaos, and too much change.

Babies respond amazingly quickly to repeated soothing songs or music. Indeed, some babies turn their heads towards a song being sung by parents that was sung to them while they were still in utero. Singing repeated soothing lullabies is an excellent way to calm unsettled, crying babies. I tended to sing 'Rock-a-Bye Baby' to my boys when they were babies. Once when I was singing it to the fourth and final son, the oldest (a then eight-and-a-half-year-old) came and whispered to me,

"Mummy that song is about child abuse. The baby falls out of the tree. You need to get another song!"

> **WILMA WALLABY**
> "The calmer we are as parents, the calmer our children will be. Take the time to relax on the couch everyday and just watch your wee one play on the floor."

So funny to think that technically he was correct. However the loving intention, the soothing singing and the constant repetition obviously works even if some of the words might suggest something quite disturbing. I love the fact that babies and toddlers and young children don't care if you sing in tune, or if you sound really lousy. They simply love singing and music — the more of that out of the mouths of humans who are present in the room, the better. Remember babies and toddlers under three are unable to take clear sound from any screens, including large TVs.

> Music holds a powerful place in our memory. Even babies as young as 8 months have shown recognition of a familiar piece of music after a two-week delay. Providing consistent experiences with the same song (at the same time, such as nap time) helps young babies remember and link that music with a particular experience.
> — Ilari & Polka, *Music Cognition in Early Infancy* (2006).

It seems that not only are repeated songs from early childhood soothing for babies and toddlers, research seems to indicate it is also a powerful stimuli to lock in memories. Researcher and associate professor of psychology at The

University of California Davis's Center for Mind and Brain at the University, Petr Janata published a study on this:

> The region of the brain where memories of our past are supported and retrieved also serves as a hub that links familiar music, memories and emotion. The hub is located in the medial prefrontal cortex region.... 'What seems to happen is that a piece of familiar music serves as a soundtrack for a mental movie that starts playing in our head. It calls back memories of a particular person or place, and you might all of a sudden see that person's face in your mind's eye. ,' Janata said. 'Now we can see the association between those two things – the music and the memories.'
> — Petr Janata, *The Neural Architecture of Music-Evoked Autobiographical Memories* (2009).

Creating moments of joy and delight with music and smell is really important for young children because it also sets up calming pathways in their minds. When my boys were ill with a fever I would hum a lullaby or sing it to them and it really helped them to settle. Recent research on the power of lullabies confirms that they soothe upset babies; apparently the number one lullaby is *Twinkle Twinkle Little Star*. Relaxation CDs with music and calming voices have the same effect and evoke feelings of safety and calmness. This is why it is so important to surround your child's life with music to calm, play and have fun to.

> Similarly with smell, the smell of vanilla always makes me feel good even though I cannot remember the original experience that evokes that response. I feel the same with roses, English lilac, lavender, many wild flowers and chocolate. This instant feel-good experience changes my emotional state very easily. I encourage you to fill young children's lives with positive experiences around smell and sound so that you give them an easy way to transform a stressful, negative mood, now and later in life. It is helpful to build these unconscious positive connections while children are young. What happens when you smell chocolate or fresh strawberries? What happens when you play a favourite song?
> — Maggie Dent, *Nurturing Kids' Hearts and Souls* (2005).

WILMA WALLABY

"Songs, lullabies and familiar stories build loving connectedness and happy memories for life."

BREATHING REALLY DOES HELP

Healthy breathing has always helped to soothe our stressed psyches. There are many breathing techniques that help restore the calmness response in our bodies. A good and simple one is taking three sighs — and pausing after the third one. Or take three deep breaths with the outward breath being longer than the inward breath, count to five and do it again. This is a simple technique that you can teach children and adolescents.

> Relaxation is much more than chilling out in front of the television. Relaxation techniques involve making a conscious effort to use the breath to calm the body and the mind.
> — Helen Graham, *Visualization: An Introductory Guide* (1996).

The benefits of correct breathing practice include:

1. Oxygenation of the blood
2. Relief of anxieties
3. Blood being sent to the brain
4. Alleviation of minor physical aches and pains
5. An increase in function of immune system
6. Lowering of blood pressure and cholesterol
7. Slowing of heart rate and pulse.

> Deep breathing oxygenates the brain and that is one reason why doing relaxation activities and exercises can be a great way to calm excited or stressed children. Encourage and model deep and healthy breathing as well as using some techniques from yoga and Tai Chi.
> — Swamia Saradanda, *The Power of Breath: The Art of Breathing Well for Harmony, Happiness and Health* (2009).

One of the creative visualisations that I've created for children is called "Calming the Angry Ant" and this is an audio track that teaches children how to calm themselves when they get angry by using colour breathing. Even from the age of two, children can learn to take big breaths to calm themselves down. It works even better when mums and dads model deep breathing, taking themselves outside to calm down or even holding their heads in their hands or closing their eyes to focus on their breath. Calmness is profoundly important to learn as a life skill especially in our ever-changing and chaotic world.

There are several other calming visualisations that I have created that work really well for children and parents. Indeed, many parents who have purchased a calming track like "Beach Bliss" or "Moonlight Magic" have found themselves enjoying it just as much as the kids. Quite simply, a voice on a CD distracts the conscious mind for a while so that it calms our thoughts and our body will calm down once our mind calms down. These calming tracks are only around 10 minutes each and have been shown to be really helpful to calming pathways in the minds of children with ADHD, anxiety, poor sleep and who are worry warts.

If you are new to visualisations, you may wish to start with one of my free downloads (available from maggiedent.com). "Sleepytime" is designed to help children to sleep better, while "Safe 'n Sound" is wonderful for anxious children and children who've had trauma.

Thankfully, one of the benefits of modern life is that it is easier than ever before for busy parents to access a myriad of visualisations and relaxation tracks from all around the world, and download them immediately to any number of devices in the household.

TIPS FOR CALMING HYPERACTIVE CHILDREN

Hyperactive children can be particularly challenging. Often, self-regulation issues can be at the root of hyperactive behaviour, and I wrote about Dr Stuart Shanker's work in this area in THE BOUNTIFUL BRAIN IN INFANCY chapter. In dealing with the challenge of hyperactive children, I have some tips for concerned parents and teachers. First, however, know that there will be times when nothing you do will make much difference. When you realise that this is such a time, make yourself a cup of tea or coffee, shut yourself in your bedroom and play some relaxing music. Take a Tim Tam if there are any left! Otherwise, you might go for a walk. Then, remember some good moments in your child's life and think positive and calming thoughts of love about them. Send him or her a rainbow of love and breathe deeply.

Important ways you can make a difference with your child's behaviour are:

1. Keep your child away from soft drink, cordial, fruit juices and anything with colouring, preservatives and added sugar. Maybe visit a nutritionist, naturopath or homeopath to get help with understanding the huge influence diet has on behaviour.
2. Have your child checked out by a chiropractor or osteopath who specialises in children, to ensure that their spinal and cranial plates are balanced.
3. Make sure your child is getting enough sleep for their age and seek help if they exhibit signs of chronic sleep issues (i.e. exhaustion, lack of

energy during the day, pervasive irritability, dark rings under their eyes, etc.)

4. Honestly check your own stress levels. Children are often emotional barometers for one, or both, of their parents.
5. Encourage as much free, unstructured outside play as possible. This may mean many trips to the park but being outside in nature helps. Try it, you may realise that your child is much harder to manage when kept inside for too long. That's why after school can be tricky if you work!
6. Learn how to give back and foot massages. Better still, learn how to give reiki or therapeutic touch and offer it to your hyperactive child.
7. Many children do not know HOW to calm down or even what calm feels like. Teach them relaxation and calmness at as early an age as possible. Read to them lots, try using relaxation products, such as essential oils or teas, at night before sleep time and teach them to breathe deeply and how to be grounded.
8. Teach them to be comfortable with silence, if not stillness! That means having a home where silence is familiar — no sounds.
9. Bathing or swimming always helps; it calms unsettled babies.
10. Try aromatherapy; the brain responds to the calming effect of many smells — lavender, sandalwood, peppermint & jasmine. There are some excellent combination essences for calming.
11. Reassure your child that even though they are highly spirited and cannot pay attention for long, you always love them. Help them to tune into what they are feeling under their hyperactivity. What is it they feel? Do they feel angry, hurt, unloved, dumb or naughty? Use life-enhancing language.
12. Surround them with calming music from classical to nature ones. Some people believe it can help change the water inside the body (we are 50-75% water) by changing the molecular structure according to the sounds of the music.
13. Give your child lots of opportunities to be creative — with drawing and painting, music, building or creative play. Allow them to become absorbed in the act of creation — this helps release emotional energy as he or she discovers the wonders and fun of creativity!
14. Build your love bridge to your child — really listen and be present with your child, at least once a day. Many hyperactive children question authority and react negatively to manipulation or inappropriate use of power. They are often very sensitive and spiritually aware underneath their mask of confidence and nonchalance so never lie to them or make up an answer. Be honest because they will know.

15. Try calming Australian bush flower essences made by Ian White, a fifth generation Australian herbalist and a naturopath. They are inexpensive and can be very effective. Bush flower essences are now available in most pharmacies. Children I have worked with often call them magic drops.
16. Finally, be very mindful of your thoughts. Hyperactive children pick up negative thoughts very quickly, and react and respond to them. Change negative words to words that are encouraging and positive. For help with this, read *Raising Your Spirited Child* by Mary Sheedy Kurcinka.
17. Hold the highest vision for your child. See him or her loved, accepted and valued just as they are. I am a huge believer that our thoughts create our reality and I have seen this play out time and time again in my own life and the lives of people I work with.
18. Consider the effect of birth order on your child — read Michael Grose's book, *Why First Borns Rule The World And Last Borns Want To Change It*.
19. If managed well in childhood, hyperactive children can mature into very capable, focused adults who are energetic, optimistic and resilient. On the other hand, being overwhelmed by a label of being difficult and nonconformist may cause them to struggle with the challenges of managing their lives as they grow older. Maintain firm boundaries, negotiate and be kind.
20. Turn it around; learn from your hyperactive child the gifts of honesty, perseverance, patience and creative problem-solving.
21. If all of the above fails, do some serious "personal growth work" to improve your ability to cope with ANYTHING! Many hyperactive and "in your face" children are here to accelerate their parents' personal healing journeys. Remember also, some of your child's behaviours may be linked to generational patterns that could do with some healing and transformation.

When to seek professional help

If you are a parent who's tried all of the things in the list above and your child is still consistently demonstrating challenging, hyperactive or oppositional behaviour that is really impacting on their everyday lives, then it might be worth investigating whether they have attention deficit hyperactivity disorder (ADHD) or similar conditions.

ADHD is not something that would normally be diagnosed in children under five, and it is also not something to label a child with lightly, nor is it easy to diagnose. Often children with anxiety are misdiagnosed as having attention disorders so it's important to really do your research and seek help from health professionals, starting with your GP who may offer you a referral to a paediatrician, psychologist or psychiatrist. It is worth involving your child's teachers/carers in any discussions around diagnosis and treatment.

The Raising Children network provides comprehensive, up-to-date information about symptoms and signs of ADHD on its website so please visit: www.raisingchildren.net.au and search "ADHD" to get a complete picture of the kinds of things health professionals look for in assessing children.

The diagnosis rates and medication of children with ADHD is highly controversial. For example, since 2005, there has been a 133% increase in the number of children who are on medication for ADHD in New South Wales in Australia (Corderoy, 2013). The situation is the same in countries like the UK and US. In cases where children genuinely have ADHD, the right medication can be a wonderful help. Medication can also have terrible side effects including one drug that has been linked to suicide.

Unfortunately, the pressure to conform and perform in schooling systems that do not really suit the needs of young children, can find teachers and parents at their wit's end when dealing with hyperactive children. It's not surprising then that the media often carries commentary about the over-diagnosis of ADHD — and with that comes a lot of misplaced judgement.

I would urge parents to be compassionate towards each other when talking about ADHD. It is hugely challenging for families who are living with this condition, and it is critical to understand that the decision to label and/or medicate a child has not come easily for those families. I've had parents whose children have ADHD write to me asking why they and their children have been treated so poorly by other parents or teachers. "Can you imagine someone judging a child with autism, or who is blind, or in a wheelchair, that way?" one mum wrote. I imagine most of us would be appalled.

The media coverage around ADHD has done little to improve understanding of the condition so it is in all of our best interests to remember that as parents, we are all doing the best we can with the resources and abilities we've been granted in life.

A note about sleep

I want to take this opportunity to emphasise the impact that lack of sleep can have on children's behaviour. A University of South Australia study into the sleeping habits of more than 690,000 children from 20 countries released in 2011 had some interesting findings. The researchers determined that today's children, aged from preschool to high school age, are sleeping an average of one hour less — they have lost about one hour's sleep in the past century.

"They're sleeping about 20 minutes less per day than their parents were when they were the same age. We've got things that make children want to go to sleep later, like computers and television, and the means to keep them awake," researcher Lisa Matricciani told *The Australian* (Edwards, 2011). Matricciani said this was partly due to technology use, schoolwork and homework, part-time employment, electrification, caffeine use and parental attitudes.

Scientists have now been able to determine the disastrous effect that lack of sleep has on developing brains. It seems sleep disorders can impair a child's IQ just as much as exposure to lead does. Tired children cannot remember what they have just learned. Also, sleep loss impacts on the prefrontal cortex that is responsible for the executive function of the brain. Among its functions are thoughts to fulfil a goal, the prediction of outcomes and perceiving consequences of actions. Poor impulse control and poor problem-solving are very common with tired children. Another key finding from brain research shows that the more you learn during the day, the more you need to sleep during the night so that the brain can process and consolidate the memories (John Medina, *Brain Rules*, 2014).

Consistent boundaries around sleep are important for everyone. Sleep deprivation and inconsistent bedtimes impact on learning, mood moderation and behaviour. The brain needs deep sleep to renew cells and grow new neurons for learning. Good sleep also contributes to better emotional stability and a more agreeable demeanour.

TIPS FOR SOOTHING SEPARATION DISTRESS

Separation distress or anxiety is very common among children and Sunderland believes this distress can influence children even as old as eight.

The changes of environment, people, routines and the number of other children they are interacting with can all cause spikes in cortisol, creating those stress symptoms you might see — crying, clinging, tummy aches, refusal to leave your side, poor appetite, restless sleep, and even outbursts and tantrums.

Remember this means the 'downstairs brain' is registering threat — and is acting accordingly. Remember too that the key stressor for children is separation from the most significant grownup who is their protector.

As a starting point, it is useful to explain to kids that new things, places and people often make even adults feel those same feelings of being a little unsettled or anxious.

Young children usually have strong imaginations and I have found that some small techniques that strengthen the connection to Mum or Dad while they are away from you can help lots:

- You could help them create an imaginary protector — They imagine having their huge protector with them while they are away from you! The two free audio downloads I mentioned earlier can help with this.
- Fill an empty, clean, small container with a lid with kisses from everyone they are fond of, and tuck it in the bottom of their backpack.
- As they leave home always place a kiss from Mummy in the same hand, left and Daddy in the right … it is also magic and stays there all day.
- Practise sending them rainbows of love from your heart to theirs at recess and lunch and ask them to send one to you when they miss you.
- Put a really small stuffed toy — maybe smelling of your perfume, Dad's aftershave or with a lipstick kiss — in the bottom of their backpack. Again they don't feel so separate and alone.
- Draw funny pictures on their lunch bag.
- Take a small bite out of their sandwich.
- Teach them how to take three big breaths and breathe out the butterflies hiding in their tummy or gently rub their tummy telling the butterflies they are safe.
- Teach them how to calm themselves by singing "Round and Round the Garden" in their hand while making circles in their hand, just as you would do — music and touch trigger feel-good hormones.
- Help build a special connection to one carer, teacher or teacher assistant who can nurture their transition by talking about that person at home, getting your child to draw pictures of them together or to give to their special carer.

These tips can be modified to help children going on school camps too when they're a bit older.

SAFE TOUCH

> Many of the infant and child behaviours that are challenging parents in our culture are unheard of in cultures that practise high-touch nurturing. Babies are biologically programmed to expect the same high-touch nurturing that evolved millions of years ago.
>
> — Pam Leo, *Connection Parenting* (2007). www.ConnectionParenting.com

Safe touch is incredibly important in all human relationships. If we reconsider a traditional kinship community, where the circle of women were constantly in close proximity to all the children, the ability to get a hug or a cuddle whenever you needed would have been really easy. There is quite interesting research from health and child development researcher James W. Prescott that shows that highly tactile societies where touch is valued and constant are much less violent than communities that deprive their children and adolescents of extensive touch (Lipton, 2005). Other research suggests children raised with lots of touch have lower levels of emotional and mental disorders later in life (Grille, 2013).

> There is a mass of research to demonstrate that the more touch a child gets in childhood, the calmer and less fearful he is likely to be in adulthood.
> — Sunderland (2007).

People who visit some developing countries often comment on happy the children seem despite living in poverty with very little in the way of possessions and toys. They notice them as being very friendly and massively engaged at playing in nature with something as simple as a stick. The Western world has created a touch-phobic environment due to a combination of fear of litigation, accusations of paedophilia and political correctness. A minority of inappropriate adults have ruined what was a very beautiful and special part of childhood.

Comfort from safe touch begins very early in the first days of life. Parents of new babies are drawn to gently stroking and kissing their new miracles. As children grow older and parents become busier, there is less and less positive safe touch that flows between them. Family rituals that can help keep safe touch as a positive part of life can include cuddling up on the couch, foot massages while the family watches TV or taking naps together on a spare mattress in the family room or a beanbag. Sometimes just the gentle rubbing on the top of the head, the shoulder or the back reassures children that we love them. Sunday mornings all piled in to Mum and Dad's bed can also be a fun way to keep safe touch a special part of children's lives.

> The parts of the brain concerned with regulation of emotion and deeply held attitudes to human relations are particularly dependent on human contact in order to develop. A mother's joyful interactions with her baby actually provide an essential building block to these areas of the brain.
> — Grille (2013).

Safe touch soothes children's nervous systems, and overloaded nervous systems are a sure sign that a child is experiencing stress. Remember stroking the forehead gently or the 'tickle point' on the back, just below the neck, are two of the most powerful trigger points to stimulate production of serotonin, which is the calming neurotransmitter. Have you noticed sometimes that you have the water from the showerhead directed at your tickle point while you are having a shower?

> Touch has been contaminated by our fear-based world. We have let our children down by withdrawing one of the most important ways to offer love and reassurance, especially for children under 10 years of age. In removing safe touch we have negated our capacity to mother our children. This is important in times of crisis and suffering. Mothering is what our children need to develop healthy mental, physical and emotional competencies.
> — Dent (2005).

My top three tips for parents to soothe our children's worlds — The three 'S's:

1. **Slow down** — walk slower, talk slower, do less and allow an extra 15 minutes than you think you need to get children ready for a scheduled event like going to school. Ask what you can take out of your life so that you can be a calmer parent, especially in the early years — avoid wearing too many hats when your children are young.
2. **Soothe more** — remember that brain chemicals flood our children's brains quite irrationally and chaotically. Reassure children that they are valued, safe, and that mistakes and accidents are normal.
3. **Create safety** — is your home child friendly? Can your children relax sometimes without being stressed to have your home looking like it's a feature house in a *House and Garden* magazine? Is there somewhere for introverted children to hide from people and the world to fill their energy cup?

Another reminder to focus on building love bridges or micro-moments of connection with each of your children, is for them to know they are valued and loved. Feeling invisible or unloved causes enormous stress to a child's nervous system, as they often can become emotionally needy and anxious about getting the love they yearn for. Remember, children do not see all the cooking, washing and cleaning as signs of love and connection. They need to hear the words, have loving touch and know that you are 'present' to them at times during any given day to *feel* loved. Having a bedtime ritual that you follow every night is an excellent way of anchoring your love for your child. The love bridges that I explored in the first chapter on CONNECTED MOTHERING are a great way to ensure your child feels secure in your love.

One of the main inhibitors for children behaving well, learning well, and having general health and wellbeing is prolonged chronic stress. Eric Jensen (2006) believes that there is up to a 50% reduction in neuron development within a week of a major stressor event. He also believes that the existing neurons wither with continued, chronic stress. This has enormous implications for children and their learning in both our homes and our schools. Many small stressors can have the same impact as one large one, such as a death of a loved one, divorce or social dislocation like moving school, town or country. This overloads their nervous system and they will exhibit distress and anxious behavior.

Sensitive children are more prone to struggling with anxiety and stress. Take time to build practical skills into their lives so that they can diffuse stress. Teach them to take deep breaths, sigh often and teach them relaxation by using calming CDs. We cannot choose our personality type and part of our responsibility as parents is to help children be aware of their natural strengths and weaknesses — and ways to overcome their weaknesses! Yoga, creative visualisation and lots of time spent in nature all help soothe sensitive nervous systems. They are also fabulous for stressed parents as well!

PARENT TIPS FOR REDUCING STRESS IN CHILDREN

- Children benefit from calm quiet spaces in their world.
- Avoid being rushed and hurried.
- Use quiet voices with gentle tones.
- Have regular quiet times in your home when all electronic stuff is turned off.
- Allow children time just 'to be' and not always be busy.
- Children sense their parents' stress and react to it — so reduce your stress.
- Ensure children have good night sleep patterns.
- Calmness can be learned — do a relaxation activity with them.
- Avoid too much noise and visual stimulation in homes.
- Avoid too much exposure to TVs, computers, smart phones and other electronic games and devices.
- Create safe home environments with boundaries and routines.
- Avoid too much significant change in children's lives.
- Avoid pressuring your children.
- Soothing and reassuring children triggers oxytocin and calms children.

— Dent, *Real Kids in an Unreal World* (2008).

Children depend on parents and other significant carers to help them develop healthy stress-regulating systems so they can manage stress and anxiety. The key is to soothe sooner, rather than later. Research shows clearly that those children who were soothed quickly as babies tend to become self-soothers later. The more love and affection, calm surroundings, safe nurturing touch, and predictable routines the better chance children have of growing the neural wiring that will allow them to be happy and psychologically strong for life. So start, now — take three deep breaths and relax.

MINDFULNESS IN CHILDREN

Children can be viewed as vulnerable and defenceless while at the same time being very capable and wise. Indeed, the latter perception is one that is held by traditional kinship communities. This view is underpinned by a notion of individual wholeness — a state that can be maintained with a healthy awareness of one's energetic and psychological wellbeing.

Living with wellbeing is a very different experience of health than stabilising symptoms or curing mental or physical disease. In contrast to a scientific worldview of health that involves "fixing or curing", wellness in Eastern and Indigenous models is based on wholeness and harmony in the energy or life force of body, mind and emotions. When energy is flowing freely and without obstruction through the channels and energy centres of the body, the person experiences good health, emotional balance, mental clarity and overall wellbeing.

To attain such knowingness these cultures practise mindfulness.

> If we allowed children more silence and stillness in our homes and schools, they would ponder more, think more and question more — for themselves. When we tell them how to see the world, what to do and how to do, we are inhibiting the growth of their unique self and denying them the opportunity to realise their own potential. Mindfulness can only happen in an environment that values the space for silence and stillness. Mindfulness for children can only occur in the presence of people who genuinely respect others, themselves and our world.
> — Dent (2005).

Babies and toddlers are almost constantly practising mindfulness. They are only paying attention to the present moment — they are not pondering about the past and they are certainly not considering the future — they are merely fully immersed in the present moment. This is one of the reasons why they struggle with living within our time-driven world and why sometimes they are so easily distracted by some other tiny, seemingly unimportant reality in their world. One of the secrets to having fabulous attunement with your baby or toddler is for you to practise mindfulness as well.

Mindfulness is a habit or practice where we pay attention to our whole selves — how we feel, sense and intuit our own 'beingness' in the now. This helps individuals to stop scaring themselves with the endless chatter of the ego-voice, or 'monkey mind' — and worrying themselves with things that are seldom real. Essentially, it is paying attention and assessing our state without judgement. It certainly allows us to develop a better awareness of ourselves with compassion and honesty.

> Mindfulness is an open awareness that can be brought to each moment and activity of life. This practice involves the discipline of staying grounded in the present moment, in the here and now, so that the mind does not run to the past or the future. The mind rests in the stillness of the moment as if it were an eternal moment.
> — Patricia Mathes Cane & Mary Duennes, *Capacitar for Kids* (2005).

Children who are allowed the space to be still and permitted to direct their own lives with respect are mindful because it is totally compatible with healthy brain development and growth. They develop at their own unique pace without being hurried by adults or well-meaning teachers. When a child is unable to master a skill or competence when an adult wants them to, it can cause confusion and stress in their sensitive psyches. Sometimes children form emotional memories of these times and they can make an incorrect assumption that they are flawed, or dumb, rather than not ready. Mindfulness allows children to come to know themselves and they can build relationships with their world on their terms. This is authentic and honouring of the sacredness of every child.

Psychotherapist and accredited Mindfulness-Based Stress-Reduction practitioner, Dr Timothea Goddard summed this up well in her paper, *Emotional Regulation through Mindfulness Training*, delivered to the 2013 Mind & Its Potential conference in Sydney, Australia:

> We all have particular cognitive filters operating — which are literally embodied in our brains. Our cognitive filters come from our temperament and constitution (what we came into the world with) and also our past experiences and therefore our current expectations. Cognitive filters give us the impression that our thoughts are facts about the world, rather than appraisals arising out of our past experience. And the more stress experiences we have had, the more these cognitive filters are going to be oriented towards seeing the world as dangerous and threat-filled. Mindfulness practice helps us start seeing how our perception is shaped by these filters. It opens people to recognise the continuous stream of semi-conscious commentary, assessment and evaluation which goes on in daily life.

Although mindfulness is an abstract concept, we can still describe many of its characteristics; what its absence causes; how it develops; and how we can introduce it into our homes and especially into our schools.

> Mindfulness includes the ability to focus one's thoughts on an objective, while tuning out irrelevant distractions. For example, when a doctor listens to your heart with a stethoscope, he hears a series of heartbeats. Within each heartbeat, there are a series of subtle sounds. He must listen to each tiny segment, by mentally tuning out the rest of the sounds. This takes a lot of practice. We all need to develop the ability to temporarily ignore the extraneous distractions of the world, and focus on what truly matters to us. This process does not involve a denial of reality, but rather, the selective direction of attention.
> — Shaun Kerry, M.D, *Mindfulness: What It Looks Like*, (www.school-reform.net).

Mindful people are in touch with their feelings. They are aware of their strengths and weaknesses. They are able to make decisions. They can think independently. Rather than simple black-and-white alternatives, they are conscious of the shades of grey that fall between. They do not control people and do not allow others to control them. They are honest, and have a sense of truth that causes them to react when a story doesn't quite 'add up'. This means they are able to tune into their inner compass or intuition. They are creative and effective problem solvers.

Lynne Hinton, academic and former principal of an inner-city primary school in Brisbane, transformed a tough school by teaching philosophy to the children from preschool. She delights in sharing stories of her years allowing children to ponder on the big questions (Search her out on ABC Conversations with Richard Fidler — it's well worth a listen). We must never forget that the most creative years of our lives are in childhood, before we become conditioned to thinking to get results or to please people or to be approved of by someone with more power! Children can think and ponder the world, themselves and how it all goes together. They are capable of doing philosophy, and of thinking creatively, and in a thoughtful and caring manner.

> You see them grapple with an idea, consider the views of others, and come to a reasoned judgement well beyond their years. You can see them imagine, wonder, reflect, question, puzzle, talk and speculate. You see them seeking clarification, giving reasons and examples, drawing conclusions and seeking alternatives. You see them get excited about paradoxes, about testing hypotheses and about thinking itself. Then you realise that through doing philosophy with children, you have created the conditions for this to occur.
> — Cam, et al., *Philosophy with Young Children* (2007).

The ability to think deeply and to ponder and question is something that needs peace and quiet, and time. The natural mindfulness of childhood is being stolen by the screen-obsessed and technology-driven world, which is keeping their little minds very busy and entertained. The brain needs times when it downloads, processes and analyses the learning that has taken place just prior to that. In early childhood there needs to be a lot of these quiet spaces because almost everything they experience is new or different.

It is not enough just to remove the main stressors out of children's lives, it is also important to encourage mindfulness activities like gazing at stars in the night sky, watching clouds, or quietly observing ants or bugs being busy in their microscopic worlds. The slower and calmer our children's worlds, the better it is for them. Ironically, they will probably end up much smarter, much healthier and certainly much happier.

> As a social psychiatrist, I examine society much like a doctor examines a patient. One of the most troubling ailments that I encounter is our school system, which — without ever realizing it — harms the majority of our students. It is my belief that our school system is the most fundamental cause of the social problems that our society faces today. Far from being expensive, the solution to this problem would cost no money. Speaking from a psychiatric perspective, our most critical mental attributes involve emotions, judgment, a sense of priority, empathy, conscience, interpersonal relations, self-esteem, identity, independence, the ability to concentrate and a number of other whole-brain functions that defy description. I will lump all of these attributes under the term 'mindfulness'.
>
> — Shaun Kerry, M.D., *Harm in the School System*, (www.school-reform.net).

I share Dr Kerry's concerns about schooling as it exists today. With the high levels of violence in our schools and society, the bullying and the shaming techniques of behaviour management, our children are being scarred psychologically and unnecessarily. We can't go back to the 'old days' of corporal punishment either. We need a different approach where children are able to develop mindfulness and patterns of awareness that encourage compassion and understanding — with this in place, our schools could be very different.

> When a child is not given enough help with his intense lower brain feelings and primitive impulses, his brain may not develop the pathways to enable him to manage stressful situations effectively. The legacy later in life is that he will not develop the higher human capacity for concern, or the ability to reflect on his feelings in a self aware

> way. Brain scans show that many violent adults are still driven, just like infants, by their ancient rage/fear and defence/attack responses deep in their brain.
> — Sunderland (2007).

The opposite of mindfulness can be the state where we feel scattered and distracted, and unable to focus very well. There are so many distractions in the modern world that are creating stress for our parents, which our children are struggling with as well.

Philosopher Damon Young spoke about distraction at the 2013 Mind & Its Potential conference. Young spoke of how each time we are distracted (for example by an email or text message) it takes a full minute to recover from our thoughts to resume what we were doing.

He spoke about how email has changed the way we work — and I think we can extend his point to text messages and social networking updates coming through on smart phones and affecting the way we interact outside of work too.

"Because of this constant stimulation," he said, "we have become habituated in being distracted".

Last year when I ran my seminar, The Importance of Silence and Stillness in Children's Lives, I asked the audience to not just turn their mobile phones to silent, but to switch them off completely — their children were being cared for in a crèche provided so staff knew where to find them in the event of an emergency. After the seminar, a young mum of a four-year-old boy came back to speak to me and said:

> Maggie I would like to share with you what happened for me today. Firstly I was annoyed when you asked me to turn my phone completely off and I really struggled doing it. I noticed for the next 15 to 20 minutes how restless and unsettled I felt. After that it felt okay. I've just gone to collect my young son from the crèche and I had forgotten to turn my phone back on. As he came over to me to greet me it suddenly hit me, how disconnected I have been. I can't remember greeting him face-to-face for ages. And just as you said he noticed that I was present and his face beamed with the biggest smile I have ever seen. He cuddled close to me and took my hand and we are now on our way to the park. I can't thank you enough for showing me how important it is to be present and to avoid letting my phone and other distractions get in the way of loving my boy — thank you so much.

We both had tears in our eyes as the crushing simplicity of what our children need from us touched us both deeply. I am so grateful that my mothering journey happened before technology swamped our homes like a tsunami.

Mindfulness also helps children develop a strong sense of their own inner compass or inner guidance. For all my years playing in nature and being away from TVs and man-made toys, I have developed a strong and accurate intuition. No amount of university education can replace my sense of knowing that comes from within. Once again, this is better developed with lots of silence, stillness and calmness.

> Childhood is a time of wonder and awe as the world grabs our attention through our fresh eyes and ears. It is not hard to find a child absorbed in the blissful moment on a swing, or spinning just to feel the world move around them. Children are natural mystics. Sometimes the wonder opens all the way to ecstasy and unity.
> — Tobin Hart, *The Secret Spiritual World of Children* (2003).

Human intuition

- A 'goodness orientation' forms in the first two years of birth.
- Everyone has an intuition.
- Quietness and time in nature build intuition.
- A key element to telepathy is having a strong emotional bond.
- Real-life experiences build intuition.
- Virtual reality stifles intuition.
- The 'higher self' is like a quiet twin.
- Favourite symbols and things reflect intuition.
- A well-developed intuition is an enormous asset, especially in a teenager's life.
- Weak intuition and inexperience can have deadly consequences.
- The intuition can disempower the inner critic.
- Transcendence is a state we all seek.
- Natural transcendence allows us to connect more fully with our inner wisdom.
- The intuition helps kids to discern who is safe and who has genuine warmth.
- Synchronicity and intuition go hand-in-hand.
- The intellect and intuition speak different languages.

Cultivating healthy intuition

You can certainly help your kids to develop their intuition and to access the wise part within themselves.

Being able to cultivate a healthy intuition in our children may very well save their lives one day. It is easy to help them nurture their intuition if you start before they are five years old, definitely before they are ten! To tap into inner guidance it helps to do three things:

- become centred and fully present
- breathe deeply and slow the body and the mind
- actively seek the quiet voice within.

— Dent (2005).

Children who have a strong intuition tend to have a much better ability to determine when they're in a situation that is potentially unsafe. This is called being able to access their "early warning system". This is incredibly important because we are unable to be with our children every moment of every day, and a strong intuition and the ability to tap into an early warning system can keep our children safer not just in childhood but also in adolescence and adulthood. Even today there are times when I park my car in underground parking stations and when I start to get out if I have any sense of feeling uncomfortable, maybe have some goosebumps or just feel cold, without question I move my car to a position where there is more light and where it is closer to an entrance. This same sense occurs when I travel on public transport or when I am returning from late-night meetings or seminars by myself.

Teaching your children the basics of protective behaviour is incredibly important in childhood. I have been staggered in my counselling work with the number of adolescents who have been sexually abused over a long period of time who were unaware that this was not appropriate behaviour from their family member. Having a strong intuition can also help children be wary of unsafe dogs, waterways and how high to climb on any given day.

Silent, solo time allows everyone to:

- Question
- Intuit
- Ponder
- Reflect
- Review
- Rest
- Process emotion
- Prepare for the future
- Come to terms with the past
- Solve problems
- Invent

- Take a break from people
- Detach from conflict
- Dream
- Find inspiration
- Find hope.

SLOW DOWN

I know that our children's world can be made better. It was never meant to be this busy, this rushed and this stressful. Research has long held the belief that happy, calm children learn best. If this simple statement of fact could be the mantra of every mum and dad of a child under eight, I think things could improve for our children — indeed our whole families. Humans are still programmed to be social animals. Social behaviour is not genetic. It happens through the constant interaction of humans with other humans over a long period of time. If we reduce unnecessary stress from our homes especially, our children will thrive and grow healthier and happier.

Silence and calmness is a basic longing within all humans. Sometimes it feels like the urge to run away from the world and hide under our doona until we feel better able to meet the demands of our day. Other times it is a state we create within ourselves where we are not fully present in our body and yet we look like we are. It is also the spacey look, the distracted moment, or the place where people may say to you "hello, anyone home?" At times, however, like after an unexpected change, a world tragedy or a mystical moment of awe, we need space to explore within ourselves how we feel about it, without interruption from others. This is a time of altering our own reality and it is a key quality of a highly resilient person. This time is needed to work through the experience until a way of coming to terms with it, or 'getting a grip on it', is found.

Quite obviously I have a deep passion for the need for more silence, stillness and calmness in the lives of today's families because it is vitally important, as it is something that helps shape the developing child in a positive way and it can profoundly improve family harmony. My first book, written in 2003, was promoting calmness, quietness and stillness in children's lives — and the world is even more chaotic 11 years on! Families who are financially challenged can still create calm environments that support children's growth. The inner world of many children today is in turmoil and the outer turmoil of the world that we have created probably contributes. I believe that children who can build a doorway to their own sense of value and worth will be better able to manage this chaotic, rapidly changing world. This means children the whole world over, not just Australian children. This doorway is found on the inside rather than the outside.

As explained by poet, priest and scholar John O'Donohue:

> "We need to return to the solitude within, to find again the dream that lies at the hearth of the soul. We need to feel the dream with the wonder of a child approaching a threshold of discovery. When we rediscover our childlike nature we enter a world of gentle possibility. Consequently, we will find ourselves more frequently at the place of ease, delight and celebration."
>
> — John O'Donohue, *Anam Cara: Spiritual Wisdom from the Celtic World* (1997).

Our world continues to be a place of conflict and uncertainty. It will continue to be so while we seek out the differences between people, cultures and countries. There is no one right way of living or being. With mindfulness and calmness we are so much more likely to use compassion and kindness in our interactions with everyone else. Maybe if we searched for the sameness within others there would be more harmony.

There is a Buddhist saying that goes like this:

> When there is peace in the heart, there will be peace in the home, there will be peace in the country and there will be peace in the world.

I'd like to conclude this chapter with a beautiful poem that I came across on Facebook, written by English woman Rebekah Knight, a mother of three girls, to remind herself to be present and not always focused on the to-do list. No wonder it has resonated with mums all around the world. You can find Rebekah's creations at *www.slowdownmummy.blogspot.com.au/*

Slow Down Mummy
By Rebekah Knight

Slow down mummy, there is no need to rush,
slow down mummy, what is all the fuss?
Slow down mummy, make yourself a cup of tea.
Slow down mummy, come and spend some time with me.

Slow down mummy, let's put our boots on and go out for a walk,
let's kick at piles of leaves, and smile and laugh and talk.
Slow down mummy, you look ever so tired,
come sit and snuggle under the duvet and rest with me a while.

Slow down mummy, those dirty dishes can wait,
slow down mummy, let's have some fun, let's bake a cake!
Slow down mummy, I know you work a lot,
but sometimes mummy, it's nice when you just stop.

Sit with us a minute,
& listen to our day,
spend a cherished moment,
because our childhood is not here to stay!

— from Teika Bellamy (Ed), *Musings on Mothering* (2012).

TOP TIPS

* Babies and toddlers benefit from having calm environments and consistent and loving care from those closest to them.
* The pressure to hurry up childhood by overscheduling and rushing is causing undue stress on our precious children.
* Stress and distress in babies and toddlers is serious, and soothing from their significant big people as soon as possible is really important.
* Soothing frequently and often is essential and will not spoil a baby or a toddler.
* Safe, nurturing touch helps children calm down and feel safe.
* Everyone needs quietness and calmness to ensure their wellbeing.
* Calmness can be learned at any age in life.
* Mindfulness is a natural state for babies, toddlers and children.
* Slowing down your life while you are parenting babies, toddlers and children will benefit everyone in so many ways.

WHAT I WISH I HAD KNOWN. ... "SLOW DOWN AND ENJOY EVERY MOMENT. EVERYTHING PASSES, EVEN THE BAD DAYS, WEEKS OR MONTHS... EVENTUALLY THINGS CHANGE." — *Gabby*

4th Thing
ROOSTERS AND LAMBS

TEMPERAMENT MATTERS

One of the 'basics' of parenting wisdom that seems to have been lost in our information-rich world is that babies are born wired to be a certain temperament. I have termed the temperament spectrum, "the rooster and lamb continuum". Firstly, imagine the cartoon character Linus (from the Peanuts comic strip); he would be a lamb. Then imagine Dennis the Menace; he would be a rooster. Even though our children will be influenced by their biological temperament, which has come through on their DNA, their sense of needing to be loved, valued and also feel that they belong is exactly the same. If you are struggling with the behaviour of one of your children, always work on the relationship rather than the behaviour. So many times they feel unloved and un-special and sometimes they make it very hard to love them.

Lambs --Roosters

ROOSTERS

> All children fear abandonment. Tricky children often fear that they won't be loved if they're not funny, thrill seeking, determined, wise-cracking, vigilant or successful and enough. Much of their forcefulness is camouflaged fear and worry.
> — Andrew Fuller, *Tricky Kids* (2007).

You will know if you have a rooster firstly because, they are strong-willed, high-energy children from quite early in life. If most nights you collapse on your couch from exhaustion because of the high energy levels of one of your children, you most likely have a rooster. I had two. My third son was a classic rooster who hated sleeping. Around the age of four, I realised the war I had with him around going to sleep was causing anxiety and conflict in the family. I knew it was time to negotiate a new deal. The new deal meant that provided he was quiet, and that he did not use the toaster or any adult equipment that could cause harm, he could turn the lights off and go to bed when he was ready. Essentially, we had no more fights and he did turn the lights off in our house from that time on. He simply needed less sleep than his mum or dad or his brothers. He loves the night hours and unsurprisingly now works in a finance investment company where he does night trading from 9pm until 5am. When he was little, I knew that he was managing our lights-out arrangement because he still bounced out of bed at six o'clock every morning with the same amount of energy as he had done before the new deal. He also liked being given the responsibility and freedom to take himself to bed. Some roosters benefit from having special 'deals' that show appreciation for their confidence and ability. When they encourage responsibility, such deals can have long-lasting positive benefits.

Some characteristics of roosters are:

- They yearn for independence.
- They prefer to do things for themselves.
- They yell louder.
- They are often very stubborn.
- They have so much energy and drive — they often exhaust you by 10am.
- They need less sleep – often wake up very early, and are last to get to sleep.
- They argue (even before they can speak!) over almost anything – food, clothes, toys.
- They want their own way and make their own choices.
- They can be manipulative and selfish.
- They think they are more important than anyone else.
- They always want to go first.
- They dislike having to share their things.
- They are impatient and impulsive.
- They learn fast and like to learn by making their own mistakes, not by what you tell them!
- They get frustrated and angry often.

- They ask a lot of questions.
- They can be entertainers — or 'party animals'.
- They sometimes explode and then run away when they get angry.
- They sometimes disappear at large public events because they like to explore on their own.
- They throw the most spectacular tantrums in the supermarket — they prefer public audiences.
- They will embarrass you in front of grandma, in-laws, teachers and doctors.
- They are very sensitive about what other people think.
- They will question almost every decision you make.
- They quite enjoy change, challenge and adventure.
- They will often make you feel you are the worst parent ever!

Roosters have a strong sense of their own importance, a powerful character, and that is possibly because they are meant to find a pathway in life where they can lead, change or drive others to a better way of being. Parents who have children with rooster tendencies need to invest time and energy to build the 'caring' traits of emotional awareness, empathy and understanding before age five or their children will tend to be dominant, bossy or even a bully. If they are unable to build those emotional competences they can also become narcissistic and overly self-focused. This can manifest in a self-absorbed, overly important "I am all that matters" approach to life that often causes problems when building friendships. Roosters need to have power at any cost, which then becomes a hungry drive — and it affects both girls and boys the same way. Typically, girl roosters can become powerful manipulators because they often have superior verbal skills to boys and even from a young age can emotionally bully parents — especially by using guilt! Never let your four-year-old daughter get away with things because she simply wears you down — or she will do it all her life! Roosters have a PhD in pester power especially in the shopping centre.

> Parenting tricky kids can be enormously hard work at times. They have the power to divide and conquer even the most loving, competent of couples and leave them bickering and squabbling.
> — Fuller (2007).

Rooster children often love challenge, change and adventure. They can get excited when these opportunities occur and can get very frustrated if they have a lamb sibling who struggles with the very same opportunities. Another annoying trait of roosters is that they tend to question your parenting — often. "But why?" is a very common plea out of a rooster's mouth. If you can, bear in mind that this questioning is not happening because your child wants to annoy you, rather because they are seeking clarification of the choice that you are making on their behalf. This can cause parents angst, especially if parents have expectations that their children are meant to do as they are told or they are meant to be seen and not heard. Ironically, if we want our children to grow up and value themselves and their choices, and to encourage self-assertiveness, then we need to value and respect their needs and wishes by really hearing them. That only happens when we really listen.

> The parenting task isn't to crush self assertion, but to foster it so the child becomes a full-fledged person who knows their own mind and is unafraid to express their voice regardless of the fact it may rattle our ego and run contrary to our movie.
> — Dr Shefali Tsabary, *Out of Control* (2014).

My first close experience with someone else's baby was my girlfriend's beautiful boy who was a lamb. So when I was first pregnant I wrongfully expected to have a similar baby who loved to sleep, was really patient and who would be fairly quiet. You can imagine my shock when my loud, active, sleep-hating baby boy arrived. To be perfectly honest, I had no idea about temperament and I simply thought that I was being a lousy mum who couldn't cope very well.

WILMA WALLABY
"Rooster children are harder to parent than lambs. They sometimes make mums and dads feel like they are bad parents!"

Top tips for parenting roosters:

1. Focus on building positive attachment.
2. Avoid shouting, shaming or criticising roosters, as they will learn how to do this to others.
3. Play card games and memory games building their capacity to wait, to take turns and to learn to lose without being too dramatic.
4. As they often get into trouble by pushing boundaries, ensure you deeply reassure them you love them when you have moments of connection like when going to bed.
5. "Don't sweat the small stuff" is a good motto for parents of roosters. Ensure you hold firm boundaries for the big stuff — safety near roads, aggression towards siblings and other children, and healthy participation in chores like everyone else.
6. Really listen to your rooster when they want to tell you how they think things could be — being heard is incredibly important to roosters.
7. Be mindful of avoiding conflict with your rooster when angry, tired or

exhausted — that goes for both of you. Allow cooling-off time before negotiating restorative justice or discipline after a conflict.

8. Work out what thing — either an activity, toy or special privilege — when removed will show your rooster that you are the parent and they are the child, and that there are unpleasant consequences for inappropriate behaviour.
9. Give them small opportunities to develop autonomy or independence that makes them feel important. Let them be the only child who collects the eggs, the mail, gets himself a snack or maybe uses the camera, Dad's telescope or a technological gadget that no one else in the family can use. One family I know encouraged their rooster to breed ducks and hens, and it engaged him for hours, and the interaction between him and his feathered friends built lots of patience and consideration for others.
10. Rooster children of school age can benefit from team games and some individual sports like swimming, BMX, pony club and cross-country running. This helps build a more healthy understanding of competiveness and it also helps to discharge their excessive levels of energy.
11. The arts are another powerful way of discharging energy and keeping them positively occupied — dance, drama, music and craft are all excellent. This also shows them activities where competition with others is not the main purpose.
12. Make time to help your rooster build their emotional intelligence especially patience, calmness and empathy.
13. Avoid them becoming dependent on (or being addicted to) competitive online games — they miss the social learning they need when playing with others.
14. Nature can be a powerful source of sustenance and calmness for roosters — bike riding, cubby building, skateboarding, gardening, sailing and fishing have all been used by parents to keep their high-energy children active and interacting with others and their world.
15. Roosters also benefit from having other significant adult relationships where they can spend time giving their parents a much-needed rest! Grandparents, aunties, uncles and non-family people like neighbours or the parents of their friends can all offer respite.
16. For boy roosters, be careful not to drown them with too many instructions and explanations as this often makes them very frustrated and annoyed.
17. Some girl roosters can often become 'tomboys' and it can be helpful to imagine they have the same needs we usually associate with most boys.
18. If you have a really exhausting and full-on rooster who completely

overwhelms you often, it is really important to cultivate another significant adult ally relationship so that you can have regular respite from their intensity.
19. Get a puppy or a kitten so they can learn how to be kind and gentle.
20. Encourage them to be your 'special' helper sometimes.

It helps to keep in mind that children need both rooster and lamb tendencies to grow into being happy, healthy kids. Roosters need to learn empathy and compassion to others or they could become a narcissistic bully, while lambs need to learn courage and confidence or they could become wimps and victims. Temperament does not have to be destiny.

> # DID YOU KNOW
> Did you know that when we talk to our kids using a quiet, kind voice and using manners, we show our kids how to speak to others, and we also show respect for our kids?

LAMBS

Lambs are typically quieter, more patient, more accommodating and generally more content with life. As babies and toddlers, lambs are delightful and they make you look like a fabulous parent.

Some of the characteristics of lambs are:

- They love sleeping.
- They often dislike noise and too much stimulation.
- They are very sensitive to being sanctioned or growled at.
- They get distressed easily when shouted at.
- They may keep a comforter like a blanket or teddy well into childhood.
- They quite like solo time.
- They are very patient and can wait while roosters go first lots!
- They get distressed easily by strange people, places and things.
- They prefer routines and predictability.
- They prefer small numbers of children to play with.
- They tend to take longer to adjust to change.
- They can take longer to warm up in social settings they are familiar with like playgroup.

- They withdraw when they feel frightened.
- They often hide in their bed or a cupboard when scared as children.
- They can easily be bullied or bossed around by roosters.
- They can struggle with social dislocation more than roosters, e.g. new teachers, schools or change of home or relationship.
- They can lack assertiveness and can be slow at making decisions.
- They can struggle with large social situations and often avoid them!
- They can struggle with shyness.

Lambs can have a tendency to be 'slow to warm' in social situations. This means that even with people they know they can take a while to be comfortable interacting. I have a very special great-nephew who is a gentle lad. Whenever I visit, even if I stay overnight, on first seeing me he often hides behind his mum or moves away to hide behind a couch. While I smile at him or wink and say "hello", I allow him to make the moves of connection. Once he has warmed up, he is very happy to play with me and allow me to hold him. Forcing children to connect or interact before they have 'warmed up' can be quite stressful for them and it can often make them even more fearful in future. The same goes for shy children — slowly building their confidence by respecting their sensitive nature is the best way to go.

As lambs often lack personal courage and confidence, it is important for parents to help build these emotional competences while they are under five if possible. Encouraging them to take risks in their play and learning, and ensuring that you build their capacity to be more assertive and capable socially can really help our lambs become stronger and more resilient. Never force a lamb to do something they are reluctant to do. This can scar them for life.

Even though the role of temperament has a big influence on parenting choices, it is helpful to think of the continuum as a guide to what competences or qualities children need to develop in order to be a blend of both rooster and lamb traits. In families, roosters and lambs can help each other — the roosters can assist to toughen up the sensitive lambs, and the lambs help to build sensitivity and gentleness in the roosters. Sibling rivalry is Mother Nature's way of softening roosters and strengthening lambs.

Do not be fooled that lambs are by nature weak, just because they are sensitive. I have found that lambs can be very determined and capable as they grow older with positive parenting and opportunities to develop mastery. Also, not all roosters are selfish and insensitive — they can become very thoughtful.

Top tips for parenting lambs:

1. Focus on building positive attachment.
2. Avoid shouting, shaming or criticising lambs as they can be crushed easily.
3. Avoid comparing them to other rooster children whether siblings or friends.
4. Ensure you spend extra time building comforting patterns when they are babies and toddlers — soothing lullabies, night lights, teddy bears, blankets, calming music, massage and bed time rituals.
5. Create small opportunities to develop mastery at small things – to gradually build their self-confidence.
6. Keep their world predictable with regular routines.
7. Affirm and encourage the caring side of their nature while teaching them to be careful not to be used by others.
8. Explain that assertiveness is different than aggression.
9. Affirm that lambs are worthy and deserving of love, affection and acceptance just the same as roosters.
10. Gradually expose them to social functions in small doses however when they have had enough, respect their needs and take them home to safety.
11. Avoid large groups of similar age children until 4-5 when they are braver.
12. Reassure them often that you are beside them and that when you leave them for a time that you ARE coming back.
13. Build close friendships with a small group of same age children and have them to play at your house until your lamb builds courage to play at other people's houses.
14. Avoid sleep over's until they feel ready – for some it can be closer to 8-10 for their first time.
15. Avoid forcing them to do things when they hesitate – encourage and be enthusiastic, and tell them "you will be able to do this when you are ready."
16. Connect deeply to nature – many lambs are serious lovers of animals and nature.
17. Allow them their own space, when they want. Many lambs have a secret quiet place they love to visit when things get tough, tiring or confusing.
18. Teach them how to take deep breaths when they feel anxious.

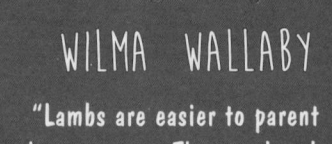

WILMA WALLABY

"Lambs are easier to parent than roosters. They tend to be gentle, caring and considerate, however often lack courage and confidence."

19. Encourage them to have conversations with you, as they often find it hard to be heard when there are roosters around.
20. As they have less energy than roosters, encourage them to have rest times or quiet times before going out to social situations. This helps them build their energy reserves up.
21. Ensure lambs get plenty of sleep.
22. Teach them relaxation strategies to help them when they feel anxious and stressed.

Often children who had been born with a lamb temperament have the deep-seated desire to help others, whether they are animals or people. They have a natural degree of empathy from an early age and can sometimes become worried when things happen, even on the other side of the world. Lambs can often have an irrational fear about the safety of their parents or people they love. It is important to be mindful of the TV programs that lambs are exposed to. They are easily scared and sometimes these moments of terror can be etched into their mind forever. I worked with an eight-year-old lamb many years ago who, while on a sleepover, saw the scary movie *Scream*. It took many months of counselling before she was able to sleep at night without night terrors or nightmares. In a way she will always have an irrational fear around dark doorways as a consequence of that experience. Even though a child may want to go and see a *Harry Potter* movie with Dad when they are five, there is a chance that even rooster children can experience a damaging moment of intense fear. Even some PG films have some scary scenes — think of the sharks in *Finding Nemo* — it can help to simply offer your children a blanket at the beginning of every film. If they feel scared suggest they close their eyes or hide under the blanket. Often these scary scenes are a tiny part of an entertaining child's film.

If you have a very sensitive lamb aged between four and 10, there are two free audio downloads available on my website that have been a great help to many children. "Safe 'n Sound" and "Sleepytime" both use the metaphor of an enormous protective character to help children feel safe in our world.

It does not matter what temperament your child has, the ability to have a calm, harmonious home environment is determined by the loving connection that the children feel from their parents and the communication that occurs between everyone.

COMMUNICATING COMPASSIONATELY WITH OUR CHILDREN

Communication seems such a simple thing to do, however poor communication is one of the key factors underlying conflict in our families. We simply misunderstand each other. For young children this happens a lot because of their inability to respond verbally. I remember having quite a shock when I asked my 10-month-old first born to take his towel into the bathroom instead of letting Mummy do it. He was walking by this stage. Sometime later when I went into the bathroom I was staggered to find his towel there. If babies and toddlers are saturated with conversation with loving adults, they are able to understand a lot more than you can believe much earlier than you can imagine. Remember that babies and toddlers are constantly downloading the cues and nuances of communication, probably before birth. What you demonstrate and model will become their template for communicating with each other later.

It is our job as parents to create safe boundaries for our children so that we can protect them. This means that quite often we are telling our children "don't" — we spend so much time telling our young children what they can't do, rather than investing our time and energy in showing them what they can do safely. So over the next few days, be mindful of how you guide your children in your home. Rather than focus on what you don't want, start expressing clearly what you do want, and then catch them doing those things, be excited and acknowledge it. Sometimes doing an exaggerated role-play, pretending you are a small child, can be funny and helpful for little children — more so than a long-winded explanation.

> Age appropriateness is the keystone of effective parenting. We do our children a disservice by putting them in situations they aren't yet mature enough to handle. In all situations of age inappropriateness, the onus is on the parent to accommodate to the situation not on the child
> — Tsabary (2014).

If you are struggling with a certain form of negative behaviour with one of your children, take some time to consider what that behaviour might mean for your child and then ask what would be the polar, positive opposite of that behaviour. Then, in a calm and encouraging voice ask your children to consider making changes. Initially there will need to be a reward for the change in behaviour especially for a rooster child. Never forget every single child is striving for their parents' love and approval, and sometimes poor behaviour is the product of a bad habit that started unintentionally. For more information on managing challenging behaviour see the chapter called the KINDNESS AND FAIRNESS REALLY MATTERS where I explore discipline.

> Parents talk too much. When our children are experiencing a strong emotion — whether through immaturity, disobedience, stress, fear or otherwise — we tend to dive right in and tell them how to fix things. But our children don't want or need our critique. They are unlikely to benefit from our judgement. Our chance to 'fix' them will come later when things have calmed down.
> — Justin Coulson, *What Your Child Needs from You* (2012).

When you next have a quiet cuppa give some thought to your pattern of communication. What happens when I ask you "not to think of a blue elephant?" This is a simple example to show you that when we use 'not' or 'don't', which are non-literal words, they simply don't register in a child's mind. Ensuring that we use language that is 'specific' really helps our children understand our expectations around their behaviour. Roosters are constantly seeking power and position, and they will challenge any unreasonable requests that you make that threaten this for them.

We are ultimately responsible for our children and it is our role to take charge when necessary. At least one parent (and better if both parents) needs to hold 'the alpha' position in the family for times when things need strength. Think when there's an unexpected accident, natural disaster or a traumatic experience of some kind. Children need to be able to look to us to be able to reassure them — it's OK — I've got this.

Yes, they may challenge us at times especially our strong feisty roosters, however if we can be consistent in setting boundaries for them — and be firm but fair — then we can have respectful healthy parent-child relationships. I often talk about being a "mean, loving mum" and that's what this is about really. You're not your child's best friend, you're their parent.

Listening to our children is a key aspect of this. Every human being has a deep need to be heard and understood. So often in my counselling rooms children and adolescents would express relief at being able to talk and share without fear. When a child is heard without judgement or over-reaction, then they will feel safer and, as they get older, more likely to be open with their parents.

Being heard

Here are some phrases you might use that let your child know you are really hearing him or her:

- Let me put this down so I can give you my full attention.
- Wait a second while I turn off the TV/radio/computer, so I can really hear you.
- Let's have some time together now.
- What would you like to do when we have our time together tomorrow afternoon?
- So what you mean is…
- Tell me more about this.
- In other words…
- Let me see if I understand you so far…
- That must have been…for you…
- Are you open to some feedback from me?

To communicate you are really listening with your body language, kneel in front of your children as they speak. Remember to keep mouth closed and ears, eyes and heart open — being fully present — and bring in your sense of humour.

When I worked as a counsellor, there were times when a troubled adolescent had attempted suicide, when they'd reached their tipping point. When I asked why they were unable to tell their parents they were at that dangerous place, so many of them responded, "I just didn't want to disappoint them again and see that look of disappointment in their eyes". How incredibly sad this is.

Our children desperately want our love and approval and they know the best chance of getting that is by doing things that please us. From an early age we need to reassure them that our love is unconditional — that means that I may not like you for a little while when you have hurt your sister, broken a window or thrown a tantrum, however I will never stop loving you. Encouraging our children to share the good, the bad and the ugly ensures that they will come to us when they are troubled. It also reduces the chances of them being manipulated by sexual deviants who ask children to keep secrets. We need to reassure them that no secret is ever too big for you as their parent and main protector. So often children and adolescents are frightened into telling lies because they are so scared of how we will respond to the truth. This is the same for both roosters and lambs.

Dr Ross W Greene in his book, *The Explosive Child* (1999), explores inflexible, explosive children and how families can help these children behave more calmly. He writes, "When patterns of communication are maladaptive, dealing with an inflexible-explosive child will be much harder". One of the patterns of adult behaviour that he has observed to cause conflict is the pattern of 'speculation', that is 'psychologising' or 'mind reading'. You can see this when a family member makes statements about another family member, often inaccurately. One example is, "John is always aggressive after dinner". "John is always worse by the end of the week." "I always know when John is going to be difficult at dinner time."

My third challenging rooster came to me when he was about eight years of age and said:

> "Mum did you know that you call me a pain in the neck quite a lot and I know that I can be at times. I am a bit worried that if you keep calling me that rather than something more positive it might damage my self-esteem."

Ouch! Needless to say he was absolutely correct and I upgraded my language immediately.

In her wonderful and resourceful book, *Raising Your Spirited Child*, Mary Sheedy Kurcinka (2006) gives positive labels to replace negative ones. This is to help reshape people's beliefs and unconscious expectations. Some of her suggestions are:

Negative	**Positive**
Demanding	Holds high standards
Unpredictable	Flexible, creative problem solver
Loud	Enthusiastic and zestful
Argumentative	Has strength, holding strong opinions
Stubborn	Assertive, persistent
Nosy	Curious
Wild	Energetic
Anxious	Cautious
Picky	Selective

— Mary Sheedy Kurcinka, *Raising Your Spirited Child* (2005).

The opposite of this poor communication style is compassionate communication.

> "Compassionate communication is a process language which focuses our here and now awareness on feelings and needs, and actions to meet those needs. The model is a practical way to put the intentions into practice."
> — Marion Badenoch Rose PhD, *The Heart of Parenting: Nonviolent communication in action*, (www.parentingwithpresence.net).

Compassionate communication requires us to be present in a calm and grounded way during the communication. Being overtired, exhausted or being distracted by technology are certainly not the best states to be in when communicating with anyone, especially our children. Have you ever noticed how chatty children become around bath time and bedtime? On most nights this is a time of more calmness. Children pick up on that as being a time of more safety and when Mum and Dad might really listen.

Here are some questions and suggestions that encourage conversations with our children that respect both children and parents. My absolute favourite phrase to use, especially for those special moments such as discovering the toilet blocked with rolls of paper or lipstick drawings on the wall is — "Now that's interesting!"

- "Does that feel fair to you?"
- "Tell me what you were hoping to do."
- "How can we make this better?"
- "What do you think needs to happen now?"
- "Sounds like you/we have a problem."
- "Whose problem is this?"
- "Does that feel kind to you?"
- "There is a problem here. How can I help you to sort it out?"
- "Check it out inside. Does it feel right?"
- "What were you trying to do here?"
- "Do you need my help right now to sort out what is happening?"
- "I know you can handle it!"
- "What would you like to do now?"
- "What would a good friend do now?"
- "I noticed that…"
- "Now that's interesting!"
- "Having a go is important — we can't all win!"

Some secrets of positive parental communication

- **Distraction** — this has to be one of the best secrets to parenting children of any age. It is much easier to use distraction with babies and toddlers than children in primary school or high school. Distraction can come in many forms, often non-verbal: suddenly looking stupid by pulling a face, pretending someone is coming unexpectedly or mirroring a certain look on your child's face for example. Good distraction happens when parents notice the energy of their child/ren is building or waning and it is time to change location, change activity or do something else that will boost the positive brain chemicals and shift the mood of the child/ren present. Inviting them to come outside, go for a walk, enjoy some afternoon tea or even have a drink of water are all minor distractions that can help children as they head towards an exhausted meltdown or frustration.
- **Respectful, caring requests** — no matter what age our children are, we must be aware that they are downloading our styles of communication. If we ask them to do things in a gentle and kind way rather than using the "my way or the highway" approach, we avoid threatening their autonomy and independence. Always using manners when interacting with our children ensures they will do the same when they leave the house. Pretend that your child is someone really well-known whom you respect — and then treat them in exactly the same way you would treat such a public figure.
- **Yes— After** — This is another useful approach especially with kids who can be difficult and who have oppositional brains. Rather than offering a straight-out "No" to their requests, it can be handy sometimes to say "Yes. After we have packed the toys away/had dinner/had a bath, etc."
- **It's just the right thing to do** — very occasionally from around the age of two it's absolutely okay occasionally to tell our kids to be the best version of themselves. You can do this by saying when the situation presents itself, "This is the right thing to do at the moment and when you do this you show the best expression of yourself."
- **The power of sorry** — there is no question that there are no perfect human beings on our planet. Of course, there will be times that we yell, misinterpret our children, misunderstand what they want and generally bugger up. One of the most powerful things we can teach our children is that when we make mistakes we own up to that mistake and we apologise. This shows them that this is the right thing to do.
- **Really listening** — being completely present to a child when you are having a conversation with them is a powerful way of showing that you love them, that you respect them and that you value them.

- **Calm down time** — while emotions are running high, it is not a wise time to resolve conflict. Pausing before reacting, and suggesting "we both have some calm down time" — at least 15 minutes — will help parents and children avoid escalating conflict. When the time of high emotion has passed — it can help to ask the child concerned what they wanted when the conflict happened. Listen carefully so you as the adult can see the situation through a child's eyes. Then you can ask them how to fix the problem rather than fix it for them.

Creating a Family solution-seeking process

The most harmonious families I know use family meetings to make big decisions. These decisions may include where to go for summer holidays or how to run the family home. Doing this helps children develop negotiation skills as well as helping them feel valued and respected. A family solution-seeking process also helps to resolve problems and conflicts. A simple, easy-to-follow process that may work for your family is described here by Chick Moorman and Thomas Haller. They suggest seven steps:

1. See the problem as an opportunity.
2. Define the problem.
3. Brainstorm possible solutions.
4. Reach consensus.
5. Commit.
6. Set a date to evaluate.
7. Evaluate.

— Chick Moorman and Thomas Haller, *The 10 Commitments: Parenting with Purpose* (2005).

Listening is the crux of human connection. It mends broken relationships and resolves conflicts. Listening carefully to our children's feelings, from the beginning of their lives, is the best insurance for their considerate and caring behaviour.

Listening is crucial; it's so important not to begrudge the time, attention and compassion it requires from us. Lending an ear to our child is an investment that cannot possibly be over estimated. In terms of better relations and our children's emotional health, it yields returns tenfold.

Children who are listened to without interruption learn to process and move through even their most difficult emotions more swiftly; emerging refreshed and renewed. Our listening becomes the model for their self-acceptance, the basis for their resilience and a corner stone for their emotional intelligence.
— Robin Grille, *Heart to Heart Parenting* (2008).

Communicating with Fairness and Kindness in mind

Just because we are talking does not mean we are communicating! So much of our communication is subtle, non-verbal, and built on cues and signs. Too much talking overloads many boys in particular and they often 'freeze up' and can't work out what is required of them. FAIRNESS AND KINDNESS is explored much more deeply in Chapter 7, however one of the things that does work when communicating with our feisty strong roosters is the art of 'suggestopedia'.

> The intended purpose of Suggestopedia was to enhance learning by tapping into the power of suggestion. Georgi Lozanov claims in his website, Suggestology and Suggestopedy,[2] that 'suggestopedia is a system for liberation'; liberation from the 'preliminary negative concept regarding the difficulties in the process of learning' that is established throughout their life in the society. Desuggestopedia focuses more on liberation as Lozanov describes 'desuggestive learning' as 'free, without a mildest pressure, liberation of previously suggested programs to restrict intelligence and spontaneous acquisition of knowledge, skills and habits.' The method implements this by working not only on the conscious level of human mind but also on the subconscious level, the mind's reserves.
> — Source: Wikipedia (http://en.wikipedia.org/wiki/Suggestopedia).

Essentially being asked to do things or having something 'suggested' can avoid the possible threat that comes from being told or demanded to do something, which for many children threatens their autonomy or independence. I recently realised, more than 15 years since I was a teacher, that I tended to use suggestion in the classroom without knowing why. This explains why many students found my style of teaching a positive experience and I'm also aware that it helped me to demonstrate respect, kindness and fairness. It was also something I tended to do as a parent.

Here are some suggestions on how to use 'suggestopedia' in your home:

- Do you want to play together or by yourself?
- In a few moments we will need to pack up...
- Choose which order you want to put your clothes on.
- Soon we will have a snack break.
- Today is storytelling in the library – is it OK to go today?
- May I invite you to stand while I clean up the crumbs on the floor where you are sitting?

- Shall we have some lunch now or after you have finished playing with that Lego?
- Maybe you could help Mummy by picking up those toys when you finish?

During my research phase for this book, I found that Grille's book *Heart to Heart Parenting* had a gem in it about listening, that will help every parent meet their child/ren in a powerful way. It reminded me of how my dad would listen to me for hours as we drove around the sheep station, or sat watching a fire burn, or rode in the truck on the way back from the grain receivables depot. How absolutely blessed was I?

Compassionate communication starts very early on the parenting journey. As Emmi Pickler, a paediatrician from Hungary, discovered back in the 1940s the best way to care for children is with the 3Rs — respectful, responsive and reciprocal communication. A key aspect of this philosophy is respect — and part of that is predictability, which is helping babies and toddlers anticipate what will happen next. As adults, we would expect to be told when someone was about to touch us or offer us food. Similarly, babies should know what to expect each step of the way when they are being dressed, changed, washed or fed. Predictability leads to a sense of security for babies. Another key aspect of the Pickler approach is to have a mindful, go-slow focus that is embedded in the care of children. This is technically called 'unhurried time' and it ensures that the mother or primary carer is fully present while the baby plays or interacts with their world without any plan at all. By offering valuable, uninterrupted quality time with babies and toddlers we indicate to the child that they are valued, which in turn enhances his/her developing self-esteem. Our sense of self is shaped in such subtle, gentle and invisible ways.

> **WILMA WALLABY**
>
> "Kids who are encouraged and acknowledged, especially for the effort that they put into things, will learn that it's up to them how strong and clever they will grow."

On Listening

When I ask you to listen to me, and you give me advice

you have not heard what I asked of you.

When I ask you to listen and you tell me why I shouldn't feel as I do,

you are trampling on my feelings.

When I ask you to listen and you feel you have to find solutions to my problems

I feel let down, strange as it may seem.

Please listen. All I ask is that you listen — not talk or do or advise — just LISTEN.

Advice is cheap. I can get that anywhere.

I can do for myself. I'm not helpless. Maybe discouraged and faltering, but not helpless.

When you do something for me that I can and need to do for myself, you contribute to my fear and reinforce my weaknesses.

When you accept as a simple fact, that I feel what I feel however irrational it may sound to you, then I can quit trying to convince you and I can then explore this irrational feeling.

When that's clear, the answers are obvious and I don't need advice.

My irrational fears make sense when I can discover what's behind them.

If you listen and understand I can work things out for myself.

So I ask again. Just listen — and if you too have something to say be patient, then I'll listen to you.

— Anonymous adaptation of a poem by Ralph Roughton, M.D.

THE DAMAGING EFFECTS OF SHAMING

Shame is the name we give to the overwhelming feeling that we need to crawl under a rock because we see ourselves as unworthy, unpleasant, dislikeable or reprehensible, and because we expect to be judged or rejected accordingly.

> Shame is like a knife that sharply delineates the limits of love in every culture, the warning signal that something we are doing risks us being ostracised.
> — Grille (2008).

Shaming starts very early and often is created through quite innocent, seemingly innocuous comments from loving parents. The impossible pressures being placed on today's parents are contributing significantly to more shaming in our children. Despite the pressure to try to live up to some family ideal, we must remember there is no perfect child, parent or teacher — never was nor will be. Humans have flaws. Children are evolving and growing, and sometimes in order to master a skill or a competence they will fail often; that's healthy, not bad.

Shaming language implies that a child is bad, naughty or in some way flawed — rather than describing them as a child who is simply learning how to manage and interpret this crazy world. Deep shame is distressing for our psyches that can happen so early in life and that makes it difficult for children and adults to come to a healthy place of self-love and acceptance, instead leaving us feeling deeply unlovable and unworthy of happiness.

Examples of shaming:

- Deliberately ignoring a child
- Being sarcastic
- Walking away as though a child does not exist
- Rolling one's eyes
- Glaring at a child with disgust
- Shouting, yelling and swearing at a child
- Using shaming language such as:
    - "You ought to be ashamed of yourself."
    - "You naughty boy!"
    - "You are acting like a selfish brat."
    - "You've been a bad little girl."
    - "Grow up!"
    - "Stop acting like a baby."
    - "Don't be a sissy."
    - "Girls don't do that sort of thing."
    - "You're hopeless."
    - "You're not even trying."
    - "Why can't you be more like your brother?"
    - "What are people going to think?"

> In his book, *The Psychology of Shame* clinical psychologist Gershen Kaufman identifies shame as a major cause of anxiety, personality disorders, compulsive disorders – phobias – and sexual dysfunction. Shame is also strongly associated with addictive disorders and eating disorders. The strongest link established by researchers is between shame and depression.
> — Grille (2008).

American shame researcher Dr Brené Brown says there is an important distinction between shame and guilt, which she feels is essential for parents to understand — and the way we talk to ourselves is paramount. Brown defines shame self-talk as thinking "I am bad", whereas guilt self-talk says "I did something bad" (Brown, 2013).

She cites a longitudinal research study of a large group of fifth-grade students, which measured whether these kids were using more shame self talk ("I'm an idiot, I'm a failure") or guilt self talk ("Boy, I made a bad choice there, I didn't do well at this"). The researchers followed these children into their senior year of high school and what they found was that "the kids who were shame prone were more likely to commit suicide, drop out of high school and engage in high-risk drug, alcohol and sexual behaviours. The guilt-prone kids were more likely to finish high school, apply for college, engage in community activities and engage in lower risk sexual, drug and alcohol behaviours" (Brown, 2013).

Perhaps the most telling part of Brown's and others' research is that the greatest predictor of whether a child will be shame prone or guilt prone is the kind of parenting they receive. She urges parents to examine their own feelings of shame, watch their own self-talk, and have honest discussions with their kids to set some non-negotiable family ground rules, such as no name-calling between anyone, including parents, and no tolerance for mean-spirited sibling behaviour. Here's how she describes her own family's attitude, which she sees as "a giant first step in cultivating a family of worthiness and whole-heartedness":

> In this household we will create a safe container for people to live, to express their emotions, to be who they are, to share their struggles – and we will work very hard to never use our vulnerabilities against each other.
> — Brené Brown, *The Gifts of Imperfect Parenting* (2013).

Having a family mandate or philosophy can be very useful in guiding the family solution-seeking processes I discussed earlier.

While it is crucial to avoid shameful communication, however, we also need to be mindful of not taking things to the other extreme by offering our children constant praise.

PRAISE AND ENCOURAGEMENT

> 'Early and often' bragged one mum of how often she praised her children. Another dad praised 'every chance I get'. Constant praise is meant to be an angel on the shoulder ensuring that children do not sell their talents short. Or is it?
> — P.O. Bronson & Ashley Merryman, *Nurture Shock* (2009).

In our efforts to look after our children's self-esteem in today's worried parenting world it seems like many children almost get stickers for breathing! Have you noticed that children don't need to be given a reward for sitting down to watch a much-anticipated movie or to eat ice cream or chocolate? That's because these activities come with a built-in reward, the immediate reward of positive emotion. In contrast, teachers and parents often encourage children to engage in less desirable tasks by offering extrinsic rewards that deliver an immediate positive emotion that's lacking in the task itself. Of course this is not what we want — and that's why it is important to set the record straight! We give children chocolate and toys for contributing to housework, stickers for sitting quietly in class and grade 'A's for handing in well-written reports. However successful this type of extrinsic motivation may appear in the short term, it presents a number of significant inhibitors to a love of lifelong learning.

> Children who are continually motivated by the immediate positive emotion associated with extrinsic rewards tend to hold a limited one-dimensional idea of wellbeing. They may also feel punished when rewards are not forthcoming. Teachers are left handing out increasingly verbose praise until we have not only lowered the standards by which we judge our children; we have made sure that high marks are almost obligatory. 'A' becomes the first letter of average.
> — Dr Helen Street, "Rewards, Punishments and Motivation" presentation to Positive Schools conference. May 23rd 2013, Perth.

Research shows quite clearly that giving children stamps and stickers to reward nice behaviour towards others actually increases the opposite effect. It decreases their capacity for sympathy and empathy, and can cause children instead to be mean. Dr Street has found this is similar to the empty yearning for fame, fortune and celebrity. Individuals can be driven towards extrinsic rewards while secretly hating what they are doing. The use of rewards also increases compliance and obedience, which at first sight may seem like a great idea in the classroom. Sadly, in the long term the increase in extrinsic rewards deprives individuals of self-determination.

> At first, I thought that commenting, acknowledging, and praising children for their achievements expressed love and built self-esteem. In time, I realized that these well-intended interventions do just the opposite: they foster dependency on external validation and undermine the children's trust in themselves. Children who are subjected to endless commentary, acknowledgment, and praise eventually learn to do things not for their own sake, but to please others. Gratifying others soon becomes their primary motivation, replacing impulses stemming from the authentic self and leading to its loss.
> — Naomi Aldort, *Raising Our Children Raising Ourselves* (2005).

Psychologist and researcher Professor Carol Dweck has found that children around the age of four develop mindsets about goodness. Many kids believe they are either good or bad — others think they can get better at being good. This reinforces the findings of the shame vs guilt research I discussed earlier. Children who hear nothing but negative feedback from their parents create mindsets or belief systems that they are 'bad' or 'useless' or 'stupid'. This mindset will inhibit them in almost every area of their life. This often happens unintentionally to roosters because they're usually getting into trouble a lot more than lambs. The mindset created by constant praise, however, can be just as inhibiting.

> A person who grows up getting too frequent rewards will not have persistence because they'll quit when the rewards disappear.
> — Dr Robert Cloninger, Washington University.

For a while praising our children at every opportunity seemed like the best course of action. Unfortunately research now shows that not to be the case. Thankfully we do not need to throw the baby out with the bathwater because praise can still be effective.

Praise works best when:

- It is specific.
- It is sincere.
- It is not excessive.
- It is to do with effort rather than achievement.
- It is intermittent.
- The reward is within context, and not too big or expensive.

> Indeed praise deflects the child's focus away from her in a will to create, play and do outward to our response to what she creates plays and does. It leads children to measure their worth in terms of what will lead us to smile and offer the positive words that they crave.
> — Reproduced from *Parenting for Peace* (2012), by Marcy Axness, with permission of Sentient Publications, LLC.

Alfie Kohn, in his book *Punished by Rewards* (1993), points out that for children, "praise sustains a dependence on our valuations, our decisions about what is good and bad rather than helping them begin to form their own judgements".

This also brings up the subjects of the compulsion of some parents to run constant verbal commentaries while our babies, toddlers and young children are doing almost anything. Have you ever wondered why we do that? Yes — language saturation is an important part of early brain development that enables a child to build language, and supports auditory processing patterns. But how much verbal saturation is healthy and when do we unintentionally flood a child's imaginary world with our endless chatter? If we want to raise self-directed, secure individuals with whom we share a strong bond of trust then maybe we need to create a balance between supportive verbal encouragement and respectful silence that honours a child's own exploration of the world, without any expectations from us as their parents. This is definitely food for thought. When I reflect on my own childhood in this context of praise, I have come to see that my non-communicative mum might actually have done me a favour by allowing me the freedom to explore my childlike adventures without a commentary, or the need to be validated or praised. In other words, I had to find that within myself.

Rather than praising, the art of *acknowledging* children is incredibly important. This is more about letting them know, "I am noticing you and the choices you are making".

Acknowledging kids positively

- Smile at them.
- Wink at them.
- Say hello using their name.
- Say, "I'm glad to see you".
- Suggest, "Let's go play together".
- Ask them to show you how to do a puzzle.
- Give them a pat on the head, back.
- Hug them if appropriate.
- Ask about their favourite toy.
- Play a hand or clapping game with them.
- Hold their hand.
- Say things like:
    - "Thank you for helping me clean up the toys."
    - "Thank you for being kind to your brother."
    - "I noticed you washing your hands after going to the toilet."
    - "I know how hard it is to be patient when you play with others."
    - "I noticed you using your quiet voice — well done."
- Sing songs with them, especially their favourite ones.
- Cuddle up and watch ABC Kids with them.
- Pretend to be an animal.

- Call them up and say hello.
- Make them laugh.

You will notice that acknowledging our children is very much about strengthening their attachment and bondedness to us in a loving, supportive way. That takes us back to connected parenting and attachment. The more loved our children feel, the more secure they feel, the better they are and the better they will behave.

UNDERSTANDING CHALLENGING BEHAVIOUR

When trying to understand your child and meet their unique needs — and whether they have strong rooster or lamb tendencies — it is also helpful to consider whether they are introverted or extroverted. These characteristics can influence how your child interacts with the world. For example, sometimes a child may bite another child in the sandpit simply because they are an introverted child who is feeling incredibly overwhelmed by having all the other children around them. By biting the closest child, they are trying to create space so they can fill their 'energy cup' backup. It is really important that we help them identify why they choose some behaviours rather than just sanctioning the inappropriate behaviour. Simply asking them "what were you hoping would happen when you did that?" can help you identify what was really going on underneath that behaviour.

Introverted Spirited Children

To keep your child's energy bank full:

- They need to think before they speak.
- They enjoy time by themselves.
- The introverted child is drained in groups.
- They need quiet, private time to refill their cups.
- They sometimes fight with other children to get some space.
- Avoid interrupting them when they are busy.
- Don't plan a full day's activity for your introvert.
- They like personal space especially on long car trips.
- They form deep lasting relationships.

Extroverted Spirited Children

To keep your child's energy bank full:

- They are outgoing.
- They enjoy being with people.

- The extrovert fills up with company.
- They like to talk, share their experiences.
- They make others feel comfortable.
- They need time with other adults and older children.
- They need lots of feedback.

— Kurcinka (2006).

We are what we eat

There is another thing to consider if you are really concerned with the challenging behaviour of your child. The more and more sophisticated we become as a society, the more complicated we seem to make things. There is so much research coming out that suggests that the additives and preservatives being put into our food — ironically to make it taste better, last longer and make life easier for time-poor people — are contributing to increased illness and poor behaviour in our children. It is not so much the immediate effect of eating food with these things in them that is concerning, but rather what the long-term, cumulative effects of consumption might be. There are increasing numbers of children developing food intolerances much earlier in life, especially allergies, with some babies being diagnosed with allergies in the first few weeks of life. Rather than food additives being the sole culprit to these changes we need to acknowledge that our environment has changed and we live in a much more contaminated and polluted environment on so many levels. Secondly, the stress levels under which we all live are also negatively impacting on the health and wellbeing of our children. Further our diet has become highly processed and refined, and producers are messing with molecules to create food that we give to our children.

Being a farmer's daughter I am always concerned when I read on the side of a commercial cake or biscuit packet that it contains milk solids and powdered eggs. These things do not exist in that state in nature. My concern is that we are overloading our precious babies' and toddlers' nervous systems in a way that makes it hard for their bodies and their immune systems to function at an optimal level. Julie Eady, author of the book *Additive Alert* (2004) suggests that parents need to take responsibility for teaching children healthy attitudes to high-quality food. She writes that the main culprits for overloading children with salt are poor-quality breakfast cereals, canned foods, canned soups, pre-packaged sauces and cooking sauces, flavour bases, packet soups, and frozen meals. The overconsumption of sugar, especially hidden sugars, is another area of concern for our children. Eady suggests that we aim for products that contain no more than 15g per 100g of sugar in total. Obviously most fruit juices, fruit bars and muesli bars are the worst culprits for excessive sugar, with up to five times more than the recommended daily intake.

Even bread can have some hidden nasties in it that can influence children's behaviour and wellbeing. The numbers to watch for on the side of your bread packets are 282, 319 and 320. I have had many parents of boys report to me how quickly their behaviour improved once they removed these numbers from their children's diets.

Eady writes about research done in a New South Wales primary school where for a two-week period the whole school went on an additive-free diet. The teachers and parents were quite staggered with the massive changes in children's behaviour, sleeping patterns and their ability to remain engaged with their schoolwork. Not all children demonstrate allergies or obvious sensitivities to additives, however giving our children the best possible diets with high-quality natural foods will ensure they have a strong immune system and that in itself is a good enough reason to be mindful of diet — at least 80% of the time. I recommend you do your research online to check out the other nasty numbers that have been shown to contribute to increases in negative health outcomes on many levels. Maybe your child's most disturbing behaviour is a consequence of chemical reactions in their body that can be turned around by removing the additives and preservatives in their food.

Giving just enough loving attention

Many years ago, I came across the work of Magda Gerber and Emmi Pikler and a 'philosophy of respect' around children's needs. It resonated with me as being very true. For each individual there is an optimum amount of attention — optimum, not maximum. If the person gets enough attention, satisfaction results. An individual who doesn't get enough will seek it in a variety of ways early in life:

- by being attractive to look at
- by being sweet and kind
- by being smart, skilled, capable, competent or talented
- by misbehaving
- by being loud
- by talking a lot
- by talking little
- by being outgoing
- by being shy
- by being sick
- by being helpless.

— Source: from Magda Gerber The RIE Manual for Parents and Professionals (1979) quoted in Janet Gonzalez-Mena and Dianne Widmeyer Eyer, Infants, Toddlers and Caregivers (2007).

Ouch — that explains why I talked so much as a child when I was away from my mum!

Temperament really does matter in our homes and often in our schools. Once we have a better understanding of the differences between roosters and lambs, and how to build more capacity in both, we can make better choices on our parenting journey. Remember even if you have already had a rooster or a lamb before, the next child who turns up may have that temperament tendency but they will of course still be unique and very we need to meet that person as honestly, as respectfully and as lovingly as possible.

TOP TIPS

* Our babies are born with a temperamental disposition.
* Both roosters and lambs have good and challenging traits.
* Ensure you preserve your energy if you have a rooster in your house.
* Caring, compassionate communication is what works best for both roosters and lambs.
* Avoid getting into power struggles with roosters.
* Keep yourself calm and grounded, and you will parent both temperament types better.
* Roosters need a bit of lamb, and lambs need a bit of rooster – help children to develop the unique strengths of either end of the temperament spectrum.

> WHAT I WISH I HAD KNOWN ..."IT'S NOT ABOUT WHO IS IN POWER. THE MORE YOU DOMINATE, THE MORE YOUR CHILD REBELS." – Colleen

RECOMMENDED FURTHER READING

Andrew Fuller, **Tricky Kids: Transforming conflict and freeing their potential** (2007).

Dr Alan Kazdin, **Parenting Your Defiant Child; The Kazdin method for managing difficult behaviour from toddlers to teens** (2002).

Mary Sheedy Kurcinka, **Raising Your Spirited Child: A guide for parents whose child is more** (2001).

David Swanson, **Help my kid is driving me crazy: The 17 Ways Kids Manipulate Their Parents, and What You Can Do About It** (2009).

5th Thing

THE MAGIC OF MOVEMENT AND PLAY

> Sight combined with balance, movement, hearing, touch and proprioception (Feedback from the muscles, tendons and joints, informing the brain about the body's status and actions at any moment in time) help to integrate sensory experience and can only take place as a result of action and practice. Movement is the medium through which this takes place.
> — Sally Goddard Blythe, *What Babies and Children Really Need* (2008).

Without plenty of natural movement, babies and toddlers run the risk of experiencing developmental delays in all areas of their life. Movement is not just about the physical body; it is a very sophisticated necessity for developing healthy brains, healthy minds and nurturing the socio-cultural development of every human being. Many people will have heard of the research into the development of children who lived in orphanages in Romania where they received minimum human contact and no space to move or play — these children continued to show deficits in cognitive processing and emotional aspects many, many years later.

The need for children to keep physically active cannot be highlighted enough. Human beings were born to be movers and living a sedentary life is really a disruption to our nature. Research shows that exercise and physical activity increases the levels of serotonin, norepinephrine and dopamine, which are crucial neurotransmitters that traffic thoughts and emotions right throughout the whole body. Essentially exercise has a profound impact on cognitive abilities and mental health — indeed it is simply one of the best treatments we have the most psychiatric problems. Not only that, physical exercise makes the blood pump through the body and stimulates the brain to work much more efficiently and soundly.

Modern society is becoming almost phobic about allowing young children the freedom to move vigorously and energetically especially in their natural world — outside. It is an interesting irony that the modern world is hell-bent on creating gadgets and equipment to improve our lives, yet which end up making it hard for our children to do what they are biologically wired to do — to move in deeply-encoded ways to ensure they gradually grow in all their competencies. Take for example the capsules that keep our babies safe in cars. Firstly, they are a fabulous invention for protecting babies in case there is an accident. However whoever designed them obviously doesn't know much about travelling with babies because they have our fragile newborns pointing to the back of the car where they can't see their beloved big people who make them feel safe. I realise this is the optimum position for safety, but it does mean that for many parents who travel often, especially rural parents who drive long distances, a loved one often needs to sit in the back so the baby feels safer! Any parent who has used a baby capsule will know it is extremely difficult to get babies in and out and that stress is not good for anyone. However, leaving your baby in the capsule for long periods of time once they're out of the car is not optimum for their spine development as their movement is severely restricted. Movement is critical to helping babies integrate their primitive reflexes. The primary early requirements of baby movement are ones that involve stretching the spine in the opposite direction because this ensures that the baby will inhibit its primitive reflexes to enable him/her to grow strong and healthy.

> ...As your child moves from not walking into walking, and from there, to running and jumping and hopping and skipping, this is not just a physical journey. It is an inward journey as well. The early movement milestones are a journey upward, not just to walking but to the higher parts of your baby's brain. The better the foundations that are laid now, the stronger will be the brain that grows from these foundations.
> — Jo Jackson King, *Raising the Best Possible Child* (2010).

One of the most disturbing trends in today's parenting is that Australian babies, toddlers and children have less freedom to move, and it impacts on their behaviour and capacity to learn. The ability for children to self-regulate their energy and emotions is created through an integrated body and brain. Movement skills have been shown to contribute to improving concentration spans and the ability of children to shift their attention at will. Poor self-regulation is contributing to too much of the restless, inappropriate behaviour we see in early years and primary school classes. It is sad to see that many of the companies that target the parent demographic keep creating products that 'containerise' our children, and stop babies and toddlers from moving naturally and without restraint. Think of walkers, prams, high chairs, bouncing gyms and weird plastic seats that can hold babies who are developmentally unable to sit by themselves — when we combine these contraptions with very little free movement, especially time on the floor, we are definitely creating unnecessary inhibitors to baby and toddler development. These containers are convenient for parents however they need to be seen through the lens of early child development and used less rather than more. One of the really important parts of baby development starts with tummy time.

> Tummy time involves placing your baby on her stomach for short periods of time to help her develop good upper body strength and strong neck muscles. Regular tummy time every day will strengthen the muscles she'll need when she learns to roll over, crawl, cruise and finally walk.
>
> Tummy time can be fun to play for you both if you get down on the floor with your baby. Try offering her toys to look at, or placing some toys within her reach that she may like to reach out and grasp. Over time she'll learn firstly to lift her head, and then to use her arms to prop herself up. Never leave your baby unattended on her tummy — you never know when she'll suddenly learn how to roll over — and never put her to bed on her tummy as this increases the risk of SIDS.
>
> Some babies protest strongly when you place them on their tummies but do persist with it in short bursts — she will learn to tolerate (and perhaps even enjoy) it and the benefits to her strength will far outweigh her complaints about playing on her tummy. A baby who only ever lies on her back for play time will take a lot longer to develop the muscles needed to hold her head up than one who has done her time on her tummy.
>
> — Source: *(www.kidspot.co.nz)*.

Please relax and stop buying stuff for babies and toddlers to "stimulate" them — this is consumer-driven nonsense. In reality and babies and toddlers are biologically wired to explore the world in ways that are best for them. The world is hugely fascinating for babies and children — even your boring lounge room. As long as they feel safe, they will learn something new every day. They need to do **something many times** to ensure the brain makes the necessary connections between the brain cells, but to adults it may look like not much is happening! Simple things matter — as long as we do them over and over again, until the baby or toddler shows us that they are ready to do something else. The delight in a child's voice when they say, "MORE, MORE!" — like when you play "Round and Round the Garden" with them — this is the true magic of parenting young ones. Babies and toddlers especially need a lot of repetition and music — preferably accompanied by movement — because it helps develop key areas of the brain plus it builds human connectedness. This is why singing nursery rhymes and playing simple touch games is SO IMPORTANT under five. In **Appendix 1**, I have reproduced the words to some of the most famous nursery rhymes that include movement. Remember babies and toddlers only take sound from moving human faces, not screens, until they are almost four years of age.

> There were many conclusions and recommendations in the original report, From Neurons to Neighborhoods. And the basic themes really focused on the importance of understanding that development is influenced by an interaction between nature and nurture; that everyone is born with a unique genetic predisposition, but **a large part of development is very much influenced by personal experience and by the environment in which children live.**
> — Dr Jack P. Shonkoff, *Leveraging the biology of adversity to address the roots of disparities in health and development* (2012).

Babies need repeated experiences in which they can self-direct and build the neural connections that create memory. *When children are bored they are wired to move on to something else*, to continue to engage their inquisitive brains. Learning how to manage boredom is a vital stage of development that over-stimulated babies and children need to master. When adults over-direct an infant's learning, with noisy toys, screens and even educational DVDs, they run a serious risk of invalidating the baby's natural curiosity and also causing the baby hidden stress. Activities that use gross motor skills, like learning to catch a large soft ball, are fun to do with a small child and are so important in terms of hand-eye coordination. Early over-stimulation causes the baby's brain to flood with stress hormones, which can cause them to be distressed and it can hard wire them to be overly sensitive to stress for the rest of their lives. So it's important to relax, sit on the couch and simply watch your baby or toddler interact with the real world through the magic of movement in their own time and in their own way.

BABY/TODDLER PLAY

- Make noise together. Sing nursery rhymes, shake and rattle things, make animal sounds, blow raspberries on their tummy, hands or feet!
- Start reading. Babies and toddlers need lots of human communication to pick up words and the facial cues that go with them. Read books as part of your bedtime routine. Your little ones will chew them, tear them and pull them apart sometimes, but keep going! Read in an animated way — and yes, they may love to be read the same book 100 times — but keep going! See Mem Fox's book, Reading Magic (2001) for more information.
- Explore safely. Create safe places in your home where your baby or toddler can explore, as this shows their natural curiosity. This might include: sitting up, crawling, pulling up, opening cupboards, picking things up, throwing them and putting them in their mouth, and eventually, walking. Try one cupboard for plastics only, peg baskets, and cushions and blankets.
- Play lots of simple games. Games like Pat-a-cake, Peek-a-boo and "This little piggy went to market" are not only fun for babies and toddlers — they help to make them smart! This builds memory pathways that build connectedness and wellbeing. The fun that a little child gets from playing with people who love them stays with them for life.

— Sourced from the Raising Children Network's comprehensive and quality-assured Australian parenting website http://raisingchildren.net.au

Remember we must never forget that child development cannot be hurried, no matter how inconvenient that may be for the adults in our 'hurry-up' world. Each child has a built-in timetable that dictates just when s/he will crawl, sit up and start to walk; and given a safe environment, their development will flow naturally. Children learn by doing and they will be noisy, untidy, messy and unpredictable. This is normal and at times parenting can be tiring, exhausting and frustrating. This too is normal.

Some of the things that can occur if our children lack movement in the first two years of life are:

- delayed motor development
- poor co-ordination/ balance
- tendency to be easily distracted, lack concentration
- language problems
- emotional immaturity
- motion sickness
- reading problems.

One thing that has changed in childhood has been the freedom of children to move and play in bare feet. It seems that parents have picked up the notion from full-day-based child care that children need to have their feet covered at all times. I have been told that young children who have been unable to experience the natural world through their bare feet, can stand on a very hot pavement without recognising the heat sensation and ending up with third-degree burns. The soles of our feet are very sensitive and intrinsically wired to our brain. Podiatrist Tracy Byrne, who specialises in podopaediatrics in London, believes that wearing shoes at too young an age can hamper a child's walking and cerebral development.

> Toddlers keep their heads up more when they are walking barefoot. The feedback they get from the ground means there is less need to look down which is what puts them off balance and causes them to fall down.
> — Tracy Byrne (in Sam Murphy, "Why Barefoot is Best for Children", *The Guardian*, August 9th 2010).

Allowing our children endless opportunities to walk and run barefoot, especially on uneven surfaces, will allow them to connect with the ground — in all its variety — so they can not only develop their physical capacity to move freely in our world, they will also create healthy brains which can function at more optimum levels.

> In a way babies and toddlers are scientists, explorers and adventurers with a passion for discovery and learning.
> — Maggie Dent.

Dr John J Ratey and Eric Hagerman in their book called, *Spark: how exercise will improve the performance of your brain* (2008) explore many studies that show quite clearly that an increase in exercise, especially in the school environment, rapidly improves student performance. It appears that when we have over 20 minutes of increased heart rate activity there is significant activity in the impulse centre of the prefrontal cortex. Students who were formerly poor performers began to work with more concentration and effort following the introduction of a program of vigorous exercise before class. Sadly we seem to be moving physical activity from our curriculums to fit in more learning. Another interesting irony! This is why walking or riding to school is not only good for our children's bodies, it's great for their brains as well.

> Serotonin is equally affected by exercise and it's important for mood, impulse control and self-esteem. It also helps stave off stress by counteracting cortisol and it primes the cellular connections in the cortex and hippocampus that are important for learning.
> — Ratey and Hagerman (2008).

Important brain development takes place as a child plays. Some of that development requires tumbling, spinning, balancing and rolling, because it stimulates the sensory system. These activities help develop the cerebellum. Studies have shown a link between dyslexia and ADHD and under-developed cerebellums, leading to poor sensory processing, inattention and hyperactivity. A group of children playing in a natural environment will naturally balance, roll, spin and tumble, and if you don't believe me just watch next time you visit a busy playground. There is less opportunity for these essential activities to occur when a child sits on a couch. Passivity is a serious concern in today's world.

PLAY AND ITS POWER TO GROW HEALTHY, HAPPY KIDS

> Many children played and learned in the streets, woods and fields without the looming presence of adults and albeit well-meaning coaches. Their experiences were real, varied and enormously engaging. These hands-on or concrete experiences with the real world prepared the brain for learning. What may have seemed to be unstructured play had a very serious purpose. It allowed children to discover the underlying rules and patterns that organize and make sense of the world. It may have set up a filing system for the storage and retrieval of information. Many of today's children are starved of real life experiences.
> —Gayle Gregory and Terence Parry, *Designing Brain Compatible Learning* (2006).

Play is the way babies and children develop their sense of self, sense of the world, and sense of where they fit in. Children are biologically wired to play. Play is very serious business for them. Opportunities for play are essential because they help a child learn many of the emotional and social competencies. These cannot be developed through direct verbal interaction with adults. Solo play, parallel play, imaginative, adult-directed and interactive play are all healthy forms of play for children to experience in childhood. However, there are so many factors that are eroding children's opportunities to play and so many busy parents tell me they simply struggle to make the time for such opportunities.

> Having sufficient time to play is important — big blocks of time without being disturbed and made to hurry is important for children and adults. We need time to chill out, relax, to let our ideas flow, have conversations with real or imaginary friends, to test our ideas and theories and replay, retest and rethink them.
> — Neville Dwyer, *Being Adventurous* (2013).

Play is a much underrated but incredibly vital part of children's development. Put simply, "play grows the brain". As Hara Estroff Marano highlighted in her book, *A Nation of Wimps* (2008):

> Play fosters maturation of the very centres of the brain that allows kids to exert control over retention, emotions and to control behaviour. This is a very subtle trick that nature plays — it uses something that is not goal directed to create the mental machinery for being goal directed.

When I ask a group of parents what play they experienced as children, and what they really loved, an interesting thing happens. These parents do not mention expensive toys or indoor games. The things they loved as kids were building cubbies, riding bikes (often without helmets, gears or brakes), catching tadpoles, building billy carts, climbing trees, and hours of playing chasey, hide-and-seek and spotlight. One parent shared with me her story of going camping with her children at a beach campsite where they could have up to 30 children playing spotlight. Mind you, some of those children were in their 40s! These play pursuits used to occur often, with little direction from adults and *costing very little money*.

> **DID YOU KNOW**
> There has been an estimated 30-50% increase in shortsightedness in children over the past two decades and this has been linked to diet, less time playing sport and being outside. Being outside strengthens eyes muscles and improves vision.

WHAT IS STOPPING OUR CHILDREN FROM BEING MORE ACTIVE AND PLAYING MORE?

According to Joanne Landy and Alice Brown, the authors of an excellent resource for educators and the carers of children called, *Kids With More Zip*

(2008), there appears to be a number of variables associated with today's modern childhood inactivity.

1. An increase in screen-based activity and labour saving devices
2. Child safety concerns that impact on children playing in the streets, local parks and walking or cycling to school
3. A decrease in play environments and play opportunities
4. Issues of modern living such as more parents working, less recreation time and an overuse of cars.

— Joanne Landy and Alice Brown.

Given that the play landscape has changed, it is not just through a reminiscent and nostalgic lens that I am talking about the playgrounds of old. Much of the play equipment that used to be in playgrounds has been removed because it was believed to be unsafe. These include the tall monkey bars, wooden see-saws and the metal may-poles — equipment that had to be treated with deep respect because you could seriously hurt yourself. If you're old enough to remember such things, I wonder did you ever get thumped in the chin when someone jumped on the other end of a see-saw? Was your bum ever thumped when someone suddenly jumped off said see-saw? Well it only needed to happen once or twice before you learnt to treat the equipment with the respect it deserved and you learned to be accountable for your actions. This is actually harm minimisation through learning how to manage and cope with potential risk and kids can do this this. An emergency nurse recently told me that they now see MORE children with injuries from the modern trampolines with the safety nets than they did before these so-called safely measures were implemented. It seems that today's largely safe playgrounds are the product of our risk-averse society, where things are built to prevent children getting hurt.

PLAY AND MANAGING RISK

Tim Gill, in his book, *No Fear: Growing Up in a Risk Averse Society* (2007), explores the long-lasting effects in the United Kingdom of removing risk from childhood.

> Activities and experiences that previous generations enjoyed without a second thought have been labelled as troubling or dangerous, while adults who still permit them are branded as irresponsible ... society appears to have become unable to cope with any adverse outcomes whatsoever, no matter how trivial or improbable.
> — Tim Gill.

Hugh Cunningham is Emeritus Professor of Social History at the University of Kent. In his book, *The Invention of Childhood* (2006), he shares Gill's concerns.

Cunningham believes that society in general has become so fixated on ensuring children are happy that we downplay their abilities and their resilience. Taking up the debate about our collective responsibility for shaping childhood, he is now an activist and lobbyist in the UK who works to ensure that children's opportunities to play and have free time without adult supervision are not forever lost.

As Gill writes, today's parents spend much more time than previous generations focusing on their children and monitoring their activities. Many parents are also constantly in touch with their children via mobile phones. The long-term effects of such strong structuring, supervision and control on children and their capacity to develop resilience is a key element of Gill's book. Children learn by being able to manage their own worlds, including the risks they encounter — with large developmental benefits. Some child health experts claim that a child can build and strengthen his or her character and personality through facing up to adverse circumstances, where there is a known possibility of injury or loss. At the same time, the child learns about the qualities of being adventuresome and innovative. Overcoming challenging situations is a key aspect of resilience and there is only one way to learn about it, and that is through experience. In his book, Gill writes about a school that banned the game of tag because of the risk of injury. A student wrote the following response, which was published in an article on the BBC website on 1 March 2005:

> **WILMA WALLABY**
> "It is important for our children to learn about risk and how to make wise choices. Mother nature is a wonderful teacher."

> To be honest, adults can be very stupid at times. They ban everything, for health and safety reasons. If they're going to ban very simple stuff like this, they might as well lock all kids in empty rooms to keep them safe. Kids should be allowed to experiment and try things. Otherwise they will grow up and they'll make stupid mistakes from not getting enough experience at childhood.
> — Gill (2007).

Gill writes of how children of previous generations learned to take care and manage risks, because they knew that playgrounds were potentially dangerous. Today, children believe that playgrounds are safe and so they take little care and do not learn healthy risk assessment or management. This is commonly known as 'risk compensation'. It is worth asking however, "What are we risking with our children if they are never exposed to risk?" There will always be some benefits as well as some concerns when exploring the question of risk in childhood. Technically our world is safer today than it has ever been, and many of our fears are irrational and fed by the media and the insurance industry.

An Australian health professional validated this perspective for me when he told me that the number of children who suffer broken wrists these days is more than the number who used to break their arms on the older-style, long monkey bars, which have been removed from many playgrounds for safety reasons.

UK data released in 2013 from the National Health Service showed that cases of children injuring themselves indoors are on the rise, despite parents' efforts to avoid risk by limiting outdoor play (Singh, 2013).

Hanging from trees and monkey bars — an activity that many children used to do for hours — had some significant benefits for children:

1. They strengthened wrists — now children are getting repetitive strain injuries (RSI) from playing games, according to the survey of British health data.
2. They gave children strong grips to help hold their pencil in Year 1.
3. They encouraged persistence as the monkey bar took many turns before a child could swing all the way across, and trees are rarely symmetrical.
4. They strengthened the shoulder girdle ensuring a strong posture — many of today's children are already experiencing posture problems and back pain, especially from the combination of weak shoulder girdle and being stooped over screens.

At a seminar I was presenting once, a teacher shared with me that the monkey bars also provided an excellent opportunity for children who struggled academically to experience competence. The king or queen of the monkey bars had something that s/he could do and feel capable about. This is a key aspect of self-esteem and builds a healthy sense of self.

Children used to learn to manage the bumps and bruises of life because they had opportunities to do so. They were not mollycoddled and wrapped in cotton wool. Accidents were seen as being part of a healthy childhood, and not a sign of poor parenting. Resilience is built from the experience of managing the things that can hurt physically, emotionally and psychologically.

Gill also explored what happened in the UK when impact-absorbing surfaces became mandatory. Firstly, the cost of the new, safer surfaces was prohibitive and many playgrounds closed or they had fewer play items. Then evidence emerged that these rubber-like surfaces may be causing more broken arms than other types of surfaces (David Yearley, Head of Play Ground Safety, Royal Society for the Prevention of Accidents, at Somerset Forum Conference, November 2006 in Gill, 2007).

In the German city of Freiburg an interesting phenomenon has been taking place. In the 1990s, the city began installing public playgrounds that made extensive use of slopes, logs, boulders, plants, sand and other natural features. Tim Gill met with the Freiburg Director of Parks, Harald Rabhein, in 2005. He asked Rabhein about playground safety in these more naturalistic playgrounds:

> "Clearly there are more hazards and they are more varied in natural play spaces compared to traditional play areas. In general, children learn to take more care and responsibility for their safety in the natural play spaces and as a result, accident rates have not increased," Rabhein said.
> — Gill (2007).

Children really need opportunities for creative, exploratory play in stress-free environments, especially in nature without restrictions on time or freedom. Anecdotal evidence shows that many preschools and primary schools are returning to having longer times for children to play outside in natural environments with dirt, trees, water and grass. Consequently, these schools are noticing an increase in children's creative play, social cohesion, better problem-solving, negotiation skills and immersion in the play experience. Children are calmer, happier, less anxious and less stressed. Cognitive learning is still taking place within unstructured play. This type of play is vital for developing social skills like sharing, taking turns, communication skills, and dealing with disappointments and delayed gratification. This is what nature play is all about.

There has been a 60% drop in outside play in one generation.

This is the finding of Curtin University academic Sonja Kuzich, reported at the Margaret River Flourish Symposium in October 2011. There is clear and consistent evidence about the many benefits for children and the wider community from exposure to and engagement with nature. Internationally, many public and private playground providers are moving to enhance playground provision by including planted landscapes and/or natural play elements into playground designs, or by giving children opportunities to play in natural semi-wild spaces.

NATURE PLAY AND NATURE-BASED PLAYGROUNDS

What the research says:

- Children who play regularly in natural settings are sick less often. Mud, sand, water, leaves, sticks, pine cones and gum nuts can help to stimulate children's immune system as well as their imagination.
- Children who spend more time outside tend to be more physically active and less likely to be overweight.
- Children who play in natural settings are more resistant to stress; have lower incidence of behavioural disorders, anxiety and depression; and have a higher measure of self-worth.

- Children who play in natural settings play in more diverse, imaginative and creative ways and show improved language and collaboration skills.
- Children who play in nature have more positive feelings about each other.
- Bullying behaviour is greatly reduced where children have access to diverse nature-based play environments.
- Symptoms of Attention Deficit Disorder are reduced after contact with nature.

— Source: Kidsafe WA (www.kidsafewa.com.au).

Children become massively engaged in nature-based playgrounds compared to in playgrounds designed by adults. It stands to reason then that we need more nature-based playgrounds and less of those brightly coloured, adult-designed jobs. High-quality play experiences definitely contribute to better cognitive development in children and they promote problem-solving, creativity, initiative and can increase children's ability to concentrate. What is most exciting about nature-based playgrounds is that every time a child visits the playground they can interact and play in a completely different way to how they played previously because the structures aren't prescribed to 'work' in a particular way. One of the key benefits of natural playgrounds is that they tend to help children develop better gross motor skills like climbing.

The key characteristics of a natural playground are:

- the use of natural products like sand, water, logs and rocks
- differing heights and levels of the ground — children love hills
- they allow children the opportunity to investigate and explore freely
- there is no fixed purpose to achieve
- some are hidden areas behind shrubs or small barriers
- they like bridges or walkways that take them from one place to another
- tunnels are a feature — children love tunnels
- the inclusion of waterways — these are purely magical to children, not just to look at but to interact with
- opportunities for children to climb and to swing with their body weight
- spaces to run freely
- the ability to move things around
- no pressure to keep things neat and tidy
- a suspension of time constraints.

Claire Warden is one of the world's leading advocates for nature play for children. She is passionate about the benefits of children being immersed in nature and through her visits to Australia she has helped promote the need for outdoor play especially in early years' centres.

In Australia bush kindergartens are beginning to appear and these wonderful centres are giving young children the opportunity to massively engage in the natural world and to discover the scientist within them. There are more and more schools across Australia interacting with the real world through their curriculum. Bold Park Community School in Perth, Western Australia, is one such school that uses the nearby lake as a form of classroom. Their whole school curriculum is woven closely with the natural world and real experiences. Massive immersion in the natural world in childhood not only allows children to grow healthy on all levels it allows them to develop a respectful consciousness around the environment and their place in it.

> **WILMA WALLABY**
> "Lots of play in nature makes our kids strong, healthy, smart and calm."

> "US research suggests that a generation of children is not only being raised indoors but is being confined to even smaller spaces. Jane Clarke, a University of Maryland Professor, calls them 'containerised kids' – they spend more and more time in car seats, high chairs and even baby seats for watching TV. When children go outside they're often placed in containers – strollers – and pushed by walking or jogging parents."
> — Richard Louv, *Last Child in the Woods* (2005).

Once again it is an interesting irony that in order to keep our children safe and healthy we are making choices that limit their movement especially out in Mother Nature. Research is suggesting that we are making our children sicker, sadder, fatter and more hyperactive. Some researchers even suggest that exposure to nature may reduce the symptoms of ADHD and that it could improve children's cognitive abilities and resistance to negative stresses and depression. Sadly we now have a new phenomenon that is called nature deficit disorder which describes the human costs of alienation from nature:

- diminished use of senses
- attention difficulties
- more physical illness
- more emotional disorders (Louv, 2005).

I would like to add that this separation from nature is also causing a weakening of the human spirit in our children. We have emotional competencies that help us build resilience, and we have spiritual competencies as well. People who have overcome huge adversity will often identify an indefinable moment when they felt strengthened by something deep within them, rather than just a rational thought. This is a spiritual aspect of themselves.

> Play is the highest expression of human development in childhood, for it alone is the free expression of what is in the child's soul.
> — Friedrich Froebel, *The Education of Man* (1826).

Children need to experience the joy of discovery — feeling rain for the first time, touching a kitten, or seeing Christmas lights. The moment of awe must be experienced while we are young in order for awe and wonder to be a powerful part of our adult life. These experiences of heightened sensation allow children to feel transcendent — somehow more expanded and larger than life. The search for transcendence can drive later experiences. Those who have had positive natural 'highs' as young children are more likely to seek natural rather than drug or high-risk thrills as they become teenagers and adults.

Happy children have a strong spirit and know that life is full of anticipation, delight and fun — the more of these experiences they have up to 10 years of age the better. The brain wires all positive experiences like a web over all future experiences and builds a sense of anticipation of how life will be. Children who have had moments of sheer fun and enjoyment will tend to anticipate and expect (and create) more of those moments as an adult.

> The most beautiful thing we can experience is the mysterious. Recognition of the mystery of the universe is the source of all true science. He to whom emotions are a stranger, who can no longer pause to wonder and stand rapt in awe is as good as dead; his eyes are closed.
> — Albert Einstein

My sons were very used to being drawn outside when there was a stunning full moon, interesting cloud formations, downpours or cloud bursts as the sun's rays shone through the clouds. And while sometimes my boys think their mother is "missing a few kangaroos in the back paddock", I know they have enjoyed some of these moments too; sometimes they get me to come and watch. I have seen the brilliant sparkle in their eyes when they return from a surfing trip to say that they were joined in the surf by a school of dolphins, or that they saw a whale close by — sheer joy and delight that is provided free of charge by Mother Earth. This connection to nature is being starved from many children's lives because of the dominance of the virtual reality world and this must be remedied if we are to heal the serious dislocation of many of today's children and teenagers. Indeed, I often wonder how many children pause to look up

— to see the sky, the trees, the birds or the sunlight? Indigenous children and adults often do this instinctively.

> Only after the last tree has been cut down;
>
> Only after the last river has been poisoned;
>
> Only after the last fish has been caught, will you find that money cannot be eaten.
>
> — 19th Century Cree Indian prophecy.

I salute the work being done in Western Australia with the organisation Nature Play WA. It was a bold move for the State Government to support such an organisation however the change in the WA playground landscape including many schools and communities has been exciting, extensive and continues to grow. I was at a primary school in Perth that had built two nature playgrounds for their students — one for the K-2s and one for the older students. The staff told me that they noticed a difference in the children's concentration and their ability to play with other children within the first week of the playgrounds opening. Some students who had been reluctant to attend school now turn up early. Children who were initially fearful of the height of the wooden bridges now run freely over them without fear.

Other schools with nature playgrounds have also reported significant reductions in truancy and bullying, improved concentration in class and improved school culture. The improved cooperative play and adventuresome nature of the play has also seen an increase in improved risk-taking and resilience. To me, simply looking at the faces of children playing in a nature playground is compelling enough evidence to give playgrounds back to children, outside, and then also allow them enough time to play deeply in these settings.

Once, when I was doing a radio interview on natural play, a listener phoned up to share her story. She lived opposite a community playground that had been upgraded to a modern, bright plastic playground. She said that I was correct in my observation that children did not stay engaged in plastic playgrounds for long. In the old playground, she noticed the children would stay there nearly all day long, still massively engaged, but not so much since it had changed. Then she told me something really funny. One of the pieces of equipment had broken and the local council had come to remove it and left a big hole in the ground. Apparently the move had attracted more children than she had ever seen, as they spent hours playing in that hole full of dirt. Ah, I love to see children enjoying dirt!

THE DIRTY LITTLE SECRET ABOUT CHILD'S PLAY

> Keeping the natural world out of the reach of children seems to be our national passion. In fact greater numbers of children are brought up in the artificial world of cement, asphalt, plastics and the virtual reality of television while fewer each year experience a world of nature and the unfolding of organic life.
>
> — Joseph Chilton Pearce, *The Biology of Transcendence* (2002).

A pretty common inhibitor to playing in nature appears to be the concern of some parents that their children will get wet and dirty. Remember wet and dirty children are most likely to be learning far more than dry, clean children. The massive sensory exposure that children experience in the natural world is one of the reasons they become smarter. Being able to cope with cold weather, rain, hot pavements and wind are all capacities that children need to develop. Being frightened of these things will cause you anxiety and stress. In Scotland, the nature play movement means that children spend up to five hours a day outside regardless of the weather. Now that is really toughening our children up and building resilience!

> The fun aspects of play also serve an important role in developing a child's psychology. The more pleasurable experiences that a child has, the more chance they have of developing a pleasure-seeking response to unknown experiences. The opposite can also occur, where the more painful experiences the child has, the more likely it is that they will seek pain rather than pleasure out of new experiences. This becomes an unconscious process that happens quite spontaneously. It is influenced by the core concepts that a child has come to believe.
>
> — John Joseph, *Learning in the Emotional Rooms* (2005).

In our fear-driven world many well-meaning parents are terrified of children being hurt emotionally or physically. A good example of this is reflected in how the birthday party game 'Pass the Parcel' has changed, so that instead of only having one winner, everyone gets a prize. Often the prizes are hand-picked so Mum or Dad has to stop the music exactly on cue so the correct prize goes to the correct child. Now while this may seem like a loving and thoughtful gesture on the part of the parents, they are actually denying their young children an opportunity to experience disappointment and failure (not to mention the thrill of chance luck). It is much easier to help children understand these big emotional moments when they are under five, rather than at 15. Overprotecting them in this way is weakening their resilience for later in life. So please allow this game to be the wonderful teacher that it is designed to be. Next time a little child says to you, "But I didn't get a prize!" lean forward and quietly say, "doesn't it suck when you don't win and you miss out on a prize? That's disappointment honey and it happens often in life. There is another game coming — good luck. I hope you do better next time."

Card games, Connect Four, Snap, Fish, Snakes and Ladders, and Pick-Up-Sticks all help children develop hand-eye coordination, memory and concentration. These are also great games that help children get used to winning and losing in socially appropriate ways. They teach children how to take turns, be patient and use strategy. Children need to understand that it is OK to make mistakes, and parents need to understand that it is OK for their children to make mistakes too and experience disappointment. This is the only way they learn that they can recover from these life realities! Some games are based on chance rather than strategy and I really believe they help children manage life when sometimes we are just in the wrong place at the wrong time with no intention of making a mistake.

Have you noticed that no one likes losing? If you are winning a game of Snakes and Ladders with a four-year-old child, you actually feel pretty good. And suddenly you end up getting that snake on the third row, and you are no longer winning ... you'll notice you don't feel so good anymore. Helping children understand the dynamics of winning and losing is incredibly important.

There is enormous pressure on children in today's competitive parenting world, to be the best child possible. This pressure can cause big problems in adolescence especially. The perfection-driven child is incredibly stressed, often to ensure that everything they do meets the exceedingly high expectation of their parents and, eventually, themselves. Sometimes this pressure forces them to cheat, to get sick to avoid a challenge, or to become incredibly rebellious without really understanding why. Boys particularly need to be drowned in experiences where they get used to losing because boys and men are biologically and culturally influenced to pursue external forms of success to help them find self-worth and value. When they fail to achieve these things they can become incredibly angry at themselves and the world. So much of our emotional and social development comes through play in experiences with other children, pets or adults. It cannot come from solo play on an iPad because tablets do not have feelings.

> ### DID YOU KNOW?
> Without play, children will often struggle more as adults because they haven't mastered the ability to get along with other people. The parts of the brain that regulate emotion and attitudes to human relationships require human contact to develop.

Only real interactions build emotional competencies; these cannot be learned by watching a screen. Playing with the same children frequently — siblings, cousins, or a close friend's children — is an excellent way for toddlers to develop. Also, although rigidly organised activities with adult intervention may seem beneficial to cognitive development, self-initiated play is often better. I have fond memories of my four sons playing for hours in the sandpit. They would make many strange noises without exchanging any real words. They had a fat time and, with hindsight, were learning vital 'boy codes' of communication — never waste words when strange grunts can suffice!

We would all like our children to get along with their siblings — not just when they are young, but when they become adults. It seems that siblings who have many peak moments of joy and delight as children get along better after they leave home. So despite your worries about sibling rivalry, which is very normal, keep in mind the need to create opportunities to have serious fun together. Again play is the best avenue to create memories that matter.

From around two years of age, toddlers are capable of learning social skills that strengthen their life-coping skills. As they start to develop their sense of 'self', these little ones have the opportunity to develop autonomy and personal independence. The stronger a person's sense of identity and independence, combined with the life skills to support these attributes, the better their resilience.

> When we play, we are engaged in the purest expression of our humanity, the truest expression of our individuality.
> — Stuart Brown, *Play: How it shapes the brain, opens the imagination, and invigorates the soul* (2009).

Children have an enormous curiosity and thirst for life when exploring their world, especially when they are with other children. Curiosity and innovative, flexible thinking are strong attributes of resilient people. Margot Sunderland in her book, *The Science of Parenting* (2007) writes about the importance of developing the mammalian brain, especially the areas associated with caring and nurturing, social bonding, playfulness and the explorative urge. This last attribute, also called the seeking system, is like a muscle — the more you use it, the more it develops. In humans this system can activate an appetite for life, an energy to explore the new and an eagerness to seek out the fruits of the world. It also stimulates our curiosity, absorbed interest and sustained motivation to achieve our goals. This is what free play and child-centred activity helps to nurture in a child's brain. The mind-numbing influence of too much TV and play within adult-centred threatens this vital brain development. This may make an individual susceptible to mental illnesses such as depression, and lead to poor motivation for life.

An under-active seeking system in adulthood could contribute to a person staying stuck in an unloving relationship or a completely soulless, boring job. These people lack that magical drive to transform the seed of disillusionment into a new adventure or an amazing new reality!

Play is essential learning. Playing verbal games with a child in his or her early years ensures the development of verbal and processing skills around visual and auditory cues. These skills help children learn to read. Such activities also help them to manage their impulses and learn about persistence, winning and losing. Singing and counting games help stimulate young children's brains. These activities develop patterning and sequencing strategies that help with cognitive processing later in life. They are very important in developing the resilience pathways.

Physical activity reduces the likelihood of obesity. It is also important for the functioning of the brain as it supports learning and memory through the repair and maintenance of neural circuits. Physical activity can reduce stress and aggression, and it helps regulate mood by increasing the release of serotonin and dopamine, which are essential for emotional and cognitive wellbeing. Being physically active may be a protective factor against depression. Vigorous play like chasing each other, jumping on a trampoline or playing ball games, have another wonderful quality to them other than having fun and getting fit. Physical activity that elevates the heart rate discharges excess energy that builds up from emotional challenges or situations of threat. Even adults feel calmer and more relaxed after physical activity. Exercise releases endorphins and chemicals that promote positive moods and a feeling of wellbeing. This is another reason why trips to parks, beaches and the bush are so important. They help burn up excess energy, release feel-good hormones and allow everyone to get plenty of fresh air.

> **WILMA WALLABY**
>
> "Play is how all kids learn the things they need to be proud, strong, kind, healthy and happy."

Play is the best way to develop a healthy enjoyment of physical activity.
That is, the activity is best treated as fun, to help build a positive attitude to physical activity. The family who plays together stays together and they will also be healthier, smarter and less aggressive.

Remember always that children are impelled by millions of years of genetic encoding to interact on a full sensory level with the events of the living world, through which they build their structures of world knowledge. They must be able to follow this innate coding and drive to connect on a full sensory level with the real world, not a virtual reality world. Baroness Susan Greenfield in her excellent book *ID: The Quest for Meaning in the 21st Century* (2008) writes of her concerns about today's changing world:

> Gradually, in each young human, the brain becomes personalized by unique experiences to become a unique entity. It is this personalization of the physical brain that, for me, is the 'mind'.
> — Baroness Susan Greenfield

Greenfield believes that in the changing landscape of childhood — where most children now play and interact in the same way with technology — that their minds could lacking the personalisation that used to occur when children were all experiencing very different experiences in the real world. She believes we may have a world full of 'anybodys' and 'nobodys' rather than unique 'somebodys' and that has to be disturbing. Authentic human play ensures this will not happen.

Another word on play comes from Daniel Goleman, author of *Emotional Intelligence* and more recently, *Social Intelligence: The New Science of Human Relationships*. Goleman studied the work of Jaak Panksepp.

> "The primal subcortical circuitry that prompts the young of all mammals to romp in rough and tumble play seems to have a vital part in the child's neural growth. And the emotional fuel for all that development seems to be delight itself."
> — Daniel Goleman, *Social Intelligence* (2006).

This writing validates the common-sense notion that children benefit greatly from experiencing sustained moments of joy and delight. It appears that these moments of delight fertilise the growth of circuitry in the amygdala and frontal cortex of the brain. Pankstepp studied the tickling response in mammals, finding that all mammals have 'tickling skin'. In his studies, Pankstepp found that children and other mammals were instinctively drawn to adults who tickle them. Apparently the tickle zone in children runs from the back of the neck and around the rib cage. I am sure many of us remember how hilarious it can be to be tickled by someone safe. The circuitry for playful joy has close ties to the neural networks that make a ticklish child laugh. This means our brain can become hardwired with an urge to play, one that hurls us into sociability.

Pankstepp argues that many children with hyperactivity, impulsivity and unfocused, rapid shifting movement from one activity to another (as in ADHD) are in fact seeking to activate the joy and delight response. He makes a radical, untested proposal to let younger children 'vent' their urge to play in an early-morning free play, rough and tumble recess; then bring them into a classroom after the urge has been sated, when they can more easily pay attention.

There are studies that suggest that 'rough and tumble play' (this also includes free-range exploration in nature) especially for boys and their dads reduces violent behaviour later in life. Play fighting, rough and tumble, and even combative role-play were once considered very normal parts of childhood. Yet today these forms of play are often misinterpreted as forms of bullying, or a precursor to bullying, and are banned. Early years' researcher, Penny Holland in her book, *We Don't Play With Guns* (2003), argues that these forms of play are outward signs of a sophisticated and largely unconscious learning process that helps to build emotional and social life skills. Children learn how to read key facial expressions and body language, and can quite clearly tell the difference between play and the real thing.

While play may seem like the fun, easy part of being a child, it is also vitally important for building connectedness and brain integration. These vital processes assist with literacy and numeracy; enhance emotional and social awareness, and competence. Play can also build mental wellbeing and provide the building blocks for being loving, caring human beings who are capable of creating intimate relationships later in life. We must let play continue throughout life.

IMAGINATIVE PLAY MATTERS

In our test-driven world, where everything needs to be measured and tested, imaginative play has been pushed aside and that worries me deeply. In my book, *Nurturing Kids' Hearts and Souls*, I wrote:

> Children's imaginations, especially when a child is not yet seven, help them experience joy. They are totally unaware of the concerns of later life. More than that, a child's imagination can nurture, protect and insulate them from many of the harsh realities of the adult modern world that surrounds them. It can feed their growing spirits and build on emotional and social competencies that will help them in adolescence and

> adulthood. Imagination and the holistic growth of healthy, happy, resilient children have suffered greatly in the last couple of generations. Modernism, the rise of a popular culture that honours 'fast and quick' living, the 'must have' mentality and family and community disintegration have all taken their toll on children.
>
> I firmly believe that a rich imaginative childhood is essential for the evolving brain. It helps to create the neuronal templates that ensure emotional stability, social awareness and the spiritual strength to cope with life in this chaotic, constantly changing world.
> — Dent (2005).

In the nine years since I wrote that book, the imaginative world of many children has almost disappeared. I have primary school teachers telling me how many of today's children struggle to do any creative writing at all unless they have seen the DVD of the story first. The imagination helps children explore and interpret life experiences as they strive for a sense of meaning. This search for meaning is not a logical process for children. Have you watched children when they are playing shops, or pretending to be Mummy and Daddy, or out mowing the lawn — they are imagining that they are grown ups. I have met children who have never built or played in a cubby either inside or outside the home. In my counselling work, I've seen that the imagination is one of the most powerful ways we can guide children back to healing after adversity or tragedy. I worry for children who have had little imaginary play in early childhood.

> One of the great tragedies for children, however is that our society has forgotten how much imaginative play contributes to the skills that lead to life success. Why? I think it is because imaginative play doesn't have a "product" that can be used as "evidence of learning" and time well spent.
> — Jackson King (2010).

Some of the best play can occur using simple things like cardboard boxes, buckets, ice cream containers and empty plastic bottles. What a great way to recycle and provide play opportunities for young children. I can remember the delight a washing machine box once gave my sons. The box became a rocket ship, a boat, a tower and a tunnel, and the morning they found it soaked through and ruined on the back lawn was a very sad day in the Dent home. Bed sheets make great indoor cubbies for when it's wet outside. Sometimes they can last weeks and you will find very interesting things inside — like vegemite sandwiches with furry green stuff growing all over them when you are finally able to help them dismantle their wonderful creations. Such a discovery could then become a wonderful science lesson on mould!

Imaginative play creates creative minds that see the world differently, problem solve innovatively and bring an incredible richness into human life. As Cambridge University psychology and education researcher Dr David Whitebread (2012) writes:

> You can't teach creativity; all you can do is let it blossom. Little children, before they start school, are naturally creative. Our greatest innovators, the ones we call geniuses, are those who somehow retain that childhood capacity, and build on it, right through adulthood.

TECHNOLOGY AND PLAY

The IT juggernaut has sent a tsunami of screens — iPads, tablets, smart phones, mp3 players, computers, internet-enabled TVs and game consoles — flooding onto the landscape of childhood and adolescence. It is hard to believe that it's barely four years since Steve Jobs launched the iPad! Never before have parents and teachers been confronted with such a sweeping, massive change in human behaviour. Research will take time to give us strong evidence about the pros and cons of the use of these devices — and there are big pluses and big minuses.

> **WILMA WALLABY**
>
> "Families who play together will feel a stronger sense of belonging. Kids need to know that they belong and they matter."

Researchers argue that, "digital media are here to stay and are going to be widely used by young children. The important issue is how to maximize the positive consequences of these new media so that they enrich rather than hinder children's play experiences." (Johnson & Christie, 2009, p.285). Salonius-Pasternak and Gelfond (2005) suggest that computer play is, perhaps, "the first qualitatively different form of play that has been introduced in at least several hundred years," and "it merits an especially careful examination of its role in the lives of children".
— Irina Verenikina and Lisa Kervin (University of Wollongong), "iPads, Digital Play and Pre-schoolers", *He Kupu* (2011).

I wrote about some of the bonuses and challenges of technology in Chapter 2. I want to be clear that I am not anti-technology ... I think, particularly as children get older, that technology has great potential to help young people learn, to express themselves, to problem-solve, and to engage with the world and the people in it. However given that this chapter is about the importance of movement and play on early development, then inevitably one of the biggest concerns with technology is that it is making our children more sedentary. Essentially the first two years are a particularly fertile time for brain growth and development, provided babies and toddlers are immersed in real-life experiences with warm loving adults. Not only is it a vital time for wiring of movement, sensory growth and tactile programming, "*the interaction from parents or consistent carers has been shown to be a major influence on whether your child will grow up to live a fulfilling life or one spoiled by persistent states of anger, anxiety or depression*" (Sunderland, 2007).

> There is a major growth spurt in the frontal lobes of a child's brain in the first two years of life. This time is a great window of opportunity for establishing nerve pathways that underpin learning and language development and also for establishing anti-anxiety chemical systems in the brain.
> — Sunderland (2007).

Babies and toddlers learn by modelling their adult caregivers' behaviour and they become fascinated by the screen world because we are fascinated by it. There are already some disturbing concerns surfacing in the allied health sector, about young children suffering from RSI from overuse of screens, short-sightedness, poor self-regulation, chronic back pain at three and four years old, and even incidents of iPad addiction with three-year-olds, which has turned them into screaming, frightening children with incredibly low social and emotional competence. We must not forget that humans are social beings who live together in units called families, within wider structures called communities. Our ability to get on with each other is profoundly important to personal and social harmony, as well as to our sense of happiness. Quite simply, to ensure our babies, toddlers and preschool age children get the very best start in life there is no question they do not *need* technology at all.

The reality is they will be using it because it is everywhere. and, as I said, there are many potential benefits to be gained. If usage is limited to short amounts of time, with an adult so that the areas of verbal and social interaction are still happening — and the children are still getting all their physical movement, endless hours of play with other children, and being spoken to and read to every single day — then the negative impacts of technology will be limited. Remember the first years of life are when we download so much information and knowledge, which shapes who we become. Children who are unable to communicate well verbally and play well with other children will struggle through school and life. There is plenty of time for technology after children turn five. They will not be behind or disadvantaged in any way; indeed research would indicate they will be in front emotionally, socially and developmentally.

Keep in mind two key things when making decisions with technology: how much movement are my children getting every day; and is the usage no more than 20% of their waking hours? These are great guideposts to what is healthy or otherwise for children under five years of age. Once they have reached all their developmental markers that require movement and real experiences, the influence of technology may be less inhibiting.

Signs that screen time may be getting out of balance include:

- tantrums when the child is unable to have technology when they want it (remember it's a privilege that needs to be appreciated, not a right)
- inability to play with other children and have fun
- difficulty sleeping
- more meltdowns and tears over small things — may mean overloaded nervous system
- young children being exposed to games that are not age appropriate
- poor conversation skills
- poor self-regulation
- difficulty losing when playing with real people
- disconnection to the outside world
- development of a bad habit of neediness — always needing to have a screen nearby
- posture problems.

Throughout early childhood, I would still suggest you keep your children as active and as connected to 'real life' rather than the 'virtual life' as possible. Adults who continue to play in their adult life — whether it's organised sport, fishing, dancing, golfing, tennis, boating or flying kites — are often more resilient and able to cope with life's challenges. Having an interest that provides joy is important for maintaining personal wellbeing. Children tend to model their parents' behaviours, and having parents who enjoy their life through play is one of the best examples to follow.

Thinking skills, communication strategies and creativity are involved with many board games, and these skills have far-reaching benefits for the developing brain. Research has revealed that the brain does not finish its maturing process until around our early 20s.

The final benefit of play has to do with its healing potential. Children who have been abused or traumatised need play to aid any healing process. In my view, play nurtures the mind, the body, the heart and the soul. It strengthens the imagination and allows real children time to be real — to play as children are biologically wired to do. We need to slow our world down to allow children to play more — and know that this is what they need most to grow healthy, happy, strong and kind.

THE COST OF LACK OF PLAY

> If we hope to groom intelligent, socially skilled and creative thinkers for the global workplace of tomorrow we must return play to its rightful position in children's lives today.
> — Kathryn Hirsch-Pasek, et al., *A Mandate for Playful Learning in Preschool* (2009).

As an author, I am constantly researching best practice in early years and adolescence. It staggers me to see the push down towards formalised learning that is happening across Australia when there is no evidence or research that validates that this can have a positive influence on young children's lives. Indeed, the only evidence I have seen shows the negative effects it has on children. The current emphasis on formalised learning in kindergarten and preschool is something that worries me deeply. This trend has come from the UK and USA, and is partly driven by decision-makers who are unaware of the key developmental stages of early childhood. Our children are not brains sitting on a seat waiting to be tested. They have minds, bodies, hearts and souls and all levels must be nurtured, especially in our early years' centres and classrooms. This is a concern shared by many experts around the world.

> In short, there is no evidence that pressuring children to read at five improves their later reading, and much concern that it is damaging. There is now a call for more rigorous education for young children. This implies additional hours of didactic instruction and testing. What we really need is a more vigorous education that meets young children's needs and prepares them for the 21st century, which is often described as a century of imagination and creativity. The children are ready. Are we?
> — Joan Almon (Co-founder, Alliance for Childhood), *Reading at five: Why?* (2013).

Dr Whitebread is one of the signatories of the UK campaign, "Too much Too soon" against early formalised learning in the UK. He is an expert in the cognitive development of young children and in early childhood education, and his latest report documents the damage that lack of play has on young children — the push down into early childhood of formal schooling at the cost of play is well documented.

> Neuroscientific studies have shown that playful activity leads to synaptic growth, particularly in the frontal cortex, the part of the brain responsible for the uniquely human higher mental functions. In my own area of experimental and developmental psychology, studies have also consistently demonstrated the superior learning

and motivation arising from playful, as opposed to instructional, approaches to learning in children. Pretence play supports children's early development of symbolic representational skills, including those of literacy, more powerfully than direct instruction. Physical, constructional and social play supports children in developing their skills of intellectual and emotional 'self-regulation', skills which have been shown to be crucial in early learning and development. Perhaps most worrying, a number of studies have documented the loss of play opportunities to children over the second half of the 20th century and demonstrated a clear link with increased indicators of stress and mental health problems.

— Source: (http://www.cam.ac.uk/research/discussion/school-starting-age-the-evidence).

In Australia the changes that have come about in the past six years under the former Labor Government have had a disastrous effect on the health and wellbeing of the children of Australia. The unintended negative side effects of NAPLAN and the subsequent posting of school results on the My School website (which, broadly, ranks schools against each other based on test results) has created an insidious pressure to push formal learning down to four and five-year-olds in the pursuit of improved outcomes in numeracy and literacy by Year 3. This is what I hear regularly from parents and other sources:

- Massive increase in suspensions of under 6-year-olds from kindy/prep for inappropriate behaviour (mainly boys)*
- Many examples of repressed and regressed behaviours of 5-6-year-old children — signs of significant distress
- Huge meltdowns in the car after school or at home
- Reluctance to attend preschool/kindy — and within six weeks of starting school
- Significant increase in ADHD (In NSW the number of children taking ADHD medications has increased 133% since 2005)#
- Increase in anxiety and mental health issues in children and adolescents
- Four-year-olds getting homework
- Seven-year-olds with two hours homework a night
- More need for specialised behaviour schools for children who are unable to mix well with other children in mainstream school
- Increases in Autism Spectrum Disorder and these children in classrooms without support
- Early years' educators being directed to teach in ways that are out of alignment with their education and experience as to what is best for young children

- Removal of play from four-five-year-old learning environments both inside and outside
- More inside activity with no movement and little student autonomy
- More depression, self harm in children from age four
- More children needing help from allied health professionals.

*— Sources: *The Courier-Mail* (Chilcott, 2013); *Channel 7* ("Violence in Schools", Today Tonight, May 27th 2013) and *The West Australian* (Hiatt, 2013).
— #Source: Corderoy, 2013.

Erik Jensen, one of the world's leading brain experts in terms of education would argue that unless children are engaged in novel, challenging and meaningful learning that includes physical activity and a degree of coherent complexity — which means there's no boredom or chaos, and there is a healthy level of stress — then it's impossible for the brain to learn, to remember, and to repair and maintain neural circuits.

We are expecting today's young children to learn in brain antagonistic environments. For Indigenous children, for the vast majority of our boys, for children who have English as a second language and for children who have additional needs we are creating environments that make it impossible for them to do well. We must revisit this as setting children up to fail like this has lifelong consequences.

Perhaps this is a contributing reason why the COAG Reform Council report on education, released in October 2013 showed that the gap for Indigenous children and disadvantaged children is growing ever wider under the new system, despite some improvements in 'outcomes' overall (Silby, 2013).

Further, Dr Peter Gray, who has written a book called *Free to Learn* (2013) wrote in a piece for *Aeon* magazine of his concern that lack of play is linked to lack of empathy — which has far-reaching consequences for our society:

> The decline in opportunity to play has also been accompanied by a decline in empathy and a rise in narcissism, both of which have been assessed since the late 1970s with standard questionnaires given to normative samples of college students. Empathy refers to the ability and tendency to see from another person's point of view and experience what that person experiences. Narcissism refers to inflated self-regard, coupled with a lack of concern for others and an inability to connect emotionally with others. A decline of empathy and a rise in narcissism are exactly what we would expect to see in children who have little opportunity to play socially.
> — Peter Gray, "The play deficit", *Aeon* (September 18th 2013).

Now for some good news, I firmly believe many educators and communities are swinging back in their approach to play — from play being ridiculously boring, safe and demonised as benign and unimportant in children's lives, to something that is valued in all its glory, as a profoundly important part of every child's growth and development on every level.

> Powerful evidence supporting this view of the role of play in human functioning has also emerged within recent developmental psychology. Here, recent studies using a range of new research techniques, including neuroscientific and other physiological measures, have shown strong and consistent relationships between children's playfulness and their cognitive and emotional development … We also now have extensive evidence of the inter-relationships between the complexity and sophistication of children's play, particularly their symbolic or pretend play, and their emotional well-being (sometimes assessed through physiological measures of stress) (Bornstein, 2006).
> — Source: Whitebread, 2013.

There is an urgency about this movement because we are losing children to the screen world and this will cause significant developmental delays to children under five if they are doing screen activities instead of physical child-directed activities more than 20% of the time. Play environments that encourage children to move, to explore, to model, to play, to problem solve, to create, to build, to question and have fun will create children who are not only capable to cope with school, they will be more than able to cope with life.

I occasionally share conference podiums with the world's leading play experts and the same shift is happening across the Western world, largely as a response to the increase in mental illness in young children. There is a growing, critical movement around nature play and Richard Louv, in his excellent and thought-provoking book, *Last Child in the Woods*, writes about the incredible possibilities that the natural world offers our children.

> Unlike television, nature does not steal time. It amplifies it. Nature offers healing for the child living in a destructive family or neighbourhood … Nature inspires creativity in a child by demanding visualization and the full use of senses. Given a chance, a child will bring the confusion of the world to the woods, wash it in the creek, turn it over to see what lives on the unseen side of that confusion. Nature can frighten a child, and this fright can serve a purpose. In nature, a child finds freedom, fantasy and privacy; a place distant from the adult world, a separate peace.
> — Louv (2005).

When a child is immersed in play, so much so that they do not notice time go by, they reach a place of incredible significance. Firstly it is a moment of transcendence from the ordinary world. Natural, drug-free, chemical-free transcendence is very healthy for later life. Secondly, that absorption is often a clue in later life about life purpose, what is important to them. For some children the activity can be watching ants, playing nurses or maybe building in the sandpit. It has a soul connection that needs to be honoured, if not treasured. Finally, the silent search for meaning that gives such a deep and profound sense of joy and wellbeing is a human need that is totally normal. It allows a really unforced and spontaneous connection between the inner and outer world to occur. This is pure magic.

BRINGING MORE PLAY INTO YOUR CHILDREN'S LIVES

- Let babies and children direct their own play — everything is interesting!
- Friendship is shaped by very early connectedness, so give your children lots of opportunities to play with cousins, close family friends and other children they see often.
- Exploratory, undirected play is really important as it stimulates the 'seeking mechanism'.
- Unstructured play gives children a sense of early autonomy and of having a sense of control in their world — and is vitally important in shaping children's innate character and personality.
- Cerebellum play — tumbling, spinning, balancing and rolling — enhances the sensory system.
- Absorbed play is magic — never interrupt a child in this state.
- Children need more play in the natural world — they can play more creatively, there is better social cohesion, better problem solving, negotiation skills, and deeper immersion in the play experience.
- Vigorous play helps diffuse excess energy and emotions, and stimulates 'feel good' chemicals in the body.
- Games help build emotional competence like learning to lose, to wait your turn, to concentrate and to finish things.
- The more play the better!
- The more families play together, the better connected, healthier and stronger they are.
- Modelling play and sport when children are young gives them a better chance of being healthy and active in life and also helps avoid obesity.
- Catching and throwing balls with young children helps develop skills that help them achieve well in school.
- 'Rough and tumble' play with Dad in particular is healthy.

An excellent research paper on the topic is, "The Importance of Play" by Dr David Whitebread, et al. University, UK. You can find this online at: (www.importanceofplay.eu).

PUTTING PLAY BACK INTO POLICY FOR KIDS FIVE YEARS AND UNDER

The evidence is in: the erosion of play in kindergarten and preschool can be damaging not only to our children's cognitive and psychological growth and development, it can also hinder their ability to function as social beings — which is still our key biological drive. The rise in aggressive behaviour being exhibited by many younger children, mainly boys, is a sign they are unable to cope with environments with barely any opportunity to play, no fun, little movement and developmentally inappropriate tasks — and we then penalise these children by suspending or expelling them! We are failing them — they are not failing school. Low social competence tend to follow right throughout life and sets children up for mental illness in adolescence and adulthood.

To ensure play is valued and encouraged I believe we need to train parents, teachers and school leaders about the key aspects of exploratory play, competitive and non-competitive play, imaginary play, modelling play, cognitive play, child and adult-directed play, and using play to help develop a love of reading, language, dance, movement and music.

I recently heard from a very competent Australian teacher, who was late to teaching and who has a deep passion for allowing children to engage massively in their learning environments. Her program is based on child-centred learning which includes many hours outside at a farm school, in the rain, climbing trees, growing veggies, building cubbies, playing with sticks, bushwalking and observing regeneration programs, propagation experiments, anything that gets them excited. In her words:

> The first class I taught with this program were with me for two years, pre-primary and Year 1 and when they completed the NAPLAN test the following year they did extremely well. Other teachers constantly feedback to me that the children from my classes are standout students — they have confidence, a broad subject knowledge, they're vibrant, their minds are turned on, they are creative and enthusiastic about learning.

That speaks volumes.

There are many other teachers focused on the same child-centred learning in our existing system and they are nurturing student growth on all levels within the mainstream schooling system. Yet, a teacher at a school two kilometres away can be doing the opposite — setting homework for four-year-olds, expecting children to complete endless hours of worksheets and sitting at their desks. I question why there is such scope for disparity, despite these schools teaching the same curriculum. Basically, it comes down to a lack of understanding about play-based learning, not only in policy, but at the coalface. However, there are many shining examples of best practice.

Award-winning Australian early years' educator Neville Dwyer, the director of the Dorothy Waide Centre for Early Learning in Griffith, NSW, describes what the learning looks like in his centre, in order to meet the five outcomes of the national Early Years Learning Framework:

> There is lots of opportunity for children to engage in meaningful, planned-for play. Within our curriculum planning we intentionally plan for play and actively create opportunities for children to engage and explore play that leads them to discoveries, new skills and new ways of thinking. Our planning model incorporates what children are interested in. This is determined by group brainstorming sessions with the children where they bring in their topics of interest and we explore what they know and what they want to learn about. This means they're engaged from the start in the learning process and how we plan for that. This allows us to then build the conceptual knowledge and skills we know children need to have success in life. Literacy, numeracy, life skills, social skills, science and creativity are all included and this is constantly assessed against the Framework in the developmental milestones to ensure that children are well within the developmental levels of their age group. Some things you won't see in our play are stencils; these are not appropriate to young children and stifle creative thinking. You won't see children sitting at tables during formal lessons or numbers or the alphabet. This is what school does and is best left when children are older, children learn in a far more organic way. Howard Gardner, educational specialist, identified that we all learn in very different ways – some by doing, some by listening, some think in logical ways, some musical, some through movement. Sometimes it's combinations of all these different learning styles. Our job as educators is to facilitate each child's learning style to get the best out of them.

This centre creates standout children who transition easily into school. So much of the learning in this best-practice centre happen outside, in nature where children are deeply engaged in the investigation, adventures and activities that fascinate them. Dwyer shares my passion for adventuresome play that allows children to engage in activities with levels of risk so they can learn to be great risk managers and risk takers later in life. For more information about adventuresome play for children, seek out Dwyer's excellent booklet, *Everyday learning about being adventurous* at: (www.earlychildhoodaustralia.org).

I am hoping you now have a greater understanding of why movement is so important in babies', toddlers' and children's lives. Passivity is the new enemy! Please ensure that you do all you can to ensure your children have lots of fun, plenty of laughter and play, especially in the early years. It helps them build physical fitness, as well as psychological wellbeing and their capacity for self-regulation, which is so important in learning and integrating into social environments like schools. Please become a champion for your children and tell other people that physical movement and play is incredibly important on so many levels.

> If we love our children and want them to thrive, we must allow them more time and opportunity to play, not less. Yet policymakers and powerful philanthropists are continuing to push us in the opposite direction – toward more schooling, more testing, more adult direction of children, and less opportunity for free play.
> — Dr Peter Gray, *Free to Learn* (2013).

TOP TIPS

* Movement right from the start, in utero, is how our children grow best.
* Movement helps create healthy brain integration and supports the functioning of the nervous system.
* Avoid things that stop your children moving naturally.
* Encourage play every single day of your child's life.
* Create a playful house where imaginary play is very welcome.
* Model healthy physical activity in your own daily life.
* Massive amounts of play are what make our kids happy, healthy, kind and smart.
* No amount of screen time can replace the learning that comes from interaction with real human beings who love us.
* Music combined with movement is hugely beneficial for the developing brain.
* Unstructured, free play in nature has positive impacts on children's development, on all levels.

Friedrich Frobel saw play as the most spiritual activity in which a child could engage:

> The child who has restricted opportunities for play is like a fruit tree which is planted in a small pot and therefore cannot bear good fruit.

> WHAT I WISH I HAD KNOWN... "TO BE INVOLVED IN THEIR LIVES ... TO LISTEN TO AND BE GENUINELY INTERESTED IN THEIR STORIES ABOUT THEIR DAYS AND THEIR FRIENDS AND THEIR PROBLEMS — AS SILLY AS THEY MAY SEEM TO US THESE ISSUES ARE HUGE TO KIDS AND THEY LOOK TO US FOR GUIDANCE IN EVEN THE SMALLEST SITUATION. HELP THEM LEARN TO BE GOOD PEOPLE, AND LEAD BY EXAMPLE. LISTENING IS A GOOD START." — Chontelle

6th Thing

GORGEOUS GIRLS AND BEAUTIFUL BOYS

PRECIOUS

In all the world there is nothing more precious
than the birth of a child.
They are a living symbol of the love
shared between their parents.
They are our future.
They are a continuance of ourselves...
They are innocents who trust without question.
They bring joy with a smile
and sadness with a tear.
They give a sense of meaning and
purpose to our lives...
They teach us to extend
our capacity to love others...
They teach us to be tolerant,
and yet for all they do for us,
all they ask in return is to be loved.
— Source unknown.

We live in a politically correct world where we tiptoe around topics that might cause controversy and upset people. While I am mindful of being as respectful as I can, I come from a place of common sense in a world of complexity and often that gives rise to healthy debate.

I want to kick this chapter off by reflecting a bit on gender and brain differences because this has been an area of much debate of late.

Many factors come into play when influencing gender such as biology, culture, genetics, environment and society. A lot of what I'm talking about in this chapter will be considered gender stereotypical, and that is because there are so many, many factors at play that inform how we view boys and girls and how we behave within in our gender identities.

In this chapter, I sometimes refer to boys' and girls' brains. There is much debate in the neuroscientific community about whether observed differences between men and women's brain structures, or the way in which they function, actually influence the way they behave. It's interesting to note too that more and more research is emerging that indicates that often boys and girls behave or perform in particular ways because that this is what is expected of them — this isn't necessarily a conscious decision or something that's 'hard-wired' into their brains (Fine, 2011).

It is useful for us to be aware that any or all of these factors may be influential on our children's behaviours because science cannot tell us for certain. As University of New South Wales Research Fellow, Amy Reichelt wrote in an opinion piece for Australia's *The Conversation* website:

> Whether the observed functional differences in male and female brains are innate or a consequence of experience remains difficult to determine. The social phenomenon of gender significantly impacts on the experiences individuals encounter through development and on a daily basis.
>
> It is important in scientific research to avoid neurosexism — jumping to gender stereotypes as conclusions to explain observations. This can lead to misunderstanding and over-selling of discoveries and observations in neuroscience.
>
> But no studies currently exist that have looked and [sic] gender differences in brain structure in a human population that hasn't been gender socialised (Reichelt, 2014).

Frankly, I think if we don't at least seek first to identify and understand what our general societal beliefs about boys and girls are and what possible biological factors might be at play, then we cannot work towards parenting our children equitably and creating more harmony in our families and our world.

Researcher Cordelia Fine writes of the way genes and biology influence us in her book, *Delusions of Gender* (2011):

> When it comes to genes, you get what you get. But gene activity is another story: genes switch on and off depending on what else is going on. Our environment, our behaviour, our thinking, can all change what genes are expressed. And thinking, learning, sensing can all change neural structure directly. As Bruce Wexler has argued, one important implication of this neuroplasticity is that we're not locked into the obsolete hardware of our ancestors. Genes don't determine our brains (or our bodies), but they do constrain them. The developmental possibilities for an individual are neither infinitely malleable nor solely in the hands of the environment. But the insight that thinking, behaviour and experiences change the brain, directly, or through changes in genetic activity, seems to strip the word 'hardwiring' of much useful meaning. As neurophysiologist Ruth Bleier put to two decades ago, we should "view biology as potential, as capacity and not as static entity. Biology itself is socially influenced and defined; it changes and develops in interaction with and response to our minds and environment, as our behaviours do. Biology can be said to define possibilities but not determine them; it is never irrelevant but it is also not determinant (Fine, 2011).

Every child matters

When we are talking about gender it is important to recognise that boys and girls (and intersex people) are equally fabulous and they absolutely have more similarities than differences. However, there is no denying that babies are born with a few key different body parts and that makes boys and girls different on some level. There are also certain predispositions and hormonal tendencies that come into play. Add to that the type of nurturing children receive, the environment in which they are raised, the expectations we have of them, and the unseen influences of the society around them — this is how we shape who our boys and girls become.

So many times after a parent seminar, I have had a parent who has children of both genders come up to me and say they wish they had known that there was such scope for inconsistency between boys' and girls' early development, physicality and emotional vulnerability. I have seen mums breathe big sighs of relief when they have heard information that reassured them that their five-year-old son was probably acting very typically for a boy his age — something they did not realise when comparing him to his three-year-old sister who was counting to 20, speaking in full sentences, colouring within the lines and able to sit calmly for much longer. Both boys and girls display some typical gendered strengths and challenges as they grow older and this chapter is written simply to build understanding, to get you thinking about how you see your children and to give possible solutions to challenging moments you may have in your home.

Every single child is born unique and different and gender is only one aspect of that uniqueness. You might notice I have a heavy focus on boys in this chapter and that is because I have become a boy champion simply to improve the outcomes for boys both in the early years and in our high schools. Also in life, boys are more likely than girls to be diagnosed with ADHD, fail or drop out of school, go to prison, die at work, suicide, have a car accident and more. Even academically, where boys traditionally prevailed, girls are outperforming boys in many areas (which is great for girls by the way!). I am also the mother of four adult sons so raising boys has clearly been something I've had experience in. If girls were struggling at the same levels, I would be a girl champion.

Rosalind Wiseman, the author of *Queen Bees and Wannabes* — the book which the Hollywood film *Mean Girls* was based on — writes that she feels parents of girls get a lot of support and resources, and that the world is well aware of "Girl World" issues.

In her book about boys, *Ringleaders and Sidekicks* (2013), she writes about how she feels our society lets boys down to some extent:

> While we still have a lot more to do ... girls have a general understanding that the complicated, mixed-message culture we live in not only gives them terrible messages about their sexuality and self-worth but also includes empowering messages that support them as they come into their full, authentic potential. We don't do any of this for boys. We don't collectively challenge boy culture.
> (Wiseman, 2013).

As you read this chapter, be open-minded that this is not intended to put boys or girls in boxes — it's important to take from this book what resonates for YOUR child. As I've said, gender identity is not fixed and we are more 'soft wired' than 'hard wired' into having more 'masculine' or 'feminine' traits. You may very well have a girl who has a lot of masculine tendencies and vice versa. I was very much that kind of girl and who knows whether that comes down to hormones during pregnancy, how I was nurtured in the first couple of years of my life, or how I was conditioned to feel — I fit so many of the characteristics of being a typical boy rather than a typical girl. Nevertheless, I love both girls and boys and only want the best for every child ever born.

GORGEOUS GIRLS

> Girls develop more quickly than boys especially in brain abilities. The oestrogen their body creates while still in the womb actually increases the rate of brain growth and they are many weeks ahead of boys at birth. The difference increases in the first five or six years.
> — Steve Biddulph, *Raising Girls* (2013).

Technically, every embryo starts off female and sometime in the first 12 weeks of life, the massive flooding of hormones stimulates the embryo to either stay female or become male. Fascinating information to start with…

I was a high school teacher for almost 17 years in co-ed schools and what I generally noticed most about girls, compared to boys, in my classrooms were the following:

- They could follow instructions better.
- Their concentration span was longer.
- They sat on their seats a lot more.
- They tended to remember details better.
- They needed less reminding about assessment dates.
- They thrived in group situations better than most boys.
- They came to class expecting to work.
- They had better organisational skills.
- They seldom needed to fart or burp in public.
- They spoke more quietly than boys.
- They tended to be more punctual to class than boys.

Given that I was teaching adolescent students — complete with swirling hormones and poorly functioning brains who were just beginning their sexual awakening — the above characteristics tended to happen in classrooms with students aged from 12 to 18. It seems there are potentially some reasons for these differences that I will explore when I am looking at boys in the latter part of this chapter. However it is important to realise that it is in earlier development, where girls seem to 'take off' quicker than boys.

> Girls think they are cleverer, more successful and hard working than boys from as young as four, according to a recent study. This is frightening news and is due to inappropriate learning and teaching strategies allied to lower expectations which results in a self-fulfilling prophecy.
> — Neil Farmer, *Getting it Right for Boys* (2012).

The ABC TV program, *Catlyst*, ran a story called "Mean Girls" in 2011, where they replicated experiments done in the US exploring the differences in the way that girls and boys tended to play. The experiments were supervised by developmental psychologist, Dr Marc de Rosnay from the University of Sydney and the program showed footage of two different scenarios.

In the first scenario, the children were sent in to play with a large castle in the centre of the room. When the boys went in, they all took up a position immediately and began playing with the castle, imagining it as a zoo. When the girls went in, they began talking and after six minutes, they were still talking. After 12 minutes, they were still talking and at 18 minutes they had finally worked out the rules of the game. At 20 minutes they began playing the game. This need to sort out the rules and to plan for how the play will unfold is more predominant in girls. So if you ever have a moment when your son and daughter go off to have a play and about 10 minutes later there is a scream because your son has hit your daughter because she is still working out the rules to the game and he just wants to play, you may have a new understanding of what is really going on.

In the second scenario, they placed a large, attractive stuffed toy in the middle of the room and sent three boys into the room to play. One boy picked up the stuffed toy, another boy tugged it out of his hands as did the third boy, and then they threw the stuffed toy away and began to play a game that had nothing to do with the toy. When the same scenario was presented to three girls and one of the girls picked up the highly desirable toy, it was instantly noticeable how different the dynamics were. Within a few moments, the two girls who did not have the toy turned their backs on the other girl, sat down and began playing their own game. De Rosnay's observations on the girls' use of ostracism to get what they wanted reflected some evolutionary explanations:

"[The girls' move] is sneaky and it depends on the power of social relationships, much more than the boys' strategy. Without a colleague, the girl who doesn't have the resource is a bit powerless. As soon as she can gang up on the girl who has the toy, then she's got power ... The boys have a higher risk strategy. They have a lower chance of propagating and they need to take higher risks in order to assert their dominance in the group."

This moment of social exclusion may be a sign that these four-year-old girls were capable of recognising how to manipulate a situation emotionally in their interactions with other children, rather than physically. When you add their tendency to have superior verbal skills it is no wonder that young girls around the age of 3 ½ can be quite skilful at emotionally manipulating their parents by using guilt. Some studies have also suggested that girls are able to tell lies much earlier than boys because telling lies requires a relatively high level of emotional savvy (Bronson and Merryman, 2009).

> ...One study found that when 18-month-old boys and girls were shown pictures of a doll and a vehicle, for example, most of the girls opted for the doll, while the majority of the boys chose the vehicle. And while 18 months is old enough to have been influenced by stereotyped gifts, research suggests that many of the differences we see are evident from birth, and may even be hardwired. And that's just the tip of the iceberg when it comes to gender research.
>
> — Anita Sethi, a research scientist at the Child and Family Policy Center at New York University (www.parenting.com), (date unknown).

It seems that no matter how hard we try to encourage our children to be gender non-specific, most seem to just follow their own pathways. Indeed there has been a lot of research into the possibility that our girls and boys are hardwired before birth to be different and as I said in the introduction to this chapter, it is controversial, and probably not as simple as that.

Apparently around six to 12 weeks into gestation the fetus gets marinated in hormones; with the male fetus being drowned in mainly testosterone and the female fetus with oestrogen and a small amount of testosterone. Essentially this is where we become a girl or a boy. After birth the unique play of the neurotransmitters in the brain appear to be different for boys and girls, with boys tending to produce naturally less serotonin and definitely less oxytocin which have been linked by some researchers to feelings of wellbeing and human bondedness. The presence of oxytocin and the absence of testosterone may be one reason why our girls are commonly less impulsive physically and why they use communication to try to ensure empathy and social cohesion in their interactions with others. This means that girls may potentially have a tendency for emotional stability and regulation more so than boys, which of course makes learning a far more predictable outcome for young girls than for young boys.

> A girl's parents are lucky; female babies are tougher and more robust than boys. We can only speculate about all the factors that contribute to this imbalance but we can say that cortisol – the stress hormone – and testosterone which boys build up, heighten the vulnerability of the immune system in male infants.
>
> — Gisela Preuschoff, *Raising Girls* (2006).

One of the most interesting challenges you may have with your 3 to 4-year-old daughter, given that she can typically be verbally confident, emotionally savvy enough to manipulate and have strength of character to demand what she wants — all fabulous attributes that she probably has developed much earlier than boys the same age — could be her pester power and that can be really hard work. She may try many different tactics to wear you down and it seems she also knows how much fuel you have in your own emotional tank before she starts demanding. How can that happen so young? I can remember watching girls "doing their mums' heads in" at playgroup, quite often feeling grateful that my boys never even bothered to try that at that young age. It is so important early on with your daughter (and indeed your sons who might exhibit this behaviour) to ensure that you have a calm, firm yet reasonable, "No!" I once worked with a mum who had an incredibly strong rooster daughter and she took to practising saying no in front of the mirror so that she could be convincing when her daughter was on the warpath.

I recently had a conversation with a very experienced early years' educator about the differences she found most often among the girls and boys in her centres. She said that over the years she has noticed that girls were becoming much more savvy in their ability to get what they want from the adults and the children in their lives. She noticed how beautifully girls could play Mum off against Dad with the classic "divide and conquer strategy". She also noticed that mums particularly rewarded their girls for being well-behaved, doing what they are told and being compliant. This might sound innocent and something to strive for but it can have a dark side to it. Children who have been encouraged to be compliant and not to question what the grownups in their world are requesting are much more at risk of being groomed and manipulated by paedophiles and sexual deviants. So next time your daughter is throwing an enormous tantrum when she doesn't want to do something you want her to do, I want you to keep this information in mind.

Another thing I noticed when taking care of my friends' daughters was the endless chatting that took place. Girls seem to love talking more than boys and being close by while they are chatting. There were times that I found this challenging because I wasn't used to the intensity of non-stop talking in my house. Certainly, this is something that I also observed as a teacher, that girls were more likely than boys to talk a lot, particularly about their feelings which boys don't seem to be encouraged to do in our culture. Just as an aside, the other thing that I found sometimes a bit startling was the screaming and squealing — girls appear to enjoy that more than boys too. I guess that means my boys did better at grunting and mumbling and it is probably what you are used to that governs your comfort.

Although there are obviously some significant biologically determined differences before babies are born — and some experts believe that at birth female babies are already four to six weeks ahead of boys developmentally — it is really what happens after birth that contributes to the differences between boys and girls in the early years.

These differences are strengthened or weakened depending on the behaviours of their significant carers and any environment in which they find themselves.

Apparently in one study people were faced with a group of infants clothed in yellow jumpsuits and they could not tell whether they were boys or girls. As soon as they learnt what sex a child was, it was noted that they reacted quite differently to the girls from the boys. They also labelled the children's emotions differently (i.e. seeing *anger* in an expression when they think the baby is a boy and *fear* when they think the baby is a girl). This social conditioning has a huge influence on the gender divide and making negative assumptions based on gender can have a significant effect on how a child grows. In some studies it's been noted that parents are more tender in the care of their baby girls then their baby boys. Maybe this is an unintentional influence of the widespread misapprehension that men need to be toughened up or that maybe boys are not even sensitive in the first place. This is so wrong.

> US psychologist, David C Geary investigated how girls and boys go about solving tasks and discovered that boys see exercises pictorially or as images whereas girls respond better to material presented in spoken or written form. He recommended teachers and parents of boys represent verbally formulated tasks, graphically, and they were successful in this.
> — Preuschoff (2006).

According to Steve Biddulph, the second six months of human life are profoundly important for us as social animals because it is when we begin to learn our people skills. This is partly because the areas of the brain that help to govern this capacity for social interaction grow around this time. Biddulph writes that girl babies appear to have more aptitude and awareness of social connection; this is a natural strength of girls however, it still must be nurtured and strengthened. Given that boys are often delayed in their development this might be a critical window if you have a baby boy, where you invest even more time and energy to ensuring he builds his emotional and social capacity to interact with other people present in his life. As our little girls grow towards their kindy and preschool years, friends are not just important, "they are the oxygen they breathe," according to Biddulph (2013). Girls tend to have more significant highs and lows in their friendships (often perceived by us as 'dramas') and I'm sure you have witnessed many tears over very tiny things that can take hours to work through with girls. With boys it is more common that they can have a fight with a friend and be best mates again within an hour.

The sexualisation of girls

One of the biggest challenges in raising girls today is the sexualisation of our girls that is happening at younger and younger ages. When we have companies that target little girls with inappropriate clothes like padded bras and g-strings for four-year-olds, high heels for children, midriff tops and micro shorts, it makes me both angry and sad. When I see little girls dancing to raunchy songs I also feel angry and sad. Biddulph expresses his concern about toxic media and I support him totally. When children watch TV it is not for entertainment like it is for us adults — it is how they learn what is *normal behaviour*. I worry about the little girls who I've heard watch *Home and Away* every night of the week and then talk about it for their show and tell sessions at kindergarten. Elsewhere in this book I have written about the concerns around children's TV so I won't repeat that here. However, we must look at the messages all media is projecting to our children. We know that our girls are struggling because of the increasing numbers of adolescent girls who are self-harming, struggling with anorexia or depression, or who are endlessly seeking ways to look thinner, sexy or more beautiful for the all-powerful selfie! Helping our girls grow into being happy, healthy and confident beings starts almost from the moment you give birth. You are the people who can choose the media that comes into your house. You are the people who can choose who you surround your beautiful daughter with. You are the one who buys the gifts and clothes. Now, more than ever, the responsibility is on you to be mindful of the need to protect your emerging little girl on her journey to womanhood.

There have been significant concerns about the increasing meanness that is appearing in girl culture. Maggie Hamilton explores this in her book, *What's Happening to our Girls?* (2008), and I've already mentioned Biddulph's, *Raising Girls* and Wiseman's, *Queen Bees and Wannabes*.

> ... Girls who are deeply stressed by the pressure to conform to a highly competitive and insecure world begin to operate in survival mode, constantly anxious and hyper-vigilant. When they have grown up too fast, and don't get enough love at home and are constantly on the edge, then there is no place for empathy or kindness. Sadly for many of them, they have never experienced it themselves.
> — Biddulph (2013).

Several years ago I had a conversation with a mum who expressed her concern about what was happening with her five-year-old daughter's circle of friends. She said that they had become quite bitchy towards girls in her preschool class who did not wear the 'right' clothes that these girls deemed to be in fashion. What really distressed this mum was that when her daughter went to a birthday party for one of these girls, she was laughed at and technically socially excluded because she was not wearing a full face of make-up. Apparently these girls had make-up bags with complete sets of everything, not a 'play' make-up kit, but actual adult make-up. This mum was at a loss as to how to manage the situation. She was lucky because she was notified that the school boundaries had changed and that she now needed to send her daughter to a different school. At the new school none of the girls were into fashion or make-up and she was instantly a much happier and less stressed little girl. Sad but true.

Of course, playing dress-ups and pretending to be grown-ups is still a healthy activity for young girls and boys. When little girls wear bras they are meant to require stuffing them with tissues or oranges, and when they wear high heels they are meant to stagger around because they don't really fit. This is what 'pretending' to be grown-up is all about. Playing with Mum's left over make-up is also quite normal. The message our girls get when these activities and items are custom made for them, however, is that growing up is to happen as soon as possible to ensure your happiness. Indeed in much of my work with troubled teenage girls this seems to be at the core of their misery. They did not have enough time being little girls, rather they were just being little girls pretending to be grown-up girls who need to look sexy. This insidious and debilitating pressure begins so early in our girls' lives. It means parents need to constantly monitor their daughter's relationships with other girls, what TV programs she is watching, what apps and games she is playing online and then, before you know it, the social media monster.

> **WILMA WALLABY**
> "A girl needs a safe circle of wise women right throughout her life to keep her safe and happy."

> Why are girls as young as five years old concerned about their looks and addicted to shopping? Why are they having sex and binge-drinking so young, responding to chat-room predators, and bullying their peers via email and text messages? Why are depression, cutting and eating disorders on the rise, and why, with so much choice, do so many just want to marry young and have babies? In a few short years our girls have become vulnerable – not just teen girls, but also young girls and baby girls. They are being forced to grow up faster than ever before. What a twelve12-year-old girl experienced at seven is not what a seven-year-old girl is now struggling with. Many of the guidelines we offer girls no longer apply, or are contradicted.
> — Maggie Hamilton, *What's Happening with our Girls?* (2008).

During my research for this book I heard about some studies that were investigating the increase in violence amongst adolescent girls. It used to be that when violent and aggressive acts took place they would most likely be committed by a boy — statistically it was a one in four chance that it was a girl.

These studies suggest it is now 50% likely to be a girl. Police have also noticed that girls who are aggressive plan out much more carefully and will often return to continue the aggression if they are not happy with the outcome. Most boys' aggressive and violent incidents were found to be the result of a spontaneous conflict that flared up suddenly. One expert believes there is a link between these violent adolescent girls and a gap in their normal girlhood journey. When girls pretend to be mummys and play with dolls and prams they are actually building empathetic pathways in their brain. This expert believes that the girls she has worked with never had these experiences and so in a way they were hardwired to be hard, mean and unable to resolve conflict in non-combative ways. Another expert believes the increase in violence in our girls is because they are really angry at the way that girls and women are portrayed and treated — and they are fighting back at an unloving and uncaring world.

It can be really helpful if you can create a network of like-minded parents who are raising daughters so that collectively you can help each other protect your precious girls from the sick and hideous aspects of the modern world. If they are surrounded by good people who model healthy ways of living and make healthy relationship choices, then this will be their template for adult life. Keep informed and then share information that will help. Our strong intentions, when combined with right action, creates reality and we are not powerless to create a positive life experience for our daughters. If we follow the wisdom of ancient kinship cultures, we would we creating safe women's circles especially to guide our girls on the journey to womanhood.

> Never let popular culture steal your daughter from you. Teach her the centrality of family, the importance of humility and the rewards of helping others. Teach her to look beyond herself.
>
> — Meg Meeker, *Strong Fathers Strong Daughters* (2006).

Without causing any more concern and trepidation I need to remind you that you can still raise girls to be awesome, fabulous women. Some tips to help:

- Let her be a little girl for as long as possible.
- Create moments of deep honest communication.
- Allow her to be really heard.
- Be welcoming of her friends.
- Build her resilience and life skills so she is capable.
- Be supportive of her choices (most of the time!).
- Model respectful attitudes to women.
- Be a healthy, functioning adult and celebrate your body.
- Have a close, warm relationship to Dad as well as Mum.
- Allow your home to be a sanctuary from the world.

> Alongside the many issues our girls currently face, there are a wealth of opportunities. It is our job to help our girls recognise these opportunities and give them the confidence and resources they need to lead lives that are even richer and fuller than our own and to find solutions to problems we can but dream of.
> — Hamilton (2008).

BEAUTIFUL BOYS

> Men's mental health issues play out at a high level right across society. Statistics of suicide, premature death, accidents, violence, crime and addiction are dominated by men. Then there's the domino effect. Men who have been victims themselves tend to hurt others in the form of physical and sexual violence, other crimes and antisocial behaviour, marriage breakdowns, alcohol and drug abuse and moral bankruptcy.
> — Georgina Barker, *'Lost Boys'*, Scoop, (Vol 65, Spring 2013).

Let me start this section about boys by repeating that girls and boys have more in common than they have differences, however it is the differences that cause parents' great confusion. As a proud mother of four sons, I was a little mystified after the birth of my youngest son at the incredibly sad responses I received from other parents. I'm sure some of them wanted to send me bereavement cards. Sometimes their responses were, "Oh no — you poor thing". I observed carefully what happened to the mothers of girls only and the response was clearly very different. Having more than two boys appeared to be a pathway that deserved sympathy and solicited a well-meaning and yet patronising expression of impending doom!

> Forget that old poem about snips and snails and puppy dog tails, says Sharon O'Donnell, a mom of three boys and the author of **House of Testosterone**. "Somehow it's been changed to boys being made of 'fights, farts, and video games,' and sometimes I'm not sure how much more I can take!"
> — Paula Spencer, *'Boys vs Girls: Who's Harder to Raise'* (www.parenting.com), (date unknown).

I have become a champion for boys in our homes and schools because with more understanding we may transform attitudes like these to celebrate boys. We may also improve the scary statistics of underachievement at school, increasing school suspensions from inappropriate and aggressive behaviour, accidents and deaths due to poor decision-making, and massive increases in abuse of alcohol and drugs alongside random senseless violence on our streets.

Anyone who has a girl and boy in their family or teaches in a co-ed school will likely observe many significant differences between boy and girl behaviour, thinking and how they see the world, and the brain may or may not have an influence on this, as I said in the introduction. Michael Gurian, author of *The Wonder of Boys* (1996) and *The Good Son* (1999), writes that the amygdala — the primary aggression centre in the brain — is larger in males than females and this could be linked to creating more aggression in males. When this is combined with massive surges of testosterone, it may give us a clue as to why boys seem more wired to like risky behaviour and 'warrior' behaviour. The effect of the neurotransmitter vasopressin has in boys, also been linked to bring out tendencies in some towards territoriality, competition and persistence. The biggest challenge we have in parenting boys is to work with these tendencies so that they can learn how to channel them in healthy and positive ways.

> "I think parents use 'which is harder?' [to parent, boys or girls?] as an expression of whatever our frustration is at the moment," says Family therapist Michael Gurian, author of Nurture the Nature. "Boys and girls are each harder in different ways." Every child is an individual, of course. His or her innate personality helps shape how life unfolds. Environment (including us, the nurturers) plays a role, too: "There are differences in how we handle boys and girls right from birth," says David Stein, Ph.D., a professor of psychology at Virginia State University in Petersburg. "We tend to talk more softly to girls and throw boys in the air."
>
> But it's also true that each gender's brain, and growth, unfolds at a different rate, influencing behavior. Leonard Sax, M.D., author of **Boys Adrift**, believes parents raise girls and boys differently because girls and boys are so different from birth – their brains aren't wired the same way.
>
> So, can we finally answer the great parenting debate over which sex is more challenging to raise? Much depends on what you're looking at, and when.
> — Spencer, 'Boys vs Girls: Who's Harder to Raise'
> (www.parenting.com), (date unknown).

Possibly, too, boys may be influenced by something deep within the genomes on the DNA where our instinctual and biological drives from the caveman days still exist. These are then tempered by the social and cultural influences of the environments in which boys find themselves. As you read this, be mindful too that some of these traits will apply to your strong-willed daughter at times and some things will simply not fit your son. Just take the insights as possibilities to better understand a parenting issue or conflict in the moment, or even better to find a solution.

Boys tend to have:

1. Lack of language skills
2. Less emotional development
3. Physically "unjoined" up and emotions expressed through action.
— Farmer (2012).

In early childhood research boys have been known to be around six to 12, even 18 months behind girls — and I meet many a mum who's concerned about how her three-and a-half-year-old daughter is running rings around her five-year-old son. This same boy by around eight tends to catch up if he is not forced to do things that he's developmentally unable to do, nor has he had repeated struggling experiences. Repeated failure creates mindsets like, "I am dumb. I am stupid". It is very difficult to change these once they are entrenched and they can become self-fulfilling prophecies; sad but true. This is where my concerns about the push down of formalised learning into the early years starts. Biddulph in his excellent updated edition of his bestselling book, *Raising Boys* (2013), argues that we need to seriously consider allowing boys to start school later than five — boys who struggle at five continue to struggle throughout school. He writes:

> Boys should stay back a year. For all kids, boys and girls, the calendar is a terrible way of deciding who should start school. Kids vary so much and with a once-a-year intake some will always be young for their year. New studies from the UK show that kids who are young for their age actually do worse in school right through. It's important to treat each child as an individual case and to think about each not in terms of 'how old?' but rather 'how ready?' In boys' cases, the answer is often, not yet.
> — Steve Biddulph, *Raising Boys* (2013).

From my own years of experience and research into the literature around boys, I would add these following differences (warning, broad generalisations ahead!).

Boys:

- **Prefer to do** — If you think for a moment what tends to happen if a man buys a flat pack from Ikea or Bunnings, he will tend to start building it without reading the instructions. The same goes for when we're out driving and we become lost. Our beloved males dread stopping to ask for directions thinking that very soon their actions will lead to the desired result. This may be due to their more superior spatial skills (think women and road maps?) and also their passion to be independent and to have the freedom for autonomous action?

- **Hear less, up to 70% less than girls.** — Apparently boys' capacity to hear, especially long-winded explanations and directions, is significantly different to how girls hear. Have you ever noticed that girls can often listen to what you're saying while they are talking as well. Please remember that if a boy is busy doing a puzzle, building Lego or watching TV he is likely to completely immersed in that singular activity and he will not hear a word you say. Try to make sure he you have his attention — especially eye contact — before you make your request.

- **Get 'information overload'** — Boys tend to struggle with too many requests at one time or quite simply too many words spoken at the one time. You may often see a glazed look on their faces, because they can't remember any of the requests because of an information overload. Try to ask boys to do one thing at a time and then ask them to do another thing. Often single words with clear non-verbal messages like waving hands and arms can get better results, like, "David — shoes (pause and point to shoes) into bag (point to bag), now, please (big smile or wink)".

- **Have shorter attention spans** — Boys' attention spans appear to be shorter if the activity they are doing no longer deserves their attention or they do not think it is worthwhile. New research suggests this maybe to do with boys processing dopamine differently from girls — as soon as the dopamine level drops, boys will start moving in order to build the level back up again. Boredom to boys is akin to failing or losing and that is why sometimes a young lad who is watching TV might also be jumping up and down on the couch.

- **Need greater stimulation** — Boys need to be sure that the activity they are about to participate in is worthwhile, interesting and something they want to do. Girls tend to be much more amenable to starting things without necessarily having a high level of interest.

Boys learn by doing – and often do not see the risk until after the event – boys are more compulsive, non-cautious, eager and liable to take risks. Girls on the other hand are more controlled, logical and analytical.
— Farmer (2012)

A mum recently shared a funny moment with her son after she had been to one of my seminars and had changed her communication style to better suit her boy. They were having a quiet cuddle when her little lad looked up at her and said, "I love you Mummy". She replied that she loved him too. They sat for awhile longer and the mum thought she could use this moment to say more — so she told her son she was proud of the way he was playing with his sister, and how he was doing well at preschool and … and … when her son interrupted her by saying, "Mummy, ssshhhhhh — no talking!" She knew she had stepped into invading his quiet space and yet it was so hard to resist!

Emotional vulnerability

Partly due to the inner struggle between hormones, brain chemicals, social conditioning and the pressure for boys to appear powerful and successful often at any cost, boys struggle emotionally on many levels. There is a mistaken perception that boys and men don't feel emotions as much as women — they do. They just process them and often communicate them very differently. It seems that boys need more time to be able to work out what big ugly feelings are really all about, whereas girls tend to move from experiencing the emotion to interpreting the emotion much quicker. When boys feel emotionally vulnerable they tend to have a default setting that takes them straight through to anger, which is a very acceptable warrior emotion but often not acceptable in everyday settings.

Sadness becomes anger.

Fear becomes anger.

Feeling misunderstood becomes anger.

Feeling rejected becomes anger.

Feeling ignored,

Feeling disrespected and invalidated,

Feeling dumb becomes anger.

Uncertainty becomes anger.

Forgetfulness becomes anger.

Frustration becomes anger.

Disorganisation becomes anger.

Feeling unloved becomes anger.

Grief can come out as anger

The stronger a boy feels emotionally connected to his adult allies, the safer his emotional world becomes and the better his behaviour will be. It is a bit sad that due to the inner warrior in our boys they often make more mistakes, break more things, forget more things and are often the ones who bear the brunt of our discipline much more often than most girls. Indeed in a controversial stand, Biddulph believes:

...That a boy should be cared for by his parents or a close family relative (apart from occasional trusted babysitter) until about age three. He argues that group care does not really suit a boy's nature and that little boys are more at risk of experiencing:

1. **Increased misbehaviour**
2. **Increased anxiety that can impair development**
3. **Weakened relationship with key caregivers.**

Essentially, Biddulph maintains that boys are more emotionally vulnerable than girls and when they feel threatened by poor attachment or lack of deep emotional bonding, they can become emotionally shut down. Many early years' educators talk about the sad/angry boy syndrome when a small boy who feels abandoned and anxious will quickly convert that into hitting or aggressive behaviour. I have found this to be the case both personally and professionally and encourage parents to keep this in the back of their minds when choosing child care for their sons. Smaller groups of children, like in family day care settings, seem to help boys in their separation from their parents. I have also seen similar behaviour in boys who have been sent away from home to boarding school — often they struggle with deep grief and a strong sense of being abandoned. This is not for all boys of course — and with some honest communication these transitions can be made easier. Gradual separations with flexibility also really help sensitive boys and girls adjust to change and can save a lot of heartache in the long run. What is definitely to be avoided is the 'toughen up' stance of last century and the use of sarcasm and shame-based language, which can have lifelong painful, negative consequences.

> For the older children in the study, both mothers and fathers reported higher rates of hostile parenting practices towards boys and were less confident in parenting them, compared with girls.
> — Farmer (2012).

In the coming weeks I would like you to be mindful to watch in large social situations how adults speak to girls and boys. The unconscious conditioning that somehow boys are tougher than girls is still playing out in the way we communicate to them. Trust me, most girls are emotionally way stronger than most boys and we really need to give our boys the time and the tools to feel and express how they are feeling.

Boys as 'warriors'

The instinctual/programmed drive of boys to be competitive has been a part of boyhood since time began. Evolutionary psychologists argue that we are wired to continue the primary patterns of our ancestors. So imagine that your little boy who wants to play very competitively, often roughly and very physically is practising to become a mammoth hunter or a deer hunter as his ancient ancestors would have done. This is why boys need a boyhood not just a childhood because those experiences I have just outlined help them to become good warriors rather than dickheads.

Before I go any further I want to clarify that when I write about a 'good warrior' in today's context, I am not suggesting that we need to nurture in our boys into a single-minded, beast-hunting thug. To me, a mature warrior man treats himself and others with respect, strives to become a better person, is not frightened to show love and other emotions. He is a man who owns life's vulnerable moments with courage, who laughs often — sometimes until he cries — and who accepts everyone he meets equally and with integrity. A true warrior is not someone equated with violence, but rather strength; and that includes strength of spirit, mind and heart, not fist. However, this process of maturation naturally takes time, and nurturing.

> **WILMA WALLABY**
> "Make time to really 'hear' your boy — both what he is saying and what he is not saying."

It seems that a boy's natural impulsiveness could be rooted in his biology. Boys tend to have lower levels of serotonin, the calming neurotransmitter, and thus their heightened state could mean it is more difficult for them to manage impulses. Combine this with the possible influence of hormones and observed brain differences mentioned before and we can appreciate the tendency for our boys to be incredibly physically active, competitive, risk-taking and seeking experiences to define their emerging manhood.

Boys definitely benefit from structure with clear rules and boundaries, but not too many. With strong emotional support and bonding, boys can grow into men who are able to manage the uniquely special qualities of being a man.

As a mother of sons I planned to keep my boys away from toy guns and swords thinking that would prevent them from becoming aggressive and violent. They were not very old when they began making them out of sticks, Lego, bananas … anything really. I realised that all of my friends' sons were doing the same thing. This then gave us an opportunity to help them learn safe ways of being. It did not take me long to realise that the soft plastic swords I could buy were probably safer than the sticks they were using. Being adventuresome with a passion for exploration with freedom was something I came to understand and appreciate quite early in my parenting journey.

The competitive hunger that many of our boys have, comes from this warrior drive within them. Allowing boys to play freely in nature not only builds their capacity to be risk-takers, it also helps to discharge excess energy. Having complete freedom away from adults is not only good for them mentally it seems to build them spiritually as well. It also gives weary mums a great opportunity to have a quiet cuppa on the couch while the boys play outside. The longer boys sit still, even if they are engaged in an activity with a screen, the more excess energy they are building that will need to be discharged. Sometimes this excess energy can suddenly pour out as irrational, aggressive play, often towards siblings.

One of the best pieces of advice I can give you as a parent of sons is to find physical activities and pursuits that they really enjoy and keep them doing these as often as possible. One of my rooster lads took up competitive swimming when he was around eight and from the very first week he began training for two hours a day, five days a week. I noticed our whole home was a calmer place to be.

Rooster boys will have a stronger warrior drive than lamb boys when they are younger. However with increasing confidence, lamb boys can often end up being much braver than their rooster brothers. It is really important to ensure that your boys get plenty of warrior play in the real world rather than just on screens. Even though they can learn strategy playing simulated games, they will not pick up the emotional and social cues that will help them on their journey to manhood.

Playing team sports is an excellent opportunity for little boys to be warriors in a real world. Learning how to be a team player is an especially important life skill for boys, who have a tendency to want to be the best at any cost. This will curb any selfish and narcissistic tendencies that can happen with boys who are roosters in their temperament.

More About Growing Good Warriors

In today's world much of the early warrior development that traditionally occurred in boyhood — and which was guided by appropriately timed rites of passage — is now taking place in adolescence with bigger bodies, higher levels of testosterone, a malfunctioning brain and much bigger, more lethal risky play. In some early years' centres in Australia hero play has been banned. This means that young kids are not allowed to pretend to be superheroes rescuing people from baddies — because they might jump off something too high. In making this seemingly harmless rule, we negate a developmentally important part of the early warrior mindset — how to be a good warrior who helps good to conquer evil. The same goes for early gun and sword play with young boys — we fear it might turn them into psychopaths but it may just help them one day find the strength to stand up and speak for someone who is defenceless against a bully.

Wiseman (2013) has an interesting take on superheroes, specifically Batman, which I'll mention here. She says when little boys watch films/TV shows depicting Batman, they see before them a stoic, strong, silent, man who's face never depicts emotion. Essentially, she suggests Batman has taught boys to suppress their emotions and put others' needs before their own. It's sad but true of our culture's expectations of boys … Batman isn't the only one projecting this message. However, it is also a great teachable moment for parents who might be sitting on the couch next to their little ones, to talk about why Batman is the way he is and to discuss how he might be feeling. I wonder if poor Batman had many friends when he was a little guy.

Boy warriors need lots of help in building emotional and social competencies to learn how to play with and get on with other children. Play is the very best way to build these competencies in our boys and for more information on that, please read the chapter on MOVEMENT AND PLAY. If you have a boy who is notoriously terrible at losing anything, may I suggest playing endless games of noughts and crosses or any other quick game that allows him to lose often. This will help him get better at losing.

Many boy warriors need lots of help to cope with disappointment and failure. Because they are wired to be winners they are also wired to see failure as a really bad thing. Helping our boys have emotional buoyancy around moments of failure is incredibly important. When a boy has broken a window accidentally he will already be beating himself up inside, so if he is confronted with a punitive or insensitive approach to the problem, he will cover up his sense of vulnerability by becoming really angry.

Boys need the following:

- **Boys like to explore the natural world in a much more physical way than girls.**
- **They need to investigate how things work.**
- **They need balls to kick, things to climb and to pit themselves against a challenge.**
- **They need structure and boundaries.**
- **They need goals and coaching in how to persist.**
- **They need a safe environment and a zero tolerance attitude towards ridicule.**

— Ian Grant, *Growing Great Boys* (2008).

When boys are struggling with emotional vulnerability they will do one of two things. They will come out fighting — acting out their emotions through angry outbursts or with irrational behaviours towards other children and their parents. Other boys who struggle with the stress of feeling overwhelmed emotionally simply withdraw and seek isolation. One of the key things to always remember with boys is that:

Any time there is a significant change in a boy's behaviour he is usually struggling with something in his world that is overloading his nervous system and troubling his mind. While he is struggling he may not be sure what it is that's causing the sense of overwhelm and distress. I have worked with boys who become very aggressive suddenly and the apparent trigger was a disaster that happened in another part of the world that they saw on TV. I repeat my previous plea to parents of boys — keep building loving connections with them, like the love bridges discussed earlier in the book, because this makes them feel very secure in their world and reduces the inner turmoil which can happen because they are not as emotionally competent as our girls at dealing with challenge.

> Their mask, or defence strategy, is to wear their anger outwardly, as they feel like a volcano building up for an eruption inside them. They are seeking love, appreciation and validation even though they are being so hard to love!
> — Maggie Hamilton, *What's Happening to our Boys?* (2010).

Something has gone wrong in the world of our boys but what has changed in the last 30 years? We seem to have stolen boyhood in the name of a sanitised, politically correct gender-friendly bland childhood.

Gurian (1996) believes that the invisible drive at the biological core of manhood is the pursuit to prove self-worth. No one can give a man his self-worth — he has to give this to himself. To find this place, boys and men seek external ways to demonstrate potency, victory and independence, and this is what helps shape their search for meaning and purpose in life from a very early age. This is the warrior unfolding from within. Boys seem to be generally competitive, active and constantly in search of moments to prove their worth and value.

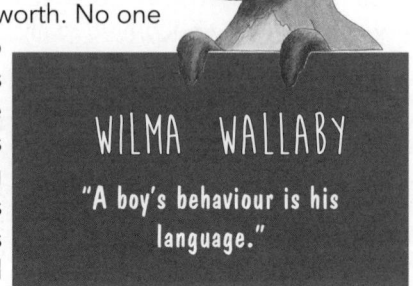

WILMA WALLABY

"A boy's behaviour is his language."

In days gone by, as in my father's generation, boys had the freedom to roam, unsupervised on adventures that allowed them to be massively engaged in pursuits that allowed them to learn and grow using life's greatest teacher — experience. It was not unusual for boys to ride their bikes up to 10 km to go fishing by themselves or with a group of other lads. Nowadays these same boys would be driven by their parents to go fishing and an adult would probably be present for the whole experience. Our modern-day phobia that our world is unsafe is creating an environment where boys are finding it more and more difficult to find that place of self-worth through external moments of potency and success, and this may be contributing to creating a generation of frustrated and angry young men.

I might add that our girls are also missing out massively thanks to this phobia, and as I noted before, female aggression is on the rise, according to statistics — they too can benefit hugely from engaging in warrior activities.

The changes in our playgrounds over the last 20 years are another example of emasculating boyhood (and indeed childhood!) as the opportunities for adventure and risk-taking have been minimised and sanitised. I spoke about this extensively in the chapter on MOVEMENT AND PLAY. We removed the monkey bars, the seesaws and the maypoles which were all wonderful opportunities to stretch oneself, hurt oneself when a poor decision was made and learn how to play well with other children. Conquering the monkey bars took persistence, commitment and enormous amounts of effort and this will never happen by playing a game on an iPad. When a boy was smacked in the chin by the wooden seesaw he learned that he had made a poor choice and he certainly never blamed the seesaw. When he was dropped on his bottom when the person at the other end of the seesaw jumped off unexpectedly, yes it hurt. From that moment of pain he knew that he needed to keep an eye on the person at the other end just in case they looked like they were about to jump off. We call that "healthy risk management". Boys particularly need to learn what happens when they make poor choices in the pursuit of conquering the world. Modern-day warriors need to become accountable for their own actions before they hit the party scenes of late adolescence. We need to celebrate the bruises, the occasional stitches and the rare broken arm because boys learn deeply from real experience and seldom learn from lectures (especially from well-meaning mums).

One profoundly important lesson for every child, but particularly our little warriors and warrior princesses, is that every choice you make will have a consequence. This means that you need to become accountable for the choices you make and if you hurt anyone else or you damage property, you will then need to take responsibility to make the right.

Helping boys with conflict

1. **Help them know what went wrong.**
2. **Help them to make it right.**
3. **Then forgive and forget.**
4. **Acknowledge the valuable learning experience — growth and awareness.**

If you can help boys with these simple steps from an early age they will learn how to cope with the mistakes, the failures and the many times that they will make poor choices. This will teach them how to be good warriors who will one day become good men. It is really important to validate boys' feelings for them when things go wrong because this is emotional coaching, which can help them right through life. It is so much better for boy to be able to identify the strong feelings he is experiencing, rather than having to default to anger because he is feeling vulnerable and confused.

Given that boys need to know how well they have performed by external measures, it must be exasperating for them playing junior sports in modern Australia with many sporting bodies electing not to keep scores until children are in their teens. Apparently this is so nobody gets upset and because sport is actually about participation. Once again, we steal another form of validation for boys that winning matters. As a mother of four sons I know every boy who plays a team sport where there is no scoring *knows who won*.

In our school system too we have feminised the curriculum in many ways, disadvantaging typical boys. By having cumulative assessment more than tests, many boys are not quite sure how well they are doing. I have seen a boy whose mum was reading his school report, which used the word 'progressing' rather than pass or fail. He had no idea what that meant so how could he work out how much effort or not to put into his schoolwork? Another change in our classrooms has been the shift towards cooperative learning, which means there is more group work. What often happens during group work is that our verbally strong girls tend to dominate group activities and do a lot of directing and organising, which really frustrates boys. Group work can be really effective and helpful with both genders if there are some careful guidelines put in place by the teacher.

When I was teaching, I introduced paired shared conversations in my English classrooms. In these conversations each partner was given a number one or two, and first up, only the number ones could talk and only for a short time of about 1 ½ minutes while the other partner had to be listening, and not interrupting. Then, they would swap over. It was really interesting that the first few times we did the activity many boys were unable to keep talking for a full minute and a half. However, after a few weeks they were well able to do it. A boy came up to me one day and said he couldn't believe how good it felt to know that he was being heard and he wasn't going to be talked over, especially by a girl. This activity is also very good to teach roosters to be good listeners instead of the motor mouths that they often are — often dominating conversations if not, complete classrooms! This exercise is also something that could be easily adapted for home life during family meetings, high-emotion conversations and conflict-resolution situations. Your family could introduce a talking stick or talking teddy or whatever object feels good for you, which one family member holds while they speak. Only the person holding the talking object is allowed to speak and no one else can interrupt. I guarantee everyone in the family will benefit from this exercise, not just the boys!

Boys can tend to demonstrate higher levels of energy than our girls and years ago vigorous play was a very valid and accepted part of the school playground. Not only did it allow kids, especially boys, to discharge excess energy, it was another way where children learnt the code of good play versus bad play. As boys tend to be less efficient at using language to resolve conflict, this is where they used to learn the non-verbal cues that it was time to leave and walk away. Dr Stuart Brown, a world-leading play expert, argues that we all develop an understanding of 'play code' in our childhood only from playing endlessly with other children. Without a play code we can badly misread social situations and interpret a threat incorrectly and without the ability to defuse the situation, this can turn into violence quickly especially with a bellyful of alcohol or other stimulants.

The link between dopamine and attention has been the subject of research for many years. Dopamine is a reward transmitter in the brain. It is created by physical activity, having fun, being creative, problem-solving, learning fascinating new information and having freedom to explore the natural world. Could we be contributing to higher levels of ADHD for our children, especially boys and Indigenous children, by not providing them with enough of these opportunities?

Not surprisingly many boys are really struggling with formalised learning. As one mum wrote:

> **We are going to an OT each week and I have learned to incorporate large amounts of physical activity into my five-year-old son's day to help him concentrate at school. I've met with a teacher to discuss ways to make the classroom situation better for everyone. Interestingly she has found all of the children are better behaved now that she has incorporated extra activities and movement into her class. It is not only my five-year-old who learns best through movement and an active classroom. I wonder how many pre-primary children are struggling with the sit and learn style and are assumed to have a learning disorder or behaviour issue as a result, just as my son did. It seems quite obvious to me that the current 'sit and learn model' is not working.**

As well as the ban on super hero play I mentioned earlier, we are also seeing early years', kindy and prep classes in some places banning tree climbing, outlawing playing chasey and removing the sand pit to be replaced by more mat time, phonics in isolation, more desk work, less free play and homework for four-year-olds. If I was a five-year-old today, I would be angry too.

Many boys' lives tend to be micromanaged, over-supervised and hyper-planned, and there is very little freedom and autonomy. The increasing depression and mental illness of our young lads in adolescence may very well be the canary at the bottom of the coalmine telling our modern world that there is some very deep instinctual drives in our boys that need to be nurtured in a healthy way rather than denied and crushed.

As Michael Gurian explains, the strong drive for external experiences to find self-worth and value is a profound and sacred journey that is the core to a healthy manhood and it starts at a boy's birth. Just the same as we need to be concerned about the negative effects of our modern world on the healthy growth and development of our girls, so too do we need to be concerned about how to help today's boys grow into being good men, and not lost souls incapable of empathy, compassion and moral strength. Again this requires a joint commitment from good women and good men who are committed to the healthy raising of our often vulnerable young boys.

> This core of manhood represents maleness at its best – self-sacrificing, devoted to service, loving, wise and powerful; and at its worst – brutal, shaming, destructive, dangerous.
> — Gurian (1996).

We need to seriously reconsider giving boys back boyhoods and opportunities for authentic growth in the company of good men, or we are going to continue seeing more and more dickhead warriors wreaking havoc in our communities.

The reality is that our boys will grow into men; the type of men they become will be based on the guidance they have received from the significant grown-ups in their lives, and on their experiences in childhood and in life in general. All boys, and men, want to be loved, valued and appreciated, and they want to be in effective, mutually caring relationships. Our home and school experiences shape who we become and boys deserve to be seen as different in some aspects but just as valuable in our schools and we must throw out the toxic shaming discipline techniques of old, and meet boys with new understanding and enthusiasm.

> The most common misconceptions about boys are that things don't matter to them, that their friendships are just about playing and hanging out. But boys have deep relationships. And if they don't have them, they want them – with their peers and with adults they trust.
> — Wiseman (2013).

Friendships do really matter to boys even though it might not seem like it from where adults sit. Because boys often have a less competent emotional awareness and poorer communication skills, sometimes friendships can be difficult for boys. Encouraging a close friendship with a little friend or a cousin as soon as you can is really important. Familiarity and frequency helps boys to develop friendships. Remember they can play in the sandpit for an hour and not exchange a word and still have a fabulous time. In many ways friendships are more to do with spending time and playing together than talking. I have also found that boys transition into preschool and school much better if they have friends who are going to be there as well. Indeed I sometimes suggest later when choosing high schools to choose one were a boy has good friends who will be attending. Maybe it has something to do with our primary need of belonging and that when we have friends we feel safer and less threatened. Long-term friendships support our boy's growth and development on so many levels. Poor friendships or short intermittent friendships seem to cause boys a lot of emotional pain and confusion.

Play, for this reason, is incredibly important to stimulate boy bondedness, and that is another reason why I have concerns with our boys who are now playing mainly with technology, often excessively and on their own. This could be contributing to even poorer levels of emotional competence and the stronger sense of feeling isolated and separate from other children. Interestingly, some research out of Queensland University of Technology in Brisbane, Australia has found that one of the most beneficial ways to play video games is together — playing video games with your children may be beneficial for your relationships.

"Playing video games with others in particular, increases a person's brain activity, improves their social wellbeing and helps them feel more connected with others," according to Dr Daniel Johnson who led the research with a team from the Young and Well CRC (Cooperative Research Centre). Johnson also says it is important to only spend moderate amounts of time playing video games, and that games should be age appropriate, and encourage creativity and cooperation (Haggmann, 2013).

> ## DID YOU KNOW?
> Did you know that a high percentage of the adolescents who commit mass murders, often in US schools, have all felt alienated and have been bullied?

In my counselling experience with boys suffering despair, depression or even ideas of suicide, I find these lads often feel overwhelmed by their emotions.

Emotions are unresolved, running rampant inside them. Many of these boys feel deeply flawed and like a failure; they believe that those closest to them do not love them. This deep sense of alienation and feeling separate came up so often when listening to these troubled lads. They were starving for deep, meaningful connection not only with their parents but also with other significant adults in their life. They often felt completely misunderstood. Many schools still use shaming, sarcasm and strong criticism when dealing with poor behaviour and many boys carry these scars right through life. We must remove the old-boy-code that existed in the 20th century because it is no longer valid; in fact it wasn't valid back then. Because they are socialised to hide their feelings, boys maybe more vulnerable than girls in terms of their inner world and we must change how we discipline boys. An excellent way to help a boy explore an inappropriate way of behaving is to walk him around an oval or up the street as you have a dialogue with him about the incident. The movement will help him to feel safe and it is less confronting and more private than sitting still face-to-face, so he will stay engaged with the communication.

Boys need to have significant adults who 'see them' and accept them. Sometimes it may be a family member, an aunty, uncle or grandfather. Sometimes it may be a school chaplain or a family friend who is trusted to keep confidentiality; or a sporting coach or teacher that a boy believes likes him. Boys need a safe person in their school to act as an adult ally or mentor, who he can trust to help him when he needs help. This is a profound need in today's schools to help boys better cope with our confusing school environment.

In my experience with boys in schools and of course with my own sons, I have discovered that boys need quiet spaces to help sort out their thoughts. I am sure that many parents and teachers overwhelm their boys with too much talk and too many questions! It took me a while to realise that my boys settled better by playing by themselves outside, especially after a full school day.

> Silence is often an excellent way of letting our sons find their own solutions rather than us imposing our own.
> — Ian Lillico, *Boys and Their Schooling* (2000).

Even though most boys are activity-based, they still need time to switch off and recharge their batteries. 'Chilling out' in front of TV or playing on computers are ways that boys do this, 'tuning out' to conversation is another, or day-dreaming. Time spent alone in their bedrooms also works well. Boys often need separation time to adjust from being at school to being in the home environment. School and home are two different battlefields, in a sense, and the armouring needs to change.

Boys value and appreciate quiet spaces to think, and yet they often are the ones making the noise! Just like girls, boys learn best when they feel safe and cared for and are in environments with adults who treat them with kindness and fairness. I believe that boys who learn how to bring more silence and stillness into their lives manage the emotional roller coaster of adolescence better than those who have no idea about how to become quiet and still.

The constant activity and busy-ness of boys may also lead them to create stress-related illnesses in later adulthood. Heightened cortisone levels, from being in a go-go-go state, can create serious problems with anxiety and later fear-based mental health problems. Constant activity can also cause sleep deprivation as winding those bodies and busy heads down for sleep is not easy. The magic of silence and stillness for boys must be taught as well as modelled because it is not a normal activity for most boys. The earlier the better!

Here's an extract from an email I received from a mum after her son started school:

> My son loved his first term; it was a stimulating, exciting new environment with all these new people to talk to. But second term, something changed. He started feeling the pressure and became aware that he was struggling and according to the speech therapist and the OT, he had deficits. When he walks into his kindy class each morning, he starts the day having to write his name and show proper pencil grip. At three he was expected to hold his pencil properly and form the letters of his name. He couldn't and he knew he couldn't. My happy, carefree, confident son started each day in tears, was clingy, experiencing night terrors, would have complete meltdowns over minor things, started exhibiting violent behaviour towards his little sister, was not making friends and did not want to go to school. It broke my heart. I felt like a failure. I'd obviously done the wrong thing in not sitting my child down and teaching how to hold a pencil ... and be a student. My poor kid was so exhausted and he was still just three.

While keeping in mind that many boys are up to six to 18 months behind girls developmentally, in the early years it is important to keep in mind that many boys struggle in the transition to school. Biddulph writes that he believes the majority of boys would benefit from starting school a year behind girls! This is a fantastic illustration of the damaging effects that the push down of formalised learning onto young children is having on our boys who need more novelty, more movement, more adventure and more people who understand and appreciate the unique differences between girls and boys. I have worked with men in very senior positions who at times struggle with a form of 'imposter syndrome.' This means that any moment they are concerned that people will realise that they aren't very smart. When I explore where this idea comes from, it often is traced back to when other students laughed at them when they couldn't read or remember something in preschool or Year 1. Such is the power of painful memories and the way they shape our minds later in life. Negative mindsets set them up for failure on so many levels. We simply need to accept that there are some things that boys tend to do differently from girls that do not support their transition into school. They think differently, they hear differently, they communicate differently, they are highly sensitive, and the list goes on.

The following is part of an email received from a mum that beautifully captures some of the concerns I have around our boys in their transition to school. I have had several similar emails explaining how boys were being sent for professional assessment because their teachers felt there was something wrong with them only to find they are within 'normal range'.

> *My boys were lucky enough to have gone through kindy a few years ago before the compulsory five full-day week went through. At that time, when the suggestion to increase the days was raised, I remember writing an email to the Minister while both my boys were bawling in the background absolutely exhausted from the day. They did NOT cope and I made the decision to brave criticism from the school by insisting they take the Wednesdays off each week to ensure a rest day.*
>
> *Both boys (one of whom is now being extended and the other who was evaluated by the school psych and noted as being very bright and in need of extension) struggled in those early years as they were not developmentally ready to sit at a desk and give up playtime — it took a number of specialists' diagnoses to convince the school that there was nothing 'wrong' with them. Each specialist told us they were just very bright and we even got quizzed as to why we were "wasting specialists time with what was clearly a 'normal' child". The reason was simple. The school needed kids to cope with the new expectations and our boys just weren't ready. Some children did appear to cope admittedly in school, but those parents shared with us how their children melted down as soon as they got home.*
>
> *What are we doing to our kids? How does this sort of policy 'enhance' education or allow our children to thrive? Any education policy should seek to do these things before all others, and the new system fails at these key aspects immensely.*
>
> *As a parent and an educator myself I cannot believe that given ALL the available research and worldwide case studies which show that these ideas are bad practice, that our policy makers are choosing to IGNORE the facts and do the exact opposite. It is our children who pay the price. If this doesn't count as child abuse, what does?*

This piece of correspondence is a perfect illustration of the mismatch between expectations placed on children, and their normal (and highly variable) developmental capabilities.

Please remember that the old-boy-code way of viewing boys — either that "boys will be boys" or that we need to toughen up boys — both need to stop immediately. Indeed in all my research around boys from birth to adulthood, it is their vulnerability that worries me the most. One of the best books to read if you have sons is, *He'll Be OK* by researcher, social advocate and New Zealand's first female prison officer to work in a men's prison Celia Lashlie. This is how she describes her thoughts about boys in adolescence:

> There were moments when their vulnerability washed over me and I was wondering how we actually manage to get so many of them safely through to adulthood...
>
> Their childlike naivety... their dependence on their peers to define their behaviour, their desire to live in the moment and their associated unwillingness to plan, all combine at a time when male hormones are raging through their bodies and the blood appears to be going down rather than up.
>
> — Celia Lashlie, *He'll Be OK* (2005).

When my first son started school he was unable to write his full name and nobody seemed to mind. Nowadays he would have had so many assessments prior to even stepping into that Year 1 classroom and most likely would have been labelled a delayed developer. He gradually settled into the school journey and, as with many boys, he didn't really 'have all his lights on' until around Year 4. In those days there was no serious concern about the gradual settling in of boys in terms of their formal schooling. That lad now has two degrees and works as a very competent professional. I have concerns that we don't allow flexibility for boys who are having difficulty in transition. It seems that with the push down of formal learning, taking a day off a week for a boy is no longer a possibility because he will miss out on something incredibly important. The fact that he will be struggling emotionally, socially and probably cognitively is obviously not anything that is considered worthy of attention. How sad.

Please consider holding your child back from starting school whether it's your son or your daughter if they are obviously socially immature, if they tire easily, have poor self-regulation, have a significant developmental delay or their ability to communicate is weak. There is no rush and no competition and you need to make decisions that suit the unique needs of your child at that time.

Sometimes an understanding of the differences of gender can help us come to a better understanding of our own unique miracle — our child. Be mindful that understanding is not shaped by stereotypes or unhelpful beliefs; they do not help our children to flourish and thrive. Every parent wants the best for their children so with more understanding, more knowledge and more choices we can help our children, especially in the early years, grow in their competence on all levels. There is no greater gift that we can give our children then the gift of a childhood for as long as possible, in as natural and uncontaminated way as possible with as much joy and delight as possible.

TOP TIPS

- There are significant differences in how our girls and boys grow and develop in the early years.
- Girls develop faster and often 18 months ahead of boys by the age of four.
- Girls are much quicker at developing language.
- Girls are often better at listening and remembering than boys.
- Boys and girls tend to communicate in different ways.
- Boys and girls often play differently.
- Both boys and girls need help to build emotional and social competencies.
- Boys enjoy physicality, competition and adventure.
- Boys are often more emotionally vulnerable than girls.
- We need to protect both boys and girls from the negative effects and influences of the modern world.

> **WHAT I WISH I HAD KNOWN** "...How fast 19 wonderful years would go and that I would be a wonderful mother; yes, I would make mistakes and that would be OK because I would love unconditionally, I would be stronger than I thought possible and my beautiful girls would be my greatest teachers." – *Cheryl*

GOOD READS ON BOYS AND GIRLS:

- Steve Biddulph's books
  latest, **The New Manhood; Raising Boys; Raising Girls**
- Maggie Hamilton's books
  What's Happening to Our Girls? Too much, Too Soon. How our kids are overstimulated, oversold and oversexed
  What's Happening to Our Boys? How the new technologies, drugs and alcohol, peer pressure and porn affect our boys
- Bruce Robinson
  Daughters and Their Dads: A book for fathers, adult daughters, husbands and father figures
- Ian Grant
  Growing Great Boys
- Richard Fletcher
  The Dad Factor
- Celia Lashlie
  He'll Be Ok: Growing gorgeous boys into good men
- Neil Farmer
  Getting it Right for Boys
- Kathy Walker
  Parenting Boys
- William S. Pollack
  Real Boys' Voices
- Arne Rubinstein
  The Making of Men: Raising boys to be happy, healthy and successful

7th Thing

EXPECTATIONS, BELIEF SYSTEMS AND MINDSETS

> Children throb with a natural connection. But the slings and arrows of outrageous misfortune start hitting early. Competitive siblings. Tough schools. Harsh media. Dangerous streets. Social injustice. All the noise of modern life. Hunger and pain. Each of these events, every childhood injury, physical and psychological, creates tension in the physical body. The result is that by the time most of us are teenagers we have lost that bubbling, continuous ability to feel life's natural beauty.
> — William Bloom. *The Endorphin Effect* (2001).

Expectations are really interesting things when you think about them. Quite often we don't even know that we consciously have expectations and yet we behave in accordance with them. One of the biggest changes that has occurred in the parenting landscape has been the arrival of parenting magazines and now parenting blogs and websites. I noticed one day when I was in a newsagent how many of these new publications were coming out. I'm quite sure there weren't any when I was breeding. Then I spent some time looking at the cover pictures and it suddenly struck me that these wonderful well-intentioned magazines were probably setting most mummies up to fail. I noticed that all the supposedly 'new mums' on the front cover were very slim and amazingly appeared to have had a full day at the day spa prior to their photo shoot — so relaxed and polished! Not only that, the baby they were holding was "oh so perfect". No wonder so many mums feel like failures.

If we have a baby and we are meeting the needs of that baby around 8 to 10 weeks of age we will probably not look like Miranda Kerr — certainly not without a support team the size of her entourage. There is a good chance we will almost have a mono brow because we haven't had time to pluck our eyebrows, let alone get around to styling the hair on our head. There will be dark rings under our eyes and probably still a reasonably generous floppy tummy. Our hair would probably need some colouring and certainly a trim. And I'm sure the outfit would have some baby's spew somewhere on the front of it. Now if people saw the odd picture of the reality of a new mum on the front of these parenting magazines, maybe expectations would be more realistic.

I remember reading a fabulous article once written by the mother of a boy who was diagnosed with autism. She had written a poem and it captured the expectation that she'd had before she fell pregnant. Simply put, she thought she was *"going on a holiday to Hawaii however, she ended up going on a holiday to Holland"*. In other words, she had expectations of a perfectly healthy, normal baby and when the reality came, she needed to adjust her expectations.

So often our expectations of uncomplicated vaginal deliveries, breastfeeding, healthy babies, full-term pregnancies and tiny sleeping babies can be shattered. As the parenting competition has accelerated, maybe the expectations have also been extended even higher than they ever were before. Recently I heard of a mum-to-be, who at her baby shower celebrated the name she had chosen for her baby with great joy and enthusiasm. Sadly, six weeks later she delivered a stillborn baby. The loss of any baby is tragic and sad beyond all understanding, however I felt so deeply for this mum because her expectations at the time of the baby shower, was that it was a definite. Sadly being pregnant, delivering babies and caring for babies can have tragic outcomes because there is no 'absolute'.

I guess as the statistics and conditions around pregnancy and childbirth have improved in western culture, so too has the sense of certainty around birth for our expectant mums. The BBC TV series, "Call the Midwife", which is based on the true experiences of a midwife in the 1950s showed how fragile the gift of a human life was just five decades ago. Most babies were delivered in homes where poverty was an unwelcome visitor. The doctor only attended when there was an emergency. With the amazing and stunning advances in medicine and science, babies that weigh under 500g and are born at 24 weeks gestation not only have a chance at survival, they can grow up to be very healthy human beings. Maybe this is giving us the false sense of surety that exists in our world today.

There is no question that as humans, it is important we have high, positive expectations however, we need to temper them with realism. Being realistic can help moderate our expectations just a little as we journey on this incredibly unpredictable, uncontrollable journey of being a parent.

Another area of unrealistic expectations that I have witnessed in my work is that of creating a really happy family. I've had mums express a deep sense of disappointment when they have experienced conflict in challenging moments with their children. Because they had experienced unsettling and unpleasant experiences in their own childhoods, they had planned and expected to create (unrealistic) 'perfect' families where there was never a cross word spoken, nor a door slammed. Humans and human behaviour are incredibly unpredictable and when you put young children into the mix, with their undeveloped prefrontal cortex, a lousy night's sleep, a sore tummy or a new tooth about to emerge, there will never be a perfectly happy child in that situation. The overload of the brain chemical cortisol will ensure that they will be unhappy and in need of great comfort from their significant loving big people.

> **WILMA WALLABY**
>
> "Always hold strong, positive expectations for your kids. Help them to dream big because this helps build possibilities and choices that will allow them to become happy, healthy, strong and kind."

As adults too, we all experience moments of not being the best person we can be, especially when we are tired or overwhelmed — and this can result in challenging family moments. Such moments happen in the most stable and loving homes — trust me I have heard this so many times. My best suggestion to you as a parent is to constantly remind yourself that there is no perfect — *no perfect* parent, no perfect child and no perfect family. This is one of the reasons why I talk a lot about the common-sense 80/20 approach to parenting, which I wrote about in the introduction to this book. This allows us to make some mistakes while still striving to do the best we can. Remember every time we make a mistake, we are giving our children a golden opportunity to learn how to be capable and resilient.

> If you're like most parents you worry that you spend too much time trying to get through the day, sometimes the next five minutes, and not enough time in creating experiences that help your child thrive both today in the future. You might even measure yourself against some sort of perfect parent who never struggles to survive who seemingly spends every waking second helping her child thrive.
> — Daniel Siegel and Tina Payne Bryson, *The Whole Brain Child* (2011).

Every individual, child or adult, behaves in accordance with their beliefs, whether these beliefs are conscious or unconscious. Our beliefs are formed by:

- the experiences we have had
- how we have interpreted those experiences
- the values that have been instilled in us by significant adults throughout our lives
- the expectations of significant adults
- perceptions gained from the media
- our culture
- society
- history

In my work as a secondary teacher for over 17 years, there were times when I became really frustrated with students and their parents when I heard the incredibly limiting expectations coming out of their mouths. What really upset me was when I met culturally negative expectations from other teachers, which held back Indigenous students in particular from any hope of academic success. I remember once when I was teaching in a rural town that every time I walked past a certain maths teacher's class, I noticed the same Aboriginal boy sitting outside every lesson. When I was on yard duty one day I had a chat with this boy and learnt that apparently his teacher didn't like Aboriginal students because he thought they were dumb and he didn't want to waste any time on them. Needless to say, I was pretty furious and as a consequence I organised to have this student join my English class. The maths teacher tried to tell me in the staffroom one day not to waste any energy on the boy because "he was dumb and probably illiterate". It took about three weeks before the boy finally put pen to paper and he wrote me a two-page story. His spelling was fine and he could write well, except he had very few punctuations skills. Although he started the story with a capital letter and he finished it with a full stop. By the end of the year he had mastered punctuation and was well on the way to becoming competent in his other subjects.

This was also the experience of the founder of the Stronger Smarter Institute, Dr Chris Sarra, whose vision is "changing the tide of low expectations" for Indigenous students. When Sarra was principal of Cherbourg State School, he had enormous success in boosting attendance rates, and improving results for Indigenous students. At the core of his philosophy is the notion of high expectations. At Cherbourg, he worked with the community, teachers and students to make sure high expectations were entrenched in the school culture. He made sure everyone in the school was committed to believing that these children were 'strong and smart' — the words became the school motto and were emblazoned on the school uniform, inspired a school song, and were the frequent catchcry of all those gathered at assembly. Sarra's work became the foundation of The Stronger Smarter Institute's philosophy and the institute now works with around 350 schools in Australia, urging them to examine the often hidden expectations they have of students and to transform these into positive, encouraging expectations that support children to succeed. You can read more about Sarra's journey in his memoir, *Good Morning, Mr Sarra* (2012).

Like Sarra, being a teacher really showed me that having high expectations of students pays off. I had the opportunity to learn about the power of expectations when I was asked to take an extra student into one of my classes because the previous three teachers were unable to manage him. On the second day he was in my classroom, I asked if he would be kind enough to take the money for a school excursion up to the front office for me. He looked perplexed and confused when I asked him, however he left the room with the money. The students in the room thought I was insane for trusting such a boy. When he returned he came up to my desk and asked, "How come you asked me to take that money up to the office?" I replied that I thought he had a face I could trust. He looked at me very surprised and said, "Trust! Is that what trust feels like? I have never had anybody trust me before!" I never had any problems with that young lad in my classroom and I'm sure it is because I refused to accept the expectations that everybody else had imposed on him. Further, I think I helped shift the expectations that he had of teachers. Such is the power of expectations.

When adults hold negative expectations about students regardless of why, they will hold those students back from achieving well. The Oakfield experiment was conducted by Dr Robert Rosenthal of Harvard University in 1975 when he did a study of 650 students and 18 female teachers. Everyone in the school was told their IQs would be tested at the beginning of the following year and a group of students would be identified as being in the top 20%. This elite group were also told that it was predicted that they would make rapid and superior progress throughout the year. The 'gifted' students did perform superiorly and did demonstrate REAL above-average increases in their IQs over the year... the interesting thing is that this supposed top 20% was chosen **randomly**, not based on real IQ scores! So they were not necessarily the brightest students — they were just led to believe they were, as were the staff who were teaching them.

Rosenthal was then interested to find out whether it was just the teachers' expectations that had created the better outcomes or was it a combination of the teachers' expectations plus the students'. So he did another experiment on rats where students were told that certain rats had been genetically bred to be superior in performance. Two groups were given 30 rats. Group A were told they had the superior stock while Group B had inferior stock. The rats were trained in the same ways, same environments and yet the ones believed to be smarter, "achieved achievement scores far above the supposed unintelligent rats". The rats came from exactly the same gene pool and stock base.

Rosenthal's conclusion was simply that the minds of the experimenters influenced the performance of the rats and the students... positively or negatively. Essentially the same goes for adults whether as parents, teachers, sports coaches or counsellors. Our expectations colour the outcomes and that is why having positive, high, yet realistic expectations is incredibly important on the parenting journey.

In my work with Aboriginal families around Australia I have found that sometimes it is the expectations of the family that is holding back an Aboriginal child's academic performance rather than staff in the school. If the parents had found schooling challenging and difficult then their negative expectations often flow unintentionally onto the children. This means that they don't value education and this can be an inhibitor that keeps children from attending school. Without attending school it is impossible to master numeracy and literacy. I have been really heartened and excited to see significant changes happening in Indigenous communities around Australia where parents are not only bringing their children to school, they are also actively encouraging and participating in the school community. This means that the culturally limiting expectations for Aboriginal children are changing and it is really exciting to see the increasing numbers of Aboriginal students graduating from high school and moving onto tertiary education. The more who graduate, the more who become professionals, the higher the expectations for all Aboriginal children across Australia. A couple of years ago I met an Indigenous surgeon at a conference in Canberra and he very proudly told me that there was now an association for surgeons who were Indigenous. Apparently you need to have a minimum of six people to form an association. He was beaming with pride when he told me.

Sometimes our children with additional needs also meet the same limiting expectations of others who may be holding incorrect perceptions around these children's potential. Just because you have met a child who was on the autistic spectrum and just because you have met a child with ADHD, this does not mean you have met **this child** who may have the same condition. All children need to be seen through the eyes of possibility, not through the blinkered lens of narrow expectations.

Because everything we do is supported by our deep-seated beliefs — patterns of poor parenting and exceptional parenting tend to follow generation after generation. No matter how much we would like to create the perfect journey through our children, it is impossible for us to control and determine destiny. I encourage parents to embrace parenthood by seeing it as a journey whereby they will be given the gift of a miracle of life — a complete unknown — and that they will simply do the best they can to take care of this helpless little being. They will do this with the best intentions of being able to lovingly, gently and patiently meet the needs of their miracle so that one day they can find the spark within their being, that brings them alive and their children can then share that spark with the world, to make our world a better place. The what, the how and everything in between is the shared sacred interaction of human beings. If we have this expectation when we become a parent, we may experience less disappointment when the child we imagined does not manifest. Every single parent wants their child to have wings and roots. If we over-control and over-parent our children we will not allow them to grow wings to fly. However if we don't give them boundaries, guidance and some roots, then there is a really good chance they'll fly off a cliff. Welcome to the ancient parenting dilemma.

> The patterns of behaviour we witness in our childhood become the template of our own way of parenting. How our parents made us feel lingers in us unresolved, becoming the lens through which we interpret our children's behaviour. To some degree we are slaves to our past and our children have a way of bringing this out.
> — Dr Shefali Tsabary, *Out of Control: Why disciplining your child doesn't work and what will* (2014).

What can be really tricky as a parent is that you may make a conscious decision to parent more fairly and more lovingly than your own parents did. And yet out of the blue, after a sleepless night or two you behave exactly the way you wish you never would. Take a breath and forgive yourself — this just shows how powerful our mind is at remembering and modelling significant life experience. So while it is important to have high positive expectations for yourself as a parent when things get tough, rather than beat yourself up, go find some help. I am a product of an aloof, emotionally unavailable mother who had a problem with alcohol and my boys tell me that I have been an awesome mum. I needed to do some work on slaying my inner dragons to ensure I didn't replicate the mothering I had in my childhood. To be honest, doing parenting courses, reading good books and chatting with as many Wilmas as you can shows that you are committed to being the best mum or dad that you can be, and I honour you and love you for being brave enough to seek ways of being better.

> The core belief I encourage adults to value is that every child ever born is born with gifts and talents that are unique to them and they can use these gifts positively to somehow make the world a better place.
> — Maggie Dent

If you were raised in a home where children were treated as though they were unimportant, stupid and annoying, you may have deep-seated beliefs that mean you will respond in ways that reinforce this even, if you don't want to. Studies have shown that the expectations we have for our children have an enormous influence on how well our children perform both at home and school. To really give all children the best opportunity to realise their full potential in life, they need to be surrounded with people who hold positive, realistic expectations and that have the tools to parent in a healthy way most of the time. A new expectation I would like you to take on board comes from Dr Gordon Neufeld (2005):

> 90% of childhood misbehaviour is the result of the developmental journey.

Essentially this means that children's behaviour, when it does not meet our expectations, is not so much wrong or bad it is mainly children being children, with a child's mind and depth of experience. If a child's behaviour is inconvenient to us as an adult, it too is not bad or wrong it is merely a normal part of the developmental journey of growing from child to adult. Next time you're frustrated and angry about your child's behaviour, pause, take a deep breath and see if you can view that behaviour through the eyes of a child.

When they smear their food all over the wall this too does not have to be seen as bad or wrong, but merely as a child using his/her senses to find meaning in their world. When they use your best lipstick to draw you a beautiful picture on the wall — again they are not wrong or bad. Their intention was from a place of love and they were using their seeking mechanism in the way that Mother Nature intended. You'll remember I wrote about the seeking mechanism in THE BOUNTIFUL BRAIN IN INFANCY chapter. The same goes for when a child unravels a toilet roll or maybe two or three, and stuffs them down your toilet to see what might happen. They're not scheming to be bad, naughty or wrong — they are merely using life's greatest teacher, experience, to learn about life. The next time you have a bugger moment like the ones mentioned, pause, and inside your mind reassure yourself that your child is a creative thinker with a passion for life who's using experience as a wonderful teacher. I recommend four steps to manage situations like this to ensure that it doesn't happen again, without using shame or exclusion.

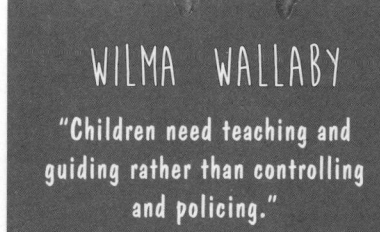

WILMA WALLABY

"Children need teaching and guiding rather than controlling and policing."

1. **Pause and take a deep breath – become present.**
2. **Enthusiastically lean forward to your child and ask, "Did you do that all by yourself?"**
3. **Now let them know why the choice they made was one you would prefer they didn't make again (e.g. "we don't play in the toilet because this is where we do poos and wees and could have germs that will make us sick"; or "we don't write on the walls, we write on paper").**

4. **Finally involve the child in a lengthy clean-up process as that acts as a natural inhibitor or deterrent to avoid doing that experience ever again.**

P.S. Remember this is a moment to share in tears or laughter later with an adult, preferably with a coffee, tea or glass of wine and remind yourself that the experience is a sign that your child has the 'desire to explore', a creative mind and a seeking mechanism which shows they are growing a smart and creative, problem-solving brain.

At the end of my first year of university I took a holiday job as a nanny in Perth for three lovely children who lived in an enormous house in one of the western suburbs. One day I heard vast amounts of giggling and laughter happening upstairs. I finally tracked the children down in their parents' enormous bathroom to find them having huge amounts of fun with the bidet! I had actually never seen a bidet and it took me a few moments to realise what it was used for. Well, the children had the tap on the bidet up high and there was water everywhere. Even though I knew this was incredibly inappropriate behaviour I also saw the funny side and how fascinating it must have been for the children. So even at the age of 18, I was able to see things through the eyes of children rather than just react through the eyes of a grown-up. I certainly made them help me clean up even though it would have been much easier if I had done it on my own. I often wonder if those children remember that moment 40 years ago.

So many times children make enormous messes when they are trying to be helpful or simply have fun — it helps to just pause a little when we come across situations that frustrate and anger us, and tell the critical voice in our head to go and find the guilt monster (also in our head) and go jump off a cliff.

Have you ever had a moment when your child asked for something, maybe a biscuit or more TV time, and you said "No" quickly? Then that began a meltdown or huge argument — cries of, "… but why?" and you may have replied, "Because I said so!"? This is a classic unconscious parenting moment driven by frustration and the 'story' from your own childhood. Next time it happens, pause and acknowledge your child's desire — it's natural to have them after all. Try the acknowledgement-then-why approach: "I know you would like more TV time however we have had the time that is healthy and acceptable in this home. Why do you want more time right now?" Sometimes they may have a good reason for wanting more time, say if we have stopped their TV time before the program they are watching is finished — how annoying would that be for us? Sometimes they may be struggling with knowing what they are meant to be doing next. Essentially taking a couple of moments to hear your child's desires and validating and respecting them can avoid the big ugly feelings that they feel when we demand they meet **our will**.

> The root of the dysfunction we experience as individuals, nations and a world lies in the belief that people need to be controlled – a belief that, no matter which culture or part of the world we come from, pervades our parenting. The need to dominate is what discipline is all about and this domination is responsible for much of the distress that has characterised our species for eons.
> — Tsabary (2014).

Let's challenge this belief about the need to dominate, and replace it with the belief that our job as parents is to teach and guide our children to navigate life by building their awareness as well as an understanding of how to live as social beings in a community. Once they have learnt the lesson from a life experience, and there is a natural consequence, do they still need to be punished? Punishment causes deep resentment when it is about power and not about fairness — more about that in the chapter on why KINDNESS AND FAIRNESS REALLY MATTERS.

One of the best bloggers in our world right now is a lovely lady called Rachel Macy Stafford who wrote the following blog at the end of 2013, which for me really captured the moment we all dread:

> I cherish the notes I receive from my children – whether they are scribbled with a Sharpie on a yellow sticky note or written in perfect penmanship on lined paper. But the Mother's Day poem I received last spring from my first-born daughter left a profound impact.
>
> It was the first line of the poem that caused my breath to catch before warm tears slid down my face.
>
> *The important thing about my mom is ... she's always there for me, even when I get in trouble.*
>
> You see, it hasn't always been this way.
>
> In the midst of my highly distracted life, I started a new practice that was quite different from the way I behaved up until that point. I became a yeller. It wasn't often, but it was extreme – like an overloaded balloon that suddenly pops and makes everyone in earshot startle with fear.
>
> So what was it about my then 3-year-old and 6-year-old children that caused me to lose it? Was it how she insisted on running off to get three more beaded necklaces and her favorite pink sunglasses when we were already late? Was it that she tried to pour her own cereal and dumped the entire box on the kitchen counter? Was it that she dropped and shattered my special glass angel on the hardwood floor after being told not to touch it? Was it that she fought sleep like a prizefighter when I

needed peace and quiet the most? Was it that the two of them fought over ridiculous things like who would be first out of the car or who got the biggest dip of ice cream?

Yes, it was those things – normal mishaps and typical kid issues and attitudes that irritated me to the point of losing control.

That is not an easy sentence to write. Nor is this an easy time in my life to relive because truth be told, I hated myself in those moments. What had become of me that I needed to scream at two precious little people who I loved more than life?

Let me tell you what had become of me.

My distractions.

Excessive phone use, commitment overload, multiple page to-do lists and the pursuit of perfection consumed me. And yelling at the people I loved was a direct result of the loss of control I was feeling in my life.

Inevitably, I had to fall apart somewhere. So I fell apart behind closed doors in the company of the people who meant the most to me.

Until one fateful day.

My older daughter had gotten out a stool and was reaching for something in the pantry when she accidentally dumped an entire bag of rice on the floor. As a million tiny grains pelleted the floor like rain, my child's eyes welled up with tears. And that's when I saw it – the fear in her eyes as she braced herself for her mother's tirade.

She's scared of me, I thought with the most painful realization imaginable. My 6-year-old child is scared of my reaction to her innocent mistake.

With deep sorrow, I realized that was not the mother I wanted my children to grow up with, nor was it how I wanted to live the rest of my life.

— Source: (*www.handsfreemama.com*).

Rachel's Stafford's book, *Hands Free Mama* (2014) explores how she has turned her family and her life around. She is no longer the mum that frightens the children when they make innocent mistakes because they are children. Her writing is beautiful and heartfelt and essentially explores her journey of changing her expectations for herself and her precious children.

MINDSETS

Our mind is constantly creating beliefs from the perceptions that our brain makes from our experiences and the memories of these experiences. These beliefs, when deeply entrenched unconsciously in our mind, become 'mindsets'.

Parents often ask me, "How do I help my child who repeats endlessly 'I am dumb' or 'I am stupid'." This mindset totally influences their behaviour and the choices they make around learning. We used to call it a self-fulfilling prophecy; these negative mindsets are a powerful inhibitor to learning, to growing and to fulfilling one's potential. So when we expect to fail, we fail. If children are shamed around a learning experience this can definitely anchor them in a negative mindset because powerful emotions help anchor memory.

WILMA WALLABY

"When kids can do things for themselves or they master a new skill, it builds their self-esteem — or how they see themselves."

There is some recent research that shows that the future of today's children, of all cultures, relies on building human connectedness, social inclusion and providing environments that allow children to develop healthy and strong. By three and a half most children have developed mindsets that greatly influence their future lives based on the most significant experience that they have had. So what really shapes our future success in life and what can we do about it?

As I mentioned in the chapter on ROOSTERS AND LAMBS, Dr Carol Dweck has explored what influences our potential for success and found that rather than it being about ability, it is more about what people believe about *why they had failed*. If we believe we failed an exam because we are dumb, we limit our future attempts at growing in ability. If we think, "I failed because I didn't understand the question or the task or I didn't work hard enough" that means we can fix that. Dr Dweck says we create flexible or fixed mindsets — the more flexible our mindset, the better our chance of success in school and life.

This is also something that renowned positive psychology researcher Professor Martin Seligman writes about in his book, *The Optimistic Child* (1995) — the notion of whether something is permanent (pessimistic) or temporary (optimistic). Children who talk about their situations as temporary or their qualities as malleable are more optimistic than their pessimistic counterparts who see their state as permanent. For example, saying, "I suck at maths", "I'm not good at school", "I'm not a good friend" or "I'm not sporty" creates a label that sticks. We need to help our children by watching our own language to ensure it's optimistic/flexible, assisting them to reframe situations when we hear them speaking like that and guiding them to understand that life is not a win/lose, pass/fail journey.

> Students for whom performance is paramount want to look smart even if it means not learning a thing in the process. For them each task is a challenge to their self-image — and each setback becomes a personal threat. So they pursue activities at which they are sure they will shine — and avoid the sorts of experiences necessary to grow and flourish. Students with learning goals on the other hand, take necessary risks and don't worry about failure because each mistake is a chance to learn — achievement goal theory.
> — Dr Carol Dweck, *Mindset* (2012).

Dweck has found that children develop mindsets about goodness as well as smartness. Many kids believe they are either good or bad — others think they can get better at being good. What is sad is that often the child who has developmental delays and who struggles in social environments will be the child who will be disciplined the most, nurtured the least and who will create a very negative mindset. Physical punishment and excessive exclusion tends to create children with the mindset that they are bad and it is pointless and hopeless to try to be anything else but bad. Preschoolers with the second mindset (the growth mindset, where they think they can get better at being good) feel ok about themselves after they have messed up and are less judgemental of others. They are also more likely to set things right, and to learn from their mistakes.

This essentially means that how we parent and care for our children in the first three to four years can either help or hinder the mindsets that our children form. If we can, we must encourage children that learning and growing is the main goal of all human experience, rather than performance itself. Children who struggle in the transition to school can also create a mindset about being dumb or useless. This is why we need to teach and guide our children with care, fairness and hope because they can learn well, they can become happy, strong and kind — if the adults who care for them, help them. It helps children to understand that even we adults struggle with transition, and we often make plenty of mistakes before we master something. In my 10 building blocks for resilience, one of the building blocks is self-mastery. This is a really helpful building block to consider if you have a child who has developmental delays. Small experiences of success make it much harder for children to create the negative mindset that they are useless or dumb. The same goes with creating moments of success by riding a bike without training wheels, by jumping off a diving board or by doing up one's shoelaces. Academic knowledge is only one form of learning in a child's life and not every child is wired to be academically brilliant. Harvard professor Howard Gardner famously defined eight multiple intelligences in his book, *Frames of Mind* (1983) and only two of them suit being brilliant at school. Every child will come with a different, innate tendency and it is our job as parents to find what their natural strengths are and build those rather than just focusing on the things they struggle with.

Sadly, and as a consequence of this perceived parenting competition that exists in contemporary culture, there is enormous pressure on our children to be perfect. Unhealthy perfectionism can be just as damaging to children as having the "I am dumb" mindset. Children naturally want to please their parents and they will strive really hard to do that often. They are also incredibly sensitive to the slightest form of criticism and, for some children, the damage from such criticism can mean they give up completely on striving to improve. One of the sad things I have noticed in my visits to early years' centres and when talking to parents is the need for adults to complete children's artwork or craftwork to make it look 'better'. Part of children's development means that the initial efforts will probably look pretty ordinary — that is actually the point. With practice children gradually improve and through their eyes whatever they do is fine. It is only when they see the disappointment in their parents' eyes, that they see that there's anything wrong with their beautiful creation. As a mother of sons, I seldom received a painting because my boys were always in the sandpit. I often hear mums asking their boys, "Did you do me a painting?" Well developmentally doing paintings is something that comes a lot later for most boys so that starts to put pressure on them because they're not as competent as most girls. I suggest you check instead to see if they have sand in their pockets or a splinter in their finger, and then celebrate because they are doing exactly what is developmentally appropriate for them at this moment.

Unhealthy perfectionism can even happen in children under five. Sometimes this is coming driven from within the child and is not a consequence of pressure from the parents. This self-driven need to achieve at a high level is one of those things that simply comes with certain temperaments or personalities, and often it comes with the first-born child. However, this need to do things at a very high level or as perfectly as possible can cause enormous angst, emotional meltdowns and irrationally aggressive behaviour. This is a really good example of how we need to build emotional resilience for some of our children. Not succeeding well enough in their eyes and not being able to do things better than other children is genuinely upsetting for these children. This is where the need to build a flexible mindset is incredibly important and it will take many moments of one-on-one parenting where you help them validate how they feel and how they can manage those big ugly feelings in the future. Remember no one likes to fail but these children with this inner drive to succeed or be perfect will need extra help to build this capacity. One of my lads was like this and in Year One he would bring home his coloured pencils every night to sharpen them so that he didn't have to waste time in class! He is still achievement-driven, highly focused and he has never needed any parental support to achieve success. It can be helpful to get children like this into music, dance or some individual competitive sports like tennis, archery or swimming so they can channel their enormous energy and enthusiasm for perfectionism in a healthy way, outside of school. Sometimes, one of the most supportive things we can say to our children when they are engaged in an activities that could be seen as competitive or performance-based (such as sport or music) is simply, "I love to watch you play."

When we link this perfectionist mindset to excessive praising about how smart a child is, then research shows clearly that this makes learning a highly stressful experience. Some research has even suggested that a perfectionist style of thinking is a "psychological risk factor to stress and anxiety symptoms, as well as for the development of bipolar disorder symptoms" (Corry, et al, 2013). Anxiousness is also an issue for children who are being pushed too soon into formalised learning that they are developmentally unable to do.

> **DID YOU KNOW?**
> Anxiety is the most significant mental health issue in childhood, and yet it frequently goes undetected and untreated. It can begin as early as age two but (as with attention disorders) we see a significant rise when children enter the school system.

With flexible mindsets plus a strong sense that they belong and are accepted, there can be a profound shift in the potential for all our children to shine. This is one of the reasons I encourage parents to allow their children to falter, fall and fail so that they are able to see themselves get back up, recover and keep on moving. Flexible mindsets are also a sign that an individual is not locked in to perceptions or expectations that are fixed and limiting.

RESILIENCE AND WHY IT MATTERS

What is resilience?

In 2007, I was approached by the Office for Children and Youth in Western Australia to work on a project to raise awareness about resilience for families and communities. In my research I found that the latest evidence-based research sat beautifully upon traditional kinship ways of raising children. I subsequently created the 10 building blocks resilience model, which is now used in many centres and communities around Australia as a way to explore how to build resilience in our children so that they can cope with our ever-changing world. Now more than ever children need the 'basics in the early years — and these basics are essential for every child. The first five years prepare our children for school. Research shows that the capacity that children turn up with in the first year of school is the best indicator to how well they will do in school for the rest of their time.

Resilience refers to the ability to successfully manage your life and adapt to change and stressful events in healthy and constructive ways. It is our survivability and ability to 'bounce back' from life's experiences, both those that are advantageous and the really challenging, traumatic ones. Two other helpful definitions of resilience are:

> ... An individual's ability to thrive and fulfil potential despite or perhaps because of stressors or risk factors.
> — Dr James Neill, University of Canberra.

> ... A universal capacity which allows a person, group or community to prevent, minimize or overcome the damaging effects of adversity.
> — The International Resilience Project (2005).

The importance of resilience in today's world

Young people have always needed effective coping skills, however the modern world is particularly challenging. It appears that many of our young people have fewer resources to be able to deal with adversity than in previous generations. Our main concerns today involve the increasing numbers of young people who are aggressive, depressed and suicidal, and who engage maladaptive coping strategies such as substance abuse and antisocial behaviour. Sleep disorders and anxiety problems are also increasingly real concerns for those who work with troubled, unwell children — some as young as two or three years old.

It is essential for parents and carers of children to improve their understanding of resilience and to actively work towards building children's resilience — keeping it in front of mind as an intention. With more understanding, parents can better prepare and protect their children from the damaging effects of an increasingly chaotic and uncertain world, *without overprotecting them*. It is an interesting irony that many parents are creating children with low resilience because they are doing too much for them. I have met four-year-olds who are unable to blow their noses, pull up their pants after being to the toilet or to feed themselves because their loving (and sometimes perfectionist!) mums have been doing it for them.

Today's world is very different from the world in which many parents were raised. The information explosion, technological advances, consumerism and rapid pace of life have created a kind of sickness. The expectation that our youth should be smarter and healthier is not always true. Experts working in research and health sciences are identifying more teenage pregnancies, depression, anxiety disorders, violence, and illicit and social drug use. There is more family disharmony and homelessness; and literacy rates and school successes are also reduced.

The most tragic example of low resilience is suicide, when an individual chooses to end his or her life because they perceive living has become too hard. That is why it is important to raise awareness in communities and homes about how we can build and enrich resilience in today's children and teenagers. It is also crucial to ask for help for yourself or someone else when feeling suicidal. Overwhelmingly, research reinforces how crucial the early years are in developing lifelong resilience.

Building resilience is a vital ingredient in parenting. It is a process that directs our interactions with our children as we strengthen their ability to meet life's challenges and pressures with confidence and perseverance.

> Thirty years of research tells us that resilient people are happier, live longer and are more successful in school and jobs, are happier in relationships and are less likely to suffer depression.
> — Reivich and Shatte (2002); Werner and Smith (2001).

Bonnie Benard was considered by many to be the mother of the concept of building resilience. She worked for many years with children who were at risk. Benard decided that, rather than focusing on what was wrong in these children's lives, she would explore what was working; what was helping them to cope with their very dysfunctional lives. With her innovative vision she identified protective factors. Communities can develop these factors to build resilience, especially in young people. The building blocks model discussed in this book — and which my book, *Real Kids in an Unreal World* (2008), explores in detail — is based on Bonnie Benard's focus on protective factors. This focus allows us to shine a light on the strengths in a child's life rather than focusing on what's wrong. In many ways we 'over-pathologise' children in today's world.

> The number of psychiatric diagnoses for childhood conditions has soared in the last two decades, increasing from about 70 conditions to more than 400. What this means is that "what was once considered within the bounds of normal is now treated as an illness requiring a cure, which more often than not comes in the form of medication".
>
> — Dr George Halasz, psychiatrist, author and speaker

Not only do we tend to focus on what's wrong with our children or what's delayed in their development, we are busy hurrying them up. This model supports the 'slow childhood down' movement that allows real kids time to be kids, instead of being hot-housed and pushed into early adolescence before they have even been able to be healthy kids. It takes lots of time, energy and loving care to raise healthy children, and with awareness it is still very possible in today's unreal world. It all starts in the first five years.

With all the new advances in modern life and more knowledge today's modern world is not producing more resilient children, teenagers or young adults. Indeed those working in both research and the health sciences are finding the reverse happening — more teenage pregnancies, more depression, more anxiety disorders, more violence, more illicit and social drug use, more family disharmony, more homelessness and often lower school success and literacy rates. This is why it is so important to lift the awareness in communities and homes on how we build or enrich resilience in today's children and teenagers. Overwhelmingly, the research validates just how crucial the early years are to developing lifelong resilience.

Some challenging questions

- How do you build the coping skills in your children so that as adults, they successfully manage the continuous change occurring in their world?
- What are some of the most important life skills to teach your child?
- How do you best support a child to grow into who they are 'meant to be', not who you think they 'should be'?
- What attributes provide your child with mental and emotional wellbeing?
- How do you build character and social competence in your child?
- How can parents be mindful of ways to prevent their child attempting suicide — at any age?
- What things can you do as a parent to build your child's capacity to manage and cope, while still allowing the child to have a childhood that is safe and life enhancing?
- What things are really important to include in your child's life that supports them to grow into a person who makes the world a better place?

- What will help your child to be a friendly, cooperative and caring person?
- What can you do to ensure that your child realises his or her full potential in life?
- How do you ensure that your child develops positive values and a healthy sense of self?
- How can you enjoy your parenting journey more?
- How do you do all of the above at the same time as running flat out on the treadmill of work and raising children?

The strongest oak of the forest is not the one that is protected from the storm and hidden from the sun. It's the one that stands in the open where it is compelled to struggle for its existence against the winds and rains and the scorching sun.
— Napoleon Hill (1883-1970).

Characteristics of Resilient People

- Ability to 'bounce back' and 'recover from almost anything'
- Optimistic, flexible thinking skills
- Have a 'where there's a will, there's a way' attitude
- Tendency to see problems as opportunities to learn and grow
- Ability to 'hang in there' or persevere and persist
- A healthy, authentic self-esteem
- Capable of setting clear, realistic and attainable goals
- A healthy social support network
- Seldom dwell on the past or the future
- Well-developed emotional and spiritual competence
- A capacity to persist rather than give up
- Learns from previous challenges and mistakes
- Capacity for detachment
- A well-developed sense of humour
- Meaningful involvement with others or their community
- Treat themselves and others with respect
- Problem-solving and conflict resolution skills
- A healthy sense of being valued and accepted
- Mental stability

— Maggie Dent, *Real Kids in an Unreal World* (2008).

The little things are the big things when children are very young. Most of the important developments are invisible and difficult to measure. Despite the pressure from advertisers and big companies that target parents, the basics that babies, toddlers and older children need are still the same as they've always been.

Fortunately, with the advance of the neurosciences and other research we are now better able to understand what helps create resilience in all of us. There are key elements that strengthen our ability to be resilient, and the more building blocks present in a child's life, the more protective factors will be present later in life. Many of these qualities are hard to measure and quantify, and this makes it difficult for some parents to know just how their child is developing — these building blocks give a universal language that can help parents to know what will matter later in life.

> The active ingredient in the environment that's having an influence on child development is the quality of the relationships that children have with the important people in their lives. That's what it's all about.
> — Shonkoff, (2012).

10 resilience building blocks for children from birth to 12
1. **Positive healthy pregnancy**
2. **Good nutrition**
3. **Safe, nurturing care within the circle of family**
4. **Plenty of play**
5. **Build life skills**
6. **Meaningful involvement with positive adults**
7. **Clear boundaries**
8. **Absence of stress**
9. **Self-mastery**
10. **Strengthen the spirit**

— Dent, (2008).

The components of this model build healthy self-esteem and strengthen children's ability to be resilient. A building block can be strengthened anytime, even in adolescence. These building blocks clearly show the different areas that a parent, school or community can focus on in order to build resilience for life. Any building block will help, and the more the better! The model is a strength-based model that encourages parents and those who care for children to build capacity in our children, one building block at a time. There are several free articles and a colour version of the building blocks model available on my website: (*www.maggiedent.com*).

> Human connectedness is the key to resilience, authentic happiness and a sense of wellbeing. This can only be achieved through the recognition, honouring and nurturing of the human spirit that exists within every child ever born.
> — Maggie Dent, Saving Our Children from Our Chaotic World (2003).

We need to be very mindful of the things that cause challenge in children's lives and we need to protect them in the vulnerable early years. Gradually they will grow braver and stronger, but in their own time. When they are frightened, hurt or sick they especially need our help to soothe them. Knowing that our role as parents is to build our children's competence on all levels so that they can cope with this strange thing called life is important. Our expectations of our role as parent or guardian of our children shapes every single action that we take.

> ...compared to those who feel that being a parent is just another job the more that we feel that our parenting role is a major purpose in our lives, the more likely it is that we will feel satisfied with our lives. We will also experience more positive emotion than those who see the role as a job – so will be happier and more satisfied with life. Importantly we will derive significant meaning from being a parent and will practice better parenting habits.
> — Justin Coulson, *What Your Child Needs from You* (2012).

TOP TIPS

* Expectations shape the way we parent and the choices we make.
* Having high, positive and realistic expectations is really important.
* We can change our expectations to be more realistic.
* The expectations we hold about our children either help or hinder them to grow.
* Belief systems become mindsets.
* Flexible mindsets are best to encourage in our children.
* Resilience really matters.
* Resilience can be built in our children from birth.

WHAT I WISH I HAD KNOWN ... "IT IS HARD WORK TRYING TO BE SUPERWOMAN. DON'T TRY AND DO IT ALL. LISTEN TO YOUR BODY AND CLOSE YOUR MIND TO EXPECTATIONS ... ACCEPT HELP AND SUPPORT, PEOPLE MAY NOT OFFER AGAIN!!! LET KIDS BE KIDS AND ALWAYS LOOK AT WHAT THEY CAN DO NOT WHAT THEY CAN'T DO." - Caroline

8th Thing

KINDNESS AND FAIRNESS REALLY MATTERS

> When a child is not given enough help with his intense lower brain feelings and primitive impulses, his brain may not develop the pathways to enable him to manage stressful situations effectively. The legacy later in life is that he will not develop the higher human capacity for concern, or the ability to reflect on his feelings in a self aware way. Brain scans show that many violent adults are still driven, just like infants, by their ancient rage/fear and defence/attack responses deep in their brain.
> — Margot Sunderland, *The Science of Parenting* (2007).

Happiness can only be achieved with a high level of emotional and social competence. This means that our children need to understand their emotional and social worlds, as well as their cognitive and physical worlds. In the chapter on THE BOUNTIFUL BRAIN IN INFANCY I explored how babies are born with billions of neurons with few connectors in between and that these connectors are only formed from experience. So even though babies are born with some predispositions that come with their DNA, it is essentially the nurturing that they receive after they are born that shapes their capacity to be a social being. In the same chapter I explored the vertical and horizontal integration of the brain and how important healthy integration is in building our children's emotional world. Keep in mind that emotional and social competence and the ability for our children to get on with other people in relationships, schools and workplaces is mainly to do with the brain. Ironically there is new research that suggests that our heart also creates micro-electronic waves that influence our brain and it is this interactive dance that creates the human mind. Hopefully, without getting too involved in the mechanics of all this, this chapter will help you understand how to build the two most important social and emotional capacities — kindness and fairness — in your child before they turn five.

> Academic intelligence has little to do with emotional life. The brightest among us can flounder on the shoals of unbridled passions and unruly impulses; people with high IQs can be stunningly poor pilots of their private lives.
> – Daniel Goleman, *Emotional Intelligence* (1996).

Goleman's book was an important milestone for me. Finally, a well-recognised and respected expert was exploring the emotional domain of us mere mortals. *Emotional Intelligence* is still seen as ground-breaking work and the knowledge Goleman brought into prominence has changed many things: the direction of people's thinking, education and consciousness. Howard Gardner probably coined the actual term 'emotional intelligence' in his book, *Frames of Mind*, in 1993.

So what are the key characteristics of emotional intelligence?

EMOTIONAL INTELLIGENCE

- Knowing your emotions and feeling states
- Managing your emotions
- Motivating yourself
- Having an ability to accurately empathise with others
- Handling relationships
- Having the ability to not be swamped by your emotions
- Believing in your ability to cope
- Persisting in the face of frustration
- Having impulse control
- Being able to delay gratification
- Feeling hopefulness

These are the characteristics of healthy emotional intelligence. A person with emotional competency would, for example, have patience in queues, resolve conflict without verbal or physical abuse, be capable of loving caring relationships, overcome setbacks quicker than others and enjoy being themselves most of the time. Emotional illiteracy and social incompetence starts early in life. Indeed, there is a high incidence of transference of low patterns of coping and resilience that is quite easy to discern by three or four years of age. When these patterns continue long-term the damaging effects can be very debilitating in later childhood, adolescence and adulthood. If you have a two-year-old at the moment who is throwing tantrums please do not think it is too late to build their emotional competence. Throwing tantrums or expressing non-compliance is actually a very important part of developing your own sense of self and it is often a sign of the frustration that toddlers feel when they are unable to express themselves. Given the limited development of their upstairs brain, this is quite normal. Of course that does not refer to the upstairs tantrum that I mentioned earlier in the book where a child knowingly chooses to throw a tantrum — remember the only rule there is, 'never negotiate with a terrorist'.

Daniel Siegel, in his excellent book *Mindsight* (2010), explores emotionally mature behaviour as being a function of the middle portion of the prefrontal cortex and it has the ability to coordinate these essential skills:

- regulating our body
- attuning to others
- balancing emotions
- being flexible in our responses
- soothing fear
- creating empathy
- having insight
- having moral awareness
- using intuition

While many of these attributes are similar to the characteristics Goleman describes, the ability to soothe fear, create empathy, and to have insight and moral awareness, seem to suggest a deeper level of emotional and social capacity can be nurtured in our children. Siegel argues that due to the plasticity of the human brain, we can build emotional and social awareness and competence at any time in life. However the best time to build this awareness is in the first years.

One example that shows what can happen when such social and emotional awareness is not built in the early years comes from a study of some of the American teenagers who committed mass murders in their school environments in the early 1990s. The studies showed that what these teenagers had in common was that when they were children, they had little opportunity to play and were largely ignored by those around them. They felt ignored, even ridiculed, in their homes and at school, and the emotional wounding and scars these experiences left on their sense of self-value was obviously deep. Compounded with a fascination for violent movies, guns and weapons, there was little possibility of a positive solution to any conflict occurring in their lives.

The final straw that breaks emotional restraint is often small and relatively insignificant. A traumatised young person may perceive that the only solution to their continued pain is to take drastic revenge for every painful experience they have ever been through.

Gayle Gregory, an educational consultant from Ontario, Canada, found the following characteristics present in the US student murderers in the early 1990s. They were:

- ignored as children
- deprived of play activity as children
- of average age 13 to 14 years
- typically very bright
- usually overweight or underweight
- in a poor relationship with Dad or he was absent
- unable to lose
- short on emotional breaks (this is knowing when to stop BEFORE things go too far)
- members of groups with like interests, for example gangs without fear
- driven to exert power with violence
- often over-users of TV, video or computer media, with a preference for violence.

Similar results have been identified in adult murderers, especially being ignored as children, experiencing a lack of play and having an absence of positive involvement or participation in family life. This shows how incredibly important healthy attachment is in the first years of life in shaping how we become, especially in adolescence.

> Our world is becoming increasingly violent. Social and political initiatives everywhere are seeking to counteract escalating trends of suicide, aggression, crime, destruction of the environment and ultimately war.
> — James W Prescott PhD, "How Culture Shapes the Developing Brain and the Future of Humanity", *Touch the Future* (Spring 2002).

In a way, our world has become a nastier and crueller place, especially in the virtual world of the Internet, incredibly violent films and pornography, which has become more prolific than I'm sure anyone ever imagined. The Internet has given trolls the opportunity to lash out at other people in incredibly nasty and vitriolic ways while remaining anonymous. Unfortunately these badly behaving individuals are creating a skewed vision of society. The world is full of good people who live caring and responsible lives in their communities. It just seems the ones with the biggest voices are those who lack the emotional and social competence to be decent people.

RAISING A MORAL CHILD

In infancy we learn what is valued, especially by our significant carers, and from this interaction we develop our own invisible value system, which shapes who we decide we are. Values are a very significant determiner of behaviour as well. Values are:

- Principles
- Standards
- Morals
- Ethics
- Ideals.

Values give us a guiding framework by which to live our lives; they are ideals that guide our behaviour and decisions, and help us distinguish between right and wrong. They also allow us to live in communities with a degree of civility if they are based on positive values, however the reverse can occur as well. The emerging values in children help to shape the choices they make that impact on their behaviour. All of these influence self-esteem. The way we are parented shapes our values and beliefs significantly, however there are other influences.

Traditional indigenous peoples historically focussed on the development of the character within their children as well as their physical growth. Responsibility for the development of a child was shared by everyone in the tribe. Physical growth was important and children were taught new skills when they were ready. They were also taught the gifts of the spirit and the heart. These are what we loosely term values, virtues, social manners and etiquette. Without these templates young people are often unaware of how to behave and what to value; they basically live a life that is codeless. The Elders ensured that the young were guided by stories, songs and by being shown how to live, often. So much of character is based on respect, fairness and kindness — isn't that interesting?

WILMA WALLABY

"Building character in our kids matters — this gives them a code to live by that helps them through life like a map. This helps us not to get lost on our journey through life."

According to John Medina, you can create moral maturity in most children. There are many definitions for what moral means and probably the most accepted one is that "morality is a set of value-laden behaviours embraced by our cultural group whose main function is to guide social behaviour". This seems to have a lot to do with the strong evolutionary requirements of social cooperation, a concept that Charles Darwin promoted alongside competition in his famous work. According to research, it seems moral awareness is a universal characteristic that is innate to a degree and of course then conditioned by our social and cultural influences.

> A willingness to make the right choices — and to withstand pressure to make the wrong ones, even in the absence of incredible threats or the presence of a reward — is the goal of moral development. Which means your parenting objective is to get your child to pay attention to and align himself with his innate sense of right and wrong. This takes time. A lot of time.
> — — John Medina, *Brain Rules for Baby* (2014). http://brainrules.net/

Families who raise moral kids tend to follow fairly predictable behaviours around rules and discipline, which tend to follow three very simple steps.

1. **Clear consistent rules and rewards**
2. **Swift punishment or deterrent consequences**
3. **Explaining the rules.**

Even though Medina has used the word 'punishment' or 'deterrent consequences' — which sounds like a parent needs to be a controlling adult, forcing children to submit to adult will — he means that children need some guidance or a gentle deterrent to prevent repeating behaviour that is unhelpful or unwanted. This can include showing a child what behaviour is fairer or kinder — rather than right or wrong — or getting the child to clean up a mess they have made. This helps them learn that they are accountable for their actions and at the same time, we respect their childlike need to experience the world as a *child* — think: putting every Band-Aid in the house on at once, smearing Dad's shaving cream on the floor or painting the cat.

If a child bites another child, picking them up quietly and walking away from the wounded child is a form of deterrent consequence that you can follow up with a calm conversation about treating others fairly, i.e. emphasising the rules of your home.

> Our children didn't come into the world to be our puppets. They came here to struggle, fumble, thrive and enjoy — a journey for which they need our encouragement. When we

> unconsciously insert ourselves into an equation in which we don't belong, we interfere with our children's ability to engage with life's ebb and flow in an organic manner. We impede the natural development of their resourcefulness.
> — Dr Shefali Tsabary, *Out of Control* (2014).

Social shifts have meant we now have less time with our children — less time to nurture their emotional growth and to instil the firm boundaries needed for the healthy growth of a moral and social code that help in later life. The reality of less time also influences a child's perception of feeling connected, being valued and of belonging. Inconsistencies are often to be found between child care as practised in the family home, in child care facilities and at school. These differences confuse children as they do not know what is appropriate and acceptable. A plethora of parenting information comes from TV, magazines, books and the Web; yet, as the world speeds up, parents have less time to read the information or to participate in parent seminars and courses. Another area of concern is the number of 'celebrity' parenting experts who do not have a child over 10 years of age who give their opinions endlessly often on breakfast television programs! Their opinions influence many young parents who are desperately seeking guidance and the opinions they are hearing are often not supported by evidence-based research, so they can be quite unhelpful. Without a Wilma in your life, you may unintentionally be downloading information that does not build your child's health and wellbeing — especially the emotional and social capacity to be decent and to have a moral code.

Wilma's guidelines for parents to keep in mind as they help their young children grow up to be caring, decent people are:

- Model unconditional love and care.
- Allowing your children space to 'be'.
- Be truthful and honest.
- Create a safe place for them to share their emotions.
- Be a positive dreamer and goal-setter yourself.
- Be real, not perfect or a know-it-all.
- Be joyful and laugh often.
- Have clear, firm boundaries.
- Model personal health and wellbeing.
- Be connected to your own spirit.
- Have relationships that you value and nurture.

The way to create healthy, happy children is for you to consciously embrace the responsibility that you have as the parent of your child and to nurture them holistically — their minds, bodies, hearts and souls. This also includes the need to allow them to feel connected and valued in their families, friendships, schools and communities, and in our natural wide world. If you hold the **9 Things** closely in your awareness as you parent your child in their first five years and you make choices based on the **9 Things**, you will be well on the way to creating the child you hope for. Rather than focus on how to build all of those capacities outlined by Goleman and Siegel, I prefer to focus on building kindness and fairness, because they seem to encompass all of them.

WHAT IS KINDNESS?

Kindness is the capacity of an individual to act from a place of genuine concern for oneself and others, and includes the qualities of empathy, compassion, generosity and consideration with the intention of making a positive difference in our world. Being kind is a choice made from the belief that every action influences others, and it honours our deepest, invisible motivation to have value and worthiness in our lives.

> One of the biggest obstacles to joy and tranquillity in the home of young children is adult agendas of what must get done. As everyone who has ever raced with the clock knows — whether it's in the workplace, out in the world doing errands or at home — one of the first casualties of time pressure is simple kindness in our demeanour and speech.
> — Reproduced from *Parenting for Peace* (2012), by Marcy Axness, with permission of Sentient Publications, LLC.

Why Kindness?

Compassion and kindness have the power to touch deeply and this often ripples through the world around us; it invites others to be caring in turn. This is a universal reality that has great power. Many people have been touched by the kindness of others after the world disasters we have witnessed recently. Kindness was the most powerful pathway to teaching I knew in my own home and in the classrooms where I taught adolescents for 18 years. It is great that science can now prove what wise, caring Elders have known for a very long time.

Recently I watched a documentary film by Neil Shadyac (better known for his Hollywood hits such as *Ace Ventura* and *Liar, Liar*) called *I AM*. In the film, Shadyac talked about Darwin's theory of evolution. Apparently his notion of 'survival of the fittest' was only a part of his theory — despite being probably the most-cited

WILMA WALLABY

"If we treat our kids with respect and kindness, this is how they will treat themselves and others."

summation of his work in popular culture. Competition definitely plays out in the human evolution story. However, Darwin also believed that another powerful drive that exists in human beings is cooperation. The documentary explored some research that was done in the animal world with deer. The researchers wanted to know how a large herd of deer makes the decision to head to a watering hole because, to an observer, they always appeared to suddenly head to the watering hole, *en masse*. The first theory was that the leader of the herd, the largest male who had fought for his position of power, must be the one who indicates when it is time to move. On closer inspection via video, the researchers found that as the herd took off, the leader was sometimes the last to realise what was happening. The decision was collective and democratic, made by members of the herd. The researchers could see different deer lift their head and look to the watering hole over a period of time and it appeared that when over 50% had indicated it was time to head to the watering hole, the whole herd moved as one. Researchers have found the same happens with large schools of fish when moving rapidly through the oceans. This appears to mean that the ability to cooperate and work together is part of our biological drive, both in the animal world and the human world. This validates the enormous need to feel we belong, which is such a crucial aspect of the research into healthy attachment for defenseless babies and toddlers.

> When a child experiences emotional and/or physical separation – perceived or real – from their special big people, their brain experiences FEAR – stress follows – then behaviour. When the child experiences emotional and/or physical connection instead of separation, this fear is taken care of, the brain is calmed and the child is released to rest.
> — Dr Vanessa Lapointe (2012).

The effects of being treated fairly and with kindness have been shown in studies in neuro-science, to make a significant difference to the way the brain integrates, and subsequently, to how individuals feel and behave. When we are treated with kindness, it allows our nervous system to relax and the pleasant sensations from endorphins, often serotonin and sometimes oxytocin to flood our body. It makes us feel safe, valued and connected. Stress and distress have significant effects of how children and adults interact with the world.

When we are kind, we don't take advantage of our power, or of other people's vulnerabilities. Instead, we seek to comfort, encourage and strengthen those around us. The strong sense of belonging that comes with being treated with kindness is tangible and powerful. It removes the distance between individuals from 'them' or 'us' to 'we'. Treating others as we would like to be treated is an ancient way of building character and human understanding. Medina explains the astonishing skill called 'deferred imitation' which develops rapidly and which research shows exists in a 13-month-old child who can remember an event a week after a single exposure. When we know this, we can appreciate how important it is to model kind, caring behaviour in front of our babies, toddlers and young children. If we have never been treated with kindness or fairness, we simply will be unable to treat others the same way.

> Brain development is especially rapid and extensive in the first year of life, more than was previously realised and suspected and is much more vulnerable to environmental influence than we ever suspected ... this influence is long lasting. ... That means that if there has been extreme neglect through the critical periods — a child who is rarely touched or talked to or soothed — it may be difficult to make up the effects of severe deprivation later on.
>
> — Anne Manne, *Motherhood* (2005).

Goleman wrote of the power of 'emotional contagion'. By this he meant that collectively we are influenced by how others feel and behave. Recent research that discovered mirror neurons, appears to validate emotional contagion. Children who are on the autistic spectrum may very well have mirror neurons that are not working or not present because they struggle so much to interact with others.

The modern world has somehow grown a culture of individualism, insensitivity, selfishness and even cruelty. As social beings, a primary need of all humans is human intimacy and connection and I believe so many of the social ills of our world — increasing violence, bullying, alcohol and drug abuse, mental illness and suicide — come from a place of disturbing alienation and separateness. If we can build a strong culture of caring, based on kindness and fairness, our children may find the world a different place when they become adults. This culture needs to start in our homes and then flow into our schools so that every child can be influenced and shaped by it.

Babies and children who are raised with a culture of care, compassion and kindness will treat others the same way, and they will expect to be treated that way throughout life. This all stems from early life experiences that build up 'filters' or a particular lens through which we see the world. If we only experienced disrespectful and unkind interactions with our significant caregivers, then that is how we will behave towards others. Just because we love children does not necessarily mean they feel loved and valued. The code of kindness and fairness will ensure that children will feel the love, and with this primary human need filled, it will allow children to have the energy to grow and flourish.

As Bruce Lipton wrote in *The Biology of Belief* (2005):

> … Children who are experiencing frequent stress will have increased illness because the adrenal hormones will directly suppress the immune system to conserve energy supplies in order to survive their stressful experience.

Remember that Lipton showed in his research that the cells in our body can only do one thing — focus on growth or protection, in order to ensure survival. So if babies, toddlers and children are surrounded by a stressful environment, they will be unable to grow as well as they could without the distress. Kind care will allow the cells in the body to grow and flourish, and that means all the cells from the heart, the kidneys, the skin and the brain!

Lipton also wrote about how all the cells in the human body respond to consciousness, or the thoughts that flow through the conscious mind. If the dominant thoughts within a child are simply around survival then they will be unable to focus on happiness, curiosity, exploration or any of the other naturally occurring biological drives of early childhood. If we combine this information with the understanding of deferred imitation, emotional contagion, mirror neurons and the innate drive of every human being to connect with others, we can see the big picture of how we build emotionally and socially competent children who grow into the same kinds of adults.

I recently heard author Shelley Davidow, who has just released her new book *Raising Stress-Proof Kids* (2014), interviewed on ABC radio and she spoke about how we are reaping what we sow as a stressed society.

> …The body wasn't really designed for long-term fight or flight so what happens is over the long-term we get things like we have today which is an epidemic of heart disease, the biggest killing disease in the western world and this didn't happen overnight …. What are we doing in society today, in the western world, where we don't really have wars and massacres and things going on, so there are no real stressors that we need to run away from? And yet, we are creating this generation of very stressed parents and children… we've got so much on and we've got so much to do. Our kids are on this freeway towards some finish line when they're about 18, and they get to the end of school and we as parents are somehow responsible for making sure that we goad them and push them and cajole them along the way to get there. We've ended up with a very stressed out society …25% of Australians suffer from anxiety in a country that is probably one of the safest, most affluent in the world. So what is it all about?

You might remember from the BOUNTIFUL BRAIN chapter where I wrote about Dr Stuart Shanker from Canada and his important message for all of us that children's capacity to self-regulate largely determines how well they will perform at school, much more than whether they can count, or be good at picture recognition or colour in within the lines. A child who has the capacity to learn to self-soothe and to self-regulate their energy and their emotions starts school with a huge advantage over a child who cannot. Being treated with kindness and fairness will give children the best opportunity to learn this vital life skill. When we treat children with anger, avoidance and abuse we threaten how their sensitive brains process information and experience the world for the rest of their lives.

To be kind requires empathy: we must consciously attune ourselves to the life experience of another being to know what will feel good for them. This means we reach across the divide that appears to be between people of different ages, cultures and gender.

BUILDING EMPATHY

The critical time for young children to develop the ability to be empathetic, gentle and kind is under four years of age. If a very young child is given the opportunity to interact with a small kitten or puppy with adult guidance, he or she can learn what being gentle and caring means. I have seen many toddlers who have nearly squeezed the life out of a kitten before they learned what gentle really meant! Without this opportunity, children may be unable to care that they are being rough or hurting others. This inability to feel empathy is a significant behavioural deficiency and could mean that an individual has difficulty in relationships, especially when it comes to intimacy. A lack of empathy is also common in teenagers and adults who were ignored as children and who experienced very little play. Despite the essential nature of social and emotional learning, many of today's adults and systems ignore or invalidate them in favour of a focus on cognitive and physical development.

> Character is shaped by life experience and cannot be seen from the outside or from physical appearances. It cannot be judged by prizes and accolades. Nor can it be judged by age or culture. Character can only be ascertained from how a person lives and interacts with others.
> — Maggie Dent, *Nurturing Kids' Hearts and Souls* (2005).

Many children who behave as bullies have problems with empathy. This emotional competency is only learned through life experience and the guidance of a caring adult. Despite research findings to the contrary, play fighting has come to be seen as a disturbing facet of childhood and one which children need to be saved from (Gill, 2007). This shift in parenting could be contributing to boys being less able to negotiate tricky social situations later in life and getting into serious trouble by misreading the social cues between play and a real threat. Children need to learn the many invisible codes of behaviour that provide life skills. This learning is being eroded by the current attitude towards demonising normal childhood misbehaviour — **children are meant to make mistakes with the choices they make because they are children — this is how they learn.**

Bullying has become such a hot topic in schools that it too may have contaminated some of today's key life skills' development for children. The original definition of bullying was that it involved "sustained, repeated maltreatment based on a power imbalance between victim and perpetrator that threatens one's wellbeing" (Gill, 2007). In recent bullying definitions it has been softened to include "any form of victimisation or harassment perpetrated by another child or young person" (J. Deakin, *Dangerous People, Dangerous Places: The Nature and Location of Young People's Victimisation and Fear*, 2006). This is of great concern as children are still developing skills to be assertive and they will make mistakes at times. Such an over-reaction encourages adults to feel under pressure to take every misdemeanour seriously and to step in and work out conflicts — we may be interrupting a normal part of social and emotional development. We need to be careful that the pressure to over-parent in today's world is not diluting the value of letting children learn for themselves how to deal with everyday unpleasantness and awkward social interactions. Wrapping our children in cotton wool can weaken their resilience later in life. At the same time, we must protect and act when real bullying occurs. However we need to learn to step back and let kids be kids when other social challenges occur. Vital emotional learning could be taking place.

To counteract perceived or real bullying, we need to teach children the skills to being a good friend. This set of social skills can help children when they start school because having friends to play with makes life less threatening, and stimulates positive neuro-transmitters that help create happiness, joy and delight. I have created an audio track called "I am a Good Friend" for children under 10 to help those who have no concept of appropriate choices around playing with other children. We must take the time to build these social skills as soon as possible before school.

This creative visualisation guides children through a journey of being a good friend and with repeated messages of being fair, kind and respectful — and it has helped many children re-wire a mindset that discourages them from being a good friend. Remember the imagination is very powerful in childhood and it works a bit like role-play. Norman Doidge writes of how our brain can re-wire itself during the process of imagining an act, just the same as if we were actually performing the act. For example, if a person imagines playing a piece on the piano, the brain fires the same as if that person was actually sitting at the piano, fingers playing the keys. The more often a child hears a visualisation, the more the brain changes — practice helps master all tasks.

> Brain scans show that in action and imagination, many of the same parts of the brain are activated. That is why visualizing can improve performance.
> — Norman Doidge, *The Brain that Changes Itself* (2007).

For example, children need help to understand that when they meet friends, they stop what they are doing, look at each other and say hello with a smile. They also say goodbye when they're leaving and sometimes kiss on the cheek, hug or shake hands. Friends take turns to talk and listen to each other. They say "please", "thank you" and "sorry". Friends share their toys with each other and wait their turn patiently. Friends comfort each other when they're sad and laugh at each other's jokes. Friends don't call each other names or hurt each other when they are upset. They say what they are feeling instead and they ask for things nicely.

Here are some ways to best support the essential brain development that will help children grow into caring people without a need to bully others:

- *Healthy management of parent emotions and the use of the right voice and energy — being calm, enthusiastic and optimistic is really helpful.*
- *Ensure there is an opportunity for respite for parents; everyone benefits with a little break from parenting young children. However, always ensure children are only with people they love, or who are able to offer a gentle loving care.*
- *Avoid shouting and criticising as it strengthens the lower brain patterns of distress, fear and rage.*
- *Have children under four experience caring for small animals like kittens, guinea pigs or puppies.*
- *Routines bring children comfort and lower the risk of an emotional overload of fear or rage.*
- *Lower other potential stressors from babies and toddlers such as shopping centres, large social gatherings, too much activity or over-stimulation from screens, and very large toys with bells and whistles.*
- *Protect children from early bullies, whether they are older siblings or at day-care. Then teach them how to become assertive, not aggressive.*

> It is important to remember that no matter how nonsensical and frustrating our child's feelings may seem to us, they are real and important to our child. It is vital that we treat them as such in our response.
> — Daniel Siegel and Tina Payne Bryson, *The Whole Brain Child* (2011).

Given that we know that the brain anchors memories more strongly when powerful emotions are present, it makes sense that if we are to build the capacity for our children to be empathetic and able to tune into other people — and to not be a narcissistic self-indulgent little brat — then we need to model and demonstrate endless moments of empathetic connection with them. If your intention from the word go is to built the ability in your children to be kind, compassionate and caring, then this intention will direct and guide the choices you make as a parent. Whatever we prioritise, guides the choices we make as humans. Even if your baby or toddler does not understand your words they will certainly know what the tone of your voice, your facial expression and what the type of touch you are using means. This is one of the reasons why pioneering paediatrician and educator Emmi Pickler encouraged the 3Rs as the foundation for her approach to caring for young children. **Responsive. Reciprocal. Respectful**. If these three things are present in 80% of our interactions with our babies and toddlers, then they will develop social and emotional intelligence to be decent people.

Being able to tune into other people is a key aspect of empathy. Even though you can teach your child the nuances of the social dance of getting on with others like using manners, taking turns, sharing and asking for things in a clear kind way, you cannot teach your child how to be emotionally warm, thoughtful and how to comfort a person in distress, or how to be naturally curious about others. Your children have to learn these attributes themselves through the multiple experiences they have with other children and humans; with Mum and Dad being their starting point.

Shelley Davidow, who I mentioned earlier, is a teacher, author and trained facilitator in Restorative Practice. She believes that the punitive/retributive disciplinary model — on which our society is based — creates narcissism in children because they become focused entirely on what they need to do to avoid punishment, rather than looking at the consequences of their actions.

Davidow writes about 'restorative parenting', which is based on a model of practice that has its roots in indigenous cultures around the world, and has become a part of parenting and education thanks to its effectiveness in criminal justice (Davidow, 2014).

She describes Restorative Practice in her book, as simply: "…to repair any harm that has been done and restore relationships. The focus is on the relationship, not on the 'crime', or on the person who commits the 'crime'".

Effectively, this approach is about getting people to take responsibility for their actions by understanding how those actions impacted on others — the beginnings of empathy. It was first used in prisons to get convicted criminals to meet with their victims and/or their families so each party could hear the other out. The victims can talk about how they've been impacted by the perpetrator's actions, and the perpetrator has a chance to try to right their wrong to some extent, by "engaging with the people they had hurt" (Davidow, 2014).

Davidow writes about how this might be applied to parenting, by looking at four parenting styles: authoritarian, permissive, neglectful and restorative.

> The punitive and authoritarian parent controls through fear. At the extreme end of authoritarianism we have dictatorships — and we know what that breeds in the civil population. The punitive parent would send the child who doesn't finish cleaning his room to the naughty corner or the bathroom, for 'not doing as he's told'. The permissive parent would make excuses for the child not cleaning his room and do it for him. The result of the permissive parent is a child who then begins to look like a dictator, who 'rules the roost' and does whatever he likes because his parents will always excuse and rescue him. There are, in fact, other choices … there is the neglectful parent, who may be abusive, indifferent or passive in response to children. Neglect can range from benign or criminal, on a sliding scale. The neglectful parent wouldn't care if the child cleaned his room or lived in a dump.
>
> If we want to create a low-stress home … [we need to look to] the restorative parent. This parent is supportive and understanding, but firm. This parent holds children *accountable* for their actions but is *also* accountable. At the heart of restorative parenting is the idea that the real currency, the thing that is valued above all else, is *relationship*. And so, no matter what happens, the restorative parent's highest endeavour is *to teach children that relationships are the things we hold in highest regard*. The restorative parent would work *with* the child and say, 'While you clean your room, I'm going to clean mine. Then in ten minutes we'll call each other in to see how lovely they look.' Or, 'You put the books back in the shelf here and I'll fold your clothes.' Over time, restorative parents make their children more and more accountable and responsible, by modelling the same behaviour (Davidow, 2014).

It is easy to see how the way we act and react as parents has a profound impact on the way our children decide to behave. It also shows clearly that modelling is a powerful way of teaching our children positive and fair ways of living when in relationships, especially families.

AVOIDING MELTDOWNS AND WARS

Imagine that you are at a school assembly for one of your older children when your two-year-old says, "I want a drink of water". Maybe you might calmly respond by saying, "Babe I can't get you a drink of water right now. However, I will, as soon as this finishes". The two-year-old starts whining and says much louder, "I want some water now, Mummy!" Again you try to placate her by saying, "We'll just have to wait til this finishes" and the two-year-old starts to lose the plot! Sound familiar?

According to behaviourist John Gottman one of the best ways to manage such a situation, especially with a young child who has poor executive function in her upstairs brain, is to acknowledge the child's feelings and empathise. So if the two-year-old at the school assembly had heard the following words, she may have felt heard: "Babe you are thirsty and I reckon a big drink of nice cold water would make you feel so much better. I wish I had a drink in my bag so that I could give it to you right now and you could drink as much as you liked". According to Gottman such an empathetic response, which helps identify the emotions that are present, acts like pouring water onto a flame as it diffuses intense emotional moments. Technically this is called 'coaching of emotions' however it can also be called taming the emotions. This has to be one of the best secrets that I've found and I have tried it on other people's children to find it works every time. It ticks all the boxes of meaningful adult interaction in that it is respectful, and it is teaching and guiding a child's awareness. As the child is heard and validated, it seems to soothe the cortisol levels in the child's brain quite quickly. So the next time your child pesters you for a biscuit and it is just before dinner, try validating that for them, "I know you want a biscuit now sweetheart because I know you like biscuits and you are going to feel frustrated and a little angry when I don't get you one because it's just before dinner. We can have a biscuit tomorrow when it isn't time for dinner".

Being empathetic and having the ability to tune into other people's emotional worlds are a really big part of being fair and being kind. As Goleman explained, emotions are contagious; we share a physiological synchrony. When we are in the company of people who are caring and empathetic, we will calm down and tend to behave in the same way. Professor Stanley Greenspan, a clinical professor of Psychiatry and Paediatrics at the George Washington University School of Medicine, suggests in his book *Great Kids* (2007) that children need to experience empathy on a regular basis to become good at expressing it. "*Empathy comes from being empathised with.*"

> If 30% of your interactions with your child are empathetic, Gottman contends, you'll raise a happy child. Does this mean 70% of the time you can cut yourself some slack? Perhaps. Really, this statistic points to the great power of paying attention to feelings.
> — Medina (2014). *http://brainrules.net/*

An excellent technique that I found to be very helpful when my youngest son was little, comes from the powerful parenting book, *Raising our Children,*

Raising Ourselves (2005) by Naomi Aldort. In her 'SALVE' technique, Naomi recommends steps that allow us to essentially calm our lower brain so we can access our upstairs brain — this is a simple example of mindfulness in play. By having parents pause and really guide children's thinking, they are then able to connect in an empathetic way that empowers them to learn to manage their own distress or big ugly feelings.

SALVE

S — Separate yourself from the child's behaviour and emotions with silent self-talk.

A — Attention on your child.

L — Listen to what they are saying or showing by their actions.

V — Validate their feelings.

E — Empower your child to resolve his own upset.

— Naomi Aldort, *Raising our Children, Raising Ourselves* (2005).

This book is an excellent one for parents who have had a challenging childhood themselves and who are keen to create a much better childhood for their own children.

EARLY COOPERATIVE PLAY

By age three or four, children spend more of their playtime interacting with each other if they are given the opportunity to do so. Initially, it is helpful if your child plays often with a small number of children who are familiar to them but in different settings — a lounge room, outside, at the park or at the beach. These slight changes to where the play occurs help them to build a stronger capacity to manage change while some things stay very familiar. In each environment the children will interact in a different way so they will have more chances to practise positive and painful interactions with children they know quite well. This keeps stress to a manageable level much of the time. Some of the interaction will be positive: imitating, planning and executing a plan together, or sharing materials. At other times, the interaction is less benign and may involve emotional pain. One child may snatch a toy away or barge in, disrupting the play. Although it may seem that these actions are intended to annoy, it's more likely that they represent that child's unskillful attempts to join in the fun. It takes a long time for some children to figure out how to assert themselves without being aggressive. On the whole, children learn best when adults assume that their intentions are good, even if they do not carry them off well. It's more helpful to show a child how to go about taking turns, than to scold him for grabbing toys.

Here are some tips that can help make early play more cooperative:

- It's helpful if you can arrange to have two or more similar toys at playtime. That way, when one child is banging pegs into holes, a second child can bang away, too, without having to wait.
- Keep the playtime short at first (30-45 minutes). If your child is having a hard time one day, you can simply leave early. There is little to be gained by sticking it out. It's more important that your child has a good time while he's there rather than to try to make the experience last. When he's ready, he'll be able to stay longer.
- Add a timer to ensure that children get used to having time blocks when they are playing with other children so that it can help them take turns fairly
- If you can, step in to redirect a child who is having a hard time playing positively before his behaviour evokes an angry reaction from another child. In this case, prevention is better than treatment!
- Give your child enough time to feel comfortable in the group. You may be a very outgoing person, but if your child is not, let him set the pace. He may want to stay near you for days or even weeks. While your natural tendency may be to push him to just get in there and play, it's more helpful to respect your child's timing and comfort level. When the unfamiliar becomes familiar, even the most slow-to-warm-up child can feel comfortable in a group.

— Sourced from the Raising Children Network's comprehensive and quality-assured Australian parenting website *http://raisingchildren.net.au*

TV AND HOW IT CAN INFLUENCE KIDS' BEHAVIOUR

We know our babies, toddlers and young children can remember and copy after just one exposure, a behaviour that occurred a week before, and by the age of 18-months-old the event could have happened four months before. This ability to imitate is wonderful if our children are imitating children and adults who behave with kindness and fairness and consideration for others. Unfortunately, TV has become the teacher for many of our precious children often under the age of two.

The first problem with TV and the developing brain is that it can poison a child's attention span and the ability to focus.

> For each additional hour of TV watched by a child under the age of three, the likelihood of an attentional problem by the age of seven increased by 10%. So a preschooler who watches three hours of TV per day is 30% more likely to have attentional problems than a child who watches no TV.
> — Medina (2014). *http://brainrules.net/*

Research seems to indicate that some children are more sensitive to this damage than others. TV is a great babysitter for weary parents; this is because the screen, with its rapidly moving images, captures a child's attention very strongly and immediately so they stop annoying you and give you some peace. So your TV can be seen as a support to get some respite, and if it is used in moderation (and only for children over two, according to government recommendations). Guidelines suggest less than 20 minutes at a time and no more than one hour per day for children aged two to five. You should also ensure your child is only watching quality programs like *Play School* on ABC TV — or programs that you have watched to ensure there was no relational aggression. This can be that 20% part of your 80/20 parenting. Having good-quality DVDs can help you monitor the media exposure that your child is getting. Given that children have this innate ability to copy things they witness please also be mindful of the programs they may see while adults are watching TV. I have worked with many young children who have become distressed and emotionally overwhelmed by things they have seen on the giant TV screen especially around natural disasters, car accidents and physical violence. Our young children have incredibly sensitive little developing brains that lack the discernment that we get as we get older. By the way, in research investigating which programs influenced children to be aggressive, *Dora the Explorer* was found to be one of the programs that did not increase aggression, however there are some three and four-year-olds who have developed Spanish accents as a resulting of watching the popular show!

> For decades we have known of the connection between hostile peer interactions and the amount of kids' exposure to TV. The linkage used to be controversial but now we see that it's an issue of our deferred-imitation abilities coupled with a loss of impulse control.
> — Medina (2014). http://brainrules.net/

One study showed that for each hour of TV watched daily by children under the age of four the risk increased by 9% that they would engage in bullying behaviour by the time they start school. PO Bronson and Ashley Merryman write in their book, *Nurture Shock* (2009), about a study conducted by Dr Jamie Ostrov and Dr Douglas Gentile into preschool children's aggression. They worked with two-and-a-half to five-year-olds in two different preschools and observed the children's TV viewing habits while also monitoring their behaviour in the playground. These two researchers expected that kids who watched violent shows like *Power Rangers* and *Star Wars* would be more physically aggressive following this exposure. And they expected that children who watched less aggressive TV programs would display less aggressive behaviour and be better at socialising. They categorised aggressive behaviour in three ways:

1. Physical aggression
2. Relational aggression — bossiness, manipulation and social exclusion
3. Verbal aggression.

The research then went on to study supposedly 'educational' programs, among which were listed shows like *Arthur* and *Clifford, The Big Red Dog*. They discovered something very interesting.

The more 'educational' media the children watched, the more relationally aggressive they became! This connection was much stronger than the connection between violent media and physical aggression. Essentially these forms of children's TV programs were teaching our children how to be mean to each other. Indeed the more time the children spent watching these programs, the crueller they became to their friends and classmates. Theoretically, the findings from this research showed that *Arthur* was more detrimental to children than *Power Rangers*.

Bronson and Merryman (2009) also write about another study, supervised by Dr Cynthia Schiebe at Ithaca College in the US, when 470 half-hour TV programs commonly watched by children were observed. The subsequent analysis revealed that 96% of all children's programming includes verbal insults and putdowns, often averaging 7.7 putdowns per half-hour episode. One of the worst offending programs was, *Sponge Bob Square Pants* and this line that the authors highlighted is a good example of the putdowns or cruel dialogue that are part of the show: *"How do you sleep at night knowing that you're a complete failure?"* Remember young children do not have a very well-developed prefrontal cortex and are not able to understand that what they are watching is not a real experience that they are witnessing. The research found that children who have been exposed to shows like these continue to use relational aggression for weeks after watching the program, whereas the children who acted out the physical aggression from *Power Rangers* often only acted out for a short time and then stop doing it.

Some serious warnings around TV (and also screens like iPads and tablets where they can watch these programs) if you have children under five:

1. Avoid TV viewing for all children under the age of two to ensure healthy brain growth and the development of appropriate social, emotional and cognitive skills.
2. Monitor and limit TV viewing for children over two to no more than one to 2 hours a day at different times (Government recommendations recommend one hour for under fives and no more than two hours for over fives).
3. Ensure children sit a good distance from the screen so that their visual senses are not overloaded.

4. Ensure that the volume is not too loud and that the TV is not left on in the background while babies and toddlers are present.
5. Ensure children are not exposed to scary images on the news.
6. Watch any program that you are going to show to children under five to ensure that it won't encourage poor social and emotional development.
7. Be mindful of young children watching programs that adolescent siblings are watching

> Our understanding of early childhood development has grown rapidly in recent years and we can now say the following with unprecedented confidence; the human brain and hearts that are met primarily with empathy in the critical early years cannot and will not grow to choose a violent or selfish life.
> — Robin Grille, *Parenting for a Peaceful World* (Second edition, 2013).

Reading picture books and traditional fairy tales that explore qualities of fairness, justice and kindness is also a great way to build the moral code of children. Young children are capable of downloading the deeper archetypes within traditional fairy tales especially the ones which teach about many of life's major issues like good vs evil, and working together to overcome challenge and resilience — the recovery after a time of adversity. Traditional indigenous communities used stories about animals to teach right ways of being and essentially that is what Aesop's Fables does as well. Many of today's young adults have never heard an Aesop's fable and may have missed some great lessons on life — think of, *The Boy Who Cried Wolf* or *The Tortoise and the Hare*.

BEING FAIR AND KIND ARE ESSENTIAL FOR BUILDING HEALTHY, HAPPY RELATIONSHIPS FROM CHILDHOOD TO ADULTHOOD.

Dr Matthew Lieberman in his article "Social Cognitive Neuroscience: The Pains and Pleasure of Social Life" (2008) has explored how powerful social exclusion is on individuals including children. Using brain imaging, he found that when a person experiences rejection or social exclusion, they experience a form of physical pain. For children who have poor attachment to their parents they will struggle to connect with other people. This sense of pain may explain why it is so hard to get children to return to school after that have experienced a serious conflict that made them feel rejected or left out. The other interesting thing he discovered was that being treated fairly activates the same parts of the brain as having our basic needs met like eating, coming in from the cold or eating chocolate. It triggers the pleasure response.

> Being treated unfairly activates the social pain and disgust circuitry. In our evolutionary past being accepted and valued by one's group is important because it means access to critical resources for survival and thriving.
> — Liebermann (In Press).

These research findings reinforced my personal belief that a meaningful life is determined by how safe, loved and accepted we are as an individual. What may seem small and unimportant — like someone playing 'Round and Round the Garden', or blowing raspberries on a toddler's tummy — profoundly shapes how attached or bonded a child feels to their significant carers. We are much braver to make mistakes if we are still valued after we mess up! Every decision we make as a parent, grandparent or teacher needs to respond to the inner response our children have to how we treat them. If we meet our children's core need to know they belong, they matter and that learning and growing is what they are supposed to do — and we treat children with kindness and fairness — we can improve every child's pathway of potential. They feel attached in a loving way.

It is widely understood that people learn by example. But adults who are respectful of children are not just modelling a skill or behaviour; they are meeting the emotional needs of those children, thereby helping to create the psychological conditions to treat others respectfully.
— Alfie Kohn, *What to Look for in a Classroom and Other Essays* (1998).

A GOLDEN SECRET TO DISCIPLINING WITH FAIRNESS AND KINDNESS

Seeing the world through the eyes of our children is the secret to being the respectful, considerate parent you really want to be. One of the most significant benefits I got out of studying neuro-linguistic programming (NLP) many years ago was an awareness that beneath every behaviour is some form of positive intention. Sometimes a child may bite another child because they are feeling crowded and overwhelmed, and they're trying to create some space for themselves. Sometimes seeking serotonin, we eat too much chocolate, so that we can calm down and be nicer human beings. Next time you approach a conflict with a young child try to ascertain what it is they wanted to happen as a consequence of the choice they made. Sometimes a child will hit a child so that that child will stop hurting another child. The reasons they may give you will be very childlike and when we see through their eyes, we can often witness what they were really trying to do.

Another thing I learned from NLP was the importance of building rapport before communicating. In a way, rapport building is a form of connecting to a child or an adult before we communicate with them verbally. This is what happens when you sit closer to a child, or you get right down to their level, or you make strong eye contact and you use their name. Any challenging communication is improved by starting with building rapport. It is especially important for boys because they are often so focused on something, they may not notice that you are communicating with them.

Now to the golden secret that will improve how you discipline your children once you master it.

The art of reframing

Reframing is the art of seeing things differently so that that your perception may change to enable you to respond more favourably in your communication. Okay so what does that really mean? Let's imagine you were driving around a roundabout in your car and a very inconsiderate driver cut in front of you and nearly wiped out the front of your car. What might be the first thoughts to go through your mind? Maybe you want to flip them the bird or speak in expletives? The reason we want to make those choices is that we have made a very quick, spontaneous choice that that person's behaviour was deliberate, it was threatening and it displayed a low level of consideration for us. Okay, so let's imagine a different response to the same scenario. What if instead of thinking about retaliation, you chose to have the thought — "Whoa, that person may have just come from a funeral home where they've seen a loved one's body, or maybe they just got sacked from their job, or maybe their partner just told them they don't want to be with them anymore. We can behave very erratically because we are distracted at such a time of intense shock". What is really interesting is that you really don't have to work very hard to reframe how you see the world in moments like this. And imagining scenarios like these is no less realistic than thinking someone has cut you off deliberately — after all, you have no idea what is happening for that other person in that car.

Now let's look at some reframes we can do around children. You might remember that in the chapter on EXPECTATIONS AND BELIEFS and THE BOUNTIFUL BRAIN IN INFANCY I wrote about how to react when your child blocked up your toilet with toilet paper or drew pictures with your best lipstick on the wall. I suggested that you see that experience as a positive sign that your child had a wonderful imagination and a healthy seeking system within their brain. This is a reframe.

I was blessed to have a near death experience when my children were quite young. My youngest was just over a year old when I almost died. When I came back from the hospital, I was so deeply grateful that I had not died, that all the minor annoying things about being a mum seemed to transform in front of my eyes. I had faced the prospect of never seeing my special beautiful boys ever again and I was so grateful that my mind had reframed how I saw my parenting role. Now you don't need to have a near-death experience to reframe how you see your children. Maybe you could reframe by thinking any of the following thoughts:

- that your child only has a short time to live
- that your child has chosen you to be his/her parent from the billions of people on our earth
- that you have been presented with a miracle to take care of — not everyone is given this gift
- that your child could disappear suddenly like Madeline McCann and you may never see them again.

What is really interesting in the art of reframing is that the reframe does not have to be possible or probable — even incredibly ridiculous reframes tend to work. I worked with a woman once who created a reframe around her very difficult, bully boss. She chose to see that he was henpecked at home and his behaviour stopped bothering her. Indeed she found it quite funny and she felt sorry for him at times. Another man told me that he managed his very difficult mother-in-law by reframing that she really loved him — she just found it really hard to express it to his face. In a way, if we could remember the awe and wonder of our children's births, we would interact with them every day in a sacred compassionate way.

DISCIPLINE THROUGH THE EYES OF A CHILD

The most challenging part of the parenting journey, after sleep deprivation, has to be discipline. You will now appreciate that a baby is not born with an understanding of what is the right way to behave to keep Mummy and Daddy happy. Essentially, this is the learned behaviour that makes up the major part of parenting. Many parenting books I have reviewed seem to encourage us to treat our child as, as Robin Grille (2008) so eloquently puts it, "a beast that needs to be tamed and some form of enemy!" Given the insights from Lieberman about how powerful exclusion and being treated unfairly are, we need to explore discipline through this new lens in order to help parents who want to raise healthy children who have a moral code.

> When we narrow our view of children to their behaviour, we end up speaking about control, discipline or if you like, the modern (but increasingly discredited) psychobabble, behaviour modification.
> — Robin Grille, *Heart to Heart Parenting* (2008).

Reviewing this adversarial focus of parenting — with a parent using power to encourage behaviour that they deem to be suitable and appropriate — is the key to creating a caring, home environment where children can learn good ways to behave and interact. This means, as discussed earlier when I was looking at Davidow's restorative parenting model, the focus needs to move from controlling and policing our children, to guiding and teaching. If you think about it for a moment — we grown-ups expect our children to behave how we prefer, by punishing them for doing the wrong thing. Logically that seems a bit mean. Our children often behave quite naturally like young children might be expected to behave with their underdeveloped higher brain, and we tell them it's 'naughty' or 'wrong'. Even when they have been shown how to behave, sometimes they forget. In your life, have you ever made a mistake — maybe spilt coffee over your desk at work or forgotten a deadline or missed a meeting? Did you consciously plan to do that? No. Well our children do not get out of bed and say, "How can I piss off Mum and Dad today?"

Jack Canfield, author the fantastic, *Chicken Soup for the Soul* series of books, taught me a great process when I attended his training many years ago.

E + R = O

What this formula means is that any experience or event, plus my reaction to it, creates the outcome. So if a child spills their drink on the couch, or they push their sibling over — it is my reaction to this that will create the outcome. When you see the experience though the eyes of a child, and see what they were responding to or what need they were trying to get met, then how you respond, will often be more compassionate. To be honest, much of children's behaviour that annoys us as parents, is simply because it is inconvenient and interferes with how we plan the world to be. It's also sometimes because we haven't dealt with our own 'stuff' and we're lashing out at our kids in order to try to grab some sense of control.

Dr Shefali Tsabary writes about this, pretty controversially, in her book, *Out of Control* (2009):

> Unless we are able to discern the difference between love and our need for our children to assuage our feeling of lack, our connection with them will be muddied. I trust it is clear by now that discipline essentially communicates, "how dare you make me feel inadequate? Because I'm now out of control. I'll show you who's really in control!!!!!"

> In other words most everyone believes parents punish their children for their misbehaviour and on the surface it would certainly appear this way. I'm saying that the real reason is different, so much so that I'm convinced we will rarely if ever punish our children for their misbehaviour. Instead we punish them for making us feel inadequate causing us to become

aware of what is lacking in our life — aware that our real self is somehow missing.

The insight that discipline is really nothing but a crutch for parents who feel helpless when confronted by their own inadequacies is nothing short of revolutionary.

These are not easy words for many parents to read, but it is important to think about where our reactions as parents are coming from, and what our intentions are in attempting to re-route our children's behaviour.

Some tips to manage conflict and tough moments:

1. Take three breaths before reacting and speaking – even walk away for a few minutes if you need to calm down
2. Lean forward or get down to a child's level.
3. Find and use your quietest voice.
4. Start by saying, "This situation is not OK because ..." The child must know that she is OK — it is the behaviour that is not OK.
5. Avoid taking things personally — it's just stuff that happens!

> Sometimes the things that our children do that are inconvenient do need to be corrected. Children do need to learn that colouring on the cream-coloured couch with red finger paint is wrong.
> — Justin Coulson. *What your Child Needs From You* (2012).

In the previous chapter I explored some reasons why children might behave inappropriately. As parents and carers it is up to us to put on our detective caps and try to work out what might be going on for our children when they do behave 'badly'.

For example, is one of your child's basic needs going unrecognised or unmet? Needs may be around food, sleep, thirst, touch, affection, recognition or acceptance. An unmet need is often linked to a perception of a lack of love.

Secondly does your child understand what is going on? Are they capable of understanding what is expected of them in this moment? Always remember that children are interpreting the world through their own eyes, not an adult's.

Finally is your child experience stress? If a child is harbouring painful, pent-up feelings or has been traumatised then they might react through emotional discharge or diffusing.

When we combine these possibilities with the knowledge of brain integration, especially upstairs and downstairs brain — remembering the upstairs brain is quite underdeveloped in young children — we can appreciate that much of our children's annoying and frustrating behaviour is simply a response to an inability to see the world through the *eyes of an adult*.

The primitive brain with its flight-fight response, is easily triggered in children when they have unmet needs like tiredness, hunger, thirst or a deep sense of being emotionally disconnected from their most significant grown-ups. So often a parent's punitive response to a child's poor choice or inability to cope, simply floods their little brain with the stress chemicals that makes everything worse. This form of authoritarian parenting often unintentionally teaches a child about submission/dominance. If we are committed to raising a child who will know how to use fairness and kindness later in life, then we need to avoid having a parent-child relationship that is based solely on power and control.

> When we realise that neediness underpins all acting out, and that emotional need easily overwhelms logic and good judgement, it becomes obvious that to go on the attack is the opposite of what is required.
> — Tsabary (2009.)

When we choose to allow the parenting journey to be one that values cooperation and respect by using compassionate communication then we will be able to teach children good ways to behave and act. Remember it is what we do 80% of the time that really matters and that even the most loving patient parents will have days when their downstairs brain will be doing the disciplining not the upstairs brain! I am not sure if Dr Spock's parenting advice was to blame for the punitive, harsh parenting practices of the 1950s and 60s but research now shows that if a child is constantly on the receiving end of criticism, commands and threats that are combined with physical hitting or smacking, then the development of their upstairs brain or their higher brain will be compromised.

"This type of parenting can also hard wire the stress response systems in the brain and the rage system in the downstairs brain to be over reactive. These children then live their lives on a very short fuse. People don't warm to children whose way of being in the world is so ruled by the fight-flight mechanisms in the reptilian part of the brain." — Sunderland (2007.)

WHY SMACKING DOES NOT WORK LONG-TERM

In *What Your Child Needs from You* (2012), Justin Coulson explores the four main arguments against smacking:

1. Violence breeds violence because adults who use physical force, model coercion as acceptable and appropriate for problem-solving. Children who were spanked more than twice a month were 50% more likely to develop aggressive behaviours than those who were not spanked at all.
2. There is strong evidence smacking children reduces their IQ mainly because the stress and anxiety that exists in these children's brains slows cognitive development.
3. Some say they smack because you can't reason with a toddler or small child. The very fact that toddlers do not have sufficient reasoning skills suggests that they need more and not less protection.
4. Smacking is simply not effective for discipline. While there may be immediate benefits to stop challenging behaviour it only lasts briefly, and the behaviour inevitably returns and when it does, it will become insidious, secretive and more manipulative. Smacking and the threat of physical punishment push the behaviour underground, turning our children into subversive but careful dissidents (Coulson, 2012).

Another important fact about punishment like smacking is that it loses its effectiveness over time and while it may appear to work with a four-year-old it will certainly not work for a 10-year-old.

My main concern is that when parents resort to smacking they have missed an opportunity to teach their children better ways of managing conflict. The debate around smacking rages on in the parenting world and that is partly because there is a perception that, without smacking, our children will be parented less and less. This is so far from the truth. People love to argue that children used to listen to adults unquestioningly when corporal punishment was legal; they did as they were told. One only has to look at the current Royal Commission into child sexual abuse to know that the consequences for doing what adults tell you unquestioningly can be life-destroying. Further, while some discipline is essential, smacking now has the depth of research to show that the long-term effects of this type of punishment create "more aggressive, more depressed more anxious children with lower IQs." (Medina, 2014).

Davidow (2014) writes that while our most treasured memories come from our childhood, so too do our deepest traumas:

> It's our job as parents and teachers to stop the 'crimes' that we keep committing against our children, robbing them of a precious few years by saturating their world with the grim pressures and stresses of adult life ... we can always work on being more conscious and proactive, rather than reactive, when we parent.

DISCIPLINE WITH RESPECT AND FAIRNESS

> A child exposed to consistent, predictable, nurturing and enriched experiences will develop neurobiological capabilities that will increase the child's chance for health, happiness, productivity and creativity.
> — Bruce Perry (2006).

Throughout this book, I've talked about many ways of parenting, and discipline and communication styles — reframing, Davidow's restorative parenting, Canfield's experience/reaction/outcome model, the family solution-seeking process and more.

What lies at the core of every one of these approaches is that what matters most in every interaction we have as a parent is our *awareness* of our heartfelt connection with our child.

The first thing I explored in this book was CONNECTED MOTHERING and how powerful that loving connection is to our children, no matter what age they are. When we have that loving connection our children are innately motivated to please us to ensure they get more love and affection. The more secure our children feel in this loving connection, the less they need to seek attention of any kind. When I hear people explain children's behaviour as 'attention seeking' I find that quite disrespectful to children. Children are love- and connection-seeking missiles, and when they are unable to reach their target then their immature brains are unsure of how to seek that love in a mature way because they are children. Exclusion of any kind creates heightened stress levels in the brain, which triggers the primitive brain into action — survival at all costs. If we can keep this thought in our mind when our children are struggling emotionally and socially, we can step forward and be what they need — a significant caring grown-up who they can really rely on to help them feel calmer and more secure.

I like the way Coulson calls this style of parenting 'mindful parenting':

> The idea of being mindful has received a lot of attention from psychologists in recent years. It seems that mindfulness is a strong relationship with our well-being and that of our children. Mindfulness is being aware of what is happening right now and remaining focused on that. It's being *present* in the present. Mindfulness requires us to be 'where our feet are'. Children who experience mindful parenting agree to statements like
>
> - my parents support me
> - my parents console me when I'm upset
> - my parents show they care about me

- my parents show a genuine interest in me
- my parents remember things that are important to me
- my parents are available to talk at any time
- my parents ask questions in a caring manner
- my parents spend extra time with me just because they want to
- my parents are willing to talk about my troubles
- my parents talk with me about my interests
- my parents value my input and my parents make me feel wanted.

— Coulson (2012).

Remember that there is no perfect in parenting but being mindful will definitely help you make better decisions as a parent, however it is no guarantee that you will get it right every time. Even if we just pause most of the time when our children do things that make us feel frustrated and annoyed — and be grateful that we have the opportunity to be parents in the first place as so many people don't.

Compassionate and respectful 'now' parenting allows both the parent and the child to be valued and respected. Next time you have a teachable moment with your child, even if it involves a spectacular tantrum, when you reflect back on that experience a couple of hours later after a nice cup of tea — ask yourself my three questions for compassionate parenting:

1. **Was that fair?**
2. **Was that kind?**
3. **What has that taught my child?**

And if you are not happy with your answers simply plan a different response next time. There is no need to beat yourself up, or think dark negative thoughts or eat the whole family block of fruit and nut chocolate; you simply allow your higher brain and your heart to guide you to making better choices next time.

> The best way to inspire your children to develop into the kind of adults you dream of them becoming is to become the kind of adult you want them to be.
> — Robin Sharma, *The Greatness Guide* (2006).

Our ability to be calm and mindful 24/7 is a primary factor in parenting with fairness and kindness. As soon as our brains are flooded with too much cortisol, then we are no longer giving our children the message that "we've got this" and so their natural response will be that they will attempt to gain control because we don't appear to be in control as their parents.

Have you ever noticed what happens if you are pushed by someone, even accidentally? Most often we will push back and this automatic push back explains what happens when we interact with our children in ways that use dominance and submission. When we use respectful and cooperative methods of interacting — the push back does not tend to take place.

At this point may I remind you that toddlers and young children who do not have moments where they push back or become a little defiant may run the risk of not developing an authentic sense of self. Keep in mind that paedophiles target children who are well-behaved and compliant because they are easier to manipulate and groom. So next time you are having a moment of push-pull with your toddler or young child keep this thought in the back of your mind.

If you find yourself losing your cool, try the parental pause:

1. You stop moving. You ground your feet.
2. Gently bend your knees.
3. Place your right hand on your heart.
4. Take a deep breath. Maybe another two deep breaths.
5. Then you slowly stand close by or kneel near your child.

Be present. Be still. Observe calmly the world through your child's eyes.

Inwardly — repeat these words silently: "My child is not bad or naughty — they are just struggling to cope with their world. This is normal developmentally. Let me be what they need right now — a safe base."

To create a sense of cooperative partnership with your children, with you still in charge, it can help if sometimes you ask your child what they would like to do next, what they might like to eat for lunch or what colour shirt they might like to wear — not every moment, however often enough for them to feel they matter.

WILMA WALLABY
"A calm mind is often a kind mind and it makes more respectful choices when parenting little ones."

Some rooster children are very clear at letting you know what they want at an unsettlingly early age! Rather than fight this, embrace it as a sign of their growing autonomy and independence. In quiet moments have conversations about how sometimes Mummy and Daddy need to make decisions that they might not agree with, however most of the time you will be respectful of the choices that they would like to make. I would give your children some examples of when parental choices may be more appropriate such as around the food they eat, using manners, being kind and respectful to other children, road safety, water safety and car safety. This approach gives your children an anticipatory view of how things may happen.

I would also suggest that you create some non-verbal signs that help your children know when their behaviour is moving into an area that is concerning for you — a sign that can be seen from a distance. That may mean Mum's glare, a frown, a shaking of the head or thumbs down sign. With one of my sons I had a very valuable learning experience when he was about two years of age. He was right into Superman at the time and we were about to head downtown to do some shopping. He came out with his blue tracksuit pants on with his red underpants over the top and his cape. For some reason I thought it looked really stupid and I suggested he take the underpants off before we went downtown. Well he erupted like a volcano and took off to his bedroom slamming the door. I remember standing there wondering what the problem was. I quickly realised that **I was** the problem, not my son nor his underpants. When I went to give him the good news that he could wear his Superman outfit any time he wanted to, I firstly apologised for not appreciating how much he wanted to go downtown with his favourite outfit on. Amazingly, his anger and frustration dissolved in front of me and he graciously said, "That's okay Mum".

Once again we are unable to be emotionally mature parents every moment of every day when we are struggling with our own stress in this busy and chaotic world. Our children need our help to develop the strong self-regulating systems in their brain so they can manage challenges in their life. Mindful parents who choose to be fair and kind still have boundaries and discipline. Discouraging poor behaviour, especially behaviour that is hurtful to others, is just as important as encouraging behaviour that is obviously helpful and positive. And ignoring bad behaviour like kicking at a chair, making whingeing whining noises and stomping down the stairs really noisily is still the most appropriate response.

Some researchers are coming to the opinion that praising the absence of bad or poor behaviour can be as effective as praising or encouraging the presence of good behaviour. Some children need help to understand what behaviour is NOT ok, so it can be useful sometimes to mix up your affirmation of positive behaviour with a statement about the absence of negative behaviour. For example, you might say, "It's great to see you using your words to tell Zoe you don't want her play with your truck, instead of biting her to show her that".

Boundaries and rules in families help children feel safe and secure, even if they don't always like them. Having no boundaries can lead to chaos and mayhem. When the house rules are based on fairness and encouraging cooperation or a team approach, they are easier to enforce.

Simple family rules might be:

1. no hitting or swearing
2. no hurting, physically or verbally
3. no damage to property
4. when you feel angry, take yourself to your quiet place
5. ask for help when you're hurting on the inside
6. use your words not your actions when you get angry.

Children need to know what the consequences will be when they break one of the boundaries or the rules. For example, if they damage something they'll need to fix it or replace it; if they make a huge mess, they'll need to clean it up; if they hit or yell at their brother, they'll need to sit down with him and talk about it, then apologise. If we keep in mind that the loving connection that we have with our children is the most important thing to avoid damaging or crushing, then the non-verbal warnings are the best place to start. Then the magic of distraction where we can completely diffuse a situation by suggesting it's time for some fruit, or a drink of water or for Mummy to sing some randomly silly song that changes the mood instantly. Avoiding making little things into big things and don't sweat the small stuff — when you are parenting like this, it reduces the amount of stress and tension in your home. If you are constantly monitoring your children's choices with endless 'don't's' and 'no's', be mindful how incredibly frustrating that would if someone was doing that to you, let alone how it feels for a child without a prefrontal cortex.

> **DID YOU KNOW?**
> ... That "sorry" has great power in re-connecting heart and mind?

Mindful or 'now' parenting will help us know when we need to use a significant consequence around a certain behaviour such as repeated biting, throwing toys or pushing other children over. We need to bring out the big guns when this happens as soon as possible. The experts suggest that the use of choices and consequences is mainly suitable for children aged five and over; however, when it is done fairly and with compassion it does work with children under five quite often. The secret is to ensure that appropriate behaviour is encouraged enthusiastically and that is largely because humans behave according to some form of motivation. We humans are definitely wired to seek pleasure and avoid pain, however young children are still developing this capacity so often a tantrum happens because they are highly motivated to have a chocolate biscuit because they love them!

In talking about serious behaviours such as repeated biting, throwing toys or pushing other children over, then this is probably the only time that I would recommend time out whereby a child needs to be removed from the situation to have some quiet, calm-down time with a caring adult nearby — not leaving them alone or feeling ostracised. Remember these behaviours are more about children struggling to cope than they are about them being 'bad' and time out can trigger the separation distress system in a child's lower brain, which in turn can activate pain centres in the brain. It should be communicated to the child that this is about them having time to calm down; it's not a punishment or time in the 'naughty chair' or the like. Calm-down time can happen right where they are — it's more like a pause button on a DVD. Time out is only appropriate for clear acts of defiance, or for the upstairs tantrum, or for disrespectful damage to property. Always remember that, *"time out is a discipline using pain that should be a last resort"* (Sunderland, 2007).

Time out is also not a replacement for communicating with your child about their feelings, actions and the impact this has had.

For children under five when there has been a concerning behaviour, I recommend getting right down to their level by kneeling in front of them and saying simple words, with gestures like 'no' and 'don't'. The voice only needs to be used at times like this because it needs to register with the child that something is really wrong. You need to send a very clear and yet respectful message that the behaviour is not to be repeated. Immediately after you have sanctioned the child, it is really helpful for them to be reminded that you still love them. So open your arms for a hug or reach forward for a very obvious puckered up kiss — this immediately starts creating calming brain chemicals in your child's brain so the amygdala and the primitive brain can go and have a nap, rather than a meltdown. For minor moments of inappropriate behaviour it is helpful to get into habits where you create 'time in' rather than time out opportunities —once your child is safely in your arms or on your lap, you can quietly explain what you want them to do next time that happens.

> **Sam, we don't throw our juice cup away when we're finished with it. We either give it to Mummy or leave it near where we were drinking it. Okay? Can you remember that the next time, please?**
>
> **Stella, please don't throw your food. If you have had enough or you are finished, simply put your spoon down and let me know that you have had enough and I will help you out of your high chair. Okay? Can you remember that for Daddy, please?**
>
> **Chase, can you please be gentle with the baby so that you don't hurt her? Babies need very gentle handling or they will get hurt and may cry. Okay? Can you remember that, please?**

Parenting with an awareness of the importance of teaching and guiding our children, rather than policing and controlling them as the alpha-adult in charge, and doing this using the higher brain, is essentially how parents who raise children capable of moral behaviour later on, behave. The discipline required for rooster children, who can sometimes possess a fearless and impulsive outlook on life, often needs to be a little stronger and firmer than it is with your lambs. Remember there is no one-size-fits all and there is no magic technique that will work every time — such is the nature of human behaviour. Such parenting simply requires consistency, love and awareness.

> When warm, accepting parents set clear and reasonable standards for their kids then offer them praise for behaving well, children present strong evidence of an internalised moral construct usually by the age of four or five. They're not everything you need in your moral toolkit, but from a statistical point of view, you won't get a good kid without them.
> — Medina (2014).

Here is an excellent tongue-in-cheek piece that has done the rounds on the Internet. It explores how to raise children with boundaries and consequences in a loving and connected way.

The Meanest Mother

We had the meanest mother in the whole world!

While other kids ate candy for breakfast, we had to have cereal, eggs, and toast. When others had a Pepsi and a Twinkie for lunch, we had to eat sandwiches. As you can guess our mother fixed us a dinner that was different from what other kids had, too.

Mother insisted on knowing where we were at all times. You'd think we were convicts in a prison. She had to know who our friends were, and what we were doing with them. She insisted that if we said we would be gone for an hour, we would be gone for an hour or less.

We were ashamed to admit it, but she had the nerve to break the child labour laws by making us work. We had to wash the dishes, make the beds, learn to cook, vacuum the floor, do laundry, and all sorts of cruel jobs. I think she would lie awake at night thinking of more things for us to do.

She always insisted on us telling the truth the whole truth, and nothing but the truth. By the time we were teenagers, she could read our minds.

Then, life was really tough! Mother wouldn't let our friends just honk the horn when they drove up. They had to come up to the door so she could meet them.

While everyone else could date when they were 12 or 13, we had to wait until we were 16.

Because of our mother we missed out on lots of things other kids experienced. None of us have ever been caught shoplifting, vandalizing other's property, or ever arrested for any crime. It was all her fault.

Now that we have left home, we are all God-fearing, educated, honest adults. We are doing our best to be mean parents just like Mum was. I think that's what's wrong with the world today. It just doesn't have enough mean mums anymore.

— Adapted from an original piece published by Bobbie Pingaro in 1967.

TOP TIPS

* Parents need to use their higher brain to parent with kindness and fairness.
* Modelling is one of the greatest teachers that parents can use.
* Building a child's empathy will help them become emotionally mature as an adult.
* By validating emotions and expressing empathy parents can avoid meltdowns in young children.
* Some TV programs for children teach them how to be mean.
* $E + R = 0$. This formula can help you parent fairly and with kindness.
* We can discipline without smacking.
* Families need rules and boundaries as they reduce the confusion and chaos around children.
* The relationship between you and your child should be at the heart of all your interactions.

Remember, with every choice you make around children, ask yourself Maggie's three BIG QUESTIONS:

- **Was that fair?**
- **Was that kind?**
- **What has that taught my child?**

What I wish I had known:

"... To be myself, communicate openly, love unconditionally and never go to bed angry. Sort the problem out even if it means you are the first to say sorry regardless of who started the situation. When you say sorry, really mean it. Do not rehash old wounds and scars. Last, but not least, enjoy the hugs and real affection." – Roslyn

9th Thing

THE SAFE CIRCLE OF COMMUNITY

> A community is only as strong as the respect it shows its weakest member.
> — Jenny Mosley, *www.circle-time.co.uk*

BELONGING

> When we feel unsafe, physically or psychologically, impulses from the reptilian and mammalian parts of our brain override our higher functions, and we can behave like a threatened animal.
> — Margot Sunderland, *The Science of Parenting* (2007).

The first biological drive in every single human being is to survive and what we instinctively are terrified of the most is being excluded from the tribe. In ancient times this would almost mean certain death. As our world becomes busier and busier we are losing the ability to stay connected in 'real time' and this impacts deeply on our ability to parent well.

> One of the most significant benefits of raising children within a traditional Indigenous community was that there were many people who were positively involved in children's lives. This created a deep sense of belonging and solidarity for the children of the tribe. Rituals and shared activities strengthened the bonds of affection and connectedness. Time spent playing or being involved with children was seen as important because the tribe's future was seen to be in their hands. The greater good of the whole tribe was always the main driving focus and this meant that people of every age were valued and appreciated. It still takes many caring people to raise one healthy, happy child.
> — Maggie Dent, *Real Kids in an Unreal World* (2008).

Anthropologists have known for some time that children who are raised in communal parenting groups fare much better. In the 19th century — a time of huge child abandonment rates all over Europe — the island of Sardinia enjoyed one of the best infant survival rates, despite being one of the poorest economies. Unlike most European mothers, Sardinian women joined together in supportive, cooperative mothering groups. Mothers who don't parent alone tend to be much happier (Grille, 2008).

Strong community support is still a fundamental part of many cultures today. All families and friends take responsibility for ensuring everyone gains the necessary social and life skills so they are valued and able to contribute to the wellbeing of the whole community. In these communities people see their role in helping to raise children as an honour and privilege. The art of cooperatively co-parenting children ensures children have the best opportunity to learn as many life skills as possible while they are young.

People who are connected to children can also offer some of these possibilities to help tired or busy parents. Respite really helps parents, especially those with challenging, highly spirited children or children with special needs. Every parent benefits from having some time out from their children and this is available when there is a strong connected network of parents, particularly mothers, who meet regularly. The bond of affection among families is important on many levels. The children benefit from playing often with the same children — like they would if they had cousins nearby. The adults, both mums and dads, tend to develop friendships and this allows for social events to happen easily and with little expense. Children also grow in their ability to spend time with other adults in other homes, and this strengthens their capacity for when kindergarten and preschool comes along.

We have heard that it takes a village to raise a child, and essentially it still does. I believe that our soaring PND rates, divorce rates and increased cases of mental illness can be in part attributed to the weakening of social capital.

We've had an overload of information and knowledge at our fingertips, and yet many people do not know who their neighbours are. We are human beings, which means we are wired to be social — living in family units within larger units called communities. It is both interesting and sad to see the amazing goodness that pours out of good human beings during times of adversity especially with natural disasters. The biggest challenges in our community of gratuitous violence, homelessness, drug addiction, mental illness and loneliness are the enormous prices that we pay for trying to live separate, individualistic, often competitively driven lives. In traditional communities, members seldom focused on individual greatness, rather they celebrated community strength, cooperation, shared commitment to the greater good of all. The healthiest families that I've met, who've had the healthiest and happiest children, are all surrounded by a network of supportive people both in family and in community. Father Chris Riley who works with Youth off the Streets in Sydney described his concerns, in a radio interview I heard once:

… Never have so many people lived so far from extended family or outside traditional communities when adults served as collective parents for all a neighbourhood's young people… these developments have reduced our social capital; the relationships that bind people together and create a sense of community. We must find ways to deal with our profound loss of social connectedness.

The pressures of modern living with its massive consumerism, fear-based media distortions and rapid pace of life have meant that our world has become more materialistic and self-focused. There have been many studies on happiness over the last decade or more and it seems that our lasting happiness is never derived from things and stuff. Anyone who has had a life-threatening moment or a near-death experience, as I did when I had three little boys, can often have a complete mind shift about what really matters in life. In a way, I am glad I had that experience because afterwards, my enthusiasm for the external trimmings of our world diminished greatly. I was grateful that I had been given another opportunity to witness my precious sons grow up to be men.

The pressures of the consumer-driven world with its sophisticated and often unseen marketing forces constantly at play, captures parents' anxious minds, and empties their wallets and purses. It is sad that marketers target parental vulnerabilities to try to make them feel inadequate, frightened and guilty — all great motivators for spending money on their children. Much of this influence transcends the traditional marketing tools of advertising and sales, so the messages are increasingly subtle.

Further, as a society we are now connecting more and more in virtual spaces rather than in real life — in social networking communities, online interest groups and interactive online spaces like MMOGs (massive multiplayer online games) and virtual worlds like Second Life. Some online communities, such as Mooshi Monsters, are designed for young children, so the opportunity (and perhaps the pressure) to connect virtually to friends and family starts early. From reading the chapter on THE BOUNTIFUL BRAIN IN INFANCY I hope you can see that the best teacher for our children, after parents, in the first five years of life, is real life experience. It is crucial that parents whose children are interacting in this new landscape when they're old enough, ensure that they have a very healthy balance of real and virtual connection. Maybe if children are kept to a 20/80 balance with technology under five, then they will have a great opportunity to have healthy holistic child development on all levels and they will then be able to manage effectively with the 80/20 balance that is in front of them. Remember technology can never replace human intimacy, which is a key ingredient to meaningful human connectedness. No matter how much we know about attachment and how a child's brain works to support learning, if a child does not feel safe they will not learn, grow or develop as well as a child who has safety and proximity to a loving adult, within a circle of other caring adults.

Our traditional communities were driven by the greater good; and the circles of care ensured that everyone was cared for, the young, old, sick — everyone, without prejudice. This ancient pattern of solidarity and collective responsibility ensured not only the continuation of the community but also the preservation of the physical world for future generations. Every child was seen as a gift and a miracle and the community valued all of its children. Maybe this one shift in consciousness is what is needed in our modern world to change things for the better. Communities today can build the same healthy connectedness or shared collective parenting as in traditional communities.

STRENGTHENING COMMUNITIES

As Robin Grille writes in his book, *Heart to Heart Parenting* (2008):

> The way the emotional centres in the brain develop is directly shaped by our relationships with our carers. By the sixth month, our stress response level is set, based on how our emotional security needs are met by others. This neurological stress response is much like a thermostat and it influences the way we face stressful situations throughout our lives. Our emotional wellbeing — in other words our ability to experience joy, love and fulfilment — comes from how closely we are able to connect to one another.

Embedded into the Wilma philosophy is the need for strong community support, especially for young families. Family, friends, regular outings and community support networks, like playgroups and walking groups, are very beneficial in the first five years of a baby's life. They offer additional interactions for the baby as well as respite for the primary carers. Parents will not always be able to provide every social need for their growing baby, and exhausted parents are less likely to have energy to play games or interact with a toddler. Games and activities build pathways to a child's ability to learn basic literacy skills later on when he or she is at school.

Relational spirituality – spirit of relationships

There is so much more that is happening at a deeper level when communities are strong and united. These are communities where people share the good, the bad and the ugly and continue to strive for the betterment of all. In a way, a strong community creates a culture that nurtures all of its members. As an attribute of spiritual intelligence, relational spirituality follows on from respect and reverence, and includes the four Cs:

- Community
- Connection
- Compassion
- Communion

The essence of the spirit of collective relationships is that communities practising the qualities of connection, compassion and communion build healthy individuals. The children they are privileged to help raise, grow-up to become healthy individuals. Connectedness is the result of people feeling they belong and that they are accepted unconditionally. No matter their age, young or old, or whether they are ill or vulnerable, their community watches over them.

Communities can help each other conquer the tough parts of life. Some communities create an opportunity each year for families to gather at Christmas or Halloween (traditionally the 'Day of the Dead') to remember departed loved ones.

Community members from all faiths attend these gatherings and at the conclusion of the ceremony, they share a cuppa and a home baked biscuit. The following words are taken from a community Christmas memorial ceremony held in Albany in 2002 that I participated in. The collective sharing in ceremonies like this is incredibly bonding and healing because people don't feel that they are suffering alone. They present a very special opportunity for pausing from our busy lives and remembering those who we will miss around the family table over Christmas.

Memorial ceremony

We have all gathered here at this special time of year to pause from our hectic and busy lives, to remember and reflect on loved ones who have

left our physical world. Christmas is a time of celebration with loved ones, a time of making extra effort to thank people, to acknowledge people and to express our love through the giving of gifts and the sharing of friendship and fellowship. The ones we love who have left us are still part of all the memories over all the years, and that is why we have created this time to pause and remember in the company of others who have also lost loved ones. We do not grieve alone. One person's pain is mirrored in everyone else's — we need to draw comfort from the shared respect and love that is being felt here tonight.

I would like to share with you a poem about the art of remembering.

A Litany of Remembrance

In the rising of the sun and in its going down
we remember them.

In the blowing of the wind and in the chill of winter
we remember them.

In the opening of buds and in the rebirth of spring
we remember them.

In the blueness of the sky and in the warmth of summer
we remember them.

In the rustling of leaves and in the beauty of autumn
we remember them.

In the beginning of the year and when it ends
we remember them.

When we are weary and in need of strength
we remember them.

When we are lost and sick at heart
we remember them.

When we have joys we yearn to share
we remember them.

So long as we live they too shall live for they are a part of us
as we remember them.

May we always remember them.

— Rabbi Roland B. Gittelshorn

Our world is in turmoil at this time. We all yearn for compassion. We all yearn for joy. We all yearn for world peace. Yet above all the peace we yearn for most is within ourselves, inner peace.

Over 2000 years ago a child was born with the aim of bringing peace to all mankind — regardless of our faith or absence of faith. The Christ child is the core reason we celebrate Christmas.

I would invite you to pause and take a minute of silence to allow our thoughts of remembrance to join together as one.

In silence, gentle silence.

THE ART OF GETTING INVOLVED

Having community events like shows, music festivals, fetes, sporting events, art shows and garden weeks not only build community cohesiveness, they lift the spirit of community. I have also heard of tulip festivals, jazz weekends, flower festivals, wine and food shows, school reunions, plastic duck races and even a 'dog in a ute' weekend! Another great initiative is community gardens, and even verge gardening projects where people work together to 'greenify' small spaces around roads and building. These activities see community members come together to create something that everyone can enjoy and benefit from. Even Halloween can be a community gathering opportunity for many streets. I was, at first, very sceptical of this American tradition coming to Australia until I witnessed it happening in my own street where I saw parents and kids connecting with neighbours in happy and cheerful ways (I still have reservations about the enormous amount of lollies and chocolates consumed, however I do know it is a 20% special occasion just like a birthday celebration).

When a group comes together in celebration of where they live and want to share their very special community or the home of their heart, with others, we are all winners. These events, even if they only occur once or twice a year, give families opportunities to build meaningful involvement with each other and give their children the chance to be positive participants in their community. All of these are opportunities for special interest groups to coordinate visitors coming to their communities to have fellowship and fun. They are often very successful spiritually, financially and socially.

Sporting clubs are an incredibly important part of our communities and they are often places where the whole family, from the babies to the grandparents, come together to share bonding times. These clubs need volunteers to survive and this is another pursuit that I recommended children to participate in — they need to help out with working bees, in the kitchen and in cleaning up afterwards!

One of the building blocks in my 10 resilience building blocks model is called 'meaningful involvement'. Meaningful involvement can be confused with quality time with a child. It is an emotional and spiritual connection that can be demonstrated even from a distance. Fathers are vitally important in this circle of love and it is very heartening to see the fathers' movement gaining credibility and synergy in Australia. An aunty who has a deep connection to a child can show that bond even when she is living a long way away, by staying in touch by phone, post, or connecting via Skype. She can call and chat about little things as well as the big things, like concerts and other social markers. She may send postcards when she goes on holidays and have a special name she calls the child that is just between the two of them. She would know the child's favourite colour, food and picture books. If the child has a special interest in frogs or bears she would keep an eye out for articles or posters that she can get for him or her. The aunty may come to most if not all birthdays and shares in Christmas and Easter family gatherings. This is what meaningful involvement is for a child. This depth of involvement is essential for wellbeing on many levels, especially in later childhood and adolescence. Parents, biological family, non-biological family, child care workers, nannies and even caring neighbours can all fill this need within children. There is only one thing for sure — the more the better, the deeper the connection the better. When these relationships happen within communities that value childhood, we give children the best possible start in life.

> Through my work I get to meet hundreds of families and their children. They are teaching me that our children want to find a place in their communities where they are heard and they feel they belong. Denied those experiences, dangerous, delinquent, deviant and disordered behaviours make a satisfying substitute. There are always gangs, drugs, crime and street life to turn to as places where one can feel connected.
> — Michael Ungar, *Turning the Me Generation into the We Generation* (2009).

In a research study done in 1998 by psychologist Raymond Starr of the University of Maryland, he found that abused and neglected children could escape the cycle of becoming abusive parents if they had one nurturing adult as their mentor to support them emotionally and psychologically. We can all make a difference in the lives of disadvantaged children. We simply have to have the courage to care and really connect.

School volunteers are another source of wonderful meaningful involvement, especially if the involvement can evolve over a few years. The EdConnect Australia program began as the Student Volunteer Program in Western Australia in and now runs across Australia supporting 6,000 with learning support and mentoring. This mentor relationship has been shown to really make a difference in the lives of children socially, emotionally and cognitively; and the volunteers are winners as well. It simply affirms that it takes a whole village to raise a child. Check out their website: www.edconnectaustralia.org.au.

Also, a community that remembers and shares the stories from its ancestors and past members builds not only a history — it builds a fertile soil for the future. School reunions are one of the ways that communities build such a sense of connection. The little village where I live in northern New South Wales holds an annual 'Honour Our Elders' day for just such a reason. Also Anzac Day gatherings — especially with the breakfast that often follows the dawn service — are a wonderful way to bring people together. Australia Day festivities, Harmony Day, NAIDOC Week celebrations and public holiday events when they happen in communities, are another way of celebrating not only your country or heritage or a day off, but also your own community — no matter where it is in the big wide land!

> When communities succeed in promoting their cultural heritage and in securing control of their collective future – in claiming ownership over their past and their future, the positive effects reverberate across many measures of youth health and wellbeing. Suicide rates fall, fewer children are taken into care, school completion rates rise and rates of intentional and unintentional injury decrease.
> — Ungar (2009).

Building communities that create resilient people

- Demonstrate care-giving environments in early childhood.
- Address low literacy at as early an age as possible.
- Encourage play and sporting activities in childhood.
- Provide parent education for new parents and the parents of adolescents.
- Make treatment and support networks available in the community for mental illness, addictions and domestic violence.
- Create employment opportunities.
- Have mentoring programs both inside and outside of schools.
- Encourage cooperative, collaborative teacher practice in schools.
- Strengthen natural kinship networking — sibling and grandparent care.
- Create opportunities for meaningful tasks and activities in the community, so that mastery experiences are possible.
- Build community links between schools and the community.
- Have a shared positive vision that values connectedness and demonstrates hope for the whole community.
- Build networks and share ideas with other communities — give and share, learn and grow.
- Have community celebration days.
- Make the town or area welcoming.

Strong, positive-thinking communities come together in times of need and tragedy, as well as for celebration. Indeed, it often takes a crisis to re-awaken a community to the importance of being connected. Real communities know that what goes around comes around, and that one day the goodness will be returned even if it is in a very different form.

Remember that strong communities raise healthy, resilient children. Crime is reduced because people value and respect the environment in which they live. People are valued and in turn they value others. So what are some ways in which we can strengthen our communities?.

Build genuine linkages

Another way to see this phenomenon of human development is as a:

> ...Question of linkages that happen within you as a person and also in the environment in which you live ... our hope lies in doing something to alter these linkages, to see that kids who start in a bad environment don't go on having bad environments and develop a sense of impotency.
> — Bonnie Bernard.

Building human linkages and social capital need to be a priority in our modern world so that we can reverse the trends that are happening right now.

There are many ways that you can be more meaningfully involved with your or someone else's child — all the while offering them opportunities to be creative, original and as expressive as they wish? Ask yourself the following questions:

- Are you comfortable with dirt, mud, paint, water and glue?
- Do you have an area around your home where your child or visitors can get 'down-and-dirty' with their creativity?
- Do you have a strategy that helps your child keep his or her creative mess outside, like a cleaning bucket or bowl and towel?
- Do you join in with your child when invited?
- Do you keep 'creations' that are given to you by children or do you quickly clean them away, as soon as possible?
- When did your child last make a cubby — inside or outside the house?

WILMA WALLABY

"Strong communities support families in caring for children, so they can thrive and grow up to be happy, healthy, strong, kind and capable."

- Have you brought home any big boxes lately for your child or the kids next door to play with?
- When did you last observe ants or butterflies with your child?
- If your child likes music, is it all on CD or do you allow them to make their own sounds and rhythms on pots and pans?
- Do you have TV-free days?
- How many sand castles and sculptures have you made?
- How many mud pies have you cooked?
- How many dozen pipe cleaners or popsicle sticks have you bought?
- How many sidewalk chalk packs have you been through?
- What does the outside of your fridge look like?
- Have you ever made capes for your child to wear?
- Have you hand-painted kids t-shirts with them?
- How many framed 'kid's bits' do you have?
- How many homemade kites have you made and flown?
- When did you last have races with leaf or bark boats in water?
- When did you last make fresh play dough?
- When did you last have fresh sand in the sandpit?
- How often have you danced with a child?
- Have you made cookies using shape cutters with a child?
- Have you made homemade chocolates in moulds?
- When did you last have a treasure hunt in the garden or park?
- When did you last play hide and seek with your child?
- Have you kept kisses or wishes in a jar?
- Has your child grown anything from seed?
- When did you take your child to the library to pick out story and picture books they wanted?
- Do you have a box of dress-up clothes?
- When did you take your child camping away from the technological world and into the natural world?

[We can't underestimate the] importance of having at least one relationship where we are held within another person's internal world ... their head, their heart – relationships that help us to thrive and give us resilience ... the neural networks around the heart and throughout the body are intimately interwoven with the resonance circuits of the brain so that when we "Feel Felt" by another, it also helps us to develop the internal strength of self regulation to become focused, thoughtful, and resourceful.

— Daniel Siegel, *Mindsight* (2010).

This concept of being 'feeling felt' by another human being is deceptively powerful. In my experiences with adolescents over 35 years I have found this is the best kept secret for supporting often confused and troubled adolescents as they journey on their way to adult would. It is often not what you do but the sense you give a young person of being really seen and really heard with an unconditional positive regard that can transform how they see themselves from then on. The same goes for our young children. Strong community networks that really value children and families build these invisible connectors as children grow. This also builds a sense of belonging that will stay with a person their entire life if as a child, they have had the strong experience of belonging.

> A major contributor to the worsening mental health of Zeds [Generation Zed broadly encompasses young people 17 and under] is less support from families, with fewer functioning adults around and a lessened sense of community.
> — Professor Ian Hickie, executive director of the Brain and Mind Institute, University of Sydney (*The Sun Herald*, April 13th 2008).

I think it is important for parents to help build on a sense of community and social justice for everyone regardless of gender, culture, age or disability. This community awareness and concern has to be modelled by the significant people in a child's life.

There are a number of ways children can learn and practise the gift of concern for others and to discover the benefits of loving service.

For modelling service and community spirit:

- Collect papers or mail for a neighbour when they are away.
- Care for friends' pets when they are away.
- Take soup to sick family, friends or neighbours.
- Help elderly people with tasks like shopping and gardening.
- Make crafty gifts that cost little and give them to people in need.
- Make cookies, scones or muffins for people in need, or for birthdays.
- Take small gifts of gratitude to teachers and carers.
- Phone and send cards or letters to thank people for kindnesses.
- Share toys and the like with friends.
- Practise random acts of kindness to others.
- Make a family friend a cuppa without being asked.
- Help with family chores without being asked.
- Pray for someone or visualise sending rainbows to them.
- Smile lots.
- Say hello to people at school or in the community who seem sad or lonely.

- Give a gentle shoulder rub to family or friend.
- Leave a loving note on family member's pillow to share why you love them.
- With permission, gather blankets for a blanket drive.
- Knit a scarf and donate it to a charity.
- Pick up broken glass on the road or path.
- Give family and friends a hug.
- Feed ducks with appropriate duck food.
- Focus on development of character in our young.
- Show children a code that includes how to behave acceptably in social settings.
- Children learn good manners from the adults who model them.
- Values-based education is essential in developing character in our young.
- Kindness to others and acts of service are character-building qualities.
- The arts help build strong perceptions of good character.
- Encourage children and young adults to read good literature and non-fiction texts.
- All life experiences build character when understood and appreciated.
- Individuals build good qualities of character at any stage of their lives.
- Good character crosses physical, mental, cultural and spiritual boundaries.
- Good character allows a person to become the best they can be.
- Every child has a unique potential waiting to be uncovered.
- Seek the highest good within each person we meet, regardless of differences.
- We are all responsible for helping our young to develop character, personal strength and wisdom — it does not happen by chance.

> ## DID YOU KNOW
> That communities that are strongly connected recover from adversity and natural disasters quicker than those that are not?

WHEN BAD THINGS HAPPEN

Adversity happens in life even to good people. It can be an accident, serious illness, death, loss of a job or the break-up of a significant relationship. These things are hard for adults to manage and even harder for children.

Research shows that it is our sense of belonging that helps us to heal faster. In caring communities it is heart-warming to see people gather together to help those who have been hurt or wounded. Rural communities are often better than city communities in responding because they are already partially separated and often come together just to survive the isolation or remoteness of where they live. Community cohesiveness can be built in our urban areas and there are many suggestions that have already been mentioned here.

Even small things matter — pots of soup, casseroles and lots of muffins show people who are hurting that others care. The 'gathering' of a community is the first step to community healing. It speaks strongly of "we're in this together so let's work together".

Remember children learn that life can be unkind, even unfair. They also learn that no matter what adversity strikes, with family and community working side-by-side, things will get better. Children become more resilient when they are involved in any recovery.

Part of my work has been with communities that are struggling with serious adversity. The drought that hit rural WA a while back was a time when the suicide rates of farmers suddenly spiked and things were really bad in those communities. While the physical reality cannot be changed — no rain means no rain and it is beyond human control — the community reality can be changed. When there is tragedy and trauma, the sense of feeling helpless, hopeless and being out of control is enormous. This then affects the ability of adults to think positively and the 'awfulising' thinking drives a cycle of despair and endless stress. One community I worked with decided to make some small changes during the months where there was nothing for the farmers to do, as they had no crops. The first was to paint their mailboxes, so that every time they drove into their driveway, they could see a freshly painted mailbox and that was one small improvement that happened during the tough times. Another community decided to have weekly working bees where 20 men would turn up one day a week to help a farmer get a big job done — a new chook house, pergola, some fencing or painting the house. These were jobs that these farmers never had time to do normally. At the end of the day, there would be a barbeque and a few quiet drinks. Then, in some communities, men were meeting once a week somewhere out in the bush — for a chat and a beer. This 'pulling together' of men was profoundly important and they were better able to keep an eye on each other.

During the floods in early 2012, which affected parts of the Riverina, the small town of Yenda was totally flooded and many of its buildings were destroyed or badly damaged including the school. I visited the community about a month after the flood and worked with the community and their children, many of whom were quite traumatised. I gave the children two yellow ribbons to take and tie around things that mattered to them, to give them symbols of hope that may lift the spirit of the town. One child tied his ribbon around one of his chooks, another around a tree in the main town park and another around his granny's front gate. When I re-visited the community the week after the children had moved back into their beautiful school — I was deeply touched with the beaming faces of these children who had walked this pathway to recovery. I wrote this poem for the Yenda community and shared it at this celebratory return.

You can

You can shed tears for what Yenda lost or you can smile because Yenda is recovering.

You can turn your back on tomorrow and live yesterday, or you can be happy for tomorrow because of yesterday.

You can remember your town as it was or you can focus on what it will be when it is rebuilt and renewed.

You can choose to be fearful, worried or stressed or you can choose to be strong, optimistic and resilient.

You can stay sad, angry and negative and turn your back or you can smile and be encouraging and enthusiastic about the recovery.

You can choose to focus on your own struggles and challenges or you can share the journey of renewal and rebuilding with others who walk beside you.

Every day when you wake up, choose to gather your best smile, your strong spirit and with pockets full of hope,

Bring the power of love and belonging into town so that your children can believe, can dream and hopefully one day share the silver lining of family and community connectedness.

Smile, open your eyes, love and go on and remember

Yenda will be a better community when it is rebuilt and it has finally recovered.

— Maggie Dent (2012).

As I get to the end of the book, I sense a circle closing. I began by writing about the dangers of over-parenting where we overly invest in our children's lives, which can weaken our children's sense of self, their resilience and maybe even inhibit their creative spark. This intensive parenting can also come at the cost of parent health and wellbeing especially with the stressors of living in a busy, chaotic world. We all need to take the time to invest in our own recreation pursuits that bring us health benefits as well as a well-earned break from the 24/7 responsibility of being a parent. This includes coffee and lunch with friends sans children. Taking time to enjoy life outside the home, especially if it is within your community can be incredibly beneficial for both parents and kids. The other relationship that we need to ensure has time and space to be nurtured is the one with your co-parent or your significant partner. Over-investing in our children's lives can leave little space for intimacy, relaxed moments of connection and taking care of the big people who matter in your life. I know of circles of friends who take care of each other's kids so that parent couples can have a weekend away or even a dinner date. I met a couple once having lunch in Bangalow — the wife was one month away from having their third child and the husband was a very busy doctor from a Brisbane hospital. Grandparents were caring for their kids so they could have a weekend away and this lunch was the first time they had been out of their accommodation because they had been sleeping and dozing for two days, just catching up. It is very important to make that time.

I have a dream. I dream that in Australia we can create a supportive network of Wilmas — wise women from within the community with high-level mothercraft skills who are on call to visit homes to help facilitate early parenting of first babies and then right through to three years of age. Yes I have suggested women even though I know there will be men with all the right attributes because I am calling on a return to ancient women's knowledge and wisdom, and with respect. Women need to be the ones to re-create the safe circles of women — including the healthy sisterhood — who will step forward wherever they can to support new mums on the tough journey of motherhood. Of course they will embrace men who are doing the mothering and the same for grandparents who are doing the mothering. It would be great if our Federal Government would support such an initiative. Maybe it could be a collective initiative with funding coming from all three levels of government. I believe we could reduce PND and also build more supportive networks that will help build that strong sense of belonging that will help parents meet the unique needs of their children. These Wilmas may also be able to identify developmental concerns and help facilitate early intervention when needed — greatly improving the outcomes for our children with special needs.

Community matters on so many levels. Families who are raising their children in a

WILMA WALLABY

"All children belong to all of us in a powerful and invisible way. It's not 'them' and 'us' — it's 'we'. Reach out and be there for all kids."

caring, safe community will have the best chance of maximising their children's potential. This means that communities need to have an 'inclusive' philosophy for all members regardless of culture or any other differentiation we can think of.

> Exclusion creates conflict, social unrest, dependency.
> — (Ungar, 2009).

Communities are where we build our implicit memories that help shape our sense of self and by building social capital and cohesiveness with commitment, compassion and communion, everyone's health and wellbeing will be better, especially that of our precious children.

TOP TIPS

* Belonging is important for every human being.
* Strong caring communities value cooperation and care for all.
* The communion of people gathered for community events is a positive experience for everyone in that community.
* Communities can create resilient children who become resilient people.
* Good communities build genuine linkages.
* Positive meaningful involvement with as many people as possible is helpful for children.
* Adversity can be overcome with strong community support.

WHAT I WISH I HAD KNOWN … "This wonderful piece of advice came from my husband's grandmother when introduced to her fifth great grandchild: "Surround yourselves with love, with loving people and loving thoughts, love is what will matter most to this child throughout his life. The material things will fade, there will never be enough money but there must always be love — no matter what!" She was a wonderful, wise woman." – Alison

CONCLUSION

As I come to write the conclusion for **9 Things** I am hoping that this book has achieved what I intended it to do when I had that inspired thought many months ago. I hope the information contained within these pages helps parents to make decisions that will help them to raise children who are happy, healthy, strong, kind and resilient. Not perfect children but rather children who will find a way to use their unique gifts and talents in some way to make our world a better place. I have a wish for every child ever born to have at least one parent or guardian in the first three years of their life who is absolutely 'nuts about them' and who is committed to building as many love bridges as possible to ensure that at the core of their being, children know they belong, they are secure, they matter and that they are loved exactly as they are.

I hope that the world helps mums and dads of children under eight to find wise Aunty Wilmas — to support, encourage and guide them on this incredibly, unpredictably challenging journey of parenthood, and to teach them that it is a sign of strength to ask for help.

I especially hope that we give permission to our kids to be kids — and that we give them the gift of a childhood with noise, chaos, unpredictability, mess, unbridled excitement, squealing joy and peak moments of mastery! Let there be laughter, let there be lingering, let there be love as our little precious beings that we have created, or agreed to care for, walk this amazing journey of life. May they know that they have come here to be themselves, not some version of our reality or of our story of who they should be. Let us gather circles of support that build human connectedness, which truly honour the value of family within communities.

Importantly, let us give deep thanks and gratitude for the precious gift of life. To complete the book I add the wise words from *The Prophet* by Kahlil Gibran,

And a woman who held a babe against her bosom said,

"Speak to us of children"...

And he said:

"Your children are not your children.

They are the sons and daughters of Life's longing for itself.

They come through you but not from you.

And though they are with you yet they belong not to you.

You may give them your love but not your thoughts,
for they have their own thoughts.
You may house their bodies but not their souls,
For their souls dwell in the house of tomorrow,
which you cannot visit, not even in your dreams.
You may strive to be like them, but seek not to make
them like you.
For life goes not backward nor tarries with yesterday.
You are the bows from which your children as
living arrows are sent forth.
The archer sees the mark on the path of the infinite,
And he bends you with his might that his arrow may go swift and far
Let your bending in the archer's hand be for gladness
For as he loves the arrow that flies
So he loves the bow that is stable."

APPENDIX 1

ROCK-A-BYE BABY

Rock-a-bye Baby, on the treetop
When the wind blows the cradle will rock.
When the bough breaks the cradle will fall, and mummy will catch you, cradle and all.

HEADS AND SHOULDERS

Heads and shoulders, knees and toes, knees and toes, knees and toes
Heads and shoulders, knees and toes
We all clap hands together
Eyes and ears and mouth and nose, mouth and nose, mouth and nose
Eyes and ears and mouth and nose
We all clap hands together

OLD MACDONALD HAD A FARM

Old MacDonald had a farm
Ee i ee i oh!
And on that farm he had a cow
Ee i ee i oh!
With a moo moo here
And a moo moo there
Here a moo, there a moo
Everywhere a moo moo
Old MacDonald had a farm
Ee i ee i oh!

Old MacDonald had a farm
Ee i ee i oh!
And on that farm he had a pig
Ee i ee i oh!
With an oink oink here
And an oink oink there
Here an oink
There an oink
Everywhere an oink oink

Old MacDonald had a farm
Ee i ee i oh!
Old MacDonald had a farm
Ee i ee i oh!
And on that farm he had a chicken
Ee i ee i oh!
With a cluck cluck here
And a cluck cluck there
Here a cluck
There a cluck
Everywhere a cluck cluck
Old MacDonald had a farm
Ee i ee i oh!

INCEY WINCEY SPIDER

Incey Wincey Spider climbed up the water spout
Down came the rain and washed poor Incey out
Out came the sun and dried up all the rain
So Incey Wincey Spider climbed up the spout again
Repeat

THIS LITTLE PIGGY

This little piggy went to market,
This little piggy stayed home,
This little piggy had roast beef,
This little piggy had none,
And this little piggy cried,
"Wee! Wee! Wee!" all the way home.

PAT-A-CAKE, PAT-A-CAKE

Pat-a-cake, pat-a cake, baker's man,
Bake me a cake just as fast as you can.
Pat it and prick it, and mark it with B.
And put it in the oven for baby and me.

REFERENCE LIST

ABC Radio, Sunshine Coast. (2014, 28 March). *Raising Stress-Free Kids*. Retrieved 7 April 2014 from https://soundcloud.com/abc-sunshine-coast/morning-author-shelley-davidow.

ABC TV. (2011, 7 April). Mean Girls. *Catalyst*. Retrieved 9 April 2014 from http://www.abc.net.au/catalyst/stories/3185243.htm)

Australian Government (2016). Australian Early Development Census National Report 2015. A Snapshot of EarlyChildhood Development in Australia. Canberra: Commonwealth of Australia.

Australian Research Alliance for Children & Youth. (2007). *School Readiness*. West Perth, WA: ARACY

Aldort, N. (2005). *Raising our children, raising ourselves*. Bothell, WA: Book Publishers Network.

Almon, J. (2013, 21 August). Reading at five: Why? *SEEN Magazine*. Retrieved 7 October 2013 from http://seenmagazine.us/articles/article-detail/articleid/3238/reading-at-five-why.aspx

Axness, M. (2012). *Parenting for peace: Raising the next generation of peacemakers*. Boulder, CO: Sentient Publications.

Barker, G. (2013, Spring). Lost boys, *Scoop*. Vol 65. Retrieved 4 April 2014 from http://scoop.realviewtechnologies.com/?iid=81811&startpage=56

Benard, B. (2004). *Resiliency: What we have learned*. San Francisco, CA: WestEd.

Berceli, D. (2005). *Trauma releasing exercises (TRE): A revolutionary new method for stress/trauma recovery*. North Charleston, SC: BookSurge.

Biddulph, S. (2013). *Raising boys* (4th ed.). Lane Cove, NSW: Finch Publishing.

Biddulph, S. (2013). *Raising girls*. Warriewood, NSW: Finch Publishing.

Biddulph, S., & Biddulph, S. (2001). *Love, laughter and parenting in the years from birth to six*. St Leonards, NSW: Dorling Kindersley.

Bloom, W. (2001). *The endorphin effect*. London: Piatkus.

Boyce, T. (2012). *What the genes remember: The new epigenetics of the early years*. Presentation to the Conference: How We Become Who We Are: The Development of Children's Mental Health.

Bronson, P. & Merryman, A. (2009). *Nurture shock: New thinking about children.* New York: Hachette Book Group.

Brown, B. (2013). *The gifts of imperfect parenting: Raising children with courage, compassion, & connection.* Audio CD. Boulder, CO: Sounds True.

Butler, D. (1980). *Babies need books.* New York: Atheneum.

Cam, P., Fynes-Clinton,I., Harrison,K., Hinton,L., Scholl, R. & Vaseo, S.(2007). *Australian Curriculum Studies Association philosophy with young children: A classroom handbook.*

Cane, P. M., & Duennes, M. (2005). *Capacitar for kids: A multicultural wellness program for children, schools and families: teacher handbook.* Santa Cruz, CA: Capacitar International, Inc.

Carr, N. G. (2010). *The shallows: How the Internet is changing the way we think, read and remember.* London: Atlantic Books.

Chapman, G. D., & Campbell, R. (2012). *The 5 love languages of children.* Chicago: Northfield Pub.

Chilcott, T. (2013, 3 June). Prep school bans soar amid rise in violence. *The Courier-Mail.* Retrieved 6 October 2013 from http://www.couriermail.com.au/news/queensland/prep-school-bans-soar-amid-rise-in-classroom-violence/story-e6freoof-1226655486006

Corderoy, A. (2013, 4 October). Suicide link to ADHD drug, *The Sydney Morning Herald.* Retrieved 19 March 2014 from http://www.smh.com.au/national/health/suicide-link-to-adhd-drug-20131004-2uzut.html

Corry, J., Green, M., Roberts, G., et al. (2013). Anxiety, stress and perfectionism in bipolar disorder. *Journal of Affective Disorders*;151(3):1016–1024. [PubMed]

Coulson, J. (2012). *What your child needs from you: Creating a connected family.* Camberwell, VIC: ACER Press.

Cunningham, H., & Morpurgo, M. (2006). *The invention of childhood.* London: BBC.

Davidow, S. (2014). *Raising stress-proof kids: Parenting today's children in tomorrow's world.* Wollombi, NSW: Exisle Publishing.

Deakin, J. (2006, 1 January). Dangerous people, dangerous places: The nature and location of young people's victimisation and fear. *Children and Society*, 20, 5, 376-390.

Dent, M. (2003). *Saving our children from our chaotic world: Teaching children the magic of silence and stillness.* Dunsborough, WA: Pennington Publications.

Dent, M. (2005), *Nurturing kids' hearts and souls: Building emotional, social and spiritual competence,* Dunsborough. WA: Pennington Publications.

Dent, M. (2008), *Real kids in an unreal world*. Dunsborough, WA: Pennington Publications.

Doidge, N. (2007). *The brain that changes itself: Stories of personal triumph from the frontiers of brain science*. New York: Viking.

Duckworth, A. L., & Seligman, M. E. P. (2005, 1 December). Self-discipline outdoes IQ in predicting Academic performance of adolescents. *Psychological Science, 16*, 12, 939-944.

Dweck, C. S. (2012). *Mindset: The new psychology of success – How you can fulfil your potential*. London: Robinson.

Dwyer, N. (2013). *Being adventurous: An everyday learning series title*. Deakin, ACT: Early Childhood Australia. Available from http://www.earlychildhoodaustralia.org.au/shop/ details.cfm?prodid=984

Eady, J., & Additive Alert Pty Ltd. (2004). *Additive alert: Your guide to safer shopping: the essential information about what's really in the food you eat, which additives to avoid and why*. Mullaloo, WA: Additive Alert Pty Ltd.

Estroff Marano, H. (2008). *A nation of wimps: The high cost of invasive parenting*. New York: Broadway Books.

Farmer, N. (2012). *Getting it right for boys: Why boys do what they do and how to make the early years work for them*. London: Bloomsbury Pub.

Fine, C. (2011). *Delusions of gender: How our minds, society, and neurosexism create difference*. New York: W.W. Norton.

Fox, M. (2001). *Reading magic: Why reading aloud to our children will change their lives forever*. New York: Harcourt.

Fuller, A. (2007). *Tricky kids: Transforming conflict and freeing their potential*. Sydney: Finch Publishing.

Gardner, H. (1983). *Frames of mind: The theory of multiple intelligences*. New York: Basic Books.

Generation Z: Rich and forgotten. (2008,13 April). *The Sun-Herald*. Retrieved 3 February 2014 from http://www.smh.com.au/articles/2008/04/12/1207856908923.html

Gerber, M. (1979). *The RIE manual for parents and professionals*. Los Angeles, CA: Resources for Infant Educarers

Gill, T. (2007). *No fear: growing up in a risk averse society*. UK: Calouste Gulbenkian Foundation.

Goddard, S. (2008). *What babies and children really need*. UK: Hawthorn Press.

Goddard, T. (2013,15 November). *Emotional regulation through mindfulness training*. A paper delivered to the Mind & Its Potential Conference, Sydney.

Goleman, D. (1996). *Emotional intelligence: Why it can matter more than IQ*. UK: Bloomsbury Publishing.

Goleman, D. (2006). *Social intelligence: The new science of human relationships*. New York: Bantam Books.

Gonzalez-Mena, J. & Widmeyer Eyer, D. (2008). *Infants, toddlers and caregivers: The Philosophy of Respect based on the work by Magda Gerber and the Hungarian paediatrician Emmi Pikler*. New York: McGraw-Hill.

Gottlieb, L. (2011, July/August). How to land your kid in therapy, *The Atlantic*. Retrieved 15 December 2013 from http://www.theatlantic.com/magazine/archive/2011/07/how-to-land-your-kid-in-therapy/308555/

Graham, H. (1996). *Visualisation: An introductory guide: use visualisation to improve your health and develop your self-awareness and creativity*. London: Piatkus.

Gray, P. (2013). *Free to learn: Why unleashing the instinct to play will make our children happier, more self-reliant, and better students for life*. New York: Basic Books

Gray, P. (2013, September). The play deficit. *Aeon*. Retrieved 3 October 2013 from http://www.aeonmagazine.com/being-human/children-today-are-suffering-a-severe-deficit-of-play/

Greene, R. W. (1999). *The explosive child*. New York: Harper & Row.

Greenspan, S. I. (2007). *Great kids: Helping your baby and child develop the ten essential qualities for a happy, healthy life*. Cambridge, MA: Da Capo Press.

Greenfield, S. (2008). *ID: The quest for meaning in the 21st century*. London: Hodder & Stoughton.

Gregory, G., & Parry, T. (2006). *Designing brain-compatible learning*. Thousand Oaks, CA: Corwin Press.

Grille, R. (2008). *Heart to heart parenting; Nurturing your child's emotional intelligence from conception to school age*. Sydney: ABC Books.

Grille, R. (2013). *Parenting for a peaceful world* (second edition). Vox Cordis Press.

Grose, M. (2003). *Why first-borns rule the world and last-borns want to change it*. Milsons Point, NSW: Random House Australia.

Gurian, M. (1996). *The wonder of boys: What parents, mentors, and educators can do to shape boys into exceptional men*. New York: Putnam.

Gurian, M. (1999). *The good son: Shaping the moral development of our boys and young men.* New York: Jeremy P. Tarcher.

Gurian, M., & Ballew, A.C. (2003). *The boys and girls learn differently action guide for teachers,* San Francisco, CA: Jossey-Bass.

Haggmann, K. (2013, 15 November). Why video games make healthy stocking stuffers. Queensland University of Technology. Retrieved 6 April 2014 from http://www.qut.edu.au/about/news/news?news-id=65855

Hamady, J. (2014, 2 February). The truth about being a parent. *Huffington Post.* Retrieved from http://www.huffingtonpost.com/jennifer-hamady/the-truth-about-being-a-parent_b_4251463.html

Hammes, M. J. (2009). "Sally Goddard Blythe discusses what babies and parents need". First published at babygooroo.com. Accessed at: http://sallygoddardblythe.co.uk/sally-goddard-blythe-discusses-what-babies-and-parents-need/

Hamilton, M. (2008). *What's happening to our girls?: Too much, too soon, how our kids are overstimulated, oversold and oversexed.* Camberwell, VIC: Penguin Books.

Hart, B., & Risley, T. (1995). *Meaningful differences in the everyday experiences of young American children.* Boston, MA: Brookes Publishing.

Hart, T. (2003). *The secret spiritual world of children.* Novato, CA: New World Library.

Hiatt, B. (2013, 17 May). Pre-primary violence on the rise. *The West Australian.* Retrieved 6 October 2013 from http://au.news.yahoo.com/thewest/latest/a/17199981/pre-primary-violence-on-the-rise/

Hirsh-Pasek, K., Michinck Golinkoff, R., Berk, L.E. & Singer, D.G. (2009). *A mandate for playful learning in preschool: Presenting the evidence.* UK: Oxford University Press.

Holland, P. (2003). *We don't play with guns here: War, weapon, and superhero play in the early years.* Maidenhead, England: Open University Press.

Horin, A. (2008, February 2). Happy in care: it's in the hormones. *The Sydney Morning Herald.* Retrieved 7 October 2013 from http://www.smh.com.au/news/national/its-in-the-hormones/2008/02/01/1201801034863.html

Ilari, B., & Polka, L. (2006). Music cognition in early infancy: Infants' preferences and long-term memory for Ravel. *International Journal of Music Education,* 24. 1.

Jackson King, J. (2010). *Raising the best possible child; How to navigate parenting myths and bring up confident, happy kids.* Australia: HarperCollins.

Jensen, E. (2006). *Enriching the brain,* San Francisco, CA: Jossey-Bass.

Joseph, J. (2005). *Learning in the emotional rooms: How to create classrooms that are uplifting for the spirit.* Australia: Focus Education.

Kerry, S. (n.d.). *Mindfulness: What it looks like.* Retrieved 5 January 2014 from http://www.school-reform.net/mindfulness_text.htm

Kerry, S. (n.d.). *Harm in the school system.* Retrieved 5 January 2014 from http://www.school-reform.net/

Kindlon, D.J., PhD. (2001). *Too much of a good thing: Raising children of character in an indulgent age.* New York: Hyperion.

Knight, R. (2012) Slow down mummy. In Bellamy, T. *Musings on mothering: About pregnancy, birth, and breastfeeding: an anthology of art, poetry, and prose.*

Kohn, A. (1993). *Punished by rewards: The trouble with gold stars, incentive plans, A's, praise, and other bribes.* Boston, MA: Houghton Mifflin Co.

Kohn, A. (1998). *What to look for in a classroom: And other essays.* San Francisco, CA: Jossey-Bass.

Krotoski, A. (2013). *Untangling the Web: What the virtual revolution is doing to you.* London: Faber and Faber

Kurcinka, M.S. (2006). *Raising your spirited child: A guide for parents whose child is more intense, sensitive, perceptive, persistent, and energetic.* New York: HarperCollins.

Landy, J., & Brown, A., PhD. (2008). *Kids with more zip: A practical guide for educators/carers focusing on long term health and movement experiences for children ages 3 to 12.* Nedlands, WA: Allan Borushek Family Health Publications.

Lapointe, V., PhD. (2012). *The development of children's mental health: How do we become who we are?* Beyond Behaviour: Understanding Children from the Inside Out. Early Years Conference. Vancouver, Canada.

Lashlie, C. (2005). *He'll be OK: Growing gorgeous boys into good men.* Auckland, NZ: HarperCollins.

Leo, P. (2007). *Connection parenting: Parenting through connection instead of coercion, through love instead of fear.* Deadwood, OR: Wyatt-MacKenzie Pub. www.ConnectionParenting.com/

Lieberman, M. PhD., & Eisenberger, N. PhD. (2008). The pains and pleasures of social life: A social cognitive neuroscience approach. InPress. Retrieved 18 September 2013 from http://www.scn.ucla.edu/pdf/Pains&Pleasures(2008).pdf

Lillico, I. (2000). *Boys & their schooling: A guide for parents and teachers.* Duncraig, WA: I. Lillico.

Lipton, B. H. (2005). *The biology of belief: Unleashing the power of consciousness, matter and miracles.* Santa Rosa, CA: Mountain of Love/Elite Books.

Louv, R. (2005). *Last child in the woods: Saving our children from nature-deficit disorder.* Chapel Hill, NC: Algonquin Books of Chapel Hill.

Manne, A. (2005). *Motherhood: How should we care for our children?* Crows Nest, NSW: Allen & Unwin.

Marion, B.R. PhD. (2004). The heart of parenting, *Byron Child Magazine.* Retrieved 4 March 2014 from http://www.parentingwithpresence.net/index.php?pageid=970

Markham, L., PhD. (2012) *Peaceful parent, happy kids: how to stop yelling and start connecting.* New York: Perigee Trade.

McKay, P. (2006). *Sleeping like a baby.* Camberwell, Vic: Penguin.

Medina, J. (2014). *Brain rules: 12 principles for surviving and thriving at work, home, and school.* Second edition. Seattle, WA: Pear Press. http://brainrules.net/

Medina, J. (2014). *Brain rules for baby: How to raise a smart and happy child from zero to five.* Second edition. Seattle, WA: Pear Press. http://brainrules.net/

Meeker, M. J. (2006). *Strong fathers, strong daughters: 10 secrets every father should know.* Washington, DC: Regnery Pub.

Moorman, C., & Haller, T. (2005). *The 10 commitments: Parenting with purpose.* Merrill, MI: Personal Power Press.

Mrozek, A. (2012, 30 August). Nurturing children: Why "early learning" doesn't help. *Institute of Marriage and Family Canada.* Retrieved 2 March 2014 from http://www.imfcanada.org/issues/nurturing-children-why-early-learning-does-not-helpNeufeld

Murphy S. (2010, 9 August). Why barefoot is best for children, *The Guardian.* Retrieved 2 February 2014 from http://www.theguardian.com/lifeandstyle/2010/aug/09/barefoot-best-for-children

Neufeld, G., & Maté, G. (2005). *Hold on to your kids: Why parents need to matter more than peers.* New York: Ballantine Books.

O'Donohue, J. (1997). *Anam cara: A book of Celtic wisdom.* New York: Cliff Street Books.

Pearce, J. C. (2002). *The biology of transcendence: A blueprint of the human spirit.* Rochester, VT: Park Street Press.

Perry, B. (1998). *How exploration and play grow a healthy brain*. Retrieved 13 April 2014 from http://www.ecmma.org/ecmma_home/links/readings/how_exploration_and_play_grow_a_healthy_brain/

Porter, L., PhD., (1994). *Children are people too: A parents' guide to young children's behaviour*. South Australia: East Street Publications.

Prescott, J.W. PhD. (2002, Spring). How culture shapes the developing brain and the future of humanity. *Touch the Future*. Retrieved 26 January 2014 from http://www.violence.de/prescott/ttf/cultbrain.pdf

Prueschoff, G. (2004). *Raising girls; Why girls are different and how to help them grow up happy and strong*. NSW: Finch Pub.

Rando, L. (2010-2013). *Caring and connected parenting: A guide to raising connected children*. Pacific Grove, CA: SAIV (The Spiritual Alliance to Stop Intimate Violence). (download available from http://saiv.org/parenting-guide/)

Ratey, J.J. MD, & Hagerman, E. (2008). *Spark: The revolutionary new science of exercise and the brain*. London: Quercus.

Reichelt, A. (2014, 24 March). Why can't a man think like a woman, and a woman think like a man? *The Conversation*. Retrieved from http://theconversation.com/why-cant-a-man-think-like-a-woman-and-a-woman-think-like-a-man-24663

Reivich, K. & Shatté, A. (2002). *The resilience factor*. New York: Broadway Books.

Rideout, V. J., Vandewater, E. A. & Wartella, E. A. (2003). *Zero to six: Electronic media in the lives of infants, toddlers and preschoolers*. CA, USA: Kaiser Family Foundation.

Robinson, B. W. S. (2001). *Fathering from the fast lane: Practical ideas for busy dads*. Lane Cove, NSW: Finch Publishing.

Robinson, B. W. S. (2008). *Daughters and their dads: Tips for fathers, adult daughters, husbands and father figures*. Perth, WA: Macsis Publishing.

Saradanda, S. (2009). *The power of breath: The art of breathing well for harmony, happiness and health*. London: Duncan Baird.

Sarra, C. (2012). *Good morning, Mr Sarra*. St Lucia, QLD: University of Queensland Press.

Seligman, M. E. P., Reivich, K., Jaycox, L., & Gillham, J. (1995). *The optimistic child*. Boston, MA: Houghton Mifflin.

Sethi, A. (n.d.). *The real difference between boys and girls*. Retrieved 23 January 2014 from http:// www.parenting.com/article/real-difference-between-boys-and-girls.

Shanker, S. (2011). *The importance of self-regulation*. Presentation for Early Childhood Australia. Retrieved from http://www.earlychildhoodaustralia.org.au/pdf/nsw_branch/importance_of_self-regulation_june_2011.pdf

Shanker, S. (2014, 6 February). *Raising children & self-regulation: An information session for parents*. A seminar delivered for the Western Australian Council of Social Service Inc.

Sharma, R. S. (2006). *The greatness guide: Powerful secrets for getting to world class*. New York: HarperCollins.

Shonkoff, J. P. (2012, 16 October). *Leveraging the biology of adversity to address the roots of disparities in health and development*. Proceedings of the National Academy of Sciences of the United States of America, 109, 17302-7.

Siegel, D. J., MD., & Hartzell, M. (2003). *Parenting from the inside out: How a deeper self-understanding can help you raise children who thrive*. New York: J.P. Tarcher/Putnam.

Siegel, D.J., MD. (2010). *Mindsight: The new science of personal transformation*. New York: Bantam Books.

Siegel, D.J., MD., & Bryson, T.P., PhD. (2011). *The whole-brain child: 12 revolutionary strategies to nurture your child's developing mind, survive everyday parenting struggles, and help your family thrive*. New York: Delacorte Press.

Sims, M. (2007). *Kids count: Better early childhood education and care in Australia*. The determinants of quality care: Review and research report. (220–245) Sydney, NSW: Sydney University Press.

Singh, L. (2013, 30 August). Keeping kids indoors doesn't make them safer. *Essential Kids*. Retrieved January 2014 from http://www.essentialkids.com.au/health/latest-health-news/keeping-kids-indoors-doesnt-make-them-safer-20130830-2suy6.html.

Solter, A. (1989). *Helping young children flourish*. Goleta, CA, USA.: Shining Star Press.

Spencer, P. (n.d.). *Boys vs. girls: Who's harder to raise*. Retrieved 28 January 2014 from http://www.parenting.com/article/harder-to-raise-boys-or-girls

Stafford, R. M. (2014). *Hands free mama*. St. Louis, MO: Turtleback Books.

Stanley, F., Richardson, S., & Prior, M. (2005), *Children of the lucky country?: How Australian society has turned its back on its children and why children matter*. Australia: Pan McMillan.

Stevenson, A. (2011, 26 October). Rise of autism puts strain on public school budgets. *The Sydney Morning Herald*. Retrieved from http://www.smh.com.au/nsw/rise-of-autism-puts-strain-on-public-school-budgets-20111025-1mi5g.html#ixzz2sQGwcDPd

Street, H. (2013, 23 May). *Rewards, punishments and motivation.* A paper delivered to the Positive Schools conference, Perth, WA.

Sunderland, M.(2007). *The science of parenting: How today's brain research can help you raise happy, emotionally balanced children.* New York: DK Publishing.

Swanson, D. (2009). *Help-my kid is driving me crazy: The 17 ways kids manipulate their parents, and what you can do about it.* New York: Perigee Book.

Tapscott, D. (2008, 30 November). How to teach and manage 'generation net'. *Business Week Online.* Retrieved from http://www.businessweek.com/stories/2008-11-30/how-to-teach-and-manage-generation-netbusinessweek-business-news-stock-market-and-financial-advice.

Taylor, M. (1999). *Imaginary companions and the children who create them.* New York: Oxford University Press.

Teicher, M. H. (2002, 1 January). Scars that won't heal: the neurobiology of child abuse. *Scientific American, 286,* 3, 68-75.

Thomas, P. (2006). *Stress in early childhood: Helping children and their carers.* ACT, Australia: Early Childhood Australia.

Tsabary, S. (2014). *Out of control: Why disciplining your child doesn't work and what will.* Vancouver, BC: Namaste Publishing.

Ungar, M. (2009). *Turning the me generation into the we generation: Raising kids that care.* Crows Nest, NSW: Allen & Unwin.

University of California, Davis. (2009, February 24). Brain hub that links music, memory and emotion discovered. *ScienceDaily.* Retrieved 26 February 2014 from http://www.sciencedaily.com/releases/2009/02/090223221230.htm

Verenikina, I. & Kervin, L. (2011). iPads, digital play and pre-schoolers. *He Kupu,* 2 (5), 4-16.

Walker, K. (2005). *What's the hurry?: Reclaiming childhood in an overscheduled world.* Australia: Australian Scholarship Group.

Werner, E. E., & Smith, R. S. (2001). *Journeys from childhood to midlife: Risk, resilience, and recovery.* Ithaca, NY: Cornell University Press.

Whitebread, D., Basilio, M., Kuvalja, M., & Verma, M. (2012). The importance of play: A report on the value of children's play with a series of policy recommendations. Written for *Toy industries of Europe (TIE).* Retrieved October 6, 2013 from http://www.importanceofplay.eu/IMG/pdf/dr_david_whitebread_the_importance_of_play.pdf

Whitebread, D. (2013). Too much too soon: School starting age: the evidence. [Web log post]. *FYI: For your information.* Cambridge Faculty of Education Library. Retrieved from http://edfaclib.wordpress.com/2013/10/07/guest-blog-post-too-much-too-soon-school-starting-age-t he-evidence-3/#more-687

Winnicott, D. (1953). Transitional objects and transitional phenomena, *International Journal of Psychoanalysis*, 34:89-97

Wiseman, R. (2002). *Queen bees and wannabes: Helping your daughter survive cliques, gossip, boyfriends, and other realities of adolescence.* New York: Crown Publishers.

Wiseman, R. (2013). *Ringleaders and sidekicks: How to help your son cope with classroom politics, bullying, girls and growing up.* London: Piatkus.

Young, D. (2010). *Distraction. The art of living series.* UK: Acumen.

Young, D. (2013, 14 November). *Distraction: A philosopher's guide to being free.* A paper delivered to the Mind & Its Potential Conference, Sydney.

CREDITS

Excerpts from THE WHOLE-BRAIN CHILD: 12 REVOLUTIONARY STRATEGIES TO NURTURE YOUR CHILD'S DEVELOPING MIND by Daniel J. Siegel and Tina Payne Bryson, copyright © 2011 by Mind Your Brain, Inc. and Tina Payne Bryson, Inc.. Used by permission of Delacorte Press, an imprint of Random House, a division of Penguin Random House LLC. All rights reserved.

Excerpts from MINDSIGHT: THE NEW SCIENCE OF PERSONAL TRANSFORMATION by Daniel J. Siegel, copyright © 2010 by Mind Your Brain, Inc. Used by permission of Bantam Books, an imprint of Random House, a division of Penguin Random House LLC. All rights reserved.

HEARTFELT THANKS

I am blessed to work with a fabulous team and this includes my graphic designer and dear friend — and longest-serving team member — Katharine Middleton. This is the seventh book we have created and birthed together. Thanks again so much Kat. To my editor and proofer, also my neighbour and dear friend, Carmen Myler — thank you for the huge job of taming my text, correcting my referencing and making me look so much better. To my gorgeous PA Laura Browning, a huge thank you for helping to keep me safe from the endless organisational aspects of my work and the mountains of emails. To my former PA Liz who shared seven years of my journey — thank you for every minute of your time that you gave to me, and for nudging and coaching me when I needed it the most. To the gifted illustrator Linda True-Arrow, many thanks for creating Aunty Wilma to look so wise and caring. To my extra proofer Michele Lockwood — many thanks for checking the book with fresh eyes. And to Jolene Daniel and Robyn Henderson, for helping with initial editing of some of the chapters — many thanks. To my husband Steve for allowing me to have peace and quiet for weeks while I wrote madly — many thanks. Finally thanks to my awesome four sons for giving me more joy and delight than they will ever know — they are and always will be the wind beneath my wings.

INDEX

ADD/ADHD, 15, 57, 62, 93, 113, 123, 125–126, 177, 182–184, 192, 198, 209, 230, 244, 253, 321
Adrenaline, 63, 64, 114, 115
Aggressive behaviour, 2, 113, 118–119, 154, 202, 217, 219, 223, 224, 227, 252, 254, 274, 280–281
Allergies, 2, 4, 167, 168
Anger
    anger in parents, 79, 246–247, 293, 298
    angry children, 39, 44, 45, 68, 80, 111, 118, 122, 124, 143, 144, 146, 188, 195, 214, 223, 226–228, 277, 279, 294
Anxiety, 5, 30, 35, 46, 57, 62, 103, 106–107, 111–112, 116–118, 123, 125, 127, 131, 143, 161, 182, 187, 195, 198, 223, 234, 253–256, 271, 289, 321
Asthma, 2, 4
Attachment and bondedness, 17–20, 23, 26, 37, 50, 76, 90, 101, 107, 111, 117, 145, 149, 166, 223, 264, 269, 282, 282, 302
Attention, 20, 33, 45–46, 57, 64, 80, 109, 124–125, 132–134, 137, 153, 157, 168, 184, 192, 221, 230, 266, 277–280, 290, 337
Australian Early Development Index/Census (AEDI/AEDC), 3, 320
Autism, 2, 52, 93, 126, 198, 240, 328

Behaviour
    challenging behaviours, 20, 99, 125, 128, 166, 250, 289
    reasons for inappropriate behavior, 44–46, 100, 113, 118, 272, 287-288
    when children are hard work, 44–46, 142, 144, 213
Behavioural disorders, 3, 15, 19, 46, 93, 182, 115, 182, 272
Being present, 23, 37, 80, 84, 124, 130, 132–133, 136, 138, 140, 153, 155-156, 159, 290
Belonging, 4, 8, 15, 17, 47, 194, 232, 267, 269, 299–302, 310–311, 313–315
Biting, 39, 45, 110, 166, 293–294
Boundaries, 37, 41, 69, 101, 119, 125, 127, 131, 145, 151, 224, 226, 245, 258, 267, 293–294, 296, 298, 311
Boys
    and language, 220–223, 227, 230, 237
    as 'warriors', 9, 219, 222-231
    emotional vulnerability of, 208, 212, 222–229, 236–237
    helping boys with conflict, 217, 228–238
Brain
    connectors, 52–53, 57, 60, 98, 104, 261, 310
    development, 38, 41, 52–56, 59, 62, 70, 76, 84, 90–93, 99, 104, 107, 110–111, 113, 130, 133, 165, 171–172, 174–178, 185, 189–191, 195-197, 203, 205, 207–208, 210, 214, 232, 263, 270, 272–274, 281–282, 288–289, 302
    formation of brain maps, 52–53, 84, 91, 108
    functioning, 64, 118, 190, 210, 225

    higher brain, 54–55, 66, 172, 197, 286, 288, 291, 296, 298–299
    impact of internet on, 78–79, 194, 264, 321
    integration: horizontal and vertical, 65–71, 104, 261
    link between experience and brain development, 59, 70, 177–178
    mammalian brain, 54, 112, 189, 299
    movement and brain development, 52– 54, 65, 76, 92–93. 96, 113, 171–174, 184, 192, 195–199, 202–205, 230–231, 235
    music and brain development, 25, 55, 57, 62, 76, 102, 113, 121, 174, 203, 205, 324, 329
    myths about children's brain development, 56–57, 70
    plasticity, 52–53, 55–58, 70, 104, 119, 208, 263
    pruning, 55, 104
    reptilian brain, 54, 112, 228, 299
    screens and brain development, 52, 57, 59, 79, 91, 99–103, 109, 120, 135, 174, 179, 189, 194–196, 200, 205, 225, 274, 280–281
Brain chemicals, 25, 62–66, 89, 111, 115, 118–119, 130, 156, 190, 195, 222, 230, 241, 288, 295
Breastfeeding, 1, 9, 25, 28, 31, 240, 325
Breathing practices, 45, 84, 103, 116, 122–124, 128, 131–132, 138, 149, 287, 327
Bullying, 4, 87, 135, 183, 186, 192, 216, 270, 273, 280, 330

Calm
    benefits of calm, 67, 108, 112, 115–117, 122–123, 131, 139, 141, 146, 152, 157, 169, 182, 274
    how to calm babies and toddlers, 23, 28, 67, 72, 119–125, 128, 131, 139, 149, 190, 266, 276–277, 290
    modelling calm, 116–122, 152, 274, 291–292
Child care, 9, 17–18, 23, 38, 40, 42, 111, 115, 126, 176, 223, 267, 306
Comforters, 116, 120
Communication
    being heard, 145,153–155, 217, 229
    building skills, 40, 83, 88, 98, 152–153, 158, 182, 196, 217, 222– 223, 232–233, 284, 290
    communication with fairness and kindness, 80, 158–160
    compassionate communication, 37, 150–160, 169, 288
    family solution-seeking process, 153–154, 157, 162, 290
    listening, 40, 80, 152–153, 156, 159–160
    non-verbal communication, 35, 45, 57, 87, 90, 98, 151, 156, 158, 189, 221, 230, 293–294
    optimistic language, 125, 250–253
    positive and negative labels, 125, 150, 154, 162, 250
    positive parental communication, 9, 17, 80, 115, 150, 152, 156–157, 175, 217
Community
    building communities that create resilient people, 253–260
    getting involved, 305–311
    importance of, 17, 299–315
Connection
    being a child's safe base, 37

    building love bridges, 35–36, 130
    connected mothering, 13, 49, 150, 290,
    link between emotional responsive parenting and stress reduction, 77, 111, 118–119, 130, 133
    micro-moments of connection, 29, 130
    tips for connecting, 20, 44–45, 50
Consumerism, 4, 38, 62, 173, 301
Corporal punishment, 135, 289
Cortisol, 63–65, 111–112, 114–119, 127, 177, 212, 241, 277, 292
Crying, 5, 14, 24–25, 27, 69, 83, 110, 120, 127

Dads/fathers
    dads and daughters, 46–48, 238, 327
    dads and sons, 46-48, 116
    father figures, 46–50, 238, 327
Death and grief, 19, 25, 41, 88, 112, 114, 117, 131, 218-219, 284–285, 299, 301, 311
Depression
    post-natal depression, 30–32
Developmental coordination disorder, 15
Developmental delays, 52, 171, 251
    Australian Early Development Index/Census (AEDI/AEDC), 3–4, 320
Diabetes (Type 1 and 2), 2-4, 19
Discipline
    the art of reframing, 250–251, 284–285, 290
    through the eyes of a child, 29, 246, 285–288
    using 'calm down time' instead of 'time out', 67, 294–295
    with respect and fairness, 290–298
    why smacking doesn't work long-term, 288–289
Distraction, 45, 58, 77, 109, 134–137, 156, 249, 294, 330
Distress, 20–21, 25–27, 54, 59, 65–67, 70–72, 83, 93, 106–119, 127, 131, 141, 147, 161, 174, 198, 215, 227, 248, 269, 271, 274–275, 278, 280, 295
DNA templates, 15
Dopamine, 63–65, 73, 87, 89, 113, 172, 190, 221, 230
Dyslexia, 15, 90–91, 177

Eighty/twenty rule, 10, 241, 280, 302
Emotional intelligence, 42–43, 73, 75, 108, 146, 158, 191, 262, 275, 322–323
    emotional contagion, 270–271
Empathy
    and compassion, 68–69, 147, 231, 268, 275
    building, 70, 144, 146, 263, 272–276, 282, 298
    expressing empathy, 277, 298
    lack of, 163, 199, 272
    roots of, 69, 150, 212, 268, 275
Endorphins, 63–65, 87, 115, 190, 269

Energy, 6, 9, 32, 40, 45, 51, 64, 72–73, 98, 100–104, 124, 130, 132, 143–144, 146, 150–151, 156, 166–167, 169, 172, 190, 201, 214, 225, 230, 242, 253, 256, 270–272, 274, 303
Expectations
    impact of negative expectations, 235, 242–244
    impact on performance, 243–244, 253
    of Aboriginal people, 242, 244
    realistic expectations, 43, 240–241, 244, 246, 260
Experience vs stuff, 36, 301

Fairness, 158, 234, 248, 251, 261–298
Family day care, 9, 40, 223
Family conflict, 67, 143, 146, 154, 157, 230, 241, 264
Family meetings, 157, 230
Family rituals, 33–34, 41, 72, 74–76, 129
FIFO (fly-in-fly-out workers), 30
Fight or flight response, 54, 64, 68, 71, 108, 114–115, 117, 271, 288
Films, 150, 226, 264
Food
    food additives, 167–168, 322
    food intolerance, 167
    high-energy foods, 100–102
Forgiveness, 80, 229, 245
Formalised education, 53, 197, 230, 235
    push down in early years, 197, 220, 235, 253
Friends
    learning to be a good friend, 41, 155, 250, 273

Games
    board games and card games, 145, 188, 196
    pass the parcel, 187
    sport, 33, 102, 105, 178, 196, 201, 229, 253
    winning and losing, 188, 190
Gender, 4, 40, 49, 88, 207–209, 212, 214, 219, 227, 237, 272, 310, 322
'Gifted' children, 243
Girls
    and language development, 220, 230, 237
    and sexualisation, 47, 161, 209–210, 213, 215–218
    and social exclusion, 211, 281–282
    and their dads, 47–48, 238, 327
    and violence, 217–219, 230, 324, 327
    'Mean Girls', 209, 211, 320
'Good-enough' parenting, 5–6, 50
Guilt, 7, 30–31, 58, 144, 162, 164, 211, 247
    guilt vs shame, 162, 164

Helicopter parenting, 6
Hitting, 110, 223, 239, 288, 293

Homework, 100, 127, 198, 203, 231
Human connectedness, 8, 23, 174, 250, 259, 302, 318
'Hurry-up' world, 1–2, 84, 107, 175, 256, 329
Hyperactivity, 123–127, 177, 184, 192, 230

Imaginary friends, 35, 82–83, 178
Imagination, 54, 81–85, 98, 127, 182, 189, 192 –193, 196–197, 273–274, 284
Indigenous peoples
    expectations of Indigenous students, 242, 244
    Indigenous children, 2, 113, 186, 199, 230
    closing the gap, 5, 9 , 199
    traditional culture and wisdom, 5, 9, 217, 314
iPad use, 53, 76, 79, 91, 103, 188, 194–195, 228, 281, 329
Intelligence, 48, 92, 98, 102, 262, 275, 303, 323
Internet use, 78, 264
    effects on brain, 78, 194, 321
Introverts and extroverts, 130, 166–167
Intuition, 134, 137–138, 263

Joyfulness, 23–24, 75, 129, 170, 267, 328

Kindergarten, 39, 42, 100, 184, 197, 202, 215, 300
Kindness, 8, 43–44, 49, 54, 56, 70, 73, 140, 151, 158, 215, 234, 248,
    261–262, 265, 268–272, 279, 282–283, 288, 291, 298, 310–311

Lambs, 37, 142, 145, 147–153, 164, 169, 250, 296
Language,
    acquisition and development, 90–97, 202, 230, 250
    learning language, 58, 62, 64, 90, 92–93, 104,109, 192, 195, 199, 250
    saturation, 76, 91, 93–94, 96, 104, 165
Laughter, 18, 65, 87–88, 120, 204, 247, 318, 320
Learning, 6, 15, 19, 32, 38–40, 42, 44, 49, 52-53, 55–59, 62–64, 70–71,
    88, 90, 92–93, 97, 99, 104–105, 109–110, 113–114, 117, 127,
    130, 135, 146, 148, 158, 161, 174, 176–177, 179, 182, 187,
    189–190, 192–193, 195, 197–199, 201–205, 208, 210, 212,
    220, 225, 229–230, 235–236, 250–253, 272–273, 283, 293,
    302, 306, 322–324, 326
Literacy, 41, 93,95,192,198,203,244,255–256, 263, 303, 307

Manipulation, 33, 124, 281
Memory
    distorted memory, 71
    emotional memory, 31
    explicit memory, 71,
    humour and memories, 86–89
    implicit memory, 31, 63, 65, 71–72
    memory pathways, 31, 71–72, 80, 175
    memory retrieval, 71

music and memory, 120–121, 174, 324, 329
Mental illness,   2, 4, 31–32, 50, 84, 200, 202, 231, 270, 300–301, 307
Mindfulness, 132–137, 140–141, 278, 290, 322, 324
Mindsets, 104, 164, 220, 235, 250–251, 253, 260
Morals, 218, 231, 263, 265–267, 282, 285, 296, 323
Mothering, 7–9, 13, 15–16, 20, 31–32, 49–50, 130, 136, 141, 245, 290, 300, 314, 325
Movement
    and babies, 26, 27, 53–54, 92–93, 171–175, 184, 195, 204, 228
    and brain development, 52–54, 65, 76, 92–3, 96, 113,
    and play, 171–205
    exercise & benefits for brain development, 122, 230
    importance of bare feet, 176
Music, 25, 52, 57, 76, 102, 109, 113, 120–121, 124, 128, 146, 149, 174, 187, 202, 205, 253, 305, 309, 324, 329

Narcissistic behaviour, 144, 147, 199, 275
Natural disasters, 98, 268, 280, 301, 311
Nature-based playgrounds, 182–186, 200
Noise
    effect on babies and toddlers, 25, 70–71, 109, 120, 131, 147
Numeracy, 93, 192, 198, 203, 244
Nursery rhymes, 84–85, 90, 92–93, 174–175
Nutrition (see also food additives), 123, 258

Oxytocin, 63, 86, 110, 119–120, 131, 212, 269
Over-parenting, 6, 313
Over-scheduled childhoods, 101, 106, 116

Parent gender roles, 9
Perfectionism
    and links to anxiety, 5, 253, 255, 321
    'perfect' childhoods, 'teacups', 2, 4–7, 43, 241, 253, 318, 321
    pressure to be perfect , 43, 160, 188, 252
Pets,   38, 72–73, 188, 310
Philosophy — teaching children, 134, 159, 242, 321
Phonics, 231
Play
    and movement, 52–54, 65, 76, 93, 96, 113, 171–205, 226, 228, 230, 233, 235
    and policy, 203–204, 235, 329
    bringing more into children's lives, 201, 202
    gun and sword play, 224, 226
    nature play, 182–183, 186–187, 200
    outdoor play, 181, 183
    playground equipment, 8, 179, 181, 183, 186, 226
    risk, 148, 179–182, 186, 204, 211, 219, 224–225, 228, 280, 329
    superhero play, 225–226, 231, 324
    technology and play, 53, 57, 77, 191, 194–196, 232
    unstructured play, 98, 124, 182, 201, 205

Praise and encouragement, 37, 57, 163–166
Preschool, 39, 41–42, 93–95, 99, 115, 126, 134, 184, 195, 197–198, 202, 214–215, 222, 232, 235, 251, 279–280, 300, 324, 327
Professional help — when to seek it, 31, 97, 125–126, 181, 199,
Proximity (i.e. attachment), 17, 37, 79, 128, 302
Punishment, 100, 105, 135, 163, 248, 251, 266, 275, 289, 295, 328
Puppets, 89, 266

Reading
    learning to read, 90–97
    reluctant readers, 96–97
Relationships
    healthy relationships, 3, 103, 217
    with self and others, 37–38
    relational spirituality, 303–305
Resilience
    10 resilience building blocks model, 40, 251, 254, 258, 305
    characteristics of resilient people, 257
    why it matters, 253–260
Respect, 8, 13, 19, 23, 32, 34, 46–47, 50, 115, 132–133, 145, 147, 149, 155–159, 165, 168,–169, 179, 184, 207, 218, 224, 247, 257, 265–266, 268, 273, 275, 277, 279, 283, 288, 290–292, 295, 299, 303–304, 308, 314, 323
Rewards, 48, 65, 78, 97, 163–165, 217, 266, 325, 328
Roosters, 142–153, 158, 164, 169, 225, 229, 250

School
    readiness, 2, 41, 93, 97, 320
Screen time
    guidelines, 109, 205, 280
    signs it is out of balance, 101, 196
Seeking mechanism, 98–99, 201, 246–247
Self-discipline, 100, 322
Self-esteem, 19, 39, 47, 80, 82, 135, 154, 159, 163–164, 181, 250, 257–258, 336
Self-regulation, 100–105, 123, 173, 195–196, 204, 327
Separation anxiety and distress, 21, 54, 66, 107, 119, 127, 184, 223, 234, 269, 295
Serotonin, 19, 63–65, 87, 113, 129, 172, 177, 190, 212, 224, 269, 283
Sexualisation of children, 4, 209, 215–218
Shame
    damaging effects of, 160–162
    shaming language, 117, 161, 223
    vs guilt, 162, 164
Skills
    communication skills, 3, 40, 83, 182, 144, 211, 232
    developing a life skills toolkit, 39–44, 87, 189
    emotional skills, 111, 131, 192
    language and cognitive skills, 3, 95, 144, 183, 220, 281
    motor and movement skills, 96, 173–174, 183, 201
    reading skills, 95, 96, 190, 198, 303

    relationship skills, 111
    socialisation and life skills, 18, 41, 157, 182, 189, 192, 201, 203, 214, 254, 256, 258, 263, 273, 300, 314
    thinking skills, 40, 196, 257
Sleep
    bedtime rituals, 28– 30, 33, 35, 75, 130, 175
    co-sleeping, 27–28
    impact on learning and memory, 127
    sleep cycles, 26–27
    sleep deprivation and exhaustion, 14, 23, 30, 89, 117, 123, 127, 143, 234, 285
    sleep disorders, 117, 127, 252
    sleep patterns, 27–28, 117, 131, 168
Slowing down childhood, 141
Smacking, 288–289, 298
Social media, 4, 78, 216
Socialisation
    long day care and socialisation, 17, 40, 176, 223
    problems with premature socialisation, 18
Solution-seeking process for families, 157–158
Soothing children, 20, 22–25, 27, 108, 110, 119–121, 127–128, 131, 141, 149, 163
Spirit, 89, 184–185, 258–259, 265, 267, 303, 310, 312–313, 324, 326
Storytelling, 94
Stress
    extreme responses, 119
    main sources of stress and anxiety, 116–121
    stress-related illness, 117, 234
    stress and learning, 49, 53, 59, 64, 70 –71, 97, 104, 110–115, 117, 127, 130, 174, 182, 187, 190, 199, 253,
Suicide, 4, 85, 116, 126, 153, 162, 209, 254–256, 264, 270, 307, 312, 321
Support networks, 2, 9, 11, 16, 136
Surprise bedroom attack, 35–36

Tantrums
    avoiding meltdowns and wars, 156, 276–278, 298
    dealing with, 69
    types (upstairs/downstairs), 68–69, 127, 263
Technology, 16, 53, 57, 77–79, 97, 127, 135–136, 155, 191, 194–196, 232, 302
Temperament, 27, 64, 116, 133, 142, 145, 147–148, 150, 169, 225, 252
Time out, 67, 157, 295
Toilet training, 39–40
Tongue twisters, 90–91
Touch
    deprivation of touch, 15, 33, 270
    link between affection and happiness, 131, 132
    safe touch, 64, 65, 102, 104, 128–130
Toys, 20, 36, 38–39, 45, 57–58, 61–62, 98, 110, 117, 120, 129, 137, 143, 156, 159, 163, 166, 173–174, 178, 274, 278–279, 294, 310
Transitions, 6, 40–41, 128, 203, 223, 232, 234–236, 251, 330

Trauma, 31–32, 110, 123, 312, 320
Tricky children, 64, 124, 142
Tummy time, 173
TV
    impact on behaviour, 91, 109, 131
    guidelines, 109, 280

Under-achievement, 219

Violence, 3–4, 9, 49, 87, 112, 117–118, 135, 207, 217–219, 224, 230, 255–256, 264, 270, 280, 289, 301, 307, 321, 324, 327

Wellbeing, 3, 6, 10, 13, 17, 33, 83, 84, 87–89, 106, 110, 119, 130, 132, 141, 163, 167–168, 175, 190, 192, 196, 198, 201, 204, 212, 232, 256, 259, 267, 273, 300, 302, 306–307, 313, 315
Working parents
    FIFO (fly-in-fly-out workers), 30
    finding balance, 9
    stay-at-home dads and mums, 16
    supporting working parents, 16

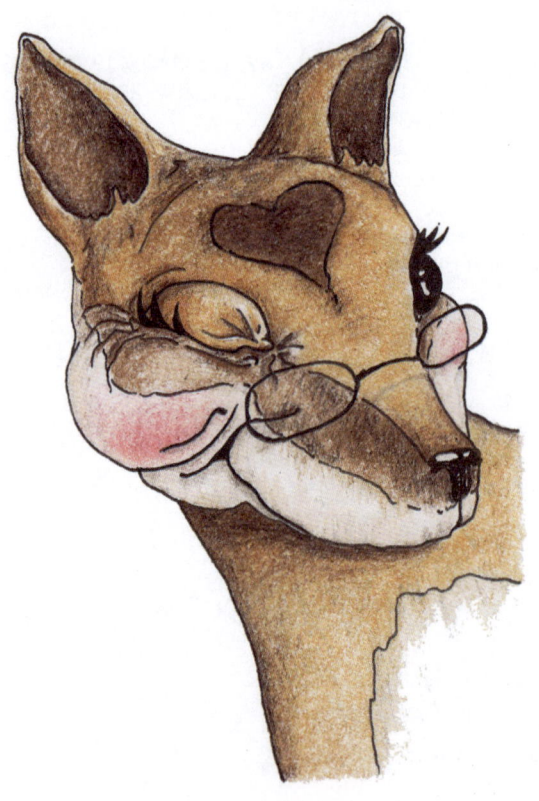

ABOUT THE AUTHOR

Commonly known as Australia's 'queen of common sense', Maggie Dent is an author, educator, and parenting and resilience specialist with a particular interest in the early years and adolescence. Maggie was a teacher for 17 years before working as a counsellor with young people and their families, in suicide prevention and in palliative care and the funeral industry.

Maggie is an advocate for the healthy, common-sense raising of children in order to strengthen families and communities. She is a passionate, positive voice for children of all ages.

Now an in-demand writer and speaker, Maggie is a regular contributor to Fairfax's Essential Kids website, Teachers Matter magazine and other parenting and education blogs. She can be regularly heard on commercial and ABC radio around Australia, and has appeared on TV programs such as Today Extra, The Daily Edition, Sunrise, ABC News Breakfast, Today and news.

She is the author of nine books, and a prolific creator of resources for parents, adolescents, teachers and early childhood educators.

Maggie is the proud mother of four sons, and an enthusiastic and grateful grandmother.

www.maggiedent.com

Facebook, YouTube, Soundcloud: /maggiedentauthor

Twitter: @queenofcommonse

Instagram: maggiedentauthor

For 24/7 access to free articles, videos, audio, downloads, online courses and tips sheets visit:

www.maggiedent.com

PRAISE FOR MAGGIE DENT AND HER WORK:

"Maggie is like a wise and entertaining aunt, whose experience and wisdom you want to drink in. She's someone I'd love to have on speed dial to ask all those tricky parenting questions, to hear her sage words of sense and calmness. She's someone who will tell you sit down with a cup of tea and keep a vague eye on your kids while they dig in the garden and climb trees. And that is the kind of advice I like to hear."
— Kirrily Martin, blogger, www.playgroupmum.com

"How do I put Maggie Dent into words? I think she shifted everyone's thinking in that room to a different place and brought us all back to our childhoods and got us to look inside our hearts to see who we really are. No matter what trials and tribulations this ever changing world throws our way we can face it with grace and get through it."
— Gloria Hackett, Inclusion Support Facilitator ECA, NT

"Maggie Dent is a writer that captures a common sense approach to working with children. Her work with school age care educators across Australia has enhanced and reinforced the vital role they play in children's lives. Maggie is someone who helps make a better world for children and inspires us to do the same!"
— Robyn Monro Miller, Network of Community Activities/National Out of School Hours Services Association

"'Real kids in an Unreal world' is a gem of wisdom, plain and simple. The book would appear to have been published from the 'tree of knowledge' and is a very good guidebook to keeping kids normal in today's fast paced world…"
— Mamamia.com (review of *Real Kids in an Unreal World*)

9 THINGS IN 9 WEEKS

A SELF-PACED ONLINE COURSE BASED ON THIS BOOK...

* Parenting support and information delivered to you in the comfort of your own home (no babysitter required)
* 9 x downloadable one-hour audio presentations in which Maggie talks about each of her '9 Things' – listen when it suits you
* Notes, resource materials and activities to enrich each week's topic
* Video and audio supplementary material
* Option to join in the online course parent community to interact with other participants, share your reflections and seek further support and information from Maggie and her team
* Access to live audio Q&A webinars.

WHAT COURSE PARTICIPANTS HAVE SAID...

"I loved this course!! The most valuable thing for me was the non-judgmental, down to earth advice offered by Maggie. Being able to listen to it all in our own time was great too."

"Practical information that calmed me and made me feel empowered."

"It's made me more confident in my decisions as a parent and also trusting my instincts."

For more information: www.commonsenseparenting.com.au

To find all of Maggie's books, ebooks, audio downloads, video seminars, cds/dvds, posters and online courses, visit the online store at
maggiedent.com

    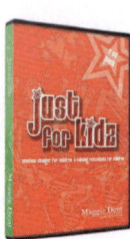 

   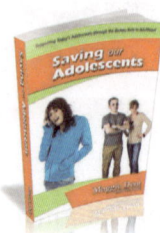